SLAVES WITHOUT MASTERS

SLAVES WITHOUT MASTERS

The Free Negro in the Antebellum South

IRA BERLIN

OXFORD UNIVERSITY PRESS
Oxford New York Toronto Melbourne

Oxford University Press
Oxford London Glasgow
New York Toronto Melbourne Wellington
Nairobi Dar es Salaam Cape Town
Kuala Lumpur Singapore Jakarta Hong Kong Tokyo
Delhi Bombay Calcutta Madras Karachi

First published by Pantheon Books, a division of Random House, Inc., 1974
First issued in paperback by Vintage Books, 1976
First issued as an Oxford University Press paperback, New York, 1981
Reprinted by arrangement with Pantheon Books, a division of Random House, Inc.

Library of Congress Cataloging in Publication Data

Berlin, Ira, 1941–
Slaves Without Masters.

Bibliography: p.
1. Negroes—History—To 1863. 2. Freemen in
the Southern States. I. Title.
E185.18.B47 301.44'93'0975 74—4761
ISBN 0-19-502905-4 pbk.

Printed in the United States of America

To My Mother

and

the Memory of My Father

Contents

Tables

Abbreviations Used in Footnotes

ACS	Letters Received, American Colonization Society Papers, Library of Congress
AHS	Atlanta Historical Society, Atlanta
AMA	American Missionary Association Papers, Amistad Research Center, Dillard University, New Orleans, La.
BCH	Baltimore City Hall
DelHR	Delaware Hall of Records, Dover
DelLP	Delaware Legislative Papers, Delaware Hall of Records, Dover
Duke	Duke University Library, Durham, N.C.
FC	Filson Club, Louisville, Ky.
GaDA&H	Georgia Department of Archives and History, Atlanta
GaHS	Georgia Historical Society, Savannah
GTS	Garrett Theological Seminary Library, Evanston, Ill.
HFPRC	Historical Foundation of the Presbyterian and Reformed Churches, Montreat, N.C.
HSD	Historical Society of Delaware, Wilmington
HSP	Historical Society of Pennsylvania, Philadelphia
HUL	Howard University Library, Washington, D.C.
JNH	*Journal of Negro History*
JSH	*Journal of Southern History*
LC	Library of Congress, Washington, D.C.
LSU	Louisiana State University Library, Baton Rouge
MCH	Mobile City Hall, Mobile, Ala.
MdDL	Maryland Diocesan Library, Baltimore
MdHR	Maryland Hall of Records, Annapolis

MdHS	Maryland Historical Society, Baltimore
MdSCS Papers	Maryland State Colonization Society Papers, Maryland Historical Society, Baltimore
MLP	Mississippi Legislative Papers, Mississippi Department of Archives and History, Jackson
MoHS	Missouri Historical Society, St. Louis
NA	National Archives, Washington, D.C.
NCA	North Carolina State Department of Archives and History, Raleigh
NCLP	North Carolina Legislative Papers, North Carolina State Department of Archives and History, Raleigh
NOPL	New Orleans Public Library
PAS	Pennsylvania Society for Promoting the Abolition of Slavery Papers, Historical Society of Pennsylvania, Philadelphia
SCA	South Carolina Archives Department, Columbia
SCH	Savannah City Hall
SCHS	South Carolina Historical Society, Charleston
SCL	South Caroliniana Library, Columbia
SCLP	South Carolina Legislative Papers, South Carolina Archives, Columbia
SHC	Southern History Collection, University of North Carolina Library, Chapel Hill, N.C.
SUL	Syracuse University Library, Syracuse, N.Y.
THS	Tennessee Historical Society, Nashville
TLP	Tennessee Legislative Papers, Tennessee State Library and Archives, Nashville
TSL	Tennessee State Library and Archives, Nashville
TUL	Howard-Tilton Memorial Library, Tulane University, New Orleans
UGa	University of Georgia Library, Athens
UVa	Alderman Library, University of Virginia, Charlottesville
VaBHS	Virginia Baptist Historical Society, Richmond
VHS	Virginia Historical Society, Richmond
VLP	Virginia Legislative Papers, Virginia State Library, Richmond
VMH&B	*Virginia Magazine of History and Biography*
VSL	Virginia State Library, Richmond
W&MQ	*William and Mary Quarterly*

Preface

The boundaries of hell, wrote Richard Wright, have never been defined. Perhaps so. After witnessing the charred remains of the concentration camps, the scarred flesh of napalmed children, the hysterical screams and eerie silence of many Sharpsvilles, who can doubt the elastic nature of evil? Our nineteenth-century forebears had few such doubts. Riding high on the wave of civilization's progress, certain that God was on their side, they denounced slavery as sin and slaveholders as evil incarnate. The Constitution, which some argued protected slavery, was "a covenant with death, an agreement with hell." Yet, as Wright's dictum suggests, the line between slavery and freedom was never quite what some abolitionists made it out to be. Once free, blacks generally remained at the bottom of the social order, despised by whites, burdened with increasingly oppressive racial proscriptions, and subjected to verbal and physical abuse. Free Negroes stood outside the direct governance of a master, but in the eyes of many whites their place in society had not been significantly altered. They were slaves without masters.

The line between slavery and freedom was not imaginary, either. No matter how hard whites squeezed black liberty, the irreducible difference between freedom and slavery remained. Freedom allowed blacks to reap the rewards of their own labor, to develop a far richer social life, and to enjoy the many intangible benefits of liberty. With hard work, skill, and luck, some free Negroes climbed off the floor of Southern society, acquired wealth and social standing. A few masterless slaves themselves became slave masters. In fact, in their own eyes, and finally even in the eyes of whites, free Negroes were not slaves.

Yet neither were they free. Instead, Southern free Negroes balanced precariously between abject slavery, which they rejected, and full freedom, which was denied them. Their world straddled one of hell's elusive boundaries.

This book explores that rough and forbidding terrain. It tells how free Negroes lived, worked, and worshipped, how they educated, entertained, improved, and protected themselves. Its purpose is not merely to describe the freemen's style of life but also to understand how they conceived of themselves as a black elite in a slave society, or, more accurately—since free Negroes were not a monolithic caste—to understand how different classes of freemen conceived of their social role.

Just as it is impossible to understand students without teachers and workers without bosses, so it is impossible to understand free Negroes without whites. Southern whites set the racial policies that affected and sometimes determined the course of free Negro life. Consequently, a second theme of this book is race relations. Here the thesis, simply put, is that in learning to deal with free blacks before the Civil War, Southern whites developed institutions, standards of personal relations, and patterns of thought which they applied to all blacks after Emancipation. Segregation, black codes, the convict-lease system, and the various forms of peonage usually associated with the postbellum South all victimized the antebellum free Negro caste. When the Emancipation Proclamation and the Thirteenth Amendment freed all blacks, whites applied the panoply of attitudes and institutions they had long used to control the free Negro caste. In many instances, the magnitude of the Emancipation and the libertarian spirit that accompanied it forbade immediate reinstatement of the old forms of white domination. But within a generation the web of constraints that had dominated the lives of antebellum free Negroes had been imposed on all Negroes. In many ways, freedom—not slavery—was the taproot of postwar Southern race relations.

Free Negroes also drew on their antebellum experience. Long at the top of black society, they maintained their position of leadership after the Civil War. Throughout the nineteenth century and into the twentieth, free Negroes and their descendants served as spokesmen for blacks. Although they were generally united with former slaves in demanding full entry into American society, their own experience in freedom deeply influenced their policies and methods. Frequently, the priorities of blacks with a heritage of liberty differed from the priorities of those who had recently received it. The experience of the free Negro caste continued to shape black life long after Emancipation had eliminated the freemen's special status.

Finally, this is a study of the slave South. As Eugene D. Genovese has remarked, "No satisfactory assessment of any slaveholding regime or of any slaveholding class will be possible until we retrace its history to take full account of its specific interaction with other classes in society, whether white or black, free or slave."[1] The status and treatment whites accorded the free Negro are an especially revealing gauge of Southern society. For just as the status of any anomalous group—children, the insane, criminals, or even intellectuals—is a telling indicator of the larger society, so the status of the free Negro is a sensitive measure of Southern attitudes on race and class. Indeed, the kind of free Negro caste—large or small, black or brown, wealthy or impoverished—that a slave society produces directly reflects the state of slavery within that society and tells much about the standing of other groups as well. The free Negro's status and treatment throw new light on the nature of the social order of the old South.

Several other ideas have shaped this book. Historians of the South have generally ignored both time and place in dealing with antebellum blacks. Kenneth Stampp—to cite only one of the best—holds time constant in his study of slavery and treats the period between 1830 and 1860 as a unit. Other scholars, constructing models of the slave South to compare with slave societies elsewhere in the Americas, have presented a monolithic South seemingly impervious to change. This has distorted the history of blacks and of the slave South generally. Whatever value such modes of explanation may have for slavery, they have none for the free Negro. The size and character

[1] Eugene D. Genovese, *The World the Slaveholders Made: Two Essays in Interpretation* (New York, 1969), p. 5.

of the free Negro caste were constantly changing, as was the place whites were willing to grant free Negroes in Southern society. I have therefore been careful to show how the situation of the free Negro caste changed over time. Although the general boundaries of this study are the American Revolution, which created the antebellum free Negro caste, and the Civil War, which destroyed it as a distinctive social group, the Prologue reviews the period before the Revolution and the Epilogue looks into the postwar years. Within the main boundaries, important temporal distinctions are observed. Part One deals with the years between 1775 and 1812, and Part Three focuses on the 1850s, both periods of trauma for Southern free Negroes.

In a like manner, special emphasis has been given to regional distinctions within the South. Historians have, of course, long noted the geographic, political, and cultural diversity of the slaveholding states. But most have agreed with W. J. Cash that if "there are many Souths, the fact remains that there is also one South."[2] The unity created by slavery and sanctified by the Civil War makes Cash's judgment difficult to dispute within the North-South perspective. But outside the context of the Civil War dichotomy, other equally valid distinctions become evident. This study assumes that there were two Souths, and that differences between the Upper South and the Lower South—as reflected in their distinctive free Negro populations —profoundly influenced much of Southern history and a good deal of antebellum American history.[3]

[2] W. J. Cash, *The Mind of the South* (New York, 1941), p. viii.

[3] For the antebellum years, I have defined the Upper South as the states of Delaware, Kentucky, Maryland, Missouri, North Carolina, Tennessee, and Virginia and the Lower South as Alabama, Arkansas, Florida, Georgia, Louisiana, Mississippi, South Carolina, and Texas. However, it should be noted that these were not always the demarcations of the Upper and Lower South. During the colonial era, for example, North Carolina was more akin to South Carolina than to Virginia—which has prompted Winthrop D. Jordan to suggest that there were two and a half Souths at the time of the Revolution (*White over Black: American Attitudes Toward the Negro, 1550–1812* [Chapel Hill, N.C., 1968], pp. 315–16)—and of course the east-west division of Tennessee has continued to the present day. Moreover, in dividing the South into Upper and Lower regions, it must not be forgotten that there were important differences within each region. The social distance between urban Delaware and the Virginia countryside or between lowland South Carolina and the Arkansas frontier was often as great as any between the Upper and Lower South.

. . .

History, in some measure, is the study of exceptions. Most historians are concerned with the richness and variety of human experience rather than with the promulgation of general laws of human behavior. Therefore it is not surprising that American historians have had a long-standing interest in the Southern free Negro—a black in a white man's country, a free man in a land where most blacks were slaves.

At the end of the nineteenth century, as American graduate schools opened their doors, historians began to take a close look at this anomalous caste. In 1899, Herbert Bolton, a pioneer student of the Americas, completed his doctoral dissertation on the free Negro in the South. It was a thin survey, but several Johns Hopkins and Columbia doctoral candidates soon issued more substantial monographs on Virginia and Maryland freemen. Ulrich B. Phillips included a chapter on the free Negro in his *American Negro Slavery*, and some of his students later wrote essays on free Negroes in various states.[4] Thereafter, interest in the Southern free Negro waned and almost disappeared. Not until the 1940s did several young black scholars revive the subject. In 1942, Luther P. Jackson published his classic, *Free Negro Labor and Property Holding in Virginia.* The following year John Hope Franklin completed his comprehensive study of North Carolina free Negroes, and about the same time, E. Horace Fitchett's essays on the free people of color of Charleston appeared.[5] Other historians, writing in the *Journal*

[4] Herbert Bolton, "The Free Negro in the South Before the Civil War," unpublished doctoral dissertation, University of Pennsylvania, 1899; John H. Russell, *The Free Negro in Virginia, 1619–1865* (Baltimore, 1913); James M. Wright, *The Free Negro in Maryland, 1634–1860* (New York, 1921); also Jeffrey R. Brackett, *The Negro in Maryland: A Study of the Institution of Slavery* (Baltimore, 1899); Ulrich B. Phillips, *American Negro Slavery* (New York, 1918), pp. 425–53, and his "Slave Labor in the Charleston District," *Political Science Quarterly*, XXII (1907), 416–39; Charles S. Sydnor, "The Free Negro in Mississippi Before the Civil War," *American Historical Review*, XXXII (1927), 769–88; Ralph B. Flanders, "The Free Negro in Antebellum Georgia," *North Carolina Historical Review*, IX (1932), 250–72.

[5] Luther P. Jackson, *Free Negro Labor and Property Holding in Virginia, 1830–1860* (New York, 1942); John Hope Franklin, *The Free Negro in North Carolina, 1790–1860* (Chapel Hill, N.C., 1943); E. Horace Fitchett, "The Traditions of the Free Negro in Charleston, South Carolina," *JNH*, XXV (1940), 139–51; *idem.*, "The Origins and Growth of the Free Negro Population of Charleston, South Carolina," *JNH*, XXVI (1941), 421–37; *idem.*, "The

of Negro History and in state and regional periodicals, contributed articles on free Negroes in other states and on related subjects like manumission and colonization. Behind these monographs were a growing number of doctoral dissertations on Southern free Negroes completed during the late forties and fifties.[6] Yet, few of these studies found their way into print, perhaps because of the lack of public and scholarly interest in black history. That, of course, changed after 1954, but no book-length study of Southern free Negroes appeared during the 1950s and 1960s. A decade after the publication of Leon F. Litwack's fine history of the Negro in the antebellum North, there was no comparable study of Southern freemen.[7] Ironically, the long-standing interest in the free Negro appeared to have run its course just when interest in black history reached its peak.

Lately, interest in the Southern free Negro caste has stirred again.[8] Several historiographic trends have contributed to this modest renaissance. The most important of these is the growing interest in comparative history, especially the world-wide comparison of slave societies. Along with Frank Tannenbaum, historians who have taken this broad view of slavery have focused

Status of the Free Negro in Charleston, South Carolina, and His Descendants in Modern Society," *JNH,* XXXII (1947), 430–51. Although not published until 1970 (University of Massachusetts Press, Amherst), James H. Johnston, "Race Relations in Virginia and Miscegenation in the South," unpublished doctoral dissertation, University of Chicago, 1937, clearly influenced these pioneering works on the free Negro, especially that of Jackson.

[6] Among the more important of these unpublished doctoral theses are James M. England, "The Free Negro in Ante-Bellum Tennessee," Vanderbilt University, 1941; Morris R. Boucher, "The Free Negro in Alabama Prior to 1860," State University of Iowa, 1950; Donald E. Everett, "The Free Persons of Color in New Orleans, 1830–1865," Tulane University, 1952; Herbert E. Sterkx, "The Free Negro in Ante-Bellum Louisiana, 1724–1860," University of Alabama, 1954; Edward F. Sweat, "The Free Negro in Antebellum Georgia," Indiana University, 1957; Leonard P. Stavisky, "The Negro Artisan in the South Atlantic States, 1800–1860: A Study of Status and Economic Opportunity with Special Reference to Charleston," Columbia University, 1958.

[7] Leon F. Litwack, *North of Slavery: The Negro in the Free States, 1790–1860* (Chicago, 1961).

[8] During the past two years three books have been published on Southern freemen: Letitia Woods Brown, *Free Negroes in the District of Columbia, 1790–1846* (New York, 1972); Herbert E. Sterkx, *The Free Negro in Antebellum Louisiana* (Rutherford, N.J., 1972); Marina Wikramanayake, *A World in Shadow: The Free Black in Antebellum South Carolina* (Columbia, S.C., 1973).

on the question of the slaves' access to freedom and their rights as citizens after emancipation as a crucial determinant and index of their status and treatment and of the nature of race relations. Making free Negroes a measure of slavery and race relations has naturally reawakened interest in the free Negroes themselves. During the past decade, a number of studies of free Negroes in various slave societies have appeared, and many more will soon reach print.[9]

A second source of this renewed interest in the free Negro caste is the general revival of social history and particularly the history of people at the bottom of the social hierarchy. This growing concern for history's disinherited, in turn, has been fostered by the utilization of nonliterary sources and the development of new methods and techniques. By closely examining census rolls, tax lists, and voting registers, historians have been able to gain considerable insight into family arrangements, occupational patterns, and the physical and social mobility of people who were either totally illiterate or who left few of the traditional written records by which they might be known. The use of such sources was, of course, not totally absent from earlier studies of the free Negro. Luther P. Jackson, for example, pioneered in the use of tax and census records to determine the free Negro's changing social status and pointed out some of the dangers of relying too closely on the latter—a warning some historians have unfortunately ignored. But the use of computers and sophisticated statistical techniques has enabled scholars to squeeze more from these

[9] Frank Tannenbaum, *Slave and Citizen: The Negro in the Americas* (New York, 1947). There is an excellent bibliography of comparative slave studies in Laura Foner and Eugene D. Genovese, eds., *Slavery in the New World: A Reader in Comparative History* (Englewood Cliffs, N.J., 1969), pp. 262–8. The most important study of the free Negro in the Americas is David W. Cohen and Jack P. Greene, eds., *Neither Slave Nor Free: The Freedman of African Descent in the Slave Societies of the New World* (Baltimore, 1972). Also valuable are Elsa V. Goveia, *Slave Society in the British Leeward Islands at the End of the Eighteenth Century* (New Haven, Conn., 1965); C. L. R. James, *The Black Jacobins: Toussaint L'Ouverture and the San Domingo Revolution,* 2nd ed. (New York, 1963); Laura Foner, "The Free People of Color in Louisiana and St. Domingue: A Comparative Portrait of Two Three-Caste Societies," *Journal of Social History,* III (1970), 406–30; Herbert Klein, *Slavery in the Americas: A Comparative Study of Cuba and Virginia* (Chicago, 1967); and Carl N. Degler, *Neither Black Nor White: Slavery and Race Relations in Brazil and the United States* (New York, 1971).

records than ever before. Historians employing the sources and methods of the new social history also promise to tell much about free Negroes.[10]

This book therefore stands at the end of one historiographic tradition and at the beginning of several new ones. Although it speaks to some of the same concerns and uses many of the same sources as the older state histories of the free Negro caste, it also attempts to formulate and answer new questions and use sources that have been previously little used or but recently unearthed. Similarly, this is not a direct comparison of Southern free Negroes with those of another slave society. But when the hemispheric perspective has been useful in clarifying the freemen's place in Southern society, it has been freely adopted. I have also used the comparative method of the inter-American studies to show how free Negroes (and hence slavery and race relations generally) differed in the Upper and Lower South. Finally, a study of free Negroes in fifteen states over the course of nearly a century precludes the kind of microanalysis of any single community which has become the hallmark of the new social history. However, I have closely examined aspects of free black life in several communities to illuminate the history of the entire caste. In doing so, I have tried to speak to the concerns and adopt the methods of this branch of social history. Thus, although this study does not belong fully either to the older tradition of free Negro studies or to the newer, emerging ones, it has been informed by all.

In the course of writing this book I have visited nearly one hundred libraries and archives. I cannot truthfully say that they were all rewarding or even enjoyable journeys, but without them this would be a different and, I am certain, a less valuable book. I would especially like to thank Ellen Burke, Ruth Davis, and Charles Shetler of the State Historical Society of Wisconsin, Arthur Miller of the Newberry Library, Deirdre Ford of the University of Illinois Library at Chicago Circle, Caroline

[10] Especially important in this regard is the Philadelphia History Project directed by Theodore Hershberg of the University of Pennsylvania; Theodore Hershberg, "Free Blacks in Antebellum Philadelphia: A Study of Ex-Slaves, Freeborn, and Socio-economic Decline," *Journal of Social History*, V (1972), 183–209.

Sung of the Library of Congress, Daphne Gentry of the Virginia State Library, Mattie Russell of the Duke University Library, John M. Price and Margaret Fisher of the Louisiana State University Library, Connie Griffith of the Tulane University Library, the Reverend Grady Powell of the Gillfield Baptist Church of Petersburg, Virginia, and the Reverend Y. B. Williams of the First African Baptist Church of Richmond, Virginia.

I have also incurred numerous intellectual debts, which I am delighted to acknowledge publicly with the understanding that they can never be fully repaid. Richard H. Sewell guided this study through its formative stages and improved those early efforts in countless ways. The late Robert S. Starobin gave freely of his unrivaled knowledge of Southern industrial development and offered encouragement when I appeared to be marching in place. In archival coffee shops in Richmond, Charleston, and elsewhere, William W. Freehling listened to my ideas on the nature of antebellum society and never failed to broaden my perspective. Much to my advantage, he read and criticized the final draft of this manuscript. Herbert G. Gutman, whose enthusiasm and high standards are a continuing inspiration, shared his research on Southern workers and made valuable methodological suggestions. I am also grateful to W. Elliot Brownlee, Eugene D. Genovese, and Louis S. Gerteis for sharp criticism at several stages of my work. Stanley I. Mallach, a model critic, read this manuscript more times than he probably cares to admit and, with a mixture of profundity and profanity, stirred me to make necessary changes. A Younger Humanist Fellowship from the National Endowment for the Humanities and the steady typing of Mrs. Mildred Singer enabled me to complete this book. I am grateful to them both.

Finally, the loving interest and critical eye of my wife, Martha, made the whole enterprise more enjoyable.

I. B.

November 1973

Stapp of the Library of Congress, Daphne Gentry of the Virginia State Library, Mattie Russell of the Duke University Library, John V. [illegible] and Margaret Fisher of the Louisiana State University Library, Carolyn Griffith of the Tulane University Library, the Reverend Canon Powell of the Gillfield Baptist Church of Petersburg, Virginia, and the Reverend V. [illegible] Williams of the First African Baptist Church of Richmond, Virginia.

I have also incurred numerous intellectual debts which I am delighted to acknowledge publicly with the understanding that they can never be fully repaid. Richard B. [illegible] guided this study through its formative stages and improved the early efforts in countless ways. The late Robert S. Starobin gave freely of his unrivaled knowledge of Southern industrial development and offered encouragement when it appeared to be [illegible] in place. [illegible] tobacco shops in Richmond, Charleston, and elsewhere. William W. Freehling listened to my ideas on the nature of antebellum society and never failed to broaden my perspective. Much to my advantage, he read and criticized the final draft of this manuscript. Herbert G. Gutman, whose [illegible] high standards are a continuing inspiration, shared his research on Southern workers and made valuable methodological suggestions. I am also grateful to W. Elliot Brownlee, Eugene D. Genovese, and [illegible] for their sharp criticism. [illegible] read this manuscript more times than he probably cares to remember and, with a mixture of perceptivity and patience, spurred me to make necessary changes. A Younger Humanist Fellowship from the National Endowment for the Humanities and the steady typing of Mrs. Mildred Snyder enabled me to complete this book. I am grateful to them both.

Finally, the loving interest and critical eye of my wife, [illegible] have made the whole enterprise more enjoyable.

[illegible]

November 197[illegible]

SLAVES WITHOUT MASTERS

Prologue

Freemen and Slaves

Forty-five years ago . . . a free African was a novelty among us.

[John S. Tyson], *Life of Elisha Tyson, Philanthropist* (1825)

BEFORE the American Revolution, few free Negroes could be found in the Southern colonies. The overwhelming majority of these were light-skinned children of mixed racial unions, generally freed after a specified term of servitude if their mother was white, or perhaps manumitted by a conscience-stricken white father. A 1755 Maryland census, the only pre-Revolutionary enumeration of Southern free Negroes, counted slightly more than 1,800 Negro freemen, 80 percent of whom were of mixed bloods. Like Maryland whites, about half of these Negro freemen were under sixteen years old, and of these, almost nine out of ten were mulattoes. Few full-blooded blacks enjoyed freedom in colonial Maryland; the free Negro caste was not only light-skinned but getting lighter. Unlike slaveowners in most places in the Americas, Maryland masters emancipated their sons as well as their daughters, with equal if not greater facility. The sex ratio, following that of slaves, favored males. In addition, about a sixth of the adult free Negroes were crippled or elderly persons deemed "past labor," whom heartless slaveholders had discarded when they could no longer wring a profit from them. In all, free Negroes composed about 4 percent of the colony's black population and less than 2 percent of its free population.[1] Almost a century after slavery had been written into law, the vast majority of Maryland blacks remained locked in bonded servitude. The routes to freedom were narrow and dismal.

Such was the case in all the Southern colonies. No other colony took a similar census, but there is no evidence that any contained a larger proportion of free Negroes than Maryland. Nowhere did officials or travelers take note, as many later would, of a large number of blacks who were free. In 1805, nearly a hundred Virginians recalled that "less than thirty years ago, the number of free negroes was so small that they were seldom to be met with." Some years later, William Gaston, the chief justice of North Carolina, investigated the subject and found "that previous to the Revolution there were scarcely any emancipated Slaves in this State; and that the few free men of color that were here at that time, were chiefly Mulattoes, the children of white women." Unsure of his judgment, Gaston queried "some aged persons"; they too confirmed that before the 1770s "scarcely an instance could be found at that time, either in Virginia or this State, of an emancipated Slave."[2]

At first, whites took but sporadic notice of these few free Negroes. Between the arrival of the first blacks and the codification of slavery in the 1660s, colonial lawmakers hardly recognized them at all. During these first forty years, some free Negroes enjoyed the full fruit of the new rich land. They earned money, accumulated property, and occasionally held minor offices. In 1651, Anthony Johnson, the best known of

[1] *Gentlemen's Magazine and Historical Chronicle,* XXXIV (1764), 261. Although free Negro men outnumbered free Negro women in 1755, a close examination of the sex ratio indicates that the balance was shifting. The number of female free Negroes under sixteen nearly equaled the number of males. This shift toward a surplus of females was more in keeping with the sexual balance of the free Negro caste throughout the Americas and in the American South during the nineteenth century. David W. Cohen and Jack P. Greene, eds., *Neither Slave Nor Free: The Freedman of African Descent in the Slave Societies of the New World* (Baltimore, 1972), pp. 7, 31, 62, 89–90; Elsa V. Goveia, *Slave Society in the British Leeward Islands at the End of the Eighteenth Century* (New Haven, Conn., 1965), p. 216; and chapter 5 below.

[2] Petition from Petersburg, 11 December 1805, VLP; *Proceedings and Debates of the Convention of North-Carolina Called to Amend the Constitution of the State* (Raleigh, 1835), p. 351.

these early free Negroes, received a 250-acre headright for importing five persons into Virginia. John Johnson, a neighbor and probably a relative, did even better, earning 550 acres for bringing eleven persons into the colony. Both men owned substantial farms on the Eastern Shore, held servants, and left sizable estates. As established members of their community, they enjoyed the rights of citizens. When a black servant claiming his freedom fled Anthony Johnson's plantation and took refuge with a nearby white farmer, Johnson took his white neighbor to court and won the return of his servant along with damages assessed against the white man.[3] But as whites secured the bonds of racial slavery, the status of those blacks who remained free suffered. In the 1660s, when slavery was given legal sanction, Virginia legislators made a lasting judgment: free Negroes "ought not in all respects . . . be admitted to a full fruition of the exemptions and impunities of the English."[4]

The racial nature of bondage in America made it necessary for whites to distinguish themselves from blacks, and the pressures to define these differences grew with the possibilities for racial equality. Whites feared that the wall of racial slavery would not keep the boundaries between black and white secure. The presence of some blacks who had slipped under that line weakened the wall that separated the races. By drawing a color line between free and slave, whites made it impossible for themselves to believe that free blacks could side with white *free* people over enslaved *black* people, a circumstance familiar in Latin America where free men of color served as soldiers and slave catchers.[5] If a white in the black man's ranks was a

[3] John H. Russell, *The Free Negro In Virginia, 1619–1865* (Baltimore, 1913), pp. 24–38, 88, 116, 119–20, 136–7; James H. Brewer, "Negro Property Owners in Seventeenth-Century Virginia," *W&MQ*, 3rd ser., XII (1955), 575–80; Susie M. Ames, *Studies of the Virginia Eastern Shore in the Seventeenth Century* (Richmond, Va., 1940), pp. 99–108; Edmund S. Morgan, "Slavery and Freedom: The American Paradox," *Journal of American History*, LIX (1972), 17–18. 8.

[4] William W. Hening, comp., *The Statutes at Large; Being a Collection of All the Laws of Virginia*, 13 vols. (Richmond, New York, Philadelphia, 1800–1823), II, 267.

[5] Cohen and Greene, eds., *Neither Slave Nor Free*, pp. 44, 68–9, 118, 136, 166, 174–5, 310–11; Carl N. Degler, *Neither Black Nor White: Slavery and Race Relations in Brazil and the United States* (New York, 1971), pp. 82–4;

traitor, what else could a black in the white man's ranks be?[6]

But most Negro freemen were not black. Throughout the Western Hemisphere, a brown skin generally assured free Negroes a social standing well above that of the black slave although below that of all whites. Planters in many parts of Latin America not only freed their offspring by black slave women, but also guaranteed their children an elevated place in society by training them for a craft or educating them for a profession. Occasionally, they endowed their mulatto children with substantial fortunes. In the colonial South, however, only a few free Negroes descended from wealthy slaveowning planters. Most mulattoes were the children of white indentured servant men and black women, and frequently, as William Gaston suggested, they were the offspring of black men and white servant women. Indeed, despite the antipathy toward such unions, masters often connived to push black men and white women into bed together because the law gave them the services of the children born of such interracial matches for thirty-one years, and it locked the white mothers into additional terms of servitude.[7] Black and white parents who liber-

---

Herbert S. Klein, *Slavery in the Americas: A Comparative Study of Cuba and Virginia* (Chicago, 1967), pp. 212–25; Gwendolyn M. Hall, *Social Control in Slave Plantation Societies: A Comparison of St. Domingue and Cuba* (Baltimore, 1970), pp. 114–19; C. R. Boxer, *The Golden Age of Brazil: Growing Pains of a Colonial Society, 1695–1750* (Berkeley, Calif., 1969), pp. 170–1, 214–15.

[6] Winthrop D. Jordan, *White over Black: American Attitudes Toward the Negro, 1550–1812* (Chapel Hill, N.C., 1968), pp. 3–265, especially pp. 122–8.

[7] Hening, comp., *Statutes Va.*, III, 86–87, 453; W. H. Browne *et al.*, eds., *Archives of Maryland*, 71 vols. (Baltimore, 1883–), I, 533–4, XXII, 552, XXVI, 259–60, XXX, 289–90, XXXIII, 112, XXXVI, 275–6; Walter Clark, ed., *The State Records of North Carolina, 1777–1790,* 16 vols. [numbered consecutively after a preceding series] (Raleigh, 1886–1907), XXIII, 65, 195; Thomas Cooper and David J. McCord, comps., *The Statutes at Large of South Carolina,* 10 vols. (Columbia, 1836–41), III, 20. The Maryland Court of Appeals later observed that the law of 1664, which enslaved for the lifetime of her husband any freeborn English woman who married a black slave, had been repealed "to prevent persons from purchasing white women and marrying them to their slaves for purposes of making slaves of them"; Helen T. Catterall, ed., *Judicial Cases Concerning Slavery and the Negro,* 5 vols. (Washington, D.C., 1926–37), IV, 2, 49; Browne *et al.*, eds., *Archives of Maryland,* VII, 204–5. For a continuing distinction in Maryland law between free Negroes and mulattoes born of white women, see William Kilty, *The Laws of Maryland,* 2 vols. (Annapolis, Md., 1799–1800), 1717, c. 13. Eugene I. McCormac, *White Servitude in Maryland, 1634–1820* (Baltimore, 1904), pp. 67–70; George M.

ated their mulatto children could rarely afford to give them more than the gift of freedom. Having little status in society themselves, these poor folk had none to pass on to their children. Likewise, the mulatto children of white indentured servant women who wriggled free of servitude at age thirty-one were in no position to compete as equals in the expanding colonial society. Broken by a lifetime of labor for masters who cared little about their fate after age thirty-one, they often found freedom a cruel reward for their long years of service. Many were barely able to support themselves in a society dominated by vigorous young white men. Thus the stigma of class was added to the burden of race to weigh Negro freemen down to the bottom of Southern society.

After the 1660s, whites sporadically chipped away at the freemen's liberty, and early in the eighteenth century, when slaves began to pour into the colonies, the status of the free Negro dropped sharply. Some Southern colonies barred free Negroes from holding office, from voting, from serving in the militia, from testifying against whites, and from having sexual relations with them. At times, Southern lawmakers mixed free Negroes indiscriminately with slaves and subjected them to the bondsmen's disabilities. Occasionally they isolated free Negroes from both slaves and whites and encumbered them with special burdens, taxing them more heavily or punishing them more severely than either. Only by fixing "a perpetual Brand upon Free-Negros & Mulattos by excluding them from the great Priviledge [*sic*] of a Freeman," declared the governor of Virginia in 1723, could whites "make the free-Negros sensible that a distinction ought to be made between their offspring and the Descendants of an Englishman, with whom they never were to be Accounted Equal."[8]

Still, whites had not fully determined the free Negro's place

---

Fredrickson, "Toward a Social Interpretation of the Development of American Racism," in Nathan I. Huggins *et al.*, *Key Issues in the Afro-American Experience*, 2 vols. (New York, 1971), I, 246–7; Donald L. Horowitz, "Color Differentiation in the American Systems of Slavery," *Journal of Interdisciplinary History*, III (1973), 526–30.

[8] Emory G. Evans, ed., "A Question of Complexion: Documents Concerning the Negro and the Franchise in Eighteenth-Century Virginia," *VMH&B*, LXXI (1963), 414. For an excellent summary of colonial regulation of free Negroes, see Jordan, *White over Black*, pp. 122–6.

in colonial society. Though the direction of white thought was clear, the pattern of colonial black law revealed the ambiguous, incomplete nature of their thinking. Colonial black codes were laced with inconsistencies. Although they often treated free blacks roughly, they left large areas where blacks enjoyed legal equality with whites. For example, Virginia barred free Negroes from holding office, yet no other colony so acted. Maryland prohibited free Negroes from mustering with the militia, but no other Southern colony issued a similar ban, and some actually required Negro freemen to attend. South Carolina and Virginia sought to ensure white dominance by whipping blacks, "free or bond," who dared raise a hand to strike a white, but they remained alone in this action. Perhaps the strictures placed on Negro suffrage best reveal the patchwork nature of colonial regulation of Negro freemen. Early in the eighteenth century, Virginia and then North and South Carolina barred free Negroes from the polls, but no other Southern colony followed their lead. By 1761, when Georgia finally joined their ranks, North Carolina had lifted its ban. And although a Negro with a gun might be at least as dangerous as one with a ballot, free Negroes usually maintained the right to hold firearms. Despite all these miscellaneous proscriptions, no Southern colony attacked the freemen's right to travel freely, as all would later do, and their right to hold property—the keystone of liberty in colonial America—remained untouched. Only on the sensitive question of interracial sexual relations did whites throughout the South reach a firm consensus: no black, free or slave, could legally sleep with a white.[9] Beyond

[9] For Virginia disfranchisement, see Hening, comp., *Statutes Va.*, III, 250–1. For militia restrictions, see Jordan, *White over Black*, pp. 125–6, and Benjamin Quarles, "The Colonial Militia and Negro Manpower," *Mississippi Valley Historical Review*, XLV (1959), 643–52. For striking a white man, see Hening, comp., *Statutes Va.*, II, 481, III, 459; Cooper and McCord, comps., *Statutes S.C.*, VII, 377. A Delaware law of similar intent prohibited the employment of Negroes to inflict corporal punishment on whites; *Laws of the State of Delaware*, 2 vols. (New Castle, 1797), I, 479. For Negro suffrage, see Hening, comp., *Statutes Va.*, III, 250–1; Clark, ed., *State Records of N.C.*, XXIII, 12–13, 208; Cooper and McCord, comps., *Statutes S.C.*, III, 16, 136, 657; Allen D. Candler, ed., *The Colonial Records of the State of Georgia*, 26 vols. (Atlanta, 1904–16), XVIII, 465–6; also Emil Olbrich, *The Development of Sentiment on Negro Suffrage to 1860* (Madison, Wis., 1912), pp. 7–22. For sexual relations, see Jordan, *White over Black*, pp. 136–78.

that the black codes were a jumble whose haphazard construction reflected the refusal, inability, or disinclination of whites to fix the free Negro's status. The confusion gave free Negroes room to maneuver in a society that often was hostile to their very existence.

In actual practice, Negro freemen had a good deal less liberty than the law allowed. Free Negroes who pressed their legal rights often found themselves confronted with subtle legal constructions or new laws proscribing just what they were doing. The sudden appearance of some black laws suggests they were a response to the first test.[10] Indeed, much of the seeming elasticity of the freemen's status owed simply to the fact that the few free Negroes did not threaten white control.

Still, no matter what the cause, the free Negro's relatively unencumbered liberty suggests a flexibility in white attitudes which would later disappear. In the colonial years, this flexibility occasionally allowed free blacks to vote despite heated opposition, to demand their "Rights as Free Born Subjects," or simply to hold their own in the white-dominated world.[11] Moreover, the white position was not so firmly fixed that it could not be abruptly reversed. In 1765, Georgia, threatened by hostile Indians and Spaniards and desperately in need of able-bodied men, encouraged free Negro immigrants to settle in the colony and offered free mulattoes all the rights of "persons born of British parents," except voting and sitting in the General Assembly.[12] The exceptions of course re-emphasized the deep feeling of difference that white colonials were unable to shake even in a moment of danger. But the sharp reversal of policy by Georgia legislators indicates how hard-pressed whites could change with circumstances. The free Negro's ambiguous yet unsettled legal status made whites susceptible

10 See, for example, the Virginia stricture against free Negroes testifying against whites, Hening, comp., *Statutes Va.*, IV, 327–8, V, 245; C. Ashley Ellefson, "Free Jupiter and the Rest of the World: The Problems of a Free Negro in Colonial Maryland," *Maryland Historical Magazine*, LXVI (1971), 1–13.

11 William L. Saunders, ed., *Colonial Records of North Carolina*, 10 vols. (Raleigh, 1886–90), II, 214–15, 903, 908, IV, 251, IX, 97–8; Ellefson, "Free Jupiter," pp. 1–13.

12 Candler, ed., *Colonial Records Ga.*, XVIII, 659; Winthrop D. Jordan, "American Chiaroscuro: The Status and Definition of Mulattoes in the British Colonies," *W&MQ*, 3rd ser., XIX (1962), 186–7.

to changes they might otherwise have resisted. In 1775, when the long-simmering crisis with Britain at last boiled over, whites would again yield to the demands of changing circumstances and spur the development of the free Negro caste.

It was not only the white man's circumstances that changed in the last quarter of the eighteenth century. By the eve of the American Revolution, blacks had been living in America for over 150 years. After a century and a half of American captivity, they were not the same people whom John Rolfe had watched march down the gangplank at Jamestown. No longer were the transplanted Africans an alien people whose minds were befogged by the horrors of the Middle Passage, whose tongues were muted by the strange language of their enslavers, and whose senses were confused by the unfamiliar landscape that everywhere surrounded them. By the 1770s, if not earlier, the vast majority of blacks were native Americans with no firsthand knowledge of Africa. Increasingly, secondhand accounts of the "great land across the sea" were losing their meaning to new generations of American-born blacks—just as the fading memories of English life were losing their meaning for new generations of American-born whites. Beyond their master's eyes, many tried to maintain the ways of the old country, difficult though that was. But since adapting to the conditions of the New World was literally a life-and-death matter, most changed. Slowly, almost imperceptibly, transplanted Africans became a new people. They spoke English, worked with English tools, and ate foods prepared in the English manner. On the eve of the Revolution, many blacks had done so for two or three generations, and sometimes more.

But black acculturation was more than a leaching process whereby an English culture, modified by New World conditions, replaced an African one. To the emerging Anglo-American culture, transplanted Africans added their own heritage, a way of thinking and acting that had survived the Middle Passage. And not just a single African heritage. A mélange of African cultures, some compatible, some antagonistic, had been thrown together in the barracoons of Africa and continued to blend under the pressures of New World enslavement. These, the diverse heritage of Africa and the dominant Anglo-American culture, in turn were molded and shaped by the peculiar status and circumstance of black people to create a new cultural type: the Afro-American.[13]

By the end of the eighteenth century, the transformation of Africans to Afro-Americans was largely complete. Just as the colonial debate with Britain pushed ideas of natural rights and universal liberty to the fore, a century of cultural change enabled blacks to listen in on that debate and turn it to their advantage. If transplanted Englishmen were prepared to assert their independence, transplanted Africans were ready to take their liberty.

Even before the first shots at Concord, the changing political and ideological climate provided an opportunity for some blacks to challenge slavery. In the summer of 1774, Bacchus, a Virginia house servant, thought he saw his chance. A "cunning, artful, sensible Fellow," Bacchus was well acquainted with his native Virginia and the capital city of Williamsburg where he had long worked for a leading physician "who trusted him much." Perhaps it was while waiting at his master's table that he overheard talk of Lord Mansfield's decision, which freed all slaves who touched English soil. Or perhaps word of that decision had slipped out in the debates in the House of Burgesses and reverberated through the grogshops, back alleys, and forest retreats where blacks congregated. In any event, the news stuck in his mind. Night after night, the possibility of freedom kept him awake and dreams of liberty followed him to sleep. When the weather turned warm, he moved toward freedom. Assuming the name John Christian, he forged a pass, emptied his owner's purse, and collected his possessions. Later his master discovered that he had headed for the coast "to get

[13] The best study of the acculturation of African slaves during the colonial period is Gerald W. Mullin, *Flight and Rebellion: Slave Resistance in Eighteenth-Century Virginia* (New York, 1972); also helpful are Melville J. Herskovits, "The Negro in the New World: The Statement of a Problem," *American Anthropologist,* XXXII (1930), 145–55, and *The Myth of the Negro Past* (New York, 1941); Norman E. Whitten, Jr., and John F. Szwed, eds., *Afro-American Anthropology: Contemporary Perspectives* (New York, 1970); Roger Bastide, *African Civilisations in the New World* (New York, 1972); John W. Blassingame, *The Slave Community: Plantation Life in the Ante-Bellum South* (New York, 1972), pp. 1–40; and from a different perspective, Philip D. Curtin, ed., *Africa and the West: Intellectual Responses to European Culture* (Madison, Wis., 1972).

on Board some Vessel bound for *Great Britain*, from knowledge he has determined of Somerset's Case."

Apparently Bacchus never made it. Weighted down with "two white Russia Drill Coats . . . blue Plush Breeches, a fine Cloth Waistcoat, two or three thin or Summer Jackets, sundry Pairs of white Thread Stockings, five or six White Shirts . . . a fine Hat cut and cocked in a Macaroni Figure," he was easily identified and probably soon taken up.[14] But his ability to forge a plausible pass and travel easily through the Virginia countryside as John Christian indicates how far some blacks had come in adapting to the conditions of the New World. After 1775, it was just such acculturated blacks—skilled, familiar with the countryside, and often literate—who were best able to take advantage of the tumultuous events of the Revolutionary years. Because so many of these blacks pressed for their liberty and because the status of the free Negro was yet unsettled, the structure of the black population would undergo a radical change in the years between 1775 and 1812.

[14] Williamsburg *Virginia Gazette* (Purdie & Dixon), 30 June 1774.

PART ONE

THE EMERGENCE OF THE FREE NEGRO CASTE, 1775-1812

Ran away from the subscriber, more than two Years ago, a Negro man named LIBERTY. . . . The fellow may have changed his Name.

Raleigh Register, 6 June 1802

1

The Origins of the Free Negro Caste

> The love of freedom, sir, is an inborn sentiment, which the God of nature has planted deep in the heart: long may it be kept under by the arbitrary institutions of society; but, at the first favourable moment, it springs forth, and flourishes with a vigour that defies all check.
>
> [George Tucker], *Letter to a Member of the General Assembly of Virginia* (1801)

THE American Revolution swelled the ranks of the tiny Southern free Negro population. Few whites desired to enlarge the number of black freemen; even those who opposed slavery and hoped for its eventual abolition could not conceive of living with blacks who were free. But the events of the Revolutionary era moved in directions few could predict and none could control. If whites tried to seal the cracks in the door to freedom, blacks pushed all the harder. In the years following the Revolution, the number of free Negroes increased manyfold, so that by the end of the first decade of the nineteenth century there were over 100,000 free Negroes in the Southern states and they composed almost 5 percent of the free population and nearly 9 percent of the black population.[1]

[1] Except where otherwise indicated, all figures have been compiled from *Population of the United States in 1860* (Washington, D.C., 1864), pp. 592–604.

The free Negro caste had grown from a fragment of the colonial population to a sizable minority throughout the South.

The War of Independence propelled large numbers of blacks from slavery to freedom. The desperate need for troops and laborers forced both belligerents to muster blacks into their service with the promise of liberty. Given the chance, most blacks gladly traded the chains of bondage for military service and eventual freedom. The British, who had no direct interest in slavery, were the first to offer the exchange. In November 1775, Lord Dunmore, the royal governor of Virginia, declared martial law and freed all slaves able and willing to bear arms in His Majesty's service. This declaration shook even the most secure Virginians, but it came as no surprise. Dunmore and other British officials had been threatening such action for several months. Slaves, ever alive to the possibilities of liberty, quickly picked up these first rumblings of freedom. Some months earlier, a group of blacks had visited Dunmore and offered to join him and take up arms. Fearful of further alienating sensitive colonials, Dunmore had brusquely dismissed them. But the blacks would not be put off, and when Dunmore officially tendered the promise of liberty, they flocked to British headquarters in Norfolk harbor.

Defeat deflated Dunmore's promise of liberty. In December, about a month after his proclamation, colonial troops routed loyalist forces, including a large number of blacks wearing sashes emblazoned with the words "Liberty to Negroes." The loss broke the back of Dunmore's attempt to discipline the rebellious Virginians, and thereafter the colonials limited him to foraging raids from his seaborne headquarters. Despite military defeat and patriot propaganda that he would sell his black followers to the West Indies, Dunmore's promise stirred slaves throughout the Chesapeake region. Whenever his flotilla neared the coast, slaves, as one dejected master put it, began "flying to Dunmore." Slaveholders became so desperate to stop their flight that they addressed directly to their slaves an article in the *Virginia Gazette* in which they alternately denied complicity in the slave trade, threatened death to runaways, and enjoined slaves to "be content with their situation, and expect a better condition in the next world."

Dunmore used his black recruits to raid the Virginia coast, and in August 1776, when he retreated to Bermuda, three hundred blacks sailed north for future military service and freedom. All told, perhaps eight hundred slaves escaped to join Dunmore, and more important, hundreds more heard of his promise of freedom and were infected with the dream of liberty.[2]

The manpower shortage that forced Dunmore to use black troops worsened as the war dragged on. British commanders, despite popular opposition in England, increasingly followed Dunmore's lead and recruited slaves with the promise of liberty. Finally, in 1779, Commander-in-Chief General Henry Clinton officially promised freedom to all slaves who would desert their masters for British service. But by then both belligerents were regularly recruiting Negro troops, and Clinton's anticlimactic proclamation went almost unnoticed.[3]

As the war turned south late in 1778, more thousands of bondsmen quit slavery for freedom behind the British lines. Some slaves fulfilled the dream that Dunmore had aroused. When Prince escaped from his Virginia plantation, his owner "expected he tried to get to Howe's army, as he once attempted to join Dunmore."[4] But many slaves, especially in the Lower South, never having heard of Dunmore's promise, Clinton's proclamation, or any other specific pledge of freedom, joined their masters' enemy as a logical alternative to bondage.

"A great many Negroes goes to the Enemy," reported a North Carolina officer in 1780. Runaways, previously few in number, increased rapidly as slaves took refuge behind enemy lines. Whenever British soldiers appeared, worried masters secured their slaves more carefully or removed them to safer ground. In spite of these and other precautions, the floodtide of fugitives continued. Some slaves waited until the British drew near, and escaped during the ensuing confusion; others, especially those who lived near the coast, fled by commandeering

[2] Benjamin Quarles, *The Negro in the American Revolution* (Chapel Hill, N.C., 1961), pp. 19–32; Williamsburg *Virginia Gazette,* (Purdie) 17 November 1775, (Dixon & Nicholson) 2 December 1775.

[3] Quarles, *Negro in the American Revolution,* pp. 111–33; Donald L. Robinson, *Slavery in the Structure of American Politics, 1765–1820* (New York, 1971), pp. 98–113.

[4] Williamsburg *Virginia Gazette* (Purdie), 3 October 1777.

small skiffs and dinghies. They were so successful that in 1781 the Maryland Council urged the General Assembly to pass special legislation to protect slave property because of the ease with which slaves "abandon the Service of their Masters who live on the Waters." Once free, these blacks often helped others to escape.[5]

When the British left at the end of the war, they took thousands of slaves with them, and other bondsmen attached themselves to the French in a last effort to reach freedom. Many of these were betrayed and sold to the West Indies, and the British gave others to loyalist planters in compensation for confiscated property. But most received their promised freedom. Some of these free Negroes migrated to Africa, the West Indies, Florida, or Canada. Others found their way back to the Southern states, and some had never left. There is "reason to believe," complained angry Virginians in 1781, "that a great number of slaves which were taken by the British Army are now passing in this Country as free men."[6]

Colonial commanders and policymakers were considerably more chary about accepting slave recruits. Many were large slaveholders and had much to lose from any disruption of slavery. Most feared that a servile insurrection or a mass defection of slaveholders would follow the arming of blacks. Although Negroes had occasionally served in some colonial militias and had fought in the first battles of the Revolution, the Continental Congress, at South Carolina's instigation, quickly barred them from the colonial army. But as the war lengthened and manpower grew critically short, colonial policy shifted. The Northern states, led by New England, began actively soliciting black recruits, and when the war moved south, the states of the Upper South grudgingly yielded to grim necessity. Yet only Maryland authorized slave enlistments and eventually subjected free Negroes to the draft. Virginia

[5] Clark, ed., *State Records of N.C.*, XV, 138; Browne *et al.*, eds., *Archives of Maryland*, XLV, 473; William P. Palmer, ed., *Calendar of Virginia State Papers*, 11 vols. (Richmond, 1875–93), I, 477–8.

[6] Quarles, *Negro in the American Revolution*, pp. 111–57; Robinson, *Slavery in the Structure of American Politics*, pp. 122–30; quotation in Petition from Henrico County, 1784. VLP.

allowed free Negroes to enlist in its army and navy, but shunned James Madison's carefully argued proposal to create a black regiment under white officers. Delaware and North Carolina followed Virginia and allowed slaves to serve in their master's stead, but that was all. South Carolina and Georgia vehemently rejected even these cautious actions. Outnumbered by blacks throughout the lowland rice swamps and desperately afraid of slave rebellions, Lower South whites ignored the urgings of the Continental Congress to arm blacks for use against the British. Clearly, they feared black skins more than redcoats.

Even in the Upper South, the enlistment of some blacks in the patriot cause did not shake the white man's allegiance to slavery. Most Southern whites believed they were using blacks as they always had: to support a way of life which rested on chattel slavery. The most prominent arguments in favor of arming blacks urged precisely this reasoning. While some states allowed slaves to earn their freedom as substitutes for their masters, others used slaves as bounties to encourage white enlistment. North Carolina did both without any sense of contradiction. In any case, the use of slave substitutes was a bow to the prerogatives of the master, not to the principles of liberty. Where blacks were enlisted, Southerners made it clear, as did the governor of Virginia, that they served because "they could best be spared." Almost always, black recruits shouldered a shovel, not a musket, keeping them well within the white man's definition of their role as subservient menials.[7]

Still, the enlistment of a few blacks widened the route to freedom. In recognition of their service, grateful masters freed many slaves, and occasionally state legislatures liberated individual bondsmen by special enactment. Most whites seemed to think this was right. The Virginia General Assembly drew back in horror at reports that some masters had re-enslaved their black substitutes, and ordered the emancipation of all such bondsmen. In other states, slaves who had served in their master's place had only a verbal promise of freedom. Some masters kept their word, others did not. Doubtless most bonds-

[7] Quarles, *Negro in the American Revolution*, pp. 3–18, 51–67; Robinson, *Slavery in the Structure of American Politics*, pp. 113–22.

men did not wait around long enough to find out.[8] Most important, the presence of a few blacks in uniform stirred others still in bondage. Many slaves ran off to join the patriot army, and hard-pressed field commanders often accepted these fugitives with few questions asked. Still others avoided all whites and escaped military service as well as slavery. At the war's end, these runaways also passed into the growing free Negro caste.

The war ended too quickly to damage slavery permanently, but the spirit of liberty it inspired outlasted the fighting. The combined impact of the equalitarianism of the American Revolution and the evangelical revivals stirred some white Americans to rethink their values and aroused black Americans to demand their freedom. As a result, throughout the new Republic, a coalition of patrician revolutionaries and evangelical sectarians joined Quakers, long the mainstay of the antislavery movement, to challenge slavery. Propelled by the same forces, blacks seized the moment to petition against slavery, institute freedom suits, and take their freedom by running away.

The struggle against slavery was nowhere easy. Most slaveholders found slavery profitable and resisted abolition. The doctrine of natural rights, which gave impetus to the first emancipation movement, also sanctified property rights, so that both abolitionists and slaveholders found comfort in the words of the Declaration of Independence. Slaveholders not only invoked the sanctity of property but began haltingly to systematize all the crude and perfunctory arguments that had been used to justify slavery. Long before Thomas R. Dew, they argued that emancipation would be economically disastrous, that Negroes were happier as slaves, and that abolition would rend the social structure by releasing a floodtide of blacks on white America. The proscription and disfranchisement of free Negroes that followed emancipation attested to the power of these arguments. But at every turn they were contradicted by

[8] Quarles, *Negro in the American Revolution*, pp. 68–93; Luther P. Jackson, "Virginia Negro Soldiers and Seamen in the American Revolution," *JNH*, XXVII (1942), 274–5; Hening, comp., *Statutes Va.*, VIII, 103, IX, 308–9.

the ideology of the Revolutionary Republic. The stark contradiction between fighting for freedom and denying it to others had undeniable power, which abolitionists never ceased to apply.

Slavery fell only in the North. There, economic and demographic changes bolstered the Revolutionary ideology. The urban professionals, merchants, and middling commercial farmers who composed the dynamic sector of Northern society were intimate with the Revolutionary rhetoric and susceptible to its antislavery application. Only a few held slaves, and none depended on slavery for their economic and social position; they proved ready allies for the abolitionists. Moreover, far from evincing contentment with their lot, slaves proved restless in bondage and anxious for freedom. Finally, blacks composed just a tiny fraction of an expanding population. Nowhere were they so numerous as to pose a threat to white political and social control. Thus, where only a few had a vested interest in slavery, where Negroes posed no threat to white supremacy, and where law and circumstances allowed blacks to push for their freedom, slavery died quickly. By 1805, every Northern state had made provision for eventual emancipation.[9]

Yet even in the North, abolition met stiff opposition. In Rhode Island and Connecticut, which had the largest proportion of Negroes in New England, antislavery forces could enact only gradual-emancipation laws. In the Middle States, where blacks were more numerous and slavery more deeply entrenched, even piecemeal abolition proved difficult. Pennsylvania enacted a gradual-emancipation act in 1780, but, despite its many Quakers, never legislated immediate abolition. Lawmakers in New York and New Jersey, where the ratio of blacks to whites was three times that of Pennsylvania, repeatedly rebuffed antislavery forces and refused to enact even gradual emancipation for another twenty years. Significantly, emanci-

[9] Arthur Zilversmit, *The First Emancipation: The Abolition of Slavery in the North* (Chicago, 1967); Jordan, *White over Black*, pp. 315–74; Mary S. Locke, *Anti-Slavery in America* (Boston, 1901); Edgar J. McManus, *A History of Slavery in New York* (Syracuse, N.Y., 1966), pp. 141–88; Edward R. Turner, *The Negro in Pennsylvania* (Washington, D.C., 1911), pp. 54–88; Thomas Drake, *Quakers and Slavery in America* (New Haven, Conn., 1950).

pation laws in both New York and New Jersey compensated slaveholders for their property.[10] Only after property rights were satisfied were human rights secured.

The same factors that bred opposition to abolition in New England and delayed emancipation in the Middle States were intensified south of Pennsylvania. Slavery was an integral part of Southern society, and slaveholding planters dominated the economy, politics, and culture. Nowhere, except in Baltimore with its mercantile ties to western Pennsylvania, was there an urban professional and merchant class whose interests might counter those of the slaveholders. With the merchants and professionals tied to the slaveholding planters, antislavery sentiment could draw but weak support from the urban elite. Furthermore, the number of blacks was ten times that in the North. Whereas in 1790 Negroes composed less than 2 percent of the population of New England, they composed a third of the population of Maryland. Similarly, Negroes made up about 8 percent of the population of New York, but nearly 44 percent of the population of South Carolina. If the problem of compensation could cause abolition to falter in the North, it could undermine emancipationist sentiment in the South. If the prospective social dislocations of emancipation worried white New Yorkers, they horrified Marylanders and totally unnerved

[10] Gradual-emancipation procedure in New York and New Jersey compensated slaveowners in two ways. First, it allowed them to enjoy the services of children born of slave mothers long after these children reached adulthood (in New York, for example, age twenty-eight for males, twenty-five for females). Second, it permitted masters to abandon these children if they so desired. The overseer of the poor would then assign such "abandoned children" to a new master, who would be paid a set fee for their support and also enjoy the benefits of their labor. As planned, the new master was none other than the original owner. Thus, slaveholders not only received the services of blacks who were eventually to be free, but they were also paid for them. By this procedure, New York and New Jersey compensated some masters well beyond the value of their property when slavery was abolished, and the enormous expense that compensation entailed eventually forced its repeal in both states.

While such compensation lead to many abuses, it did have the distinct advantage of discouraging slaveowners from selling their slaves to some slaveholding region in the wake of emancipation. Where masters were not compensated by the state, they often compensated themselves in this manner. See Zilversmit, *First Emancipation*, pp. 180, 182, 194–9; Turner, *Negro in Pennsylvania*, pp. 80–1.

TABLE 1

PERCENTAGE OF POPULATION NEGRO IN 1790

Region / State	Percentage
New England	
Maine	0.6%
New Hampshire	0.6
Vermont	0.3
Massachusetts	1.4
Rhode Island	6.3
Connecticut	2.3
Middle States	
New York	7.6
New Jersey	7.7
Pennsylvania	2.4
Upper South	
Delaware	21.6
Maryland	34.7
Virginia	40.9
North Carolina	26.8
Kentucky	17.0
Tennessee	10.6
Lower South	
South Carolina	43.7
Georgia	35.9

SOURCE: U.S. Bureau of the Census, *Negro Population of the United States, 1790–1915* (Washington, D.C., 1918), p. 51.

South Carolinians. Between Maryland and North Carolina, antislavery sentiment was precarious; farther south, it was all but inconceivable.

Despite these dismal prospects, in the years following the Revolution a few Southerners challenged slavery. The ideas and events that stimulated abolition in the North were national, even international, in scope.[11] Lockean ideology was an intimate part of the Southern heritage, as it was of the Northern. It was only natural, and tactically wise, for Southern

[11] David B. Davis, *The Problem of Slavery in Western Culture* (Ithaca, N.Y., 1966).

abolitionists to draw liberally from the ideas of the Declaration of Independence. Yet the burden of the antislavery argument, again for tactical reasons, rested on the detrimental effect of slavery on white society. Abolitionists argued that slavery contradicted the basic tenets of republican ideology and threatened to subvert the moral foundations of the new Republic. It sapped the new nation of virtue, and, as many republicans believed, "Virtue is absolutely necessary for the happiness and prosperity of a free people." By allowing slavery to fester within the body politic, abolitionists believed Americans courted catastrophe. "I have no hope," observed a Maryland emancipationist in 1789, "that the stream of general liberty will flow for ever, unpolluted, thro' the foul mire of partial bondage, or that those who have been habituated to lord it over others, will not in time be base enough to let others lord it over them."[12]

Slavery, of course, did more than threaten the nation's righteousness. Throughout history slaves had risen up and overthrown their masters. If Southerners had forgotten the lessons of ancient history, they needed only to examine their own past. The insurrections and conspiracies that punctuated the colonial years had etched the threat of rebellion in the slaveholder's mind. Yet, as Americans, slaveholders not only feared revolt, they had to expect it. As abolitionists reminded them, the desire for liberty was inherent in human nature and impossible to stifle; surrounded by liberty but unable to enjoy it, blacks would naturally rebel. Even if constrained by rigorous oppression, they would remain potential incendiaries eager to join foreign enemies and domestic dissidents.[13]

The Christian equalitarianism unleashed by the religious revivals of the late eighteenth century complemented and

[12] Petition from Frederick and Hampshire County, 1786, VLP; Philanthropos [David Rice], *Slavery Inconsistent with Justice and Good Policy* (Lexington, Ky., 1792), p. 13; William Pinkney, *Speech of William Pinkney, Esq., in the House of Delegates of Maryland, at their Session in November, 1789* (Philadelphia, 1790), p. 9; also see [George Tucker], *Letter to a Member of the General Assembly of Virginia, on the Subject of the Late Conspiracy of Slaves* (Baltimore, 1801). For the importance of "virtue" in republican ideology, see Gordon S. Wood, *The Creation of the American Republic, 1776–1787* (Chapel Hill, N.C., 1969), pp. 65–70 and *passim*.

[13] [Rice], *Slavery Inconsistent with Justice*, pp. 9–12; [Tucker], *Letter to the General Assembly*, pp. 3–14.

strengthened the idealism of the Revolution. Like Revolutionary ideology, the religious awakenings transcended sectional boundaries. Methodist and Baptist evangelicals crisscrossed the nation and in hundreds of camp meetings made thousands of converts. Propelled by the revolutionary idea that all men were equal in the sight of God, they accepted black and white converts with equal enthusiasm. The equality of the communion table proved contagious, and some of the evangelicals broke the confines of otherworldly concerns to make a connection between spiritual and secular equality. True to his name, Freeborn Garretson, a Maryland Methodist, "endeavoured frequently to inculcate the doctrine of freedom in a private way" in his black converts.[14]

Others were less circumspect. Francis Asbury and Thomas Coke, the leaders of the American Methodist Church, circulated antislavery petitions and worked to institutionalize antislavery principles in their church. In 1784, at the special Christmas Conference in Baltimore, the Methodists agreed to expel members who failed to free their slaves as their *Discipline* prescribed. Despite intense opposition, Methodist evangelicals continued to preach an antislavery gospel and did not retreat from the 1784 rule until late in the 1790s. Baptist abolitionists, in part because of their denomination's congregational polity, could not duplicate the Methodists' stand. In 1785, the General Committee of the Virginia Baptist Church, at the urging of David Barrow, declared "hereditary slavery to be contrary to the word of God," but failed to enact antislavery principles. Some individual Baptist churches and associations, however, did adopt an antislavery stance. Antislavery delegates to one Virginia association recommended that its members join with the Virginia Abolition Society in petitioning against slavery, and another association inserted a detailed plan for gradual emancipation into its minutes.[15] Despite opposition in and out-

[14] Nathan Bangs, *The Life of the Rev. Freeborn Garretson,* 2nd ed. (New York, 1830), p. 59; Robert McColley, *Slavery and Jeffersonian Virginia* (Urbana, Ill., 1964), pp. 148–62; Wesley M. Gewehr, *The Great Awakening in Virginia, 1740–1790* (Durham, N.C., 1930); John B. Boles, *The Great Revival, 1787–1805: The Origins of the Southern Evangelical Mind* (Lexington, Ky., 1972).

[15] Donald G. Mathews, *Slavery and Methodism: A Chapter in American Morality, 1780–1845* (Princeton, N.J., 1965), pp. 3–29; Garnett Ryland, *The*

side the churches, some Methodist and Baptist evangelicals joined with Quakers to fill the ranks of the antislavery movement.

The opponents of slavery mounted their strongest challenge in the Upper South. Tobacco had long been that region's staple crop; it required intensive care and depleted the soil, but as long as it was readily marketable it remained dominant. Throughout the eighteenth century, however, wheat production had grown steadily in Maryland and Virginia as a glut of tobacco from newly settled western land drove prices down. The dislocations in mercantile ties and the depression which accompanied independence speeded the shift to cereal crops and transformed the agricultural patterns of the Upper South. In addition, the absence of British goods during the war spurred the development of a host of light industries. Peace and the return of foreign competition destroyed many of these new industries, but state subsidies helped some survive. These industries, together with the general expansion of commercial activity in the region, swelled the cities of the Upper South. Baltimore, Richmond, Fredericksburg, and Petersburg grew as never before. In all, the change in agricultural patterns, the nascent industrialization, and the concomitant urbanization profoundly altered the character of the region. Many Americans thought the Upper South would follow the pattern of development exemplified by Pennsylvania and not that of the states farther south. In the 1780s, even George Washington spoke of Virginia as one of the Middle States.[16]

Baptists of Virginia, 1699–1926 (Richmond, Va., 1955), pp. 150–5; W. Harrison Daniel, "Virginia Baptists and the Negro in the Early Republic," *VMH&B*, LXXX (1972), 65–8; Carlos R. Allen, Jr., "David Barrow's *Circular Letter* of 1798," *W&MQ*, 3rd ser., XX (1963), 440–51; J. H. Spenser, *A History of Kentucky Baptists*, 2 vols. (Cincinnati, Ohio, 1885), I, 182–5.

[16] Lewis C. Gray, *History of Agriculture in the Southern United States to 1860*, 2 vols. (Washington, D.C., 1933), II, 602–17; Gordon C. Bjork, "The Weaning of the American Economy: Independence, Market Changes, and Economic Development," *Journal of Economic History*, XXIV (1964), 541–60; Avery O. Craven, *Soil Exhaustion as a Factor in the Agricultural History of Maryland and Virginia, 1606–1660* (Urbana, Ill., 1926), pp. 72–121; Mary Jane Dowd, "The State of the Maryland Economy, 1776–1807," *Maryland Historical Magazine*, LVII (1962), 90–132, 229–58; Jacob M. Price, "The Beginnings of Tobacco Manufacture in Virginia," *Virginia Magazine of History and Biography*, LXIV (1956), 3–29; George Washington to Robert Lewis, 18 August 1799, in John C. Fitzpatrick, ed., *The Writings of George Washington*,

Economic changes in the Upper South and emancipation in the North created doubts about the viability of slavery and drove slave prices down. After a century of steady increase, the price of slaves slumped in the decade following the war. Between 1783 and 1795, according to one estimate, it fell by almost one-half. Thereafter slave prices rose, recouping the postwar losses and surpassing the prewar highs.[17] In the meantime, the switch from tobacco culture left a residue of surplus labor, and fears that slavery would wither away buttressed the Revolutionary ideology. Most masters sold their surplus slaves farther south, but the economic changes often gave antislavery sentiment an entering wedge. A few slaveowners yielded to the insistent equalitarian rhetoric and freed their slaves or allowed them to purchase their liberty.[18]

The ideological and economic changes of the post-Revolutionary years encouraged some nonslaveholders to challenge

---

39 vols. (Washington, D.C., 1931–44), XXXVII, 338–9; John R. Alden, *The First South* (Baton Rouge, La., 1961), pp. 9–10. For a comparative perspective on how dislocations in a slave economy stimulate manumission, see Degler, *Neither Black Nor White*, pp. 44–5.

[17] Evidence of slave prices before 1800 is disparate and often unreliable. In addition to the usual problems with such evidence, estimating the value of slaves during the post-Revolutionary years is made even more difficult because transactions were made in a variety of currencies of uncertain value. Regional differences between North and South, the Upper and Lower South, further compound the problem. After surveying the evidence for the United States, Ulrich B. Phillips concluded that "the range [of slave prices] in 1783 was a little lower than it had been on the eve of the war, while in 1795 it was hardly more than half as high"; *American Negro Slavery* (New York, 1918), pp. 366–71. Also see Jordan, *White over Black*, pp. 320–1, and Zilversmit, *First Emancipation*, pp. 40–6, 231–41. The question of viability, apart from profitability, has been raised in a more limited economic context by Yasukichi Yasuba, "The Profitability and Viability of Plantation Slavery in the United States," *Economic Studies Quarterly*, XII (1961), 60–7.

Since this book went to press, more accurate information on slave prices during the post-Revolutionary period has become available. New data collected by Robert William Fogel and Stanley L. Engerman reveal that while slave prices dropped sharply during the 1770s, they recovered most of their loss by the mid-1780s and remained at nearly that level until late in the 1790s, when they resumed their steady increase. Unfortunately, however, Fogel and Engerman do not distinguish between the price of slaves in the Upper and Lower South, and while they rightly emphasize the rapid recovery of slave prices in the 1780s, they also admit that slave prices remained "soft" throughout that decade and most of the one that followed. *Time on the Cross: The Economics of American Negro Slavery* (Boston, 1974), pp. 86–9.

[18] George Drinker to Joseph Bringhurst, 10 December 1804, PAS.

slavery. These Southerners spoke out not merely in horror at the immorality of bondage or in fear for the safety of the Republic, but in their own interest. As farmers, they were no longer able to compete with slaveowners for the best land, and as artisans, they suffered grievously from skilled-slave competition. They saw slavery locking them into a subordinate position in Southern society. Most of all, nonslaveholders disliked the invidious comparison of their own work with that of black slaves. "To labour," complained one emancipationist, "is *to Slave;* to work, is to work *like a Negro. . . .*" Thus, no matter how they felt about blacks, nonslaveholders had good reason to despise slavery, and they welcomed the opportunity to strike it down. Unhappily for the slaves, sneered one anti-abolitionist, "the greatest advocates for manumission, have been a set of men that had very little property to lose. Perhaps none." While patrician slaveholders disparaged slavery but did nothing about it, nonslaveholding farmers, artisans, and tradesmen filled the ranks of the antislavery movement. David Rice, a leading emancipationist, described the membership of the abortive Kentucky Abolition Society as "in low or but middling circumstances," and the Maryland Abolition Society was composed almost exclusively of merchants, skilled mechanics, and petty tradesmen.[19] Class antagonism, long masked under a veneer of racial solidarity and deference politics, suddenly struck against slavery.

The rise in antislavery sentiment in the Upper South heartened emancipationists, but their ideals never penetrated the Lower South. There, economic changes only reinforced the militant opposition to emancipation. The need for slave labor stimulated by the rise of cotton culture and fears generated by

[19] [Rice], *Slavery Inconsistent with Justice,* p. 14; Annapolis *Maryland Gazette,* 25 November 1790; David Rice to William Rogers, 4 November 1794, letterbook copy, PAS. The Maryland Abolition Society listed 165 members in Baltimore in 1797. Of these, 94 were merchants, 11 were professionals (6 lawyers, 3 physicians, a dentist, a teacher), 54 were skilled mechanics and tradesmen (8 potters, 7 tailors, 5 cabinetmakers, 2 druggists, 2 tavern keepers, 2 blacksmiths, a carpenter, a scrivener, a clockmaker, a weighmaster, a printer, and other artisans), and 6 did not list their occupations. Membership list, Maryland Abolition Society, with "Report to the American Convention," 1797, PAS; also "Report of the Delaware Abolition Society to the American Convention," 11 December 1797, PAS.

the numerical superiority of slaves in the coastal rice plantations extinguished every spark of antislavery idealism. Southern attachment to slavery also increased as plantation culture expanded west. In the newly settled Southwest, the demand for slaves was even greater than in the older states of the Lower South, and the Revolutionary experience which had fostered antislavery ideals was but a fading memory. Expansion into the West not only consumed slaves but emancipationist ideals as well.

Even in the Upper South, antislavery sentiment was fragile and confined to a small group of men and women. In the 1790s, when the flames of Revolutionary idealism flickered low, the economy settled into its familiar antebellum pattern, and the fears of insurrection intensified, the always weak Southern antislavery movement would collapse.

As in the North, the first fruits of the abolition movement in the South appeared soon after independence. In 1782, Virginia repealed its fifty-nine-year-old prohibition on private acts of manumission. Slaveholders were now free to manumit any adult slave under forty-five by will or deed. Five years later Delaware passed a similar act, and in 1790 Maryland, which already permitted manumission by deed, extended the law to include manumission by will. North Carolina lawmakers debated the liberalization of their manumission statutes several times during the 1780s but continually rebuffed antislavery forces. North Carolina slaveholders could free their slaves only for meritorious service and with the permission of the county court. By 1790, manumission was a slaveholder's prerogative throughout the South, except in North Carolina.

Liberalized provisions for manumission were extended to the new states and territories of the South. Kentucky adopted the Virginia law in 1792, and the Missouri Territory accepted a similar rule in 1804. Tennessee adopted the restrictive North Carolina act, but in 1801 the state vested county courts with greater discretion in determining "meritorious service."[20]

[20] Hening, comp., *Statutes Va.*, VI, 39–40; *Laws of Delaware*, II, 884–8; *Md. Laws*, 1790, c. 9, and repassed, 1796, c. 67; Locke, *Anti-Slavery in America*, pp. 121–2; *N.C. Laws*, 1788, c. 20; Francis N. Thorpe, comp., *The Federal*

Southern abolitionists scored their greatest success in the pages of the statute books.

Almost immediately slaveholders took advantage of the greatly liberalized laws. Throughout the South, but especially in the Upper South, hundreds of masters freed their slaves. Although manumission at times had nothing to do with antislavery principles, equalitarian ideals motivated most manumitters in the years following the Revolution. Slaveholders, many of whom opposed a general emancipation, freed their slaves because they were deeply troubled by the contradiction between slaveholding and the sanctity of the family, the inalienable rights of men, and the lessons of the gospel. "I cannot satisfy my conscience," wrote a Virginia emancipator, "to have my negro slaves separated from each other, from their husbands and wives." A Maryland slaveholder freed her slaves in 1802 because slavery contradicted "the inalienable Rights of Mankind," and another Virginia master manumitted his slaves because "it is contrary to the command of Christ to keep fellow creatures in bondage." Often Revolutionary ideology and Christian ideals were so intertwined that slaveholders blurted them out in the same breath. A Kentucky manumitter was convinced slavery was "inconsistent with republican principles; that it is in violation of our bill of rights, which declares, *that all men are by nature equally free;* and above all, that it is repugnant to the spirit of the gospel, which enjoins universal love and benevolence." Some emancipators, of course, merely mouthed antislavery rhetoric while ridding themselves of unwanted or unprofitable bondsmen, and of course emancipationist principles profited from the general insecurity of slave property, but the constant reiteration of antislavery ideals suggests that most manumitters took them to heart. Moreover, large-scale manumission seemed to legitimate the act in the eyes of many doubtful masters and encourage them to do likewise. "The history of emancipation in Maryland," one abolitionist observed, "has proved that manumission begets manumis-

---

and State Constitutions, 7 vols. (Washington, D.C., 1909), III, 1272–3; E. M. Violette, "The Black Code of Missouri," *Proceedings of the Mississippi Valley Historical Association,* VI (1912–13), 299–300; *Tenn. Laws,* 1801, c. 21. Not wishing to tax the master's right in any way, South Carolina and Georgia did not restrict manumission during the colonial years.

sion, that they increase even in a geometrical proportion."[21] Individual men enacted principles which abolitionists failed to translate into public policy.

While wholesale private emancipation released thousands from bondage in the Upper South, the Lower South remained largely aloof from the manumission fever. Manumission increased in South Carolina and Georgia, but it was much more selective. Whereas Upper South slaveholders often displayed their belief in the principles of liberty by indiscriminately freeing their slaves at once, Lower South masters tended to pick and choose, generally liberating only their illicit offspring, special favorites, or least productive slaves. Nevertheless, antislavery feeling sometimes did cross the line between the Upper and Lower South. The large number of masters who ignored the law and freed their slaves in North Carolina, a state which straddled the Lower South and was deeply influenced by Lower South intransigence, indicates the power of antislavery ideas to touch slaveholders even where abolition was fiercely denounced. In fact, so many North Carolina masters tried to free their slaves that hard-pressed county courts relaxed their definitions of "meritorious service." Furthermore, many slaveholders avoided the courts, ignored the law, and simply freed their slaves. Suggesting a general practice, one master petitioned the General Assembly to emancipate a slave whom he had "suffered for several years to live to himself." Most North Carolina manumitters did not even bother to request retroactive legislative approval. The unauthorized increase of freemen so infuriated the North Carolina legislature that it repassed the restrictive 1777 manumission act in 1788 and again in 1796, complaining that "divers persons, from religious motives, in violations of the . . . law continue to liberate their slaves."[22] But legal restrictions failed to slow the increased tempo of manumission.

Quakers were the most conspicuous violators of the North

[21] Catterall, ed., *Judicial Cases Concerning Slavery*, I, 183–5, 317, IV, 114; Anne Arundel County Misc. Manumissions, 4 January 1802, MdHR; [John S. Tyson], *Life of Elisha Tyson, Philanthropist* (Baltimore, 1825), p. 25.

[22] John Hope Franklin, *The Free Negro in North Carolina, 1790–1860* (Chapel Hill, N.C., 1943), p. 22; Petition from Duplin County, 1799, NCLP; *N.C. Laws*, 1788, c. 20, 1796, c. 5; also John Hope Franklin, "Slaves Virtually Free in Antebellum North Carolina," *JNH*, XXVIII (1943), 284–311.

Carolina manumission law. Not only did Friends free their own slaves, but in 1808 they agreed to act as the trustees of Negroes emancipated by non-Quaker slaveholders. These blacks, nominally owned by the Quakers, were in fact free and collected their own wages, controlled their families, and sometimes held property. By 1814, over 350 North Carolina Negroes had been turned over to the Quaker trustees.[23]

The very nature of the process makes it impossible to determine how many masters freed their slaves by merely setting them out on their own, yet the number of such cases to reach North Carolina courts suggests that the practice was almost commonplace. The custom of allowing persons legally enslaved to go at large as free men brought frequent laments from North Carolina jurists, who complained bitterly about the creation of "a species of *quasi* emancipation, contrary to the law, and against the policy of the State." The peculiar status of the quasi-free Negroes confounded attempts to control the growth of the free Negro caste in North Carolina. Sheriffs might arrest illegally freed blacks and even occasionally sell them back into slavery, but community pressures seemed to frown on that practice. Usually law officers simply turned them over to their old masters, who doubtless set them out on their own once again.[24] The growth of the North Carolina free Negro population lagged but slightly behind that of the Upper South.

The general liberalization of manumission law tended to reduce the number of quasi-free slaves, but every state had some. In 1811, a Virginia "slave" petitioned for his emancipation, claiming his master had promised him his freedom and "with an eye to that end allowed him to purchase real property and enjoy the benefits of it, and in no respect did he treat him as a slave." Similarly, Delaware whites complained that "under the

[23] Catterall, ed., *Judicial Cases Concerning Slavery,* II, 52; Stephen B. Weeks, *Southern Quakers and Slavery* (Baltimore, 1896), pp. 224–31. Even before the Quakers instituted the trusteeship system, they probably were holding "slaves" who were virtually free; Weeks, *Southern Quakers,* p. 227 n.

[24] Catterall, ed., *Judicial Cases Concerning Slavery,* II, 161–2, 188–9; Petitions from Perquimans and Pasquotank Counties, N.C., 5 May 1778, Manumission Papers, SHC; Records of Sale of Negroes "taken up and committed as emancipated contrary to law," 14 July 1788, 16 October 1788, 17 July 1789, and others undated, Perquimans County Records, NCA; *Raleigh Register,* 7 September 1809.

name and Character of Free Negroes many idle and evil-disposed Slaves" lived as free men, "whereby their legal Owners are for a long time deprived of their services."[25] These quasi-free Negroes, legally slaves but free in fact, greatly enlarged the growing free black caste.

The relaxation of the strictures against manumission reflected the main thrust of antislavery activity, but Southern abolitionists pressed their cause with equal vigor in the courts. Although freedom suits provided only piecemeal emancipation, establishing a single precedent often led to the emancipation of many slaves. "Whole families," recalled a Maryland abolitionist, "were often liberated by a single verdict, the fate of one relative deciding the fate of many." Awakened to the possibility of freedom, slaves flooded the courts with their petitions. A Maryland attorney reported that he was besieged with "repeated Applications from Negroes who are solicitous to obtain their freedom."[26] Confronted with the growing number of freedom suits, Southern courts occasionally responded sympathetically by liberalizing the rule of descent and expanding the range of evidence acceptable in freedom suits.

The Butler case reflected the post-Revolutionary change in judicial opinion in Maryland. In 1771, Mary and William Butler, the grandchildren of a Negro slave and a free white woman named Eleanor and "commonly called Irish Nell," sued for their freedom in a Maryland court, claiming descent from a free white woman. Maryland was the last colony to make the child of a mixed union follow the status of the mother. A 1664 law to prevent "shameful matches" had enslaved white women who married slaves and made their children slaves for life. The law was repealed in 1681, but a number of mulatto children had already been enslaved. Although the rule of descent from the mother, standard in all other states, was well established in Maryland by 1770, the presence of slaveborn descendants of white women created judicial chaos. As a result, the Butlers secured their liberty in a lower court only to have the case

[25] Petition from Washington County, 10 December 1811, VLP; Petition from Sussex County, 1786, Slavery Collection, HSD.

[26] [Tyson], *Life of Elisha Tyson,* p. 15; S. Greaves (?) to Meirs Fisher, 27 May 1790, Robert Pleasants to James Pemberton, letterbook copy, 22 April 1795, PAS.

reversed by the Court of Appeals. Sixteen years later, however, their daughter, also named Mary, initiated another suit and won her freedom.[27]

Mary Butler's success established an important precedent and almost immediately increased the number of freedom suits by slaves who claimed descent from a white woman. Of course, the usual absence of written proof made it difficult to demonstrate descent from anyone, but the Court of Appeals sympathetically allowed hearsay evidence. Eleanor Toogood, for example, received her freedom in 1783 because her great-grandmother reputedly was a white woman who married an "East Indian Indian," Basil Shorter was freed in 1794 because he was lineally descended from Elizabeth Shorter, a free white woman, and Anthony Boston won his liberty because his great-great-grandmother had a "yellow colour complexion with long straight hair." Admitting hearsay evidence greatly enhanced a slave's chances for freedom. "Hundreds of negroes," complained the attorney general of Maryland in 1797, "have been let loose upon the community by the hearsay testimony of an obscure illiterate individual."[28]

The North Carolina Supreme Court went even further than Maryland jurists in liberalizing the rule of descent. Although the North Carolina court upheld the presumption that all blacks were slaves, in 1802 it reversed the burden of proof for mulattoes, declaring them free men until proven slaves. Mixed-bloods might be the descendants of white, Indian, or free mulatto parents, the court decided, and, "considering how many probabilities there are in favour of the liberty of these persons, they ought not to be deprived of it upon mere presumption. . . ." Although Virginia courts neither distinguished mulattoes from blacks nor were they challenged by an ambiguous law of descent, they too reflected growing libertarian sentiment in their liberal interpretation of the manumission law of 1782. In 1804, the General Court upheld a 1781 will manumitting six slaves, noting with authority: "Devises in favour of . . . liberty ought to be liberally expounded." Again the Lower South generally remained aloof from the trend, but

[27] Catterall, ed., *Judicial Cases Concerning Slavery*, IV, 2–5, 49–50.
[28] *Ibid.*, IV, 49, 4, 52, 51, 54.

occasionally even South Carolina courts rang out in favor of freedom.[29]

Bitter experience cautioned blacks against depending too heavily on white benevolence or justice. Many slaves did not wait for their masters to offer freedom or for the courts to certify their liberty; they bought it by their own hard work. Masters sympathetic to the libertarian spirit of the age, but unwilling to suffer the economic losses that accompanied manumission, often permitted their slaves to purchase freedom. At the same time, the transformation of the Upper South economy increased the practice of allowing slaves to hire themselves out and widened opportunities for blacks to save some cash. Many slaves bought their liberty with money they earned while hiring their own time. A Virginia emancipationist explained the decline of slavery in the Northern Neck as partly the result of the "practice among lenient slaveholders of setting a moderate value on the time of slaves and suffering them to hire out at the best terms they could get."[30] Although it is impossible to estimate the number of self-purchases in the years following the Revolution, with the price of slaves relatively low and with the expectations for freedom high and white attitudes flexible, the percentage of slaves buying their freedom was probably higher than at any time thereafter.

Although the Lower South remained aloof from the postwar manumission fever, its free Negro population nevertheless increased rapidly. Beginning in 1792, the revolt on Saint-Domingue sent thousands of refugees fleeing toward American shores. Most were white, but among them were many light-skinned free people of color who had been caught on the wrong side of the ever-changing lines of battle. Although Americans welcomed these white refugees, with whom they sympathized and even identified, they feared the influx of brown émigrés. The states of the Lower South, ever edgy about slave rebellions, quickly barred West Indian free people of color from entering their boundaries, and other states later

[29] *Ibid.*, II, 18–19, 54, I, 109–10; Donald J. Senese, "The Free Negro and the South Carolina Courts, 1790–1860," *South Carolina Historical Magazine*, LXVIII (1967), 140–2.

[30] George Drinker to Joseph Bringhurst, 10 December 1804, PAS.

followed their lead.[31] Although many free Negro refugees avoided these states and migrated elsewhere, some of the panic-stricken free people of color who fled in the wake of Toussaint's revolution continued to flock into the nearby ports of Charleston and Savannah. During the winter of 1793, opposition to their presence burned high in those cities. A mass meeting in Charleston urged the expulsion of "the French negroes," and petitions supporting similar demands flooded into the South Carolina legislature from throughout the low country. In Savannah, nervous officials barred any ship that had touched Saint-Domingue from entering the harbor. Later the federal government added its weight to these edicts, but the congressional ban on free-Negro entry was no more successful than state and municipal legislation in stopping the flow of West Indian coloreds into the South.[32] South Carolina and Georgia suddenly acquired a large free Negro population.

The rapid increase of free Negroes in the years following the Revolution swelled the expectations of those remaining in bondage. For the first time, freedom was the property of a large class of blacks. Many slaves who saw their friends and relatives shed the shackles of slavery began thinking of what had previously seemed unattainable. While some of these bondsmen saved to buy their freedom and others took their masters to court, many more struck for liberty by running away. The increase in fugitives that had begun during the tumult of the war continued into the post-Revolutionary years.

Slaves, of course, had always run away. Generally, most

[31] Jordan, *White over Black*, pp. 382–4. For a general account of events on Saint-Domingue, see C. L. R. James, *The Black Jacobins: Toussaint L'Ouverture and the San Domingo Revolution*, 2nd rev. ed. (New York, 1963); James G. Leyburn, *The Haitian People* (New Haven, Conn., 1941), chap. 1.

[32] Papers Relating to Santo Domingo, 1791–1793; Petition from Charleston, 11 December 1797, ? September 1798, SCLP; Grand Jury Presentments, Beaufort, November 1793, Charleston, November 1792, September 1798, SCA; Rusticus Letters, 1794, SCHS; Charleston *City Gazette*, August–December 1793; Proceedings of the Savannah City Council, 5 July 1795, SCH; John Lambert, *Travels Through Lower Canada and the United States of North America*, 3 vols. (London, 1810), II, 404; Charles Fraser, *Reminiscences of Charleston* (Charleston, 1854), pp. 43–4; *Annals of Congress*, 7th Cong., 2nd Sess., pp. 1564–5.

absconded to redress personal grievances like an increased work load, the sale of a loved one, or a vigorous "correction." In a like manner, a change of circumstance resulting from the death of a master or the threat of being sold precipitated the flight of other fugitives. Still others ran away for a brief respite from the dismal plantation routine. These runaways generally made little preparation and were either quickly captured or soon returned of their own volition. Escaping into the woods for a few days was relatively easy; translating escape into freedom required planning, assistance, and a good measure of luck.

Even with preparation, only a few slaves made good their escape. Many had no knowledge of where to find freedom, and some had been so dulled by bondage that they did not know how to look. In America, law and custom had identified freedom with whites. By definition, the virtues of a free human being—independence and self-reliance—were not the virtues of a slave; by law, blacks were presumed to be slaves. Countless laws and customs relentlessly reinforced the identification of black with slavery and white with freedom. Moreover, even the most self-assured black fugitive would have difficulty passing as a member of the light-skinned colonial free Negro population. The successful runaway bondsman generally went to sea as a sailor, perhaps with the hope of securing his freedom in a distant port, or else he headed for a newly settled region where planters, strapped for labor, might hire and protect him with few questions asked. A few men and women took to the woods and lived the precarious outlaw's life; the lucky ones were adopted by neighboring Indian tribes. Significantly, the most stringent colonial runaway laws were aimed at outlying slaves, who lived in the woods or swamps and raided nearby plantations.[33]

The changes unleashed by the American Revolution impelled slaves to consider anew the possibilities of escaping to freedom. Rumors of abolition in the North and the rumblings of emancipation in the South inspired some blacks to strike out for their liberty. The success of a local runaway or freedom

[33] Mullin, *Flight and Rebellion,* pp. 106–12, 129.

suit, the equality accorded blacks by evangelical sectarians, and the triumph of Toussaint L'Ouverture on Saint-Domingue awakened many more. In the Upper South, where manumission daily increased the number of free Negroes, some whites spoke out against slavery, and most blacks were second- or third-generation Afro-Americans, many bondsmen took their liberty simply by leaving their masters. The number of fugitives also increased in the Lower South, though the scale was not nearly so great. But throughout the South, successful runaways added to the free Negro population.

Slaves lost little time in testing the rumors of freedom in the North. In 1795, when a Virginia bondsman absconded, his master was sure he was going to Philadelphia, as "some time before his elopement he inquired very particularly the way there, said he heard negroes were free there." Rap Gowing was "on his way to Pennsylvania," his Virginia owner reported, "where he has been informed, by those who now call themselves 'Friends of Liberty,' he will find an asylum." So many fugitives headed north that many slaveholders assumed that was the destination of their slave. "I suppose he may go to Baltimore, and from hence push for Pennsylvania," wrote an Eastern Shore master, and William Paca of Annapolis understood his "complete waiting man" had taken "the Philadelphia road."[34] Throughout the antebellum period the North Star remained a symbol of freedom to enslaved blacks.

Like abolition in the North, large-scale manumission in the South encouraged slaves to leave their masters. The sudden liberation of men and women long known as equals shook those who remained in bondage. When news of a large emancipation in Richmond reached Petersburg, several slaves immediately left their owner and tried "to pass as part of the negroes that obtained their freedom under the will of John Pleasants." Slaveowners understood the disturbing effect freeing some slaves had on all slaves. A Maryland master, like many other slaveholders, thought it "natural" that his slave would attempt to pass as free, "as a number have been set free in

[34] Richmond *Virginia Gazette,* 15 April 1795, 13 October 1799; Annapolis *Maryland Gazette,* 5 June 1800, 26 June 1794.

the neighborhood which he just left."[35] Similarly, news of a successful freedom suit not only induced other bondsmen to take their owners to court but caused many slaves simply to run off when their suits failed. In Maryland, the success of Mary Butler, Eleanor Toogood, and Basil Shorter in winning their liberty provided a heady example to others. For example, Ralph ran away to Annapolis "to prove his freedom as a descendant of Nell Butler." Apparently he failed, but upon his return he "refused to go to work with other negroes, and left his master again immediately." Having come so close to freedom, Ralph could no longer tolerate bondage. Other slaves, adopting a common strategy, took the name of some family who had recently won their liberty. The Butler name was so commonplace in Maryland runaway advertisements that one planter estimated that the descendants of Irish Nell numbered 750! Even below the Potomac, where new repressive laws stifled freedom suits and juries were generally hostile, sometimes word of the Butlers' success in Maryland had the same effect, and everywhere the presence of newly freed bondsmen awoke some slaves to the possibility of liberty.[36]

The acceptance of blacks as equals in the sight of God by many evangelicals also revolutionized black expectations. Although many white preachers, responding to pressure from planters, tried hard to inculcate the Biblical doctrine of "Servants, obey your masters" along with the regular dose of Christianity, the revolutionary nature of Christian universalism was irrepressible. Bondsmen constantly found connections between spiritual and temporal equality. Cooper, a Virginia slave, was a typical runaway, one who, "being sensible and artful in conversation, reads well, and frequently assumes the character of a Baptist preacher." Some evangelicals made no apology for slavery and frankly preached equality to blacks. Sam "was raised in a family of religious persons, commonly

[35] Richmond *Virginia Argus,* 5 September 1800; Annapolis *Maryland Gazette,* 29 June 1803.

[36] Annapolis *Maryland Gazette,* 18 June 1796, 27 August 1789, 18 January 1798; Baltimore *Maryland Journal,* 17 February 1792; "Information given of ? sometimes in the Month of July," 17 September 1789, Robert Carter Papers, Duke; Fredericksburg *Virginia Herald,* 8 July 1790; Annapolis *Maryland Gazette,* 23 June 1803.

called Methodists, and has lived with some of them for years past, on terms of perfect equality," complained a Maryland master. "The refusal to continue him on these terms . . . has given him offense, and is the sole cause of his absconding."[37] Sam was not the only black sectarian who quit slavery. Other slaves used their attendance at church services and camp meetings as an opportunity to make their escape. Not surprisingly, many masters viewed the evangelicals as dangerous subversives and sometimes kept their slaves from religious meetings. Yet it was difficult for Christian masters to deny the opportunity of salvation to their charges, even though many black converts were the first runaways.

Toussaint's success in overthrowing the French slaveholders of Saint-Domingue and the eventual establishment of a black republic buttressed the impact of Revolutionary ideals. At the very least, his achievement told American blacks that whites need not rule permanently. Slaveholders, who watched events on Saint-Domingue with dreadful fascination, understood this only too well. After 1792, most Southern states barred the entry of slaves touched by the revolution, who had been accompanying refugee masters into the South. Virginia failed to adopt the preventive legislation, thereby allowing large numbers of refugees and their infected slaves to pour into the Norfolk area. Throughout the tidewater region, fear of impending insurrection grew. Some of the newly arrived blacks quickly absconded, and even when they did not, their presence heightened slaveholder fears. "The insolence of those people is common talk on the Court Green, particularly since the arrival of the French from C[ap Français]," fretted one Virginian. Despite the increased activity of the police, militia, and slave patrols, the heightened black self-esteem, which the whites deemed insolence, continued to grow. Some slaves planned insurrections of their own, and many more ran away. "Within a few weeks past," wrote a Virginian to the governor, "several negroes have eloped from their masters' plantations & . . . one in particular came to his master with a sword made out of a Reap hook, and told him to his face that he would not serve

[37] Richmond *Virginia Gazette,* 23 March 1791; Baltimore *Maryland Journal,* 23 June 1793.

him unless he was allowed certain privileges which his master denied; he then went off, & has not returned."[38]

Whatever a fugitive's motive, the greatly enlarged free Negro population enhanced his or her chances for making a successful escape. The free Negro caste, for the first time, was large enough and dark enough to camouflage large numbers of runaways. With so many newly (and illegally) freed blacks traveling through the countryside, it was no longer possible for whites to know every free Negro in their neighborhood or realistically assume that every unknown black was a slave. Although many whites automatically stopped every strange or unsupervised black man and woman and demanded proof of their status, the number of unknown free Negroes doubtless taxed the zeal of even the most vigilant white. This novel situation forced many slaveholders to append a special caution to runaway advertisements. "It is probable this fellow may endeavour to pass for a free man, as there are many free blacks passing about the country," read a typical Maryland notice. Runaways challenged the white man's presumption that all blacks were slaves by hiding among the growing free Negro population. It seemed the number of free Negroes always exceeded the number of Negroes freed. "I will venture to assert," complained an angry neighbor to one prominent manumitter, "that a vastly greater number of slave people have passed & are passing now as your free men than you ever owned."[39]

The nascent urbanization of the South compounded the problem of recovering fugitives and aided the passage of many blacks from slavery to freedom. The growing cities of the South, with their countless back alleys, warehouses, and grogshops, provided a resting place for fugitives on the run. Even if their destination was the North, many runaways first headed for a nearby city where they might mix with free and fugitive blacks and perhaps find an odd job on the bustling docks or new factories to help finance their escape. Richmond, like most Southern cities, was so inundated by strange blacks, many of them runaways, that in 1787 the Common Council instructed

[38] Palmer, ed., *Virginia State Papers,* V, 625, VI, 651, VII, 425, 470, 475–6.

[39] Annapolis *Maryland Gazette,* 9 August 1792; Richmond *Virginia Gazette,* 11 December 1793; [Rev. Thruston] to Robert Carter, 5 August 1796, Robert Carter Papers, LC.

the constable to make it his daily practice to "traverse the streets and lanes of the city and apprehend all negroes and mulattoes, who do not belong to any citizen, and cannot give a good account of their business." Apparently this had little effect, because a year later the Common Council ordered a census taken of all Negroes "not being domestic servants or slaves and appearing to be free." Nevertheless, complaints about the growing free black caste soon echoed in the state legislature. The General Assembly denounced the "great inconveniences that have arisen in many, if not all the towns within this commonwealth, from the practice of hiring negroes and mulattoes, who pretend to be free but are in fact slaves," and legislated against free Negroes' entering cities and against slaves' passing as free. Still, runaways were a continuing problem for Southern municipalities.[40]

Economic changes also made it easier for fugitives to elude their masters. The transformation of the Upper South economy swelled the number of tenant farmers and tradesmen who were always in need of an extra hand but were rarely in a position to purchase slaves. These men, often antislavery in sympathies, might employ strange blacks with few questions asked. The ability of runaways to find a safe haven, even for a few days, often made a successful flight possible. Moreover, as the chances of success increased, slaves planned their escapes more carefully and probably further increased the proportion of fugitives who managed to pass from slavery to freedom.

The enlarged free black population not only camouflaged fugitive slaves but actively encouraged and aided their flight to freedom. So often did runaways take refuge with free friends and relatives that masters usually looked first to them when searching for their missing property. Thomas Jones thought Sam would go to Baltimore, where he had "several relations (manumitted blacks), who will conceal and assist him to make his escape," and "Bet went off in company with a mulatto free fellow named Tom Turner, who follows the water for a living and calls her his wife." As Bet's escape suggests, kinship ties

[40] Minutes of the Richmond Common Council, 24 January 1787, 27 July 1788, VSL; Samuel Shepherd, comp., *The Statutes at Large of Virginia from . . . 1792, to . . . 1806, Inclusive,* 3 vols. (Richmond, 1835), I, 238; Richmond *Virginia Gazette,* 14 May 1786.

motivated many of the free Negroes who aided slaves. Blacks often took extraordinary chances to free their families. John Cotton, a North Carolina fugitive, not only successfully freed himself but returned from Philadelphia to liberate his wife and five children. Yet, even more important than the protection, shelter, food, and passes that free Negroes provided was their example: they were the living proof that blacks could be free. "Henny," noted a Maryland slaveholder in 1783, "will try to pass for a free woman, as several have been lately set free in this neighbourhood."[41]

Occasionally whites befriended runaway slaves. Although Southern racial ideology generally succeeded in dividing whites and blacks, similar living and working conditions occasionally fostered close personal ties. In the post-Revolutionary years, when equalitarian ideals challenged racial prejudice and a large number of newly arrived Irish apprentices worked alongside slaves, interracial friendships sometimes developed. With hardly a hint of surprise, George Pinter's master noted that his slave went off "in company with a couple of Irish servants [from] where they had been at work together for some time past." Before he departed, Tom "informed one of my other negroes," declared a Halifax master, "that a white man had given him a pass, and that he intended to pass as a freeman." Some whites saw fugitive slaves as a source of cheap labor and encouraged them to leave their masters, and others found that interracial cooperation could be profitable for whites as well as blacks. One duped slaveholder complained that soon after Harrison sold him Peter, the slave absconded and "the Irishman also went off. . . . It is suspected those two fellows have joined themselves together again, and . . . that it is their design for Peter to be sold as often as they find it convenient, if either of them is in need of money." Intimate ties with blacks motivated still other whites. Jacob, a slave, went off "with a certain Betty Larkey, who is an Irish woman . . . by whom he had a mulatto son." Jacob and Betty took their son with them, perhaps to get "settled in some town to the northward." Ap-

[41] Baltimore *Maryland Journal,* 25 June 1793; Annapolis *Maryland Gazette,* 6 May 1790; Richmond *Virginia Gazette,* 2 May 1792; Annapolis *Maryland Gazette,* 6 July 1797. Also William McKean to John Dunlap, 10 October 1816, letterbook copy, Roslin Plantation Papers, VSL.

parently their attempt to build a new life was successful, for two years later they were still at large.[42]

Runaway slaves valued this assistance because they needed all the help they could get. Southern law presumed blacks to be slaves and provided that all suspected Negroes be jailed, advertised, and, if unclaimed, sold to the highest bidder. Fugitives who resisted capture could be declared outlaws and legally killed. Whites enforced runaway laws with varying degrees of rigor, but all blacks were suspect. Sometimes forged papers were enough to fool suspicious whites. When Moses ran off, he was stopped the same day, but he flashed a pass and was permitted to go on. Other passes were not as convincing, and other whites were more suspicious. A North Carolina jailer committed a Virginia Negro whose freedom papers he "suspected to be a forgery," and a Maryland sheriff revealed just how precarious the freemen's liberty could be when he requested Robert Loveless's "owner (if any) . . . to release him . . . or he will be sold."[43] Against the suspicions of the local sheriff or any white who might stop them, runaways could match only their wits and "smooth tongue." A Virginia master warned whites to keep up their guard, as Brunswick "appears rather silly which induces those that has had him in custody to indulge him, by which he effects his escape."[44]

Brunswick's success suggests that quick thinking and careful preparation provided the runaway's best defense. No matter how many friends might help, during most of his flight a fugitive was on his own. If freedom was his goal, he changed his name, procured a pass or a set of freedom papers, and purloined food, clothing, money, and often a horse or a gun. Prince, a carpenter and joiner, not only took food and clothing, but prepared himself for freedom by taking "two planes, two drawing knives, and some tools belonging to these trades." Prince was no exception. Ned, "a rough shoemaker carried off

[42] Baltimore *Maryland Journal*, 2 April 1793; Halifax *North-Carolina Journal*, 28 August 1797; Charleston *City Gazette*, 1 September 1793; Savannah *Georgia Gazette*, 1 January 1789; Richmond *Virginia Gazette*, 27 October 1790; *Raleigh Register*, 8 December 1801; Richmond *Virginia Gazette*, 2 May 1792, 20 August 1794.

[43] Annapolis *Maryland Gazette*, 3 June 1808, 31 October 1799; *Raleigh Register*, 9 March 1807.

[44] Richmond *Virginia Gazette*, 16 March 1791.

a parcell [*sic*] of old shoemaker's tools," and Dick ran away with "a hand saw, jack, and a long plane."[45] Many runaways planned new management, but business as usual.

The elements of a successful escape were not grasped at once; indeed, it seemed that most runaways tried several times before they reached freedom, if they ever did. "He is an old and artful offender" and "she will pass as a free woman as she did before" were the staples of runaway advertisements. But some things even experience could not buy. Many slaves, broken by the crippling effects of plantation slavery, remained oblivious to the new possibilities for freedom. But others, alive to the libertarian impulse of the age, quickly took advantage of the new avenues to freedom created by the emergence of the free Negro caste. These were special men and women, for it took a special kind of person to leave the familiarity of a relatively small, if harsh, world and risk the almost certain punishment that would follow failure. Slaveholders seemed to understand this and often noted the character traits that set these slaves apart: Roger was "resolute at anything he undertakes"; Stuart spoke "with great confidence"; John was "self-important"; and Rezin had "a great share of pride."[46] Not surprisingly, slaveholders tried to shatter this self-esteem either with suffocating paternalism or, if necessary, with brute force. This self-confidence was never completely extinguished by bondage, but it flourished only under special conditions. Most of the runaways were skilled artisans, mechanics, and house servants. Almost all were acculturated Afro-Americans; many were literate; and some had traveled widely. These blacks had seen more of the world, had a wider range of experience, and were not blinded by the narrow alternatives of plantation life. Before they ran off, most fugitives were already part of the black elite.

The spectacular increase in manumissions and runaways and the influx of West Indian people of color altered the size and

[45] Richmond *Virginia Gazette,* 4 April 1792, 7 May 1794; Halifax *North-Carolina Journal,* 1 October 1793.

[46] Fayetteville *North-Carolina Chronicle,* 24 May 1790; *Richmond Enquirer,* 20 January 1807; Baltimore *Maryland Journal,* 25 June 1793; Baltimore *Federal Gazette,* 30 October 1806.

TABLE 2

FREE NEGRO POPULATION, 1755–1810*

	Pre-1790	*1790*	*1800*	*1810*
United States		59,466	108,395	186,446
North		27,109	47,154	78,181
South		32,357	61,241	108,265
Upper South		30,158	56,855	94,085
Lower South		2,199	4,386	14,180
Delaware		3,899	8,268	13,136
D.C.		—	783	2,549
Kentucky		114	741	1,713
Maryland	1,817[a]	8,043	19,587	33,927
Missouri		—	—	607
North Carolina		4,975	7,043	10,266
Tennessee		361	309	1,317
Virginia	1,800[b]	12,766	20,124	30,570
Georgia		398	1,019	1,801
Louisiana	165[c]	[1,303][d]	[1,768][e]	7,585
Mississippi		—	182	240
South Carolina		1,801	3,185	4,554

[a] 1755 [d] 1785
[b] 1782 [e] ca. 1803
[c] 1769

* Between 1790 and 1810, the federal census enumerated free Negroes as "all other free persons" (1790) and "all other free persons, except Indians not taxed" (1800, 1810).

TABLE 3

PERCENT INCREASE OF FREE NEGROES, 1755–1810

	Pre-1790	*1790–1800*	*1800–1810*
United States		82.3%	72.0%
North		73.9	65.8
South		89.3	76.8
Upper South		88.5	65.5
Lower South		99.5	223.3
Delaware		112.1	58.9
D.C.		—	225.5
Kentucky		550.0	131.2
Maryland	342.7%[a]	143.5	73.2
Missouri		—	—
North Carolina		41.6	45.8

TABLE 3—CONTINUED

	Pre-1790	*1790–1800*	*1800–1810*
Tennessee		−14.0	326.2
Virginia	609.2[b]	57.6	59.1
Georgia		153.0	76.7
Louisiana	689.7[c]	[37.7][d]	[329.0][e]
Mississippi		—	31.9
South Carolina		76.8	43.0

[a] 1755–1790 [d] 1785–ca. 1803
[b] 1782–1790 [e] ca. 1803–1810
[c] 1769–1785

TABLE 4

PROPORTION OF NEGROES FREE, 1755–1810

	Pre-1790	*1790*	*1800*	*1810*
United States		7.9%	10.8%	13.5%
North		40.2	56.7	74.0
South		4.7	6.7	8.5
Upper South		5.5	8.1	10.4
Lower South		1.6	2.1	3.9
Delaware		30.5	57.3	75.9
D.C.		—	19.4	32.1
Kentucky		1.0	1.8	2.1
Maryland	4.0%[a]	7.2	15.6	23.3
Missouri		—	—	16.8
North Carolina		4.7	5.0	5.7
Tennessee		9.6	2.2	2.9
Virginia		4.2	5.5	7.2
Georgia		1.3	1.6	1.7
Louisiana	3.5[b]	[7.3][c]	[12.0][d]	18.0
Mississippi		—	5.0	1.3
South Carolina		1.7	2.1	2.3

[a] 1755 [c] 1785
[b] 1769 [d] ca. 1803

SOURCES FOR TABLES 2–4: *Gentlemen's Magazine and Historical Chronicle,* XXXIV (1764), 261; St. George Tucker, *A Dissertation on Slavery* (Philadelphia, 1796), p. 72; Lawrence Kinnaird, ed., *Spain in the Mississippi Valley, 1765–1794,* in *Annual Report of the American Historical Association for the Year 1945,* 4 vols. (Washington, D.C., 1946), II, pt. 1, 196; *Appendix to an Account of Louisiana Being an Abstract of Documents in the Offices of the Departments of State and the Treasury* (Philadelphia, 1803), pp. 84–7; *Annals of Congress,* 8th Cong., 2nd Sess., pp. 1574–6; *Population of the United States in 1860* (Washington, D.C., 1864), pp. 600–1.

character of the Southern free Negro caste. The change can best be viewed in Maryland. Between 1755 and 1790 the free Negro population of Maryland grew over 300 percent to about 8,000, and in the following ten years it more than doubled. By 1810, almost one-quarter of Maryland's Negroes were free, and they numbered nearly 34,000; this was the largest free Negro population of any state in the nation.

Free Negroes registered similar gains throughout the Upper South. In 1782, the year Virginia legalized private manumission, St. George Tucker estimated the number of Virginia free Negroes to be about 2,000.[47] By 1790, when the first federal census was taken, the number of Virginia free Negroes had grown to 12,000. Ten years later, the caste numbered 20,000 and by 1810 it stood at over 30,000. During the twenty years between 1790 and 1810, the free Negro population of Virginia more than doubled. In all, the number of Negro freemen in the Upper South grew almost 90 percent between 1790 and 1800 and another 65 percent in the following decade, so that freemen composed more than 10 percent of the region's Negro population.

In Georgia and South Carolina, which sternly refused to enlist blacks in the Revolutionary cause and stifled the development of antislavery sentiment, considerably fewer masters freed their slaves and fewer fugitives found freedom. But the arrival of light-skinned refugees from Saint-Domingue expanded the free Negro population in the Lower South well beyond the bounds of natural increase. Georgia's tiny free Negro population of 400 in 1790, probably all but nonexistent before the Revolution, totaled 1,800 in 1810, a gain of well over 300 percent. Likewise, the number of Negro freemen in South Carolina more than doubled during those twenty years to total over 4,500. Nevertheless, these states lagged far behind the Upper South. In 1800, free Negroes from Georgia and

[47] In 1796, St. George Tucker estimated that there were 1,800 free Negroes in the state in 1782, the year Virginia liberalized its manumission code. Seven years later, he apparently revised his estimate to 2,800. Whether this is a re-estimation of the free Negro population or merely a correction of a typographical error is unclear. St. George Tucker, *A Dissertation on Slavery* (Philadelphia, 1796), p. 72; St. George Tucker, ed., *Blackstone's Commentaries*, 5 vols. (Philadelphia, 1803), II, app. 66. I have used Tucker's first estimate. For a different interpretation see Russell, *Free Negro in Virginia*, p. 11 n.

South Carolina composed a mere 7 percent of the Southern free Negro population. Even after the purchase of Louisiana with its large free Negro caste, only 13 percent of Southern free Negroes resided in the Lower South. Moreover, while the free Negro population of the Upper South grew darker through indiscriminate manumission and the addition of many black fugitives, that of the Lower South remained light-skinned. A crack, which would widen during the antebellum years, appeared in the ranks of the growing free Negro caste.

By 1810, the 108,000 free Negroes were the fastest-growing element in the Southern population. Although the number of Southern whites and slaves also increased rapidly during the early years of the Republic, the growth of the free Negro population outstripped both. In Virginia, for example, the free Negro caste doubled between 1790 and 1810, while whites increased 24 percent and slaves 31 percent. In Maryland during the same period, the comparison was even more startling. Maryland free Negroes increased fourfold, while the white population grew 12 percent and the slave population a paltry 8 percent. In Delaware, the expansion of freedom undermined slavery. In 1790, the Delaware free Negro caste of about 4,000 was less than the state's slave population. Twenty years later its 13,000 free Negroes outnumbered slaves more than three to one, and Delaware slavery was permanently impaired. Even South Carolina and Georgia free Negroes multiplied more rapidly than whites and slaves in their respective states. Moreover, since the law presumed all blacks to be slaves and some free Negroes had been illegally freed if not outright fugitives, many free Negroes doubtless avoided census marshals, and the census substantially underenumerated the free Negro caste.

The increase in size also altered the character of the free Negro caste. Large-scale indiscriminate manumission and the successful escape of many black fugitives darkened the free Negro population. In the Upper South, where the manumission movement had its greatest impact, the balance between mulatto and black freemen may have been shifted to the blacks.[48] Furthermore, since most of the runaways were young men and

[48] The United States census did not distinguish between mulattoes and blacks until 1850, and at that time it indicated that about 40 percent of Southern free Negroes were of mixed racial origins. This is a sharp shift from the racial

women, the increased number of successful fugitives infused the free Negro caste with a large group of restless youth. By the beginning of the nineteenth century, the free Negro caste was no longer the tiny group of mulattoes and cripples it had been before the Revolution. It included blacks as well as mixed-bloods, vigorous young as well as elderly former slaves. Throughout the South, the greatly enlarged caste was an important and, in some areas, an indispensable part of the labor force, an ever-present example to slaves, and a direct contradiction to the white man's racial ideal.

---

composition of the colonial free Negro population as suggested by the Maryland census of 1755. An enumeration of free Negroes in the District of Columbia taken soon after the Federal District was established indicates that the shift in the character of the free Negro caste from brown to black (although, compared with slaves, still disproportionately brown) took place during the years immediately following the Revolution.

The District was carved out of Maryland and Virginia. No information is available on the racial composition of Virginia free Negroes during the colonial era, but the 1755 census indicates that Maryland free Negroes were overwhelmingly mulatto. Yet in 1807, black freemen outnumbered mulatto 279 to 215 in the District of Columbia. U.S. Commissioner of Education, *Special Report . . . on the Condition and Improvement of Public Education in the District of Columbia* (Washington, D.C., 1871), p. 195.

2

From Slavery to Freedom

> It may fairly be inferred that the negroes, if once emancipated, would never rest satisfied with any thing short of perfect equality.
>
> [George Tucker], *Letter to a Member of the General Assembly of Virginia* (1801)

THE post-Revolutionary era marked the first flowering of Afro-American life. The simultaneous growth of the free Negro caste and emergence of a new generation of American-born blacks released the creative energies of black people with a force not equaled until the Reconstruction period nearly a century later. Newly freed blacks moved at once to give meaning to their freshly won liberty and to give form to the rapidly maturing Afro-American culture. They chose new names, took new residences, found new jobs, reconstructed broken families, and organized their own churches, schools, and fraternal societies. Although encouraged by the rising expectations that accompanied freedom and the promise of American life as reflected in the charter of the new Republic, free blacks were also confronted by the repressive reality of American racism. Thus, the society and culture that emerged from this first attempt to remake black life in America represented both the powerful demands of newly liberated blacks and the stern resistance of entrenched slaveholding whites.

Free Negroes commonly celebrated emancipation by taking a new name. A new name was both a symbol of personal liberation and an act of political defiance; it reversed the enslavement process and confirmed the free Negro's newly won liberty just as the loss of an African name had earlier symbolized enslavement. Emancipation also gave blacks the opportunity to strip themselves of the comic classical names that had dogged them in slavery and to adopt common Anglo-American names. Very few Caesars, Pompeys, and Catos remained among the new freemen. In bondage, most blacks had had but a single name; freedom also allowed them the opportunity to take another.[1] Robert Freeman, Landon Freeland, and Robin Justice chose names that celebrated their new status. Many, like Tom, who took the name "Toogood" when he ran off, flaunted the increased self-esteem that accompanied freedom. Others, following an ancient tradition, borrowed names from their trades or skills: James Carter was a drayman, Henry Mason a bricklayer, Charles Green a gardener, and Jacob Bishop a preacher with obvious aspirations. Similarly, James Cook took his name "from his being skilled in the art of cooking and house service," and the origins of Jockey Wheeler's cognomen can be safely surmised. More significantly, some identified themselves by their pigment and origin and took names like "Brown," "Coal," "Africa," "Guinea," and "Negro." Yet slave society, which identified wealth, power, and authority with whites, was not easily denied. Some blacks called themselves "White," and others borrowed the name of some local notable, more often than not a slaveholder. A few took their master's name with the hope that they could capitalize on the close connections with whites it suggested. William Ellison, an ambitious South Carolina black who later worked his way into the planter class and married his daughters to white men, adopted his owner's name with the full realization "that such a change although apparently unimportant would yet greatly advance his interest as a tradesman." But Ellison was an exception. Most newly liberated blacks found their master's name more of a burden than a blessing. Only a few took the name of their emancipator.[2]

[1] A significant number of bondsmen did carry surnames (usually different from their master's, although possibly that of a former master) out of bondage. See, for example, Anne Arundel Manumission Records, MdHR.

[2] For Tom Toogood, Annapolis *Maryland Gazette,* 18 June 1795; for Carter, *ibid.*, 3 July 1794; for Mason, Petition from Henrico County, 22 December 1847, VLP; for Green, Richmond *Virginia Gazette,* 15 July 1795; for Bishop,

Newly freed bondsmen also tried to escape the stigma of bondage by deserting the site of their enslavement. Runaways did it as a matter of course, and some free Negroes were forced to leave by their former masters. But even when invited to stay, many manumitted blacks left. Bondage had limited the physical mobility of blacks, and now many seemed determined to compensate for their confinement. By snubbing their former masters, free Negroes demonstrated their liberty. Free Negroes often went out of their way to break the bonds of dependence which had weighed so heavily in slavery. Much to the displeasure of one Delaware mistress, her former servant ignored her offer of "a good place" with a Philadelphia friend and found a job on her own. "I cannot help thinking," moaned the rejected aristocrat, "it is too generally the case with all those of colour to be ungrateful."[3] Everywhere

---

Minutes of the Portsmouth Baptist Association, 1794, p. 6; for Cook, Baltimore *Federal Gazette,* 14 March 1806; for Wheeler, Anne Arundel County Manumissions, Liber no. 1, A, p. 289, MdHR; for Ellison, Marina Wikramanayake, *A World in Shadow: The Free Black in Antebellum South Carolina* (Columbia, S.C., 1973), p. 94. Other names are taken from a survey of the free Negro registers cited below. County clerks in almost all Southern states were required by law to keep a list describing every free Negro in the county and indicating how and when they were freed. If the free Negro was manumitted, the register of free Negroes often noted the manumitter's name. County clerks kept these registers with varying degrees of fidelity, and many Negro freemen—most notably fugitives and illegally freed Negroes—did not register. Those registers that have survived courthouse fires and housecleanings clearly indicate that few freed Negroes took their emancipator's name. In Anne Arundel County, Maryland, for example, about one Negro in fifteen took his or her manumitter's name; Anne Arundel County Certificates of Freedom, 1807–1816, in Anne Arundel County Manumissions, Liber no. 1, A, 1810–1864, MdHR. Other registers of free Negroes, although not as detailed, indicate much the same pattern. The best collections of free Negro registers are in the Maryland Hall of Records; the Virginia State Library (in addition, many Virginia clerks seem to have listed free Negroes in the County Order Books, in *VSL*); South Caroliniana Library, University of South Carolina, Columbia; South Carolina Archives, Columbia; Georgia Historical Society, Savannah; and the Georgia Department of Archives and History, Atlanta. For an excellent discussion of the pattern and meaning of the names newly emancipated blacks took during the Civil War and Reconstruction, see Joel Williamson, *After Slavery: The Negro in South Carolina During Reconstruction, 1861–1877* (Chapel Hill, N.C., 1965), pp. 309–11.

[3] Robert Carter to Spenser Ball, 23 April 1796, Carter Letterbooks, LC; A[nn] Ridgely to Henry M. and George C. Ridgely, 17 November 1796, Ridgely Family Papers, DelHR; Johann D. Schoepf, *Travels in the Confederation,* 2 vols. (Philadelphia, 1911), II, 150.

emancipated blacks tested their liberty by asserting it.

Fleeing the memory of servitude, looking for new opportunities, searching for loved ones, free Negroes moved in all directions. Many went to the North, some emigrated to Canada or Haiti, and a few found their way back to Africa. Yet, most of those who abandoned the place of their enslavement remained in the South. Lonely and fearful, some returned to their old neighborhoods, where they had friends and relatives. Others continued to wander aimlessly, living off the land while searching for a new life and giving every state a transient free Negro population which encouraged "dangerous" thoughts among already restless slaves. These bands of black freemen were a magnet for runaways, and occasionally they grew so large that officials called out the militia to disperse them.[4]

Most migrating free Negroes chose their destination with care. Many sought out loved ones in the hope of reconstructing shattered families and sharing the exhilaration of liberty. Some free blacks, like whites, searched for new opportunities in the West, but more often free Negroes looked to the expanding urban frontier. Cities, where the relative anonymity of urban life provided an added measure of liberty, were the most important refuge from the memory of plantation slavery. Throughout the South, municipal officials joined the mayor of Petersburg in lamenting that "large numbers of free blacks flock from the country to the towns." Although cities added police and passed special ordinances to curb this unwanted migration, urban free Negroes increased in numbers more rapidly than did the free Negro caste generally. While the free Negro population of Virginia more than doubled between 1790 and 1810, that of Richmond increased almost fourfold and that of Norfolk tenfold. Similar tales could be told of Charleston and Savannah, but the rise of Baltimore's free Negro caste was the most spectacular. In 1790, slightly more than 300 free Negroes resided in Baltimore; twenty years later, they numbered over 5,000.[5] Yet even the growth of the urban free Negro

[4] Petition from Sussex County, 1786, Misc. Slavery Collection, HSD; S.C. House Journal, 1788, pp. 266–7, SCA; Charleston Grand Jury Presentment, November 1792, SCA.

[5] Petition from Petersburg, 11 December 1805, VLP; also see Charleston Grand Jury Presentment, September 1798, SCA; figures compiled from *Returns*

TABLE 5

URBAN POPULATION GROWTH, 1790–1810

City	Free Negroes 1790	Free Negroes 1810	Percent Increase, 1790–1810 Free Negroes	Percent Increase, 1790–1810 Whites	Percent Increase, 1790–1810 Slaves
Baltimore[a]	323	5,671	1,655.7%	203.7%	272.3%
Alexandria	52	836	1,507.7	127.7	174.0
Richmond	265	1,189	348.7	137.9	153.4
Petersburg	310	1,089	251.3	92.0	71.7
Norfolk	61	592	870.5	197.8	195.6
Charleston	586	1,472	151.1	43.0	51.9
Savannah[b]	112	530	373.2	1.4	−73.2

[a] Includes the eastern and western precincts for 1810.
[b] Includes Chatham County in 1790.

SOURCES: *Return of the Number of Persons Within the Several Districts of the United States* (Washington, D.C., 1802); *Aggregate Amount of Persons Within the United States in the Year 1810* (Washington, D.C., 1811).

population was but symptomatic of the wholesale movement of freed men and women, as newly emancipated blacks rejected their slave past and fled the memory of their master's plantation.

Migration, no matter how tempting, was never easy. For many newly freed blacks, it meant abandoning enslaved loved ones. Although Southern law refused to recognize the slave family, bondsmen developed strong family ties.[6] A relatively equal sexual balance between men and women, the heritage of a strong family life in Africa, and perhaps the absence of other institutional ties such as those with church or state may have strengthened family relations among slaves. Moreover, many masters found it profitable to promote slave family life, for it added stability to the plantation and encouraged the production of profitable offspring.

The bonds of kinship made newly liberated blacks reluctant

of the Whole Number of Persons Within the . . . United States (Philadelphia, 1791), pp. 47, 50, 54–5, and *Aggregate Amount of Persons Within the United States in the Year 1810* (Washington, D.C., 1811), pp. 53, 55a, 79–80.

[6] Herbert Gutman's recent work on the Negro family demonstrates that blacks were able to maintain strong family ties through the years of servitude. Herbert Gutman, "Persistent Myths About the American Negro Family: A Critical Reexamination of E. Franklin Frazier's *The Negro Family in the United States*," unpublished paper courtesy of the author.

to leave without their families and friends. Negroes, themselves fresh from bondage, often helped loved ones purchase their liberty. Since most free Negroes were poor, buying the freedom of a friend or relative took years of austere living, and it was not unusual for a free Negro to save for five to ten years in order to liberate a single bondsman. In spite of such obstacles, some free blacks dedicated much of their lives and fortunes to helping others escape bondage. Graham Bell, a Petersburg free Negro, purchased and freed nine slaves between 1792 and 1805. In 1792, Bell emancipated five slave children, probably his own, whom he had bought three years earlier. In 1801, he purchased and freed a slave woman, who later paid him fifteen pounds for the service. The following year, noting "that God created all men equally free," he emancipated two more slaves, and in 1805 he manumitted his brother. Bell's persistence was unusual, but not unique. In New Bern, North Carolina, John C. Stanly, a wealthy free Negro, purchased and emancipated his wife and children in 1805, and two years later he freed his brother-in-law. During the next eleven years, Stanly freed another eighteen slaves.[7] Other free Negroes, anxious to reunite their family or friends, had not the patience, money, or inclination to buy liberty and instead plotted runaway schemes and aided fugitives. Once free, these blacks did not forget those left behind. With the memory of slavery still fresh in the mind of most freemen, caste unity between free Negroes and slaves was probably higher than it would be again until the general Emancipation of 1863 and 1865.

Yet, free Negroes were not completely at one with slaves. The patterns of racial separation and discrimination inherent in American slavery soon permeated the free Negro caste. As the free Negro population grew, newly emancipated blacks began to distinguish themselves from those who remained in bonds. Much as they might sympathize with the slaves, free Negroes now had an interest of their own to defend. Although racial ties generally transcended these status differences, the

[7] Luther P. Jackson, "Manumission in Certain Virginia Cities," *JNH*, XV (1930), 285–6; Franklin, *Free Negro in North Carolina*, pp. 31–2. For an example of the difficulty free Negroes had in purchasing the freedom of a bondsman, see Petition from Southampton County, 9 December 1811, VLP.

insoluble distinctions between free and slave remained. Some Negro freemen advanced themselves in the free world with scarcely a backward glance. Occasionally, free Negroes gave these often unspoken distinctions an institutional form. In one Norfolk Methodist church, free Negroes seated themselves separately from slaves, a novel pattern in an era when whites and blacks still mixed indiscriminately at many religious meetings. Similar social distinctions also developed among free Negroes. Class differences, denominational differences, and—perhaps most insidious of all—color differences racked the growing free Negro caste.[8]

A degree of color consciousness had probably always existed among Southern free Negroes. During the colonial era, most Negro freemen owed their liberty to their "white blood" and some had benefitted from close relations with whites. The appearance of a large number of free blacks, as opposed to mulattoes, may have intensified the free Negro's consciousness of color. The old mulatto free Negro caste doubtless felt some hostility to the new darker and more assertive freemen. But it was the influx of light-skinned West Indian émigrés that made this division explicit and branded it upon the free Negro's mind. Unlike most American free Negroes, West Indian free people of color were neither poor nor former slaves. They came from a society where free Negroes had composed an important element of the population and where whites were a distinct minority. By force of numbers alone, they often controlled the balance of power between white planters and black slaves and between independence-minded colonial whites and metropolitan administrators. Siding first with planters against their slaves and then with metropolitan authorities against the planters, tree Negroes had secured numerous liberties and advanced their economic standing. Although freemen suffered galling legal and social discrimination, they had a place in West Indian society and they made the most of it serving not only as soldiers in time of distress but also as tradesmen, merchants, and overseers. The most successful purchased slaves and occasionally pushed their way into the planter class. These elite

[8] Kenneth and Anna M. Roberts, eds. and trans., *Moreau de St. Méry's American Journey (1793–1798)* (New York, 1947), p. 48; Lambert, *Travels Through Lower Canada and the United States,* II, 414, 416.

free Negroes, usually mulattoes, often successful tradesmen or artisans, and sometimes slaveholders, had been among the first to flee Saint-Domingue when the course of the revolution turned against the French.

Although light-skinned West Indian émigrés brought to the United States—as whites feared—the knowledge that a successful black revolt was possible, they also carried—as whites only slowly recognized—an understanding that elite colored men could suffer when black slaves won their freedom. Many had fought under the French against the slave armies, and only Toussaint's success had driven them from their homeland. For refugees seared by that memory, the hierarchical three-caste system, which uniformly rewarded those with a lighter skin by distinguishing blacks from mulattoes and mulattoes from quadroons, held a special meaning. They carried it ashore with their few treasured possessions.[9] As these light-skinned émigrés flowed into the ports of the Lower South, distinctions between blacks and browns suddenly appeared. During the 1790s, mixed-blood free Negroes in Charleston, a center for Saint-Domingue refugees, established the exclusive Brown Fellowship Society, a benevolent association open to free brown men only and a symbol of mulatto exclusiveness throughout the antebellum years.[10]

Selecting a new name or residence and emancipating loved ones were symbolically important acts which marked a clean break with bondage and an effort to begin life anew. But whatever psychic satisfaction free Negroes derived from their new names, new addresses, and reunited families, these provided little of the substance of liberty. Newly emancipated Negroes were still black in a society which presumed that only whites were free, and propertyless in a society which measured status mainly in dollars.

A few Negroes moved from slavery to freedom in relative comfort. Their masters, partly to ensure an orderly transition

[9] James, *Black Jacobins,* pp. 36–44; Hall, *Social Control in Slave Plantation Societies,* especially pp. 113–36, and Hall's essay on Saint-Domingue free Negroes in Cohen and Greene, eds., *Neither Slave Nor Free,* pp. 172–92.

[10] WPA, Brown Fellowship Society Papers, SCHS; E. Horace Fitchett, "The Traditions of the Free Negro in Charleston, South Carolina," *JNH,* XXV (1940), 144–5.

from slavery to freedom and partly for humanitarian concerns, provided for them after emancipation. George Washington and Robert Carter, both of whom manumitted several hundred slaves, composed elaborate plans to support their former bondsmen and to assure that they would not burden the community. Washington provided for apprenticeship and tenancy for the able-bodied and lodgings and pensions for the aged.[11] Carter gave his older hands small plots of land for the remainder of their lives and allowed some of his former slaves to become tenants. In 1793, in conformity with other arrangements he would later make, Carter awarded small lots to all of his newly emancipated slaves over forty-five, assigning three freemen to each lot. He also made special arrangements with his black foremen, house servants, and others he thought especially trustworthy. In 1792, as his plan of emancipation went into effect, Carter permitted James Bricklayer, George Cooper, Gloucester Billy, Sam Harrison, and Prince to rent houses and garden plots and to hire their wives and children. They were also allowed to take firewood from his land, but he insisted that they pay their own tithe. In addition, some of those Negroes had to perform their former tasks without pay. Prince continued to receive and deliver grain, and his son, Harry, took care of Carter's stock as he had before. Besides his new responsibilities as a free man, Sam Harrison had to shave Carter, dress his wig, and do the customary duties in the study.

Carter's interest in the future of his slaves went beyond humanitarian concern. By providing for gradual manumission, allowing some of his former slaves to become tenants, and keeping his most experienced and responsible hands at their old jobs, Carter minimized the economic dislocations of large-scale emancipation. Since he expected his tenants to hire most of his former field hands, Carter foresaw no drop in either production or profits. As predicted, most of the slaves Carter emancipated seem to have hired themselves out to his tenants and other neighboring farmers.[12]

[11] Fitzpatrick, ed., *Writings of Washington*, XXXVII, 276–7; Eugene Prussing, *The Estate of George Washington, Deceased* (Boston, 1927), pp. 154–60.

[12] Benjamin Dawson to Robert Carter, 7 September 1793, Carter Papers, VHS; Robert Carter to Benjamin Dawson, 22 July 1794, Carter Letterbooks, LC; Proposal to Prince and others, 13 February 1793, Carter Papers, VHS; Robert Carter to Thomas Stowers, 3 May 1793, typescript, Carter Papers, Duke.

Occasionally, less prominent slaveholders initiated similar postemancipation schemes. Levin Bell, an Eastern Shore farmer, rehired the two men he had freed and gave them one-sixth of his farm's produce. Bell was ecstatic with the results of his sharecropping arrangements, and abolitionists collected his testimony as emancipationist propaganda. "I find by experience," wrote Bell, "I am the gainer . . . and they seem to be happy and cheerful and do more than twice the labour than when they were in a state of bondage, and make themselves a comfortable livelihood."[13]

Most slaveholders did not have the resources, ideals, or enthusiasm necessary to imitate such plans. Only a few provided their bondsmen with a means of making a living. Occasionally, some benevolent masters gave their former slaves small gifts of clothing, a few sticks of furniture, or a little money. Rarely did they provide more than this. Since most manumitters were motivated by the ideology of the Revolution and since that ideology required nothing but the bestowal of freedom, slaveowners saw no reason to go beyond emancipation. For most Negroes, slavery was a poor school for freedom, and emancipation at first added nothing to their inheritance. Once freed, they usually found themselves without property or steady work. Sometimes they had to hire themselves back to their former masters on long-term contracts at low wages.[14]

Many freed blacks suffered a sharp decline in occupational status. Men and women valued for their skills as slaves often had trouble finding good jobs once they were free. Frequently, they were proscribed from trades they had dominated or monopolized in slavery. From the first, white workers objected to free Negro competition. In 1783, white carpenters and bricklayers in Charleston, complaining that aggressive black tradesmen undercut their wages and lowered their standard of living, demanded legislation to prohibit Negroes from working on their own account.[15] Such legislation was not passed at this time, but workingmen in other cities soon echoed these com-

[13] Levin Bell Manumission, 1787, PAS.

[14] Wright, *Free Negro in Maryland*, pp. 157–8.

[15] Petition from Charleston Carpenters and Bricklayers, 19 February 1783, SCLP.

plaints and helped push free Negroes into an ever-shrinking range of menial occupations.

Newly emancipated blacks faced similar problems in renting or purchasing land. Landlords often refused to grant blacks credit so that they might buy farms and even balked at renting land to free Negroes. Some whites refused to allow blacks on their land in any capacity once they were free. When Caesar Rodney, a leading Delaware emancipationist, rented land to a black tenant, he first prepared an elaborate apology to his slaveholding father. "I know you do not like to have any of this colour on your land," Rodney concluded, "but for my own part I have a good opinion of this fellow and I think he will endeavour more to give you satisfaction than any white person you could have got." Similarly, Christopher Collins, one of Robert Carter's overseers, disapproved of renting farms to free Negroes "unprepared with Teams and Tools for its cultivation," and Carter's neighbors objected even more vigorously. In fact, everyone but the freemen opposed the idea. Collins did his best to discourage the blacks from renting farms, but they persisted. "I advised them against renting it," he reported to Carter, "& represented to them the Difficulties that were likely to attend; but found that they were desirous to undertake it." Carter sided with the blacks and they got the land, but not all white landlords had the prestige, let alone the interest, to overcome popular opposition to renting land to blacks who were free.[16]

The legacies of the peculiar institution continued to burden blacks as they struggled to find a place in free society. After years of dull, pitiless bondage, some newly freed blacks lived high, invested their small wages in fancy clothes, and played the dandy. Others celebrated their emancipation with a well-deserved vacation. For many blacks, the connection between slavery and labor was so intimate that freedom literally meant idleness. These free Negroes lived off the land, worked only when necessary, and occasionally enriched their diet by raiding a planter's henhouse. Slaveholders pointed to them as confirmation of their belief that Negroes were naturally indolent and

[16] C. A. Rodney to Thomas Rodney, 28 March 1792, Caesar A. Rodney Papers, HSD; Christopher Collins to Robert Carter, 21 December 1792, Carter Papers, VHS.

would work only under the firm direction of whites. But more perceptive observers had other explanations. "It is natural to suppose," noted one French traveler, "that a slave, harassed by continual labour, driven by the scourge to toil in the open fields whether he is healthy or sick, considers liberty merely as a release from labour."[17]

Although accompanied by proscription and exclusion, freedom also created new opportunities. Allowed to enjoy the fruits of their own labor, blacks purchased farms, opened shops, and entered trades from which slavery had barred them. Suddenly blacks appeared as painters and poets, authors and astronomers, ministers and merchants. The wave of black showmen licensed to perform in Baltimore during the 1790s suggests some of the new routes to success opened by freedom. In 1795 the city commissioners granted a license to "Wm Nisbitt a bl[ac]k man to Exhibit on the Slack Rope, Tumbling, &c., for one Month from this date on paying 8 Doll[ar]s." Apparently business was good, because Nisbitt was back again in 1796. That same year, Robert Wilson, a free Negro, paid one dollar to hold an exhibit for three months; a license was given to a "Negro Rope Dancer"; and permission was granted to exhibit "a Negro turned White as a Show." If the Baltimore records are at all representative, the South was invaded by black vaudevillians. Doubtless, many did not meet as warm a reception as William Nisbitt. Daniel Fortner, a black "dancing master," tried to open a school in Franklin County, Kentucky, but was jailed "upon suspicion of being a slave."[18] Even under the most favorable conditions, few blacks could walk the "slack rope" and fewer still could turn white.

The new opportunities of freedom allowed some free Negroes to accumulate property and attain a modicum of economic security. William Flora, a Revolutionary veteran, purchased

[17] Lambert, *Travels Through Lower Canada and the United States,* II, 176; Schoepf, *Travels in the Confederation,* II, 222; Duc de La Rochefoucauld-Liancourt, *Travels Through the United States of North America . . . 1795, 1796, and 1797,* 2 vols. (London, 1799), II, 281–2.

[18] *Records of the City of Baltimore (Special Commissioners), 1782–1797* (Baltimore, 1909), pp. 288, 296, 330, 316; Frankfort (Ky.) *Palladium,* 7 November 1799. The Negro who turned "white" was doubtless Henry Moss; William R. Stanton, *The Leopard's Spots: Scientific Attitudes Towards Race in America* (Chicago, 1960), pp. 5–7.

several lots in Portsmouth, Virginia, soon after his discharge from the army. Later he opened a livery stable, which he operated for the next thirty years and then willed to his son. While many free Negroes followed Flora's example and built their prosperity on bounties received for fighting in the Revolution, others found success plying their trades in the growing cities of the South. Urbanization and nascent industrialization tended to counter the racial proscriptions that often greeted job-seeking free Negroes. The short supply of white artisans and craftsmen forced some employers to put aside their prejudices. A few skilled free Negroes improved their economic status markedly. By 1787, James McHenry, a Maryland shoemaker who had just purchased his freedom, was renting a farm for thirty-five pounds a year and owned "a house and other stock more than sufficient for his farm." Henry Carter, a Virginia free Negro, boasted a similar success story. Emancipated in 1811, within six years he not only had "funds sufficient to purchase his wife Priscilla but some other property, personal & real." In some cities, free Negroes controlled sizable businesses and employed other free Negroes in positions of authority.[19]

Much to the discomfort of whites, the transformation of the Southern economy, especially that of the Upper South, enabled free Negroes to expand their liberty and make real economic gains. The decline of tobacco, the growth of cereal farming, and the resultant increase in tenancy in Maryland and northern Virginia, for example, gave free blacks a chance to work on their own. Although the opportunity to work outside the direct supervision of whites was often reason enough for many blacks to sign on as tenants, many hoped a few years of tenancy would enable them to build a reputation and gain credit enough to buy their own farms. With thousands of whites leaving the tidewater region for new opportunities in Kentucky and Ohio, free Negroes could occasionally purchase good land at bargain prices and make their dream a reality.[20]

[19] Jackson, "Virginia Negro Soldiers and Seamen," pp. 269, 272, 283; Talbot County, Md., Manumission, 1787, PAS; Petition from Charles City County, 21 December 1815, from Petersburg, 9 December 1805, VLP; William Poole to the American Convention, 1796, PAS.

[20] For the growth of tenantry in the Northern Neck of Virginia see Robert Carter Papers, LC, VHS, Duke.

The growth of a black property-holding class seemed everywhere to follow the emergence of the free Negro caste. In Talbot County on the Eastern Shore of Maryland, there were but 18 free Negro property owners in 1793. Ten years later their number had increased to 88, and by 1813 there were 102 Negro freemen who owned, among them, property valued at five thousand dollars. Although the free Negro population of Talbot County increased greatly during these years, its increase nowhere matched the fivefold growth of free Negro property owners.[21] The development of a black propertied class was not as rapid everywhere in the South, but Talbot County represented the general trend. Although most blacks remained, as in slavery, poor and propertyless, some Negro freemen rose to modest wealth and respectability. Despite enormous obstacles, a few free Negroes assumed their place among the property-holding middle class.

Throughout the South, a new black elite slowly emerged: Daniel Coker in Baltimore, Peter Spenser in Wilmington, Christopher McPherson in Richmond, John Chavis in Raleigh, Peter Mathews in Charleston, and Andrew Bryan in Savannah. Born in the decade before the Revolution, these men came of age with the emergence of the free Negro caste. Many owed their liberty to the changes unleashed by the American Revolution, and they shared the optimism and enthusiasm that accompanied freedom. Generally wealthier, more literate, and better connected with whites than were most blacks, they took up the leadership of the enlarged free black caste and pressed for greater freedom. Pointing to the ideas of the Declaration of Independence and the principles of Christian equalitarianism, they petitioned Southern legislatures to relieve them of the disabilities inherited from the colonial years. Norfolk free Negroes, in a typical action, asked that they be allowed to testify in court against whites so they could prove their accounts. South Carolina freemen petitioned for relief from a special head tax that pushed them into a condition "but small removed from Slavery." And from Nashville came a plea that free Negroes "ought to have the same opportunities of doing well that any Person being a citizen & free man of the

[21] Wright, *Free Negro in Maryland*, p. 184.

State . . . would have, and that the door ought not to be kept shut against them more than any other of the Human race."[22] Anxious to expand their newly won freedom, some Southern black leaders took their pleas directly to the newly formed federal government. Occasionally, a few bold free Negroes, like Daniel Coker, publicly condemned slavery and demanded a universal emancipation.[23]

But free Negroes protested in vain. The most restrained pleas seemed to lead to harsher repression, which further anchored Negro freemen to the bottom of free society. The experience of Charleston free Negroes indicates again how vehemently whites opposed any improvement in the status of blacks. In 1791, Peter Mathews, a free Negro butcher, along with several other free Negro artisans and tradesmen, petitioned the state legislature to expand their rights as free men. The law barred them from testifying in court against whites—"for which cause many Culprits have escaped punishment"—made it impossible for them to collect their debts, and subjected them to numerous frauds. At the same time, they were tried without a jury in courts in which slaves could testify. For many years, Mathews went on, free Negroes had supported the government, paid their taxes, and upheld the peace. "Your memorialists," he tactfully concluded, "do not presume to hope that they shall be put on an equal footing with free White Citizens of the State in general [but] humbly solicit such dictate in their favor by repealing the clauses [of] the Act before mentioned. . . ." Although Mathews measured his words carefully and tailored his request so as not to threaten white dominance, his petition received no hearing from the legislature. However, it did not go unnoticed. Three years later, when fears of insurrection ran high, white vigilantes broke into Mathews's house searching for a cache of arms. Mathews, a substantial tradesman of good repute, had little choice but to try to explain publicly that an "old pistol without flint, a broken sword, and an old cutlass" he

[22] Petition from Norfolk, 7 December 1809, VLP; Petition from John and William Morriss, [1793], SCLP; Petition from Casper Lott, 4 August 1803, Petition from William Nodding, 31 August 1803, TLP; *Annals of Congress*, 4th Cong., 2nd Sess., pp. 2015–18, 8th Cong., 1st Sess., p. 790.

[23] Daniel Coker, *A Dialogue Between a Virginian and an African Minister* (Baltimore, 1810).

kept in his attic were not the beginning of the revolution.[24] Perhaps he convinced Charleston vigilantes, perhaps not; in any case, the experience of Peter Mathews was just further proof that whites would tolerate no alteration of their standards of race relations.

Frustrated by unyielding white hostility, black leaders increasingly turned inward and worked to strengthen black community life. They organized institutions where blacks might pray, educate their children, entertain, and protect themselves. African churches, schools, and fraternal orders not only served the new needs of the expanding free Negro caste but also gave meaning to black people's liberty and symbolized their new status.

Yet even while shouldering the new responsibilities of freedom, blacks did not immediately form separate institutions. The development of the African church, for example, was not merely a product of the growth of the free Negro caste. At first, most blacks looked to the white-dominated evangelical churches, which made acceptance of the gospel the only criterion for salvation and welcomed blacks into the fold. Free Negroes along with slaves and poor whites found this open-membership policy, the emotional sermons, and the generous grants of self-expression an appealing contrast to the icy restrictiveness of the older, more staid denominations. Although racially mixed congregations were often forced to meet at odd hours to avoid hostile sheriffs and slave patrols, black membership in the evangelical churches grew rapidly. By the end of the century, thousands of Negroes, many of them free, had joined Methodist and Baptist churches. In 1800, blacks composed one-fifth of the Methodists in Virginia, and they outnumbered whites in several Maryland and South Carolina churches.[25] Although comparable statistics are unavailable for the Baptists, Negroes might have constituted a higher proportion of the membership of that denomination.

[24] Petition from Thomas Cole, Mathew Webb, P. B. Mathews, and other free Negroes, 1 January 1791, SCLP; Charleston *City Gazette,* 7 September 1793.

[25] *Minutes of the Annual Conferences of the Methodist Episcopal Church for the Years 1773–1828* (New York, 1840), p. 92; F. A. Mood, *Methodism in Charleston,* ed. Thomas O. Summers (Nashville, Tenn., 1856), pp. 30, 40, 48, 71, 83, 86–91, 97–8, 106–7, 116.

The newness of the evangelical denominations together with their Christian equalitarianism sometimes fostered new racial patterns. In some evangelical churches, blacks and whites seated themselves indiscriminately, and occasionally free Negroes shared the rights of church members with whites. In 1781, when Francis Asbury, a future bishop of the Methodist Church, finished preaching to a Virginia meeting, he turned the assembly over to "Harry, a black man." "This circumstance," Asbury noted in his diary, "is new and white people look on it with attention."[26]

By the last decade of the eighteenth century, the presence of black preachers, although by no means commonplace, no longer surprised white congregations. Throughout the Upper South, free Negroes ministered to whites. William Lemon, "a man of colour," and pastor of the largely white Petsworth Church in Gloucester County, Virginia, was a delegate to the local Baptist association in 1797, 1798, and 1801. Whites regarded Henry Evans, a free Negro preacher in Fayetteville, North Carolina, as the "best preacher of his time in that quarter." Evans, a Virginia-born Methodist, preached briefly to blacks, only to be driven out by hostile whites. He continued to hold secret prayer meetings and slowly began attracting whites to his congregation. The familiar spectacle of nonbelievers who came to scoff and remained to pray was reenacted in an interracial setting. Before long, whites accepted Evans, and he continued to preach to a mixed but segregated congregation until his death in 1810. While Evans ministered to Fayetteville Methodists, John Chavis, a free Negro Presbyterian missionary, rode a North Carolina circuit, converting whites as well as blacks. In Georgia, David George, Jesse Peters, George Liele, and Andrew Bryan, all Negro Baptist ministers, occasionally preached to whites.[27]

[26] Elmer T. Clark *et al.*, eds., *The Journal and Letters of Francis Asbury*, 3 vols. (London and Nashville, Tenn., 1958), I, 403. The pioneering and still invaluable work on the Negro church is Carter G. Woodson, *The History of the Negro Church* (Washington, D.C., 1921), pp. 100–23.

[27] Ryland, *Baptists of Virginia*, p. 156; William Wightman, *Life of William Capers . . . Including an Autobiography* (Nashville, Tenn., 1858), pp. 124–9; Margaret B. DesChamps, "John Chavis as a Preacher to Whites," *North Carolina Historical Review*, XXXII (1955), 165–72; Walter H. Brooks, "The Priority of the Silver Bluff Church and Its Promoters," *JNH*, VII (1922), 172–96; John W. Davis, "George Liele and Andrew Bryan, Pioneer Negro

In racially mixed congregations sometimes both races shared control of church affairs. The 1792 constitution of the Emmaus Baptist Church of Charles City County, Virginia, allowed all "free male members" to vote. Not until almost fifty years later was church suffrage restricted to "free white male members." In a like manner, the action of the Roanoke Baptist Association barring free Negroes from business meetings in 1797 not only prescribed the inequality that would thereafter rule but suggests the equality that had once reigned. Even in Charleston, the power of evangelical idealism allowed new relationships to develop. The black membership of the Charleston Methodist Church, which greatly outnumbered the white, controlled their own finances and discipline and elected church officers to attend the quarterly conferences. Frontier conditions may have reinforced evangelical equalitarianism. In 1806, a Tennessee Baptist Church resolved: "The Black Brethren . . . enjoy the same liberty of Exercising public gifts as white members have or do enjoy."[28]

The pressure of Christian equalitarianism forged new racial modes and brought whites and blacks together in places where previously they had never met. It was not unusual for black churchmen to attend synods and association meetings with whites. Several free Negroes represented their churches in meetings of regional Baptist associations. In 1794, when one Virginia church called this practice into question, the Ports-

Preachers," *JNH*, III (1918), 119–27. But other black ministers, not as "famous" as these, preached in almost total obscurity; see Annapolis *Maryland Gazette*, 26 June 1800, 13 January 1803; John Asplund, *The Universal Register of the Baptist Denomination in North America, 1790, 1791, 1792, 1793 and a part of 1794* (Boston, 1794), pp. 50–1. During the formative post-Revolutionary years the transforming radicalism of evangelical Christianity cut through racial lines in the North as well as the South. Richard Allen's African Church in Philadelphia attracted white as well as black converts. In 1798, during a great revival, Allen and his colleague, Jupiter Gipson, reported: "Our Congregation Nearly Consist of as many Whites as Blacks, many Never attended any place of Worship [and] come some through Curiosity & many of them are awakened & Join the Society So that Nearly as many whites as Blacks are Convinced & Converted to the Lord." Richard Allen and Jupiter Gipson to Ezekiel Cooper, 22 February 1798, Ezekiel Cooper Papers, GTS.

[28] *Sesquicentennial Jubilee—First Baptist Church, Norfolk, 1800–1950* (Norfolk, Va., [1950]); Minute Book of the Emmaus Baptist Church, 1790, February 1840, VaBHS; Ryland, *Baptists of Virginia*, p. 158; Mood, *Methodism in Charleston*, pp. 129–33; Minutes of the Mill Creek Baptist Church, 15 November 1806, TSL.

mouth Association firmly announced that it saw "nothing in the Word of God, nor anything contrary to the rules of decency to prohibit a church from sending as a delegate, any male member they shall choose." Four years later, the association accepted Jacob Bishop as its first black delegate.[29]

Although Christian equalitarianism momentarily bent the color line, it could not break it. In most churches, membership did not assure blacks of equal participation. Indeed, free Negroes, like slaves, were usually seated in a distant corner or gallery and barred from most rights of church membership. One Virginia congregation painted some of its benches black to avoid any possibility of confusion.[30]

As free Negroes found themselves barred from white churches and discriminated against in mixed churches, they attempted to form and control their own religious institutions. This was no mean task. Free Negroes not only lacked capital and organizational experience, but they also met fierce white opposition. In 1795, after the white pastor of the Portsmouth, Virginia, Baptist Church quit, "the black brethren of the Church seemed anxious for Jacob Bishop [a black preacher] to take oversight among them." Pressure was immediately placed on the Negroes, and they soon surrendered the heretical idea. They agreed to "be subordinate to the white brethren, if they let them continue as they were."[31]

Despite white opposition, some free Negroes determined to use their new liberties. In Williamsburg, Virginia, blacks ultimately established their own church, over the bitter opposition of whites. In the 1780s, when Moses, a black man, tried to preach to a group of Williamsburg Baptists "composed, almost, if not altogether, of people of colour," he was taken up and whipped. His successor, Gowan Pamphlet, was more successful, but he too encountered stiff opposition. The local Baptist association refused to recognize the church, and when Pamphlet persisted in preaching, the association excommunicated him

[29] Ryland, *Baptists of Virginia,* p. 155; *Minutes of the Portsmouth Baptist Association,* 1794, p. 6, 1798, p. 3.

[30] Roberts and Roberts, eds. and trans., *St. Méry's Journey,* p. 64.

[31] Lemuel Burkitt and Jesse Read, *A Concise History of the Kehekee Baptist Association from Its Rise Down to 1803,* rev. ed. (Philadelphia, 1803), pp. 258–9.

and some members of his congregation. In spite of these obstacles, Pamphlet's church continued to meet and to expand. In 1791, announcing that they numbered over five hundred, blacks again petitioned the Dover, Virginia, Baptist Association for membership, and two years later the association grudgingly received the church with Pamphlet as its minister.[32]

Independent black churches sprang up throughout the South. In the 1770s, David George founded the Silver Bluffs Church near Augusta, Georgia. Soon after, George Liele and Andrew Bryan established what would become the First African Baptist Church of Savannah. The number of independent African churches grew even faster in the Upper South. Evangelical circuit riders traveling through the region noted numerous black congregations, and some of the larger ones were reported in church registers. As free Negroes migrated west, they took their churches with them. In 1801, "Old Captain," a Virginia-born free Negro who moved to Kentucky with his former master, founded an African Baptist church in Lexington. Later John Berry Metchum carried black religion into St. Louis, and London Ferrell brought it to Louisville.[33] Slaves composed a large part of the membership of many of these churches, but the freedom of their ministers gave them a stability that otherwise would have been inconceivable.

[32] Robert Semple, *A History of the Rise and Progress of the Baptists in Virginia* (Richmond, Va., 1810), pp. 97, 114–15; Minutes of the Dover Baptist Association, typescript, 1793, VaBHS; Thad W. Tate, Jr., *The Negro in Eighteenth-Century Williamsburg* (Charlottesville, Va., 1965), pp. 158–63. Pamphlet served as a delegate until 1807; *Minutes of the Dover Baptist Association*, 1807. The following discussion of the independent Negro church movement draws on Woodson, *History of the Negro Church,* pp. 71–99.

[33] John Rippon, *The Baptist Annual Register for 1790, 1791, 1792 and a Part of 1793* (n.p., [1793]), pp. 332–7, 339–43, 540–1, 544–5; John Rippon, *The Baptist Annual Register for 1798, 1799, 1800, and a Part of 1801* (n.p., [1801]), pp. 366–7; Brooks, "Priority of Silver Bluff Church," pp. 172–96; Davis, "George Liele and Andrew Bryan," pp. 119–27; "Letters Showing the Rise and Progress of the Early Negro Churches of Georgia and the West Indies," *JNH,* I (1916), 69–92; James M. Simms, *The First Colored Baptist Church in North America* (Philadelphia, 1888); Journal of Ezekiel Cooper, especially for the 1790s, GTS; Ryland, *Baptists of Virginia,* p. 157; Jackson, "Virginia Negro Soldiers and Seamen," p. 285; Semple, *Rise and Progress of Baptists in Virginia,* p. 361; Spenser, *Kentucky Baptists,* II, 563–4; *Diamond Jubilee of the General Baptist Association of Kentucky* (Louisville, Ky., 1943), pp. 128–9; John B. Metchum, *An Address to All the Colored Citizens of the United States* (Philadelphia, 1846); Boston *Liberator,* 17 October 1854.

The independence afforded by the Baptists' congregational polity aided Negroes in forming their own religious institutions, but not all of the newly established African churches were Baptist. In Maryland, Methodists received most of the black converts. Although the Methodist Church wrote antislavery principles into its *Discipline* and encouraged black local preachers and class leaders, many Methodists shared the racist assumptions of Negro inferiority and subordination.[34] Blacks found that white Methodists held all the important church offices, controlled finances, and regulated church discipline. Most irksome to free Negroes—many of whom were attracted to the church by its equalitarian gospel—was the physical separation of whites and blacks. Although it is unclear when various Methodist churches began to segregate Negroes, in the 1780s several Baltimore freemen withdrew from the Methodist meetinghouse in a dispute over seating arrangements. Perhaps encouraged by the recent success of Philadelphia blacks in organizing a Free African Society, a few Baltimore free Negroes attempted to establish their own church. In 1787, led by Jacob Fortie, several black Methodists began meeting in private houses. Soon after, they established the Colored Methodist Society.[35]

Although the rank discrimination of the white-dominated church fostered black separatism, clearly many blacks welcomed the split. It allowed them, probably for the first time, to control their own religious life. While some Negroes continued to attend the regular meetinghouse, Fortie's society gained adherents, and even those who remained within the

[34] Mathews, *Slavery and Methodism*, pp. 3–29. The status of blacks within the church clearly caused problems for even the most committed Methodist equalitarians. Ezekiel Cooper, a leading Methodist abolitionist, mused over the question of a separate black hierarchy; see undated note, vol. XIV, p. 25, Cooper Papers, GTS.

[35] James A. Handy, *Scraps of African Methodist Episcopal History* (Philadelphia, n.d.), pp. 13–16, 22–4; Daniel A. Payne, *A History of the African Methodist Episcopal Church* (Nashville, Tenn., 1891), pp. 5–8. It is a matter of dispute which was the first African Methodist Church. David Smith, a contemporary AME minister, declared that the Baltimore AME was formed three weeks earlier than the Philadelphia church. It seems more likely that the two groups, perhaps in contact with each other, were motivated by the same forces and moving toward the same goal; David Smith, *Biography of David Smith of the A.M.E. Church* (Xenia, Ohio, 1861), pp. 25–33.

regular Methodist organization were becoming restless under white domination. Bishop Asbury, visiting Baltimore in 1795, found that "the Africans of this town desire a church, which, in temporals, shall be altogether under their own direction, and ask greater privileges than the white stewards and trustees ever had a right to claim."[36]

Asbury, who tried to discourage black Methodists in Philadelphia from taking an independent course, probably rejected the plea for greater autonomy. Yet the independent church movement continued to grow. In 1797, citing "the many inconveniences arising from white and colored people assembling in public meetings—especially public worship," Fortie invited some other black Methodists to join his separatist group. The same year, Fortie, Don Carlos Hall, Stephen Hill, and Charles Hackett, all freemen, purchased a building on Fish (later Saratoga) Street and founded what would become the first African Methodist Episcopal church in Baltimore.[37]

The establishment of an independent African Methodist Church stirred the blacks still attending the old church. Soon after, whites and those Negroes agreed to divide the church property, and the blacks established another separate African meetinghouse. The following year the remaining black Methodists abandoned the old mixed church and organized the Sharp Street AME Church.[38] Later, Baltimore AME leaders met with black churchmen from Philadelphia, Wilmington, Delaware, Salem, New Jersey, and Allenborough, Pennsylvania, and in 1816 organized an independent denomination, the African Methodist Episcopal Church.

Yet even as the AME Church grew, black Methodists were unable to penetrate much beyond Maryland, and the AME churches clung to the borderlands of the South. While Northern whites, who shared many of the racial assumptions of Southerners, made few objections to blacks' forming their own religious institutions and generally welcomed their departure from white churches, slaveholders viewed any independent

[36] Clark *et al.*, eds., *Journal and Letters of Francis Asbury*, II, 65.
[37] *Ibid.*, II, 119; Handy, *Scraps of African Methodist Episcopal History*, pp. 13–16; Payne, *History of the African Methodist Episcopal Church*, pp. 3–8.
[38] Wright, *Free Negro in Maryland*, pp. 212–13.

black organization as an intolerable threat. Even white ministers found themselves under attack for their work with black congregations. In Charleston, "Methodists were watched, ridiculed, and openly assailed. Their churches were styled 'negro churches,' their preachers 'negro preachers.'" When a white missionary tried to preach to a mixed congregation in Richmond, he was threatened with the lash and run out of town. Small wonder that many black preachers left the South and the development of new African churches was abruptly halted.[39]

Still, whites failed to erase all the gains of the postwar years. In many communities African churches limped on, and in some cities they flourished. The Savannah African Baptist Church, under the leadership of Andrew Bryan, grew so large that the old meetinghouse could no longer contain its membership. By 1812, the church had split twice and produced two healthy offspring, the Second and Third African churches.[40]

Where whites barred the development of African churches, blacks were quick to find other institutions to serve the same purposes. In Charleston, where the independent church movement made little headway, wealthy light-skinned free Negroes formed the Brown Fellowship Society. Although limited to free brown men only, the society expressed the freemen's desire to control their own affairs. It not only provided insurance benefits for the survivors of deceased members but contributed to the support of Negro orphans, purchased cemetery lots for its members, and sponsored a school for free Negro children.

[39] Alexander McCaine to Ezekiel Cooper, 30 September 1802, Cooper Papers, GTS; Mood, *Methodism in Charleston*, p. 64. Jacob Bishop went north, George Liele to the West Indies, David George to Canada, Daniel Coker and Lott Cary to Africa; Coker, *Dialogue Between a Virginian and an African Minister*, p. 40; David Benedict, *A General History of the Baptist Denomination in America and Other Parts of the World*, 2 vols. (Boston, 1813), II, 509; Rippon, *Baptist Annual Register, 1790–1793*, pp. 332–7; Brooks, "Priority of Silver Bluff Church," pp. 182–3; Davis, "George Liele and Andrew Bryan," pp. 120–1; Daniel Coker, *Journal of Daniel Coker, a Descendant of Africa . . .* (Baltimore, 1820); James B. Taylor, *Biography of the Elder Lott Cary* (Baltimore, 1837). For the strikingly different reaction of white Northerners to the formation of black churches, see Jordan, *White over Black*, pp. 422–6.

[40] Rippon, *Baptist Annual Register, 1798–1801*, pp. 263, 366–7; Jesse Lee to Ezekiel Cooper, 27 May 1807, Cooper Papers, GTS.

Other Charleston free Negroes, perhaps not as well placed as the members of the Brown Fellowship Society, joined African Masonic lodges and formed their own fraternal societies.[41]

The early development of African schools followed the same tortuous path as that of the independent churches and benevolent societies. In the years immediately following the Revolution, the momentary respite in racial hostility encouraged some free Negroes and sympathetic whites to establish integrated academies. In 1802, for example, Baltimore Quakers reported teaching several "mixed schools," and about the same time a few Alexandria teachers accepted both white and black pupils. But the emotions and ideals that united poor whites and blacks in evangelical churches were absent from the founding of schools. Schools were middle-class and upper-class institutions, and class distinctions alone excluded most Negro freemen. Handicapped by a lack of funds and surrounded by hostile whites, integrated schools languished. By the turn of the century, the ebbing of Revolutionary equalitarianism and the rising fears of servile revolt forced those few remaining integrated academies to close their doors or segregate their classrooms.[42]

The disappearance of "mixed" schools and the general exclusion of free Negroes from white schools moved a few interested whites, especially Quakers, to establish academies for black children. About 1781, Robert Pleasants, a Virginia Quaker abolitionist, proposed a school for "the children of Blacks and people of Color" which would form "their minds on the principles of virtue and religion, and in common and useful litera-

[41] WPA, Brown Fellowship Society Papers, SCHS; James B. Browning, "The Beginnings of Insurance Enterprise Among Negroes," *JNH*, XXII (1937), 422–3; Charleston Grand Jury Presentment, 1791, SCA; "Report of the Committee on Courts of Justice," 4 February 1791, SCLP. A copy of *Rules and Regulations of the Brown Fellowship Society Established at Charleston* (Charleston, 1844) is in E. Horace Fitchett, "The Free Negro in Charleston, South Carolina," unpublished doctoral dissertation, University of Chicago, 1950, app.

[42] "Constitution of the African School Society," in Minutes of the African School Society, Wilmington, 1809–1835, HSD; William C. Dunlap, *Quaker Education in Baltimore and Virginia Yearly Meetings with an Account of Certain Meetings of Delaware and the Eastern Shore Affiliated With Philadelphia* (Philadelphia, 1936), p. 485; U.S. Commissioner of Education, *Special Report*, pp. 353 ff.; *Raleigh Register*, 25 August 1808. The best survey of early Negro education is Carter G. Woodson, *The Education of the Negro Prior to 1861* (New York, 1915).

ture . . . as the most likely means to render so numerous a people fit for freedom and to become useful citizens." Pleasants later founded a school on his own land, outside Richmond. Abolition societies also aided in the establishment of African schools. In 1794, the American Convention of Abolition Societies urged its constituents to establish schools for emancipated Negroes. Like Robert Pleasants, the Convention also emphasized the utility of education in preparing newly emancipated slaves for liberty. Schools would not only teach "those mechanic arts which will keep them most constantly employed," but would also make free Negroes "less subject to idleness and debauchery, and thus prepare them for becoming good citizens of the United States."[43]

Despite praise lavished on education as a device for integrating former slaves into free society, emancipationists had difficulty establishing African schools. Once under way, these schools were small, their enrollment limited, and their classes infrequent. After five full years of operation, the school begun by the Delaware Abolition Society still met once a week. Most abolitionists could not imitate even these feeble efforts. The Richmond Abolition Society, unable to fund its own school, appealed to the American Convention for aid. But the Convention did nothing, and Richmond emancipationists could do little but recommend that free Negro children be apprenticed to sympathetic craftsmen or farmers.[44] If abolitionists had difficulty generating enthusiasm for educating newly liberated blacks, small wonder that most whites remained unconcerned.

Naturally, the strongest supporters of the African schools were the blacks themselves. Free Negroes, like whites, looked increasingly to education as a prerequisite for upward mobility and greater participation in American society. Baltimore free Negroes saw their school as a commitment to "the improvement

[43] Weeks, *Southern Quakers and Slavery*, p. 215; Dunlap, *Quaker Education*, pp. 173–7, 458–9; *Minutes of the Proceedings of a Convention of Abolition Societies* . . . (Philadelphia, 1794), p. 14, hereafter cited as *American Convention Minutes*.

[44] *American Convention Minutes*, 1805, p. 34; James Wood to the American Convention, 20 May 1798, PAS; Minutes of the Delaware Abolition Society, 20 January 1805, HSD; Minutes of the Delaware Abolition Society, 8 January 1806, HSP; Alexandria Abolition Society to the American Convention, 28 May 1801, PAS; Dunlap, *Quaker Education*, p. 445.

and happiness of the present and future generations."[45] As white-sponsored schools failed, freemen organized their own academies.

Blacks applied the lessons they had learned in establishing their churches to the building of African schools. Usually the development of the two institutions was closely intertwined. Soon after their establishment, most African churches sprouted educational auxiliaries with ministers doubling as schoolmasters. The Sharp Street African Church in Baltimore, like many others, also served "as a school for the education of black children of every persuasion." Although African churches bore most of the burden of educating black children, some independent schools flourished. In Charleston, for instance, the members of the elite Brown Fellowship Society subsidized the Minor's Moralist Society for educating indigent free Negro children.[46]

Like black churches, African schools were not popular with whites, who generally saw them as nurseries of subversion. The fact that they too believed education was a mechanism for perfecting liberty and securing social improvement only made African schools seem more dangerous. In an age of revolutions, whites moved quickly to stamp out many of the most promising black schools.

The destruction of the Richmond African school suggests the depth of white hostility to any attempt free Negroes might make to improve their status. In 1811, Christopher McPherson, a free Negro of considerable talent and modest wealth who also styled himself "Pherson, the first son of Christ," hired Herbert H. Hughes, a white schoolmaster, and opened a night school for free Negroes and slaves who had the consent of their master. Classes began at dusk and ran until nine thirty, and Hughes taught "the English language gramatically, Writing, Arithmetic, Geography, Astronomy, &c. &c." for a fee of about $1.25 per month. The results were most promising. The school opened with twenty-five pupils, and McPherson noted that "from frequent application since, 'tis expected the number will

[45] *Baltimore American*, 6 June 1805 (misdated 5 June 1805); Richmond *Virginia Argus*, 12 March 1811.

[46] *Baltimore American*, 6 June 1805 (misdated 5 June 1805); Daniel A. Payne, *Recollections of Seventy Years* (Nashville, Tenn., 1888), pp. 14–15.

shortly be doubled." McPherson was so pleased with his initial success that he publicly boasted of the school in the Richmond *Argus*, and recommended "to the people of colour throughout the United States (who do not have it in their power to attend day schools) to establish similar institutions in their neighborhoods." Excited over the new possibilities, he hoped "that everyone who loves his Country, and has it in his power will generously further and foster every institution of the kind that may be established throughout this happy Union."[47]

Richmond whites were less enthusiastic. Within days after McPherson's notice appeared, several leading citizens confronted Samuel Pleasants, the editor of the *Argus*, and demanded that the advertisement be withdrawn. "They deem it," Pleasants reported, "impolitic and highly improper that such an institution should exist in this City." Pleasants disagreed, but dutifully yielded to public pressure. Herbert Hughes, the white schoolteacher, was made of sterner stuff. He took space in the *Argus*, defended the school, and attacked the idea that it was impolitic to educate Negroes as Rousseauistic sophistry. Reiterating his support of the school, Hughes declared "without Education in some degree *they are* in a state of bastard civilization," and he pledged to teach until authorities closed the school.[48]

That apparently was not long in coming, for soon after Hughes made his appeal, Richmond officials summoned McPherson to court to show why his school should not be declared a nuisance. The case was delayed, but the police continued to harass McPherson and probably drove Hughes out of town. Despite the greater threat implicit in the police action, in April, when the court again delayed his case, McPherson advertised his desire to establish "a seminary of learning of the arts and sciences" as soon as he could find a "proper tutor." But before he could act, the police again jailed McPherson and shipped him to the Williamsburg Lunatic Asylum.[49] McPherson

[47] Christopher McPherson, *A Short History of the Life of Christopher McPherson, alias Pherson, Son of Christ, King of Kings and Lord of Lords*, 1st ed., ca. 1811 (Lynchburg, Va., 1855); Edmund Berkeley, Jr., "Prophet Without Honor: Christopher McPherson, Free Person of Color," *VMH&B*, LXXVII (1969), 180–9; quotation in Richmond *Virginia Argus*, 12 March 1811.

[48] Richmond *Virginia Argus*, 14 March 1811, 16 March 1811.

[49] McPherson, *Short History of McPherson*, pp. 6–11, 24.

doubtless had "mad" religious delusions, but these had not prevented him from functioning for years in a manner acceptable to Richmond whites; only when he established his school was he thrown into the madhouse. His lesson was obvious: any black man who would attempt to found a school was "crazy."

The establishment of African churches and schools in the years immediately following the Revolution reflected the new needs and rising expectations of the growing free Negro caste. During the antebellum years, African churches, benevolent societies, and schools—often operating clandestinely—provided an institutional core for black life. In these institutions black people baptized their children, educated their youth, and provided for the sick, aged, and disabled. Leaders of these institutions, especially ministers, moved into dominant positions in black communities; and African churches, especially the hierarchical AME, provided a means of advancement for talented black youth. Yet, in building these institutions, blacks did more than provide for their own comfort, security, and mobility. In the years immediately following the Revolution, Negro freemen saw African churches and schools, like the selection of a new name or migration to a new city, as a means of establishing a new identity as a free people.

This search for a new identity was part of a larger cultural transformation. The growth of the free Negro caste allowed Afro-Americans the first opportunity to express themselves unfettered by the shackles of slavery. The new names they chose, their patterns of mobility, and the institutions they created reveal how far transplanted Africans had come in assimilating to American life. Yet free Negroes called their churches African churches and their schools African schools. Within these institutions the new Afro-American culture flourished. The growth of the free Negro caste marks nothing less than the emergence of that culture.

3

The Failure of Freedom

> Tell us not of [Revolutionary] principles. Those principles have been annihilated by the existence of slavery among us.
>
> Richmond *Virginia Argus,* 17 January 1806

FOR ALL the heady equalitarianism of the Revolutionary years, white racial attitudes remained essentially unchanged. Slavery, though on the defensive throughout the Upper South, proved remarkably resilient. In the 1780s, as Southern emancipationists realized that slavery would not wither away, they began to organize themselves more tightly. Following the example of their Northern counterparts, the "friends of equal liberty" established abolition societies in Delaware, Maryland, and Virginia. These societies sprouted branches and auxiliaries, all of which informally affiliated with the Pennsylvania Abolition Society and joined in the formation of the American Convention of Abolition Societies in 1794.[1]

[1] Thomas Collins to Benjamin Franklin, 11 April 1788, PAS; *The Constitution of the Delaware Society for Promoting the Abolition of Slavery* (Philadelphia, 1788); Baltimore *Maryland Journal,* 15 December 1789; *Constitution of the Maryland Society for Promoting the Abolition of Slavery* (Baltimore, 1789); *The Constitution of the Virginia Society for Promoting the* ABOLITION OF SLAVERY (n.p., 1790); *Constitution of the Alexandria Society for the Relief and Protection of Persons Illegally Held in Bondage,* 1790; the latter two are in PAS Papers. Also see Gordon F. Finnie, "The Antislavery Movement in the Upper South Before 1840," *JSH,* XXXV (1969), 320–42; Monte A. Calvert, "The Abolition Society of Delaware, 1801–1807," *Delaware History,* X (1963), 295–320.

Although weak and shadowy organizations, they soon became the focal point of Southern opposition to slavery.

As might be expected, the antislavery societies weakened as one traveled south from Pennsylvania. The Richmond society was clearly the weakest. In 1794, when its members failed to muster a quorum at two succeeding meetings, Robert Pleasants, its Quaker president, feared the society would "drop altogether." Pleasants, a confirmed opponent of slavery, rallied the Virginians, but the society remained in constant danger of dissolution. South of Virginia, opposition to slavery proved impossible to organize. Although the American Convention meeting in Philadelphia and Baltimore sporadically petitioned Lower South legislatures, their memorials fell on deaf ears. When they pressed their case in North Carolina, emancipationists glumly discovered that the public viewed their petitions with "an indignant and jealous eye" and considered "the preservation of their lives, and all they hold dear on earth, as depending upon the continuance of slavery." Opposition to slavery fared no better in the new slave-hungry states to the west. In 1797, slaveholders blocked Thomas Embree's attempt to establish an abolition society in Tennessee, and the efforts of David Rice in Kentucky suffered the same fate.[2]

The strongest Southern abolition societies stood on the periphery of power. In the North, abolitionists recruited leading men into their ranks. Benjamin Franklin, Alexander Hamilton, and John Jay all lent their names, if less often their time, to the antislavery cause. Southern emancipationists could muster little such support. Leading Southerners owned slaves and had much to fear from meaningful abolitionist agitation. Although some slaveholding Southerners went beyond the perfunctory condemnations of slavery, few had the nerve to say so publicly. Edmund Randolph confessed to Benjamin Franklin that he favored emancipation, but carefully added that he wrote "merely as a private man" and could only hope someday

[2] Robert Pleasants to James Pemberton, 11 December 1794, PAS; *American Convention Minutes,* 1795, p. 18, 1800, p. 5, 1803, p. 27 (quotation), 1804, p. 25; Asa Martin, "The Anti-Slavery Societies of Tennessee," *Tennessee Historical Magazine,* I (1915), 262; David Rice to James Todd, 26 April 1797, Carter Tarrant to the Philadelphia Abolition Society, 27 May 1809, PAS.

to speak as "a *citizen.*"[3] Moreover, unlike later reform movements, the first antislavery crusade failed to produce a single professional reformer committed to ending slavery. The nonslaveowning artisans and tradesmen, who composed the backbone of the Southern antislavery movements, sincerely opposed slavery, but were hard pressed to make a living and lacked the leisure to pursue freedom suits and lobby legislative assemblies.[4] While concern for their own livelihood absorbed the energies of these men and limited their power, planters and their allies dominated Southern society.

Nevertheless, in the 1790s abolitionists reaped the benefits of greater organization. They petitioned legislatures more frequently, prosecuted freedom suits more forcefully, helped protect free Negroes from re-enslavement, and occasionally founded schools for newly emancipated blacks. But far from drawing the South closer to emancipation, increased antislavery agitation only aroused slaveholder resistance. In 1791, in an action symptomatic of the heightening opposition to emancipation, the Maryland House of Delegates condemned the state abolition society and came within two votes of declaring it "subversive to the rights of our citizens." When the abolition society petitioned for an official apology, the House censured its memorial as "indecent, illiberal, highly reprehensible, and, moreover, as untrue as it is illiberal." The legislature then attacked abolitionist-supported freedom suits. Legislators made all those who aided freedom suits liable for the defendant's expenses as well as court costs; required, in the case of failure, full payment before a second suit could be initiated; and prevented the removal of freedom suits from southern to more sympathetic northern counties.[5] Maryland abolition never recovered from the shock of legislative censure and new repressive legislation.

[3] Zilversmit, *First Emancipation*, pp. 162–7; Edmund Randolph to Benjamin Franklin, 2 August 1788, PAS.

[4] "Report of the Delaware Abolition Society" to the American Convention, 11 December 1802; David Rice to James Pemberton, 16 January 1790, PAS.

[5] [*Resolutions Passed*] *At a Meeting of "the Maryland Society for Promoting the Abolition of Slavery" . . . held in Baltimore, the 4th of February, 1792* (n.p., n.d.); Annapolis *Maryland Gazette*, 12 December 1791; *Md. Laws*, 1791, c. 75.

Emancipationist strength was already waning when the news from Saint-Domingue reached American shores. It did not take long for slaveholders to envision an American Saint-Domingue; on this subject, American slaveholders showed no lack of imagination. "When we recollect how nearly similar the situations of the Southern States are in the population of slaves, that a day may arrive when they may be exposed to the same insurrections," wrote the governor of South Carolina to the Saint-Domingue Assembly, "we cannot but sensibly feel for your situation & have particular interest in hoping that such support will be afforded you . . . to effectively crush so daring & unprovoked a rebellion." Yet whatever else they thought about the Saint-Domingue insurrection, few Americans believed it was unprovoked. Americans knew what happened when men were oppressed. As the world's most successful revolutionaries, they understood the contagious nature of the principles of liberty and feared, as Jefferson put it, "if something is not done, & soon done, we shall be the murderers of our own children," for the "revolutionary storm, now sweeping the globe, will be upon us."[6]

To quench the flames of revolution that seemed to flicker all around them, slaveholders strove to eliminate the tiny emancipationist groups located throughout the Upper South. In 1795, Elisha Dick, a prominent Virginia physician, broke into an Alexandria antislavery meeting and accused emancipationists of "infusing into the slaves a spirit of insurrection and rebellion." Abolitionists ignored the intruder, but the petitions he sent to the Virginia legislature received a warm reception. The Virginia General Assembly, copying Maryland's action, responded with legislation designed to destroy the antislavery societies and thwart the growing number of freedom suits. The new law, aimed directly at abolition societies, changed the procedure for freedom suits. It required a pretrial judgment of the admissibility of a suit, allowed only court-appointed lawyers for a plaintiff, and provided a one-hundred-dollar fine for anyone aiding unsuccessful court action. In 1798, another act de-

[6] Charles C. Pinckney to Colonial Assembly of Santo Domingo, September 1791, SCLP; Jefferson to St. George Tucker, 28 August 1797; Paul L. Ford, ed., *The Writings of Thomas Jefferson,* 10 vols. (New York, 1892–9), VII, 168; Jordan, *White over Black,* pp. 375–402.

barred abolition society members, but not slaveholders, from juries hearing freedom suits.[7] As expected, these laws made it almost impossible for a slave to win his freedom in Virginia courts. Virginia emancipationists complained that it was difficult for slaves to get good counsel. And worse, freedom suits were almost always prosecuted in the county courts, "where the common county justices preside, & those justices [are] often considerable slaveholders; under these circumstances the claimant must appear as clear as the sun at noon before it would be admitted for tryal [*sic*]." Slaveholders' law, slaveholding judges, and slaveholding juries destroyed "almost every suggestion of hope that any person . . . can obtain liberty by due process of law."[8]

In the face of growing opposition, the major religious denominations retreated from their antislavery outposts. In 1796, the Methodist General Conference again condemned slavery, but retracted its strong antislavery rule of 1784. Eight years later, the Methodist antislavery façade collapsed as the Conference ordered the publication of a separate Southern *Discipline* with the antislavery rules deleted. The Baptists, who had briefly flirted with a denominational endorsement of emancipation in Virginia and Kentucky, now confirmed their opposition to abolition. In 1791, when the Virginia General Committee queried the district associations on slavery, one association sharply advised them not to interfere with it. Baptists refused to see slavery in moral terms, complained a Kentucky abolitionist, and had "reasoned themselves into a kind of belief that black is white." Still the Baptists, with their congregational organization, had attacked slavery with greater consistency and determination than the older, more staid denominations. In 1789, when Kentucky Presbyterians debated abolition, they concluded that "freedom was desirable," but meekly added that it could not "at all times be enjoyed with advantage." Prodded by David Rice, the Presbyterians went on to condemn slavery

[7] Arch. McClean to William Rogers, 15 February 1796, PAS; Palmer, ed., *Virginia State Papers*, IX, 178; Shepherd, comp., *Statutes Va.*, I, 363–5, II, 77–9.

[8] George Drinker to Joseph Bringhurst, 10 December 1804, Petition from Alexandria Abolition Society to the Virginia General Assembly, 1796 (copy), PAS.

but allowed local churches to deal with the question of emancipation, a compromise that asserted their piety and assured their inaction. As opposition to abolition mounted, the Methodist and Baptist churches also found comfort in this hollow compromise. By 1800, Quakers were again alone in their commitment to abolition.[9]

With the attacks of the Virginia and Maryland legislatures and the collapse of denominational support for abolition, antislavery societies declined in membership and activity. Throughout the Upper South, the public opinion which abolitionists had so assiduously tried to cultivate grew increasingly hostile. The demand for slaves stimulated by the expansion of cotton culture in the Lower South further undermined the abolitionist cause. Masters who had leaned toward emancipation when a glut of slaves crowded Upper South plantations seemed to change their minds as slave prices soared. "Interest, all powerful Interest," moaned David Rice, "closes the eyes and hardens the heart to a great degree: it gives the least plausible pretense the force of the strongest argument."[10] By 1796, the secretary of the Delaware Abolition Society gloomily predicted that organization's imminent dissolution, and a year later the Virginia Abolition Society reported to the American Convention that the 1795 anti-abolition law had so decimated its ranks that it had nothing to report. In 1798, the Maryland society, weakened by legislative censure, disbanded. The desertion of "men of weak nerves and of apathetic constitutions" was just part of

[9] Mathews, *Slavery and Methodism*, pp. 3–29; Ryland, *Baptists in Virginia*, pp. 150–5; David Rice to William Rogers, 4 November 1794, letterbook copy, PAS; Andrew E. Murray, *Presbyterians and the Negro—A History* (Philadelphia, 1966), p. 18. Changes in the Baptist and Methodist churches made them more susceptible to pressure from slaveholders. After a generation of growth, both of these evangelical churches were much more closely identified with the "established" interests of the South. This was reflected in their services and membership as well as in their retreat from opposition to slavery. Robert Semple, an early church historian, noted that by the 1790s Baptist preachers "were becoming much more correct in their manner of preaching: A great many odd tones, disgusting whoops and awkward gestures, were disused: In their matter also, they had more of sound sense and strong reasoning. Their zeal was less mixed with enthusiasm, and their piety became more rational. They were much more numerous, and of course, in the eyes of the world, more respectable. Besides, they were joined by persons of much greater weight, in civil society." (*Rise and Progress of Baptists in Virginia*, p. 39.)

[10] David Rice to William Rogers, 4 November 1794, letterbook copy, PAS.

the problem. After two decades of frustrating agitation, death claimed many stalwart abolitionists, and others migrated west, where they hoped to escape slavery or find a more favorable climate for their antislavery opinions.[11]

Whether inspired by Revolutionary principles, Christian equalitarianism, or their own interests, the emancipationists proved to be no match for the planters. Against the real benefits slavery gave these whites, the antislavery argument fared poorly. Slave society successfully provided economic prosperity and controlled what was considered a dangerous if not inferior caste. While abolitionists argued that slavery would lead to economic stagnation, immorality, decadence, and revolution, slaveholders countered with greater truth that it created prosperity, leisure, "civilization," and political stability for the most powerful part of Southern society. Not all Southerners were slaveholders, but economic dependencies, kinship bonds, ambition, and racial solidarity tied many nonslaveholders to the slaveholding class. David Rice entered a lasting judgment on the failure of Southern abolitionism when he noted that many favored emancipation, "but the majority are poor: the rich hold Slaves, and the rich make the laws."[12]

By the summer of 1800, when Gabriel Prosser, a black carpenter, and his fellow slaves made plans to take Richmond, organized Southern abolition was sadly declining. The hysteria following Gabriel's rebellion drove it into near-oblivion. In 1804, one Virginia abolitionist rightly described the state society as "a mear Mishien for manufacturing Addresses to the Convention, a fungus lump growing out of Society at large that only serves to show its bad health." Although the Southern abolition societies occasionally reported to the American Convention, they were impotent after 1800.[13] Southern slaveholders had smashed the most important internal challenge their peculiar institution would face.

[11] William Poole to the American Convention, 1796, John Anthony to the American Convention, 3 May 1796, George Drinker to Joseph Bringhurst, 10 December 1804, PAS; Allen, "David Barrow's *Circular Letter* of 1798," pp. 440–51.

[12] David Rice to James Pemberton, 16 January 1790, PAS.

[13] Alexandria Abolition Society to the American Convention, 28 May 1801, George Drinker to Joseph Bringhurst, 10 December 1804, PAS.

. . .

As slaveholders systematically destroyed opposition to slavery, they began to fashion a defense of an institution which even they increasingly deemed peculiar. At first, the proslavery argument was inchoate and often contradictory, but it rested on the simple premise that free Negroes could never be part of white America. Since blacks could not live as equals with whites, emancipation would lead inexorably to a physical amalgamation of black and white or the creation of two separate and eventually warring societies. In the minds of most whites the threat of insurrection was tied tightly to that of amalgamation. Indeed, the end results of amalgamation and a successful slave revolt were precisely the same: a loss of white identity. Blacks, it was believed, not only threatened to make war on their white oppressor, but to unite with his daughter and destroy a white posterity.

Yet the South was not of one mind about slavery. In the Upper South, chattel bondage continued to embarrass many whites. Recognizing blacks as human beings, if culturally inferior ones, and accepting the ideas of the Declaration of Independence, they abhorred the idea of slavery and were uncomfortable holding people in bonds. They sympathized with the main thrust of the antislavery argument: that slavery had a detrimental effect on whites and was subversive to the Republic. They complained bitterly that the British had foisted slavery on their unwilling ancestors. But the alleged cultural inferiority of blacks, their inability to work without white direction, and their threat to white dominance made emancipation impossible. Slavery was thus a necessary evil, and the leaders of the Upper South bemoaned the terrible burden whites had to bear. Yet the necessary-evil argument was more than just an apology for slavery. It soothed the consciences of those hostile to slavery and stayed the criticism of many emancipationists, while it gave slaveholders a good excuse to keep their slaves.[14]

In the Lower South, no such view prevailed. The planters of South Carolina and Georgia felt little embarrassment about holding slaves, only distress that they did not have more. They slapped down every challenge to slavery, not by subtle in-

[14] Jordan, *White over Black*, pp. 301–4; McColley, *Slavery and Jeffersonian Virginia*, pp. 114–40, 163–81.

direction, but by direct assault. During the war, they had refused to arm blacks, and with independence no abolition societies appeared and few masters manumitted their slaves. Emancipation, as one Savannah newspaper noted, was simply "not a prudent subject of discussion in Georgia."[15] If the Upper South believed slavery was a necessary evil, the Lower South considered it merely a necessity.

Growing economic differences widened the rift within the South. While an excess of slaves crowded Upper South plantations owing to the change from tobacco to wheat culture, the Lower South, with its expanding cotton culture, desperately needed black laborers. These complementary interests would ultimately knit the South together, but the possibility of importing slaves directly from Africa put the Upper and Lower South temporarily at odds. Closing the African trade would assure Virginia and its neighbors a market for their surplus slaves and would fatten the prices they would fetch in Charleston. Opposition to the trade not only brought real rewards, but it also allowed the Virginia statesmen to stand, for once, with "enlightened" world opinion against chattel bondage. Not surprisingly, Virginians saw heinous immorality where South Carolinians saw only cold economic necessity. Yet the differences between the Upper and Lower South transcended crude calculation. South Carolinians began to defend the trade with the same moral ardor as Virginians used to condemn it. More than one South Carolinian thought the trade "could be justified on the principles of religion, humanity and justice." While the Upper South toyed briefly with emancipation, the Lower South continued to import Africans. In 1803, South Carolina reopened the African slave trade after it had been legally closed for a decade.[16]

Rather than lamenting the evils of slavery, the leaders of the Lower South celebrated the institution and declared it a boon to both white and black. In 1790, before Toussaint or Gabriel had etched himself on the Southern mind, William Loughton Smith, a South Carolina congressman, gave a full-blown elab-

[15] Savannah *Columbian Museum & Savannah Advertiser,* 11 March 1796.

[16] Jonathan Elliot, ed., *The Debates in the Several State Conventions on the Adoption of the Federal Constitution,* 5 vols. (Washington, D.C., 1836–41), IV, 284; W. E. B. Du Bois, *The Suppression of the African Slave-Trade to the United States of America, 1638–1870* (Cambridge, Mass., 1896), pp. 86–7.

oration of the positive-good argument, declaring "that negroes were by nature an inferior race of beings" and therefore better off as slaves.[17] Occasionally, the assumption of innate Negro inferiority was echoed in the Upper South. Thomas Jefferson leaned toward the idea that blacks were naturally inferior to whites, but remained tentative in his judgment. The universal belief in the unity of creation contradicted the idea that blacks were a distinct species. The novelty of that idea astounded Upper South emancipationists. "Gracious God!" roared William Pinkney of Maryland. "Can it be supported that thy almighty providence intended to proscribe these victims of fraud and power, from the pale of society, because thou hast denied them the delicacy of an European complexion!" Pinkney lashed out at the arrogance of presuming "the Ruler of the universe had made darkness of skin, the flatness of a nose, or the wideness of a mouth, which are only deformities or beauties as the undulating tribunal of taste shall determine," the standards of humanity.[18] Yet these were precisely the standards emerging in the Lower South.

The diverse defenses of slavery pointed to a split in Southern ranks which would grow steadily throughout the antebellum years. Yet both the necessary-evil and the positive-good arguments arose from a common fear and hatred of blacks who were free and the implicit threat free Negroes posed to slavery. Whether the Negro was culturally or innately inferior, whites would not tolerate free Negroes living among them. Once freed, Negroes degenerated into unproductive, irresponsible vagrants and quickly became a burden on the white community. To stay alive, they stole uncontrollably from plantations and became the "agents, factors, and carriers" of slave-pilfered goods. Free Negroes refused to work, maliciously destroyed property, stirred unrest among the slaves, and depreciated the value of all property. Emancipation, predicted a group of some eighty Virginians in 1782, would be "productive of Want, Poverty, Distress and Ruin to the Free Citizens;

[17] *Annals of Congress,* 1st Cong., 2nd Sess., pp. 1453–64; also 1st Cong., 1st Sess., pp. 338–41.

[18] Thomas Jefferson, *Notes on the State of Virginia,* ed. William Peden (Chapel Hill, N.C., 1955), pp. 61, 138–43; Pinkney, *Speech of William Pinkney,* pp. 15–16.

Neglect, Famine, and Death to the helpless black infants and superannuated Parents; Horrors of all the Rapes, Murders, and Outrages, which a vast Multitude of unprincipled, unpropertied, vindictive, and remorseless Banditti are capable of perpetrating . . . and lastly Ruin to this now free and flourishing Country."[19]

In a slave society, the free Negro was an incorrigible subversive. "If blacks see all of their color slaves," observed a Virginia lawmaker, "it will seem to them a disposition of Providence, and they will be content. But if they see others like themselves free, and enjoying rights they are deprived of, they will repine." Events on Saint-Domingue magnified the fear of free Negro subversion inherited from the colonial years. Southern whites were well aware that unrest among the free people of color had triggered the revolt which eventually established the Haitian Republic, and they worried about restlessness among their own growing free black population. Already well-informed free Negroes, observed the citizens of Petersburg, were complaining, "What is liberty . . . without social intercourse?" In an age of revolutions, these remarks needed no interpretation, for "with such language among the free people of color a train was laid, a mine sprung in St. Domingo that totally annihilated the white population." The growth of African churches and the willingness of free Negroes to aid fugitive slaves pointed to a growing sense of black self-esteem which was plainly contagious. During Dunmore's rebellion, noted one Virginian in the aftermath of the Gabriel conspiracy, blacks "sought freedom merely as a good; now they also claim it as a right."[20]

The free Negroes' fervent attempt to shake off the habits of slavery, purchase property, build churches and schools, and establish an identity as a free people heightened white fears. Ironically, the more the free Negro became like them, the more enraged whites became. It was easy for a people who professed to love freedom to despise a slave; whites needed

[19] Petition from Halifax County, 10 November 1785, VLP. For other proslavery petitions with the same emphasis see Fredrika T. Schmidt and Barbara R. Wilhelm, eds., "Early Proslavery Petitions in Virginia," *W&MQ*, 3rd. ser., XXX (1973), 133–46.

[20] Richmond *Virginia Argus*, 17 January 1806; Petition from Petersburg, 11 December 1805, VLP; [Tucker], *Letter to the General Assembly*, p. 7.

reasons to hate blacks who were free. The growth of the free Negro caste and the development of Afro-American culture as manifested in the independent black churches and schools forced whites to define more carefully than ever the differences between free and slave, white and black. It was no accident that an articulate defense of slavery appeared with the emergence of the free Negro caste.

The emergence of the free Negro caste also necessitated a sharper definition of the freemen's status. During the colonial years, whites had allowed the few light-skinned free Negroes to share with them many of the rights of a free people, but a large, dark-skinned free Negro population just barely removed from slavery induced whites to reconsider the status accorded free Negroes. Whites could no longer tolerate the ambiguity of the colonial black codes. They demanded free Negro subordination, yet the law allowed Negro freemen some measure of equality. And equality was not something whites were about to share. The libertarian rhetoric that accompanied the Revolution pushed the idea of equality into a central place in the emerging national ideology. The belief that all men had a natural right to equal treatment before the law elevated the status of many whites, freeing them from unwanted taxes and allowing them to participate in the political process for the first time. As possession of these rights became the defining element of American nationality, whites became increasingly reluctant to give them to a people they despised. Therefore, as the free Negro caste grew, Southern legislatures eliminated the inconsistencies in the old colonial black codes, prevented free Negroes from enjoying the new liberties provided by the Revolution, and enacted new regulations to assure the subordination of black freemen. Throughout the South, free Negroes found their mobility curbed, their economic opportunities limited, and their civil rights all but obliterated. The separation and discrimination inherent in slavery continued into freedom; those free Negroes who measured their liberty against that of whites everywhere found it wanting.

The proscriptive process commenced immediately following the Revolution and accompanied the liberalization of slave codes and the growth of antislavery ideals. Legislatures might relax manumission requirements, but they showed their fear and hatred of the newly emancipated blacks by limiting their liberty in the same breath. In 1782, for example, the same Virginia law which legalized private manumissions also provided that free Negroes could be sold into servitude for defaulting on their taxes. A year later, when Maryland legislators provided for the emancipation of illegally imported slaves, they also ruled that no Negro thereafter manumitted should "be entitled to the rights of free men," except to hold and defend property. Southern lawmakers systematically sealed the leaks in the colonial black codes which allowed Negro freemen a measure of equality with whites. Maryland lawmakers went on to bar emancipated blacks from holding office, voting, and testifying against whites. Four years later, while it relaxed its manumission rule and forbade the export of slaves to certain places, Delaware enacted a similar ban.[21]

The equalitarian promise of the Revolution was not entirely barren, but the new rights free Negroes acquired in the first flush of freedom did not usually last long. With independence, most Southern states adopted new constitutions. Written in a fit of equalitarian zeal, many of these documents spoke grandly of the rights of man and at times did not distinguish as to the kinds of men who had rights. In Delaware, Maryland, and later Kentucky new constitutions enfranchised free Negroes, subject to the same property qualifications as whites. The new North Carolina constitution kept the colonial provision for free Negro suffrage, and Tennessee later copied it. But as the free Negro caste grew, Southern legislatures hastily trimmed these newly awarded rights. Kentucky, Delaware, and Maryland barred free Negroes from the polls. Only in North Carolina and Tennessee did the Revolutionary heritage survive.[22]

[21] Hening, comp., *Statutes Va.*, VI, 39–40; *Md. Laws*, 1783, c. 23; *Laws of Delaware,* II, 887. Maryland and Delaware seem to have created two classes of free Negroes, those free before 1783 and 1787, respectively, and those freed after. The former could vote, hold office, and testify against whites; the latter could not. I have found no evidence that this distinction existed in fact, and it was quickly eliminated by constitutional restrictions that applied to all freemen. Thorpe, comp., *Federal and State Constitutions,* III, 1705, I, 574.

[22] Thorpe, comp., *Federal and State Constitutions,* I, 563, 574, III, 1269, 1278, 1691, 1698, V, 2790, 2796, VI, 3418.

After recasting colonial codes and erasing gains of the Revolutionary years, Southern legislators added disabilities to the free Negro's steadily shrinking liberty. New restrictions were enacted fitfully as different states responded to the greatly enlarged free Negro caste, but the growing fear of rebellion speeded the proscriptive process. Throughout the 1790s, free Negroes found their freedom further restricted and their liberty usurped.

The unobstructed right to travel allowed Negro freemen increased economic opportunities and made them difficult to control. Slaveholders feared that mobile free Negroes would intermingle with slaves, encourage them to run away, and foment insurrection. Thus, Southern legislatures devised new methods to limit mobility and prevent mixing with slaves. Virginia took the lead, and in 1793 prohibited the immigration of free Negroes into the Commonwealth. About the same time, Georgia required that all free black immigrants give proof of their industry and honesty within six months of their arrival or face deportation. Two years later, North Carolina limited free Negro immigrants by requiring entering Negroes to post a bond of two hundred pounds. Those who failed to do so were arrested, jailed, and then sold at public auction. In 1800, South Carolina banned free Negro entry.[23] Other states hesitated to enact similar prohibitions; however, in 1806, when Virginia ordered newly manumitted blacks to leave the state, they acted quickly. The following year, noting the Virginia law, Kentucky prohibited the entry of free Negroes. A year later, when Maryland whites complained that "many beggarly blacks have been vomited upon us," the state legislature enacted a similar ban. Delaware still resisted. In 1807, it partially restricted the entrance of free Negro migrants, but repealed the law the following year. Three years later, however, Delaware capitulated and enacted a total prohibition, and Georgia slapped a twenty-dollar tax on all Negro freemen entering the state.[24]

[23] Shepherd, comp., *Statutes Va.*, I, 239; Robert and George Watkins, comps., *A Digest of the Laws of the State of Georgia, from Its First Establishment . . . to the Year 1798* (Philadelphia, 1800), p. 530; *N.C. Laws,* 1795, c. 16; Cooper and McCord, comps., *Statutes S.C.*, VII, 436–7.

[24] Shepherd, comp., *Statutes Va.*, III, 252; William Littell, comp., *Statute Law of Kentucky,* 5 vols. (Frankfort, 1809–19), III, 499–501; Russell, *Free*

The prohibitions on interstate migration left state lawmakers with the problem of how to control free Negroes within their borders. All manumission laws prescribed the issuance of freedom papers to identify free Negroes, but these certificates were easily forged and freemen often moved far from where they were emancipated, making it difficult to verify their status. Freeborn blacks, who carried no papers, compounded the problem of free Negro control. The inadequacy of the freedom-paper system was especially disturbing in cities where newly freed and fugitive slaves tended to congregate and become almost indistinguishable. To prevent slaves from passing as free and to control free Negroes, Southern legislatures revised and reinforced the freedom-paper laws and established a system of registering Negro freemen.

North Carolina, with its large quasi-free population, initiated the new system of control. A 1785 North Carolina law, regulating the hiring of slaves in certain towns, ordered all urban free Negroes to register with the town commissioners and to wear a shoulder patch inscribed with the word "FREE." In 1793, the Virginia General Assembly, complaining of the "great inconvenience" of slaves passing as free in the cities, required urban free Negroes to register with the town clerk. The clerk would record their name, sex, color, age, stature, identifying marks, and how they were freed. The "Register of Free Negroes" was to be kept in the town hall and a copy, which had to be renewed annually for a fee of twenty-five cents, issued to every free Negro. A similar system was adopted for rural free Negroes, but since they posed less pressing problems of control, they had to re-register only every three years. A free Negro who failed to register was fined five dollars and could be sold into servitude in default of payment. Free Negroes without papers and unable to prove their freedom were, of course, treated as fugitives. In 1805, Maryland adopted the Virginia system with only slight modification, and a year later Tennessee enacted a similar measure. The Lower South lagged behind. But in 1799, when state officials failed to act, the Savannah City Council

Negro in Virginia, p. 71; *Md. Laws,* 1806, c. 66; *Del. Laws,* 1807, c. 42, 1808, c. 49, 1811, c. 16; Augustin S. Clayton, comp., *A Compilation of the Laws of the State of Georgia, Passed . . . 1800–1810, Inclusive* (Augusta, 1812), pp. 655–6.

passed a registration law. Later, the Georgia Assembly reinforced the Savannah law and passed its benefits on to other municipalities, by subjecting all urban free Negroes to the same regulations as slaves.[25]

The new registration system was not without problems. Many Negro freemen forged their papers, and others, claiming they had lost them, applied for new certificates and quickly passed them on to slaves. To combat these abuses, Virginia, Maryland, and Tennessee provided stiffer penalties for forgery and regulated more strictly the reissuance of certificates of freedom.[26] Free Negroes and fugitive slaves continued to evade the system and turn it to their own advantage, but the registration system worked well enough to become the basis of free Negro control throughout the South.

These new strictures did not end the attempt to control the free Negro. It took constant prodding, close supervision, and an intricate system of incentives to make blacks work in slavery; whites had little hope that Negroes, once freed, would continue to be productive. Even as whites perfected the registration system, they designed other laws to extort free Negro labor, punish those deemed socially useless or potentially dangerous, and bring free Negroes under closer supervision by whites. In 1796, when Maryland codified its hodgepodge of black laws, it required that all indigent free Negroes be jailed and either give security for their good behavior or be expelled from the state. Free Negro vagrants who remained in the state were to be sold for six months, and at the end of their service the process was to be initiated again. An 1801 Virginia law of similar intent declared that all registered free Negroes who "intruded" into another county could be arrested and, if judged vagrants, fined, and sold in default of the fine and court costs.[27] Other states attempted to extort free Negro labor directly. In 1808, Georgia legislators, complaining about the "dangerous tendency" of permitting "free negroes

[25] Clark, ed., *State Records of N.C.*, XXIV, 727–8; Shepherd, comp., *Statutes Va.*, I, 238; *Md. Laws*, 1805, c. 66; *Tenn. Laws*, 1806, c. 32; Savannah Ordinances, 31 December 1799, SCH; Clayton, comp., *Laws of Ga.*, 369.

[26] Shepherd, comp., *Statutes Va.*, II, 417–18; *Md. Laws*, 1807, c. 164; *Tenn. Laws*, 1807, c. 100.

[27] *Md. Laws*, 1796, c. 67; Shepherd, comp., *Statutes Va.*, II, 300–1.

and persons of color to rove about the country in idleness and dissipation," empowered the justice of the peace and any three freeholders to bind out all such free Negro men between eight and twenty-one. Maryland and Delaware soon passed similar laws, and in 1810, Georgia took the unprecedented step of inviting free Negroes to take white guardians to supervise their affairs.[28] By the beginning of the nineteenth century, the freemen's liberty was precarious indeed. At any time, any white could demand proof of a free Negro's status; even if his papers were in order, an unemployed free Negro could be jailed and enslaved and his children bound out to strangers.

Whites especially feared free Negroes' consorting with slaves, implanting the idea of freedom, and helping slaves to abscond or rebel. Attempting to stop the flood of runaways at the end of the century, legislatures strengthened fugitive-slave laws to provide for additional penalties for harboring slaves and increased rewards to informers. As might be expected, free Negroes bore the brunt of the increased penalties. In many places, free Negroes guilty of harboring slaves were whipped while white offenders faced only fine or imprisonment. Slaveholders were especially anxious to stop the traffic in freedom papers. In Virginia a free Negro guilty of supplying a slave with such papers was adjudged a felon and might suffer death for a second offense; in Maryland he could be fined three hundred dollars or sold in default into seven years of servitude. In 1793, perhaps in response to the growing number of successful runaways, Congress activated the fugitive slave clause in the Constitution enabling masters to reclaim escaped slaves in any state of the Union.[29]

As the fears of servile insurrection mounted, Southern lawmakers lashed out at free Negro subversion, real and imagined. The hysteria unleashed by events on Saint-Domingue eroded the freemen's legal rights like a torrent of rain on a grassless slope. In 1795, while prohibiting the entry of black West Indian émigrés, North Carolina legislators ordered grand

[28] Clayton, comp., *Laws of Ga.,* 462–3, 655–6; *Md. Laws,* 1808, c. 54; *Del. Laws,* 1811, c. 164.

[29] For representative runaway codes see *Md. Laws,* 1792, c. 72, 1796, c. 67, 1802, c. 96; Shepherd, comp., *Statutes Va.,* II, 177; *U.S. Statutes at Large,* I, 50.

juries to indict all free Negroes deemed "dangerous to the peace and good order of the state and county." These trouble-makers were to be jailed pending trial and, if found guilty as charged, sold into slavery. For like reason, Maryland prohibited free Negroes from keeping guns and dogs without a license, and Delaware barred free Negroes from all towns on Election Day. But in trying to prevent a black insurrection, whites went far beyond punishing subversive activity, no matter how loosely defined. In various places, free Negroes could be fined or whipped for entertaining slaves, meeting in groups of more than seven, attending school, or holding church meetings. North Carolina forbade free Negroes to marry slaves without compensating the slaveholder.[30]

To further denigrate free Negroes, Southern lawmakers increasingly equated them with slaves. Every state, except Delaware, barred free Negroes from testifying against whites in court while allowing slaves to testify against freemen. In 1811, Georgia went a step further and denied free Negroes the right to a jury trial, ordering them tried like slaves before a local justice of the peace. Increasingly, although still not regularly, free Negro criminals were punished more severely than whites. In some places, Negro freemen could be punished by long terms of servitude. Often sale into servitude was so defined that free Negroes were doubtless enslaved for life. A Delaware law, for example, punished free Negroes guilty of horse stealing with sale to the West Indies or some other place "for a term not exceeding fourteen years."[31]

Finally, whites legally curtailed free Negro economic opportunities. When Maryland slaveholders complained that free Negroes induced their slaves to steal produce which free-

[30] *N.C. Laws,* 1796, c. 16; *Md. Laws,* 1806, c. 81; *Del. Laws,* 1798, c. 3; Cooper and McCord, comps., *Statutes S.C.,* VII, 440–3; Clark, ed., *State Records of N.C.,* XXIV, 890–1; Alexander Edwards, comp., *Ordinances of the City Council of Charleston* (Charleston, 1802), pp. 67–8, 110; *Digest of the Ordinances of the City Council of Charleston, from the Year 1783 to . . . 1818* (Charleston, 1818), pp. 74, 179–80; Savannah Ordinances, 8 December 1806, SCH; Minutes of the Savannah City Council, 13 April 1810, SCH; *N.C. Laws,* 1791, c. 4.

[31] L. Q. C. Lamar, comp., *A Compilation of the Laws of the State of Georgia, 1800–1819* (Augusta, 1821), pp. 797–9; *Laws of Delaware,* II, 887; *Del. Laws,* 1811, c. 164.

men then bought and resold as their own, the General Assembly slapped a new prohibition on free-Negro trading. In 1796, the legislature barred Maryland free Negroes from selling agricultural produce without a special permit from a local justice of the peace. Virginia and Georgia forbade the licensing of free Negro river captains and pilots, thus barring them from a lucrative and prestigious aspect of a trade that blacks dominated. Municipal officials in Charleston and Savannah proscribed free Negroes from a variety of occupations and required that they procure special licenses for trades that whites practiced freely.[32] After limiting their ability to earn a living, South Carolina, Georgia, and Virginia burdened Negro freemen with special taxes.[33]

Whites answered the free Negroes' insistent drive for independence by methodically stripping them of their liberty. By the beginning of the nineteenth century, the ambiguity that characterized the status of the free Negro during colonial years was gone and the equalitarian enthusiasm of the Revolutionary years had run its course. Whites had pushed free Negroes into a place of permanent legal inferiority. Like slaves, free Negroes were generally without political rights, were unable to move freely, were prohibited from testifying against whites, and were often punished with the lash. Indeed, the free Negro's only right that escaped unscathed was his ability to hold property—a striking commentary on the American idea of liberty.

In robbing free Negroes of their liberty and rigorously distinguishing their rights from those enjoyed by free white persons, Southern lawmakers raised still another problem: Who was a Negro? During the colonial era, only Virginia and North Carolina had bothered to define legally what made a person black. Both colonies carried the search for African ancestry back three generations, and at times, North Carolina

[32] *Md. Laws,* 1805, c. 80; Shepherd, comp., *Statutes Va.,* II, 313; Clayton, comp., *Laws of Ga.,* pp. 332–3; Clark, ed., *State Records of N.C.,* XXIV, 890–1; Edwards, comp., *Ordinances of Charleston,* pp. 73–4; *Digest of Charleston Ordinances, 1783–1818,* p. 38; Savannah Ordinances, 31 December 1799, SCH.

[33] Herbert Aptheker, "South Carolina Poll Tax, 1737–1895," *JNH,* XXXI (1946), 132–6; W. McDowell Rogers, "Free Negro Legislation in Georgia Before 1865," *Georgia Historical Quarterly,* XVI (1932), 33; Russell, *Free Negro in Virginia,* pp. 112–4.

legislators peeked into the fourth generation removed. Any free person with an African parent, grandparent, great-grandparent, and sometimes a great-great-grandparent—that is, up to one-eighth or one-sixteenth Negro—was deemed black and subject to laws regulating free Negroes. In rummaging through family trees to the third and fourth generations, Virginia and North Carolina gave legal force to the commonplace colonial notion that anyone who displayed the physical attributes of an African past or was unable to shake the memory of his or her African paternity was to be considered black as a full-blooded Negro. Other colonies seemed to follow this rule, although none chose to write it into law. Perhaps because there were so few free Negroes, they were so light-skinned, and they shared so many rights with whites, it simply did not matter. Mixed-blood free Negroes were obviously distinct from the overwhelmingly black slaves, and whites did not seem particularly averse to absorbing those few mulattoes light enough to pass into the white caste. In fact, because they were unwilling to create a separate mulatto caste and endow it with special rights as was done in parts of the West Indies, whites may have considered passing as a means of dealing with the lightest, most acculturated, and most successful members of the colonial free Negro population.[34]

The rapid deterioration of the status of the greatly enlarged and darkened free Negro population and the concomitant elevation of whites in the post-Revolutionary decade necessitated a sharper and more realistic definition of who was black and who was white. For one thing, much more was at stake than during the colonial era, when the differences between the status of free whites and free blacks were small and often ill-defined. A free Negro who could pass for white now had considerably more to gain, and a white who slipped into the free Negro population had considerably more to lose. Light-skinned freemen could be expected to try to muscle their way across the color line, and Southern courts, making hairline decisions between those who were an eighth or a sixteenth

[34] Jordan, *White over Black*, pp. 163, 167–8; H. R. McIlwaine, ed., *Journal of the House of Burgesses, 1752–1755* (Richmond, Va., 1909), pp. 339, 342, 348, 359–61.

black, might condemn some swarthy whites to the degraded free Negro caste. To avoid such mishaps, in 1785 Virginia lowered the color line and defined a Negro as a person having one African ancestor in the previous two generations. Kentucky, upon entering the Union, adopted the Virginia rule, and most of the other states of the Upper South later followed suit.[35] The Lower South, where the free Negro caste infused with large numbers of brown-skinned émigrés remained largely a mulatto group, refused to act. Perhaps fearing that any attempt to define who was white and who was black would push too many persons of both colors to the wrong side of the color line and create racial chaos, South Carolina and Georgia still made no effort to describe what made a brown man or woman white or black.

The contempt Southern leaders showed for the free Negro's liberty encouraged still less scrupulous whites to enslave free Negroes by force. Attracted by a quick profit, some whites engaged openly in manstealing. In the post-Revolutionary years, kidnapping blacks became so widespread that complaints reach the halls of Congress and several Southern states enacted stiffer penalties for the offense. Virginia and North Carolina made kidnapping a capital offense, and in Delaware kidnappers could be punished by thirty-nine lashes and have both ears nailed to the pillory for an hour and then cut off.[36]

Vigorous official disapproval provided insufficient protection for free Negroes. Working in isolated rural areas, at odd hours, kidnappers acted with impunity. "The great increase of the practice of kidnapping," observed horrified emancipationists in 1801, continued "in defiance of every principle of moral and legal obligation." Although most kidnappers were petty criminals, some operated on a large scale. In 1800, a resident of

[35] Hening, comp., *Statutes Va.*, XII, 184; William Littell and Jacob Swigert, eds., *A Digest of the Statute Law of Kentucky,* 2 vols. (Frankfort, 1822), II, 1164.

[36] *Md. Laws,* 1796, c. 67; Hening, comp., *Statutes Va.*, XII, 531; James Iredell, comp., *Laws of the State of North Carolina* (Edenton, N.C., 1791), pp. 370–1; *Laws of Delaware,* II, 1093–4.

Richmond reported a kidnapping ring working between Delaware and Virginia which had recently sold several hundred slaves into the state for fifty or sixty dollars each. "There can be no doubt but every one was kidnapped, because to buy them at full price of a slave in Delaware, in order to sell them here would be a losing game." He estimated that hundreds of stolen blacks had been sold into Virginia during the previous five years.[37]

Legal, financial, and logistical problems made kidnapping difficult to prevent. Except in Delaware, Negroes were not allowed to testify against whites, and blacks were usually the only witnesses to the crime. The inability of free Negroes to testify in their own defense hampered the prosecution of kidnappers and doubtless further encouraged manstealers. Moreover, unlike free Negroes, kidnappers were familiar with the law and usually arranged to have witnesses who would testify on their behalf. When a Baltimore emancipationist brought one alleged kidnapper to trial, he despaired of conviction because the kidnapper "employed the ablest counsel in our city to defend him."[38]

Abolitionists, who helped protect free Negroes against kidnappers, often saw their best efforts frustrated by the sheer magnitude of the task. In 1802, an agent of the Delaware Abolition Society pursued a kidnapper from New Castle to Norfolk only to find that the young black girl had been placed on a Florida-bound slave ship three days before he arrived. Such frustrations wearied emancipationists, and their efforts to liberate kidnapped free Negroes sagged. In 1810, Elijah Morris, a Delaware free Negro sold to Tennessee, sent word of his enslavement to the Pennsylvania Abolition Society through a sympathetic Nashville jailer. The society, which in its declining years acted as a clearinghouse for kidnapping information, passed on the message to its colleagues in Delaware, who collected proof of Morris's freedom but failed to find an agent to deliver it. The information apparently arrived too late to prevent his sale. Ten months later, the aboli-

[37] *American Convention Minutes,* 1801, pp. 43–4; Richmond *Virginia Argus,* 12 September 1800.

[38] Elisha Tyson to William Masters, 9 April 1812, PAS.

tionists closed the book on Morris's freedom, noting ruefully that "justice cannot be done."[39]

Stiff penalties signified official disdain for manstealing, but public apathy and a general reluctance to enforce kidnapping laws revealed that disdain for the free Negro's liberty was stronger. After many attempts to prosecute kidnappers, an exasperated Delaware lawyer concluded that the "propensities of juries to lean on the merciful side of the question, when the crime was committed against a black person, was so strong, as to raise a high degree of suspicion that the accused would be acquitted, if they prosecuted for kidnapping."[40] Whites who believed free Negroes would be better off as slaves could muster little enthusiasm for prosecuting other whites who simply followed that presumption to its logical conclusion.

Slowly the door shut on Negro freedom. Whites increasingly looked with suspicion upon those who freed their slaves. "It appears to me . . . ," wrote an angry neighbor to Robert Carter, "that a man has almost as much right to set fire to his own building though his neighbor[']s is to be destroyed by it, as to free his slaves. . . ."[41] If the opponents of manumission dared to challenge Robert Carter, one of the most powerful planters in Virginia, little wonder that they intimidated lesser men. After 1800, the number of manumissions declined sharply. The glare of hostile public opinion not only dissuaded many would-be manumitters but also encouraged avaricious heirs and creditors to challenge the slaves' right to freedom. Once promised liberty, slaves often faced new hurdles which delayed freedom or quashed it altogether.

Public opposition was soon transformed into legislative prohibitions. In 1800, South Carolina lawmakers tightened manumission procedures, regulating the freeing of slaves for the first time. Two years later, Georgia prohibited masters from liberating their slaves and vested that right solely in the legislature, and in 1805 the Mississippi Territorial Council enacted

39 Minutes of the Delaware Abolition Society, 12 October 1802, HSD; Mathew Neale to Warner Mifflin, 4 January 1810, Joseph Christy to Daniel Mifflin, 26 October 1810, ? to Daniel Mifflin, 16 December 1810, PAS.

40 Minutes of the Delaware Abolition Society, 21 December 1803, HSD.

41 [Rev. Thurston] to Robert Carter, 5 August 1796, Carter Papers, LC.

a similar law. Fear of free Negroes forced the Lower South states, which so tenaciously guarded the rights of the master, to limit them for the first time. In the Upper South, states that only a decade earlier had relaxed manumission restrictions reconsidered their actions. At first emancipationists held their own, but slowly the legislative initiative slipped to their opponents. In 1806, after several frustrating years, Virginia restrictionists required all blacks to leave the state a year after being freed or face summary re-enslavement. When opponents of the law claimed its repressive nature contradicted the principles of the Revolution, restrictionists snapped, "Tell us not of principles. Those principles have been annihilated by the existence of slavery among us."[42]

Judicial opinion also followed the flow of public opposition. Emancipationists who pressed freedom suits found that "attorneys on the opposition make such subtle constructions of our laws, the laws themselves being unfavourable, and the prevailing disposition of judges unfriendly to our cause . . . that they baffle many hopeful cases." Still, a successful freedom suit depended on more than liberal laws and judges. Slaves needed competent lawyers to stand up to their masters in court, but public hostility discouraged most attorneys from taking such cases. An interested Maryland lawyer admitted his slave clients had a good case, but frankly declared, "I am not yet Abolition-mad enough to run the hazard of the expense." The courts proved an inadequate avenue to freedom.[43]

As slaveholders and their allies stamped out the sparks of antislavery idealism, slowed the rate of manumission, and made successful freedom suits all but impossible, the expectations that stimulated the increase in runaways withered and the number of fugitives declined. Those few slaves who set out to free themselves faced a tighter system of enforcement and higher rewards for their capture. Stiffer punishments dis-

[42] Cooper and McCord, comps., *Statutes S.C.*, VII, 442–3; Clayton, comp., *Laws of Ga.*, p. 27; Harry Toulmin, comp., *A Digest of the Laws of the State of Alabama* (Cahawba, Ala., 1823), p. 638; Shepherd, comp., *Statutes Va.*, III, 252; Jordan, *White over Black*, pp. 575–82; quotation in Richmond *Virginia Argus*, 17 January 1806.

[43] "Report of the Delaware Abolition Society to the American Convention," 11 December 1802, S. Greaves (?) to Miers Fisher, 27 May 1790, PAS; *American Convention Minutes*, 1805, pp. 22–3.

couraged many who dared to aid them. Moreover, the strictures on free Negro migration and the registration system made it increasingly difficult for strange blacks to blend into the free Negro population. Although slaves would continue to make good their escape throughout the antebellum years, fugitives would probably never again be so numerous and so successful.

Curbing the growth of the free Negro caste and denigrating the free Negro did not sooth white anxieties. In many ways, the legislative restrictions heaped on free blacks only intensified white fears. For if, as many whites believed, the love of liberty was inborn, it could never be permanently confined. "It is an incontrovertible maxim," observed one Virginia legislator, "that man will never be content with lesser liberty when he has sufficient intelligence to perceive, and enough power to demand the greater." Keeping liberty cramped would only make the inevitable moment of liberation more explosive.[44] Therefore, even as they debased the free Negro's liberty, whites groped for ways to rid the South of free Negroes altogether.

Deportation quickly became the most pervasive and durable solution to the free Negro problem. In the years immediately following the Revolution, as the free Negro caste began to grow rapidly, some Southerners called for its removal. Although their proposals were sometimes part of long-range emancipation plans, the deportationists premised them on the incompatibility of free Negroes with white America and naturally focused on the removal of those blacks who were free. Most colonizationists deplored slavery but found the free Negroes even more objectionable. Not surprisingly, deportation schemes found their greatest support in the Upper South, which had the largest free Negro population.[45]

A large-scale colonization effort would be expensive and, in the eyes of many, impossible without coercion, and forcible deportation was repugnant to most whites. Nevertheless,

[44] [Tucker], *Letter to the General Assembly*, p. 6; *Richmond Enquirer*, 15 January 1805.

[45] The best account of the early colonizationist movement is Jordan, *White over Black*, pp. 542–72. Also useful are P. J. Staudenraus, *The African Colonization Movement, 1816–1865* (New York, 1961), chap. 1; Henry N. Sherwood, "Early Negro Deportation Projects," *Mississippi Valley Historical Review*, II (1916), 484–508.

colonization quickly became the *idée fixe* of a generation mindful of the evil effects of slavery and fearful of slave rebellions, but unable to conceive of alternative patterns of race relations. The tenacious support practical men gave an impossible plan suggests the pathetic hope of whites to be rid of blacks, especially free ones.

In his *Notes on Virginia,* Thomas Jefferson unveiled the first important removal proposal. In 1777, when Virginia was revising its legal code, an emancipation plan was presented that would free slaves born after a certain date, provide apprenticeships until they were adults and "colonized to such a place as the circumstances of the time should render most proper." The inability of whites to live with free blacks made their removal necessary. "Deep rooted prejudices entertained by whites; ten thousand recollections, by the blacks, of injuries they have sustained; . . . the real distinctions which nature has made; and many other circumstances, will divide us into two parties and produce convulsions which will probably never end but in the extermination of one or the other race." Ever fearful of a reversal of racial roles, Jefferson insisted on Negro removal as a precondition for emancipation.[46]

Other Southerners announced similar conditions for Negro freedom. In 1790, a Maryland "TRUE FRIEND OF UNION" assaulted an abolitionist appeal, but conceded that "a general emancipation might take place—on exportation" of the freed slaves. The same year, Ferdinando Fairfax, a Virginia planter, outlined the first detailed colonization plan. Since amalgamation was repugnant to all whites and manumitted slaves could never be allowed the rights of citizens, Fairfax suggested their removal to Africa. With the aid of the new federal govenment, he thought, a separate Negro state suitably distant from America could be established. Similarly, St. George Tucker's emancipation proposal incorporated a plan for colonization of freemen in the West. By denying free Negroes "the most valuable privileges which civil governments afford," wrote Tucker, "I wish to render it their inclination and their interest to seek those privileges in some other country." To help hustle the free Negroes out of America, Tucker proposed additional

[46] Jefferson, *Notes on Virginia,* pp. 137–43.

fetters to the free Negro's liberty. In addition to those rights Virginia had already denied, Tucker would prohibit free Negroes from bearing arms, willing and transmitting property, and holding land except on short-term leases. "Though I am opposed to their banishment," declared Tucker, "I do not wish to encourage their residence among us." Not all colonizationists were as specific as Fairfax and Tucker, but the subject found a ready audience throughout the Upper South. When the Duc de La Rochefoucauld-Liancourt visited Virginia in the 1790s, he found the state rife with talk of Negro removal.[47]

Colonization sentiment rarely penetrated the Lower South. Congressman William L. Smith, one of the few South Carolinians to consider the scheme, denounced it as inhumane as well as impractical. Behind his condemnation stood a belief that deportation was merely a front for abolition. Yet, it was not simply that the small, generally light-skinned free Negro population of the Lower South made whites look upon Negro removal as an emancipationist plot rather than as a solution to the free Negro problem. The emerging positive-good defense of slavery, which depicted blacks as hopelessly inferior beings, made whites more tolerant of the free Negro's presence. If blacks were innately inferior, limiting their liberty would not goad them to rebellion. Once whites carefully defined their place in the Southern caste system, freemen might even become useful members of society. Where whites felt secure holding slaves and saw little threat from inferior blacks, they felt less need to rid themselves of free Negroes.[48]

Throughout the 1790s, the leading men of the Upper South maintained a deep interest in colonization, but they did little. It appeared the scheme would wither under the weight of its own impracticality. But Gabriel's rebellion dramatically revived interest in the idea. Following the abortive insurrection, the Virginia legislature began secretly considering Negro removal. After long deliberation, the General Assembly instructed

[47] Annapolis *Maryland Gazette*, 16 December 1790; Ferdinando Fairfax, "Plan for Liberating the Negroes with the United States," *American Museum*, VIII (1790), 285–7; Tucker, *Dissertation on Slavery*, pp. 77–104; La Rochefoucauld-Liancourt, *Travels Through the United States*, II, 357.

[48] *Annals of Congress*, 1st Cong., 2nd Sess., p. 1455. South Carolina, where the positive-good argument had its deepest roots, also had the mildest free Negro codes; Jordan, *White over Black*, pp. 409, 411–12.

Governor James Monroe to ask President Jefferson if there were not some place outside the state "whither persons obnoxious to the laws or dangerous to the peace of society may be moved."[49] Monroe wrote to Jefferson inquiring if the federal government or a friendly foreign nation would set aside a place where the large number of insurrectionary blacks now in the Richmond jail might be sent. Monroe found mass executions distasteful and feared they would further excite blacks. He also cautiously suggested that the legislature's resolution might be understood to apply to others who were not immediately under sentence for insurrection. "As soon as the mind emerges, in contemplating the subject, beyond the contracted scale of providing a mode of punishment for offenders, vast and interesting objects present themselves to view." The following year, the Virginia legislature clarified the "vast and interesting objects" that might accrue beyond the establishment of a penal colony. In addition to criminal slaves, the legislature suggested that free Negroes might be sent to the "asylum."[50] The discussion that had begun with the hope of ridding Virginia of slavery and Negroes quickly focused on the least desirable elements, the criminal slaves and free Negroes. In the mind of many Virginians, there seemed little to distinguish them.

The Virginia removal proposal aroused Jefferson's long-standing interest in deportation, and he and Monroe quickly struck up a lively correspondence on the subject. Jefferson ruled out the possibility of the colonization of Negroes on mainland North America, but he was sanguine about their removal. He thought the West Indies offered "a more probable and practical retreat" for Negroes. The West Indies was already inhabited by blacks, its climate suited the black constitution, and its blacks were insulated from whites; indeed, Jefferson declared, "nature seems to have formed these islands to become a receptacle of the blacks transplanted into this hemisphere."

[49] Resolutions reprinted in Archibald Alexander, *A History of Colonization on the Western Coast of Africa* (Philadelphia, 1846), pp. 63–72; removal had been forcefully suggested to the legislature by George Tucker in his public *Letter to the General Assembly.*

[50] Monroe to Jefferson, 15 June 1801, in Stanislaus M. Hamilton, ed., *The Writings of James Monroe*, 6 vols. (New York, 1898–1902), III, 292–5; Alexander, *Colonization on the Western Coast of Africa*, pp. 63–72.

Later, Jefferson turned his attention to Africa, which he also saw as "offering a most desirable receptacle for the blacks." Indeed, almost any place seemed the proper "receptacle" for the Negro, except America.[51]

Like other colonization schemes, this one was quickly forgotten as other more pressing matters pushed their way to the fore. Jefferson's growing concern with American involvement in the European crisis curbed his interest in Negro colonization. But the repeated proposals for removal, like the proscriptive laws, manstealing, and restrictions on emancipation, made clear the free Negroes' place in the white mind.

[51] Jefferson to Monroe, 24 November 1801, 2 June 1802, in Ford, ed., *Writings of Jefferson,* VIII, 103–6, 152–4; Monroe to Jefferson, 13 February 1802, 11 June 1802, in Hamilton, ed., *Writings of Monroe,* III, 336–8, 351–3.

4

The Free People of Color of Louisiana and the Gulf Ports

> They are a very numerous class in this city[,] say ⅓ or ¼ of the population[,] many very respectable & under this government enjoy their rights in common with other subjects . . . they may be made good citizens or formidable abettors of the black people . . . if they should ever be troublesome."
>
> Benjamin Morgan to Price Chandler, 7 August 1803

EARLY in the nineteenth century, as the doors to freedom slammed throughout the seaboard South, the number of Southern free Negroes suddenly surged upward. The purchase of Louisiana in 1803 brought a large number of free Negroes within American borders. Like the white population of Louisiana, these French- and Spanish-speaking creoles stood apart from their seaboard counterparts. In their numbers, origins, traditions, and place in society, the *gens de couleur* of Louisiana were unlike the free Negro caste of Revolutionary America. In 1810 and 1819, when restless Americans pushed Spain out of West Florida and Florida, smaller free Negro populations around Mobile and Pensacola were brought under the American flag.

The free Negro population of the Gulf region was almost

entirely the product of extramarital unions between white men and black women. Early French adventurers in this region, unlike English mainland colonists, did not settle with their families, and the preponderantly male population quickly formed liaisons with black slave women. By the middle of the eighteenth century, such matches had become so commonplace that whites customarily recognized their mulatto children, and some provided for their upbringing and education. Few white men thought it necessary to hide what English mainland colonists called "shameful" and "unnatural" relations. Although the children of these mixed racial unions followed the status of their mother, a liberal manumission policy encouraged masters to free their black mistresses and their light-skinned children. By 1769, when Spain gained control of Louisiana, mulattoes composed better than half of the small free Negro population centered in New Orleans, and the remaining free blacks were mostly women.[1]

Under Spanish rule, the free Negro caste expanded rapidly. Spanish manumission policy proved even more lenient than that of the French. Spanish law automatically freed slaves who had been abandoned by their masters or allowed to act as free for a period of years, and generally liberated slaves for performing meritorious services for the colony. When a master disputed a slave's right to freedom, the courts generally favored liberty. Most important, Spanish officials encouraged slaves to purchase their freedom. If a reluctant master refused to relinquish his valuable property, a slave could petition the court to set a price on his liberty. Within the context of the expanding commercial economy of New Orleans and the relatively immature plantation economy of the hinterland, this liberal policy induced hundreds of owners to free their slaves or to allow them to buy their liberty. Still, illicit sexual relations between white men and black women remained the greatest source of free Negro increase. "The military officers

[1] Donald E. Everett, "Free Persons of Color in Colonial Louisiana," *Louisiana History*, VII (1966), 29–40, 46–7; Laura Foner, "The Free People of Color in Louisiana and St. Domingue: A Comparative Portrait of Two Three-Caste Slave Societies," *Journal of Social History*, III (1970), 408–10; Lawrence Kinnaird, ed., *Spain in the Mississippi Valley, 1765–1794*, in *Annual Report of the American Historical Association for the Year 1945*, 4 vols. (Washington, D.C., 1946), II, pt. 1, 196.

and a good many inhabitants," lamented a Spanish bishop, "live almost publicly with colored concubines, and they do not blush at carrying the illegitimate issue they have by them to be recorded in the parochial registries as their *natural children.*" A census of Upper Louisiana at the turn of the century revealed that mulattoes composed 80 percent of the free Negro population.[2] All told, between 1769 and 1785 the number of free Negroes in Louisiana jumped from only 165 to over 1,300. By the end of the century, about 2,000 Negro freemen lived in Louisiana.[3]

By any standard, Louisiana free Negroes enjoyed a considerably higher status than the small free Negro population in the English seaboard colonies. Still, most French and Spanish settlers remained intensely hostile toward blacks who were free. Like English colonists, they characterized free Negroes as indolent, vain, and dangerous. Because they too treasured white dominance, they worried that the presence of so many light-skinned freemen would blur the color line and topple white rule. Although free Negroes suffered few legal disabilities, they met unyielding opposition whenever they pressed for full equality with whites. Free Negroes found social discrimination pervasive and galling. Spanish officials even regulated the dress of free Negro women to assure whites a monopoly of frills and feathers.[4] Neither fair skin nor blood relations assured Louisiana free Negroes of the affection or respect of whites. Not only did most free Negroes bear the

[2] Samuel P. Scott, trans., *Las Siete Partidas* (Chicago, 1931), pp. 981–4; Everett, "Free Persons of Color in Colonial Louisiana," pp. 43–7; *Annals of Congress,* 8th Cong., 2nd Sess., p. 1576; Charles E. A. Gayarré, *History of Louisiana,* 4 vols. (New York, 1854), III, 408.

[3] Kinnaird, *Spain in Mississippi Valley,* II, pt. 1, 196; *Appendix to An Account of Louisiana, Being an Abstract of Documents in the Offices of the Departments of State and the Treasury* (Philadelphia, 1803), pp. 84–7. Spanish censuses included West Florida with Louisiana. In 1803, Americans found that the last Spanish enumeration, which counted 1,768 free Negroes in about 1800, was "manifestly incorrect—the population being underrated." I have conservatively estimated the free Negro population of Louisiana in 1803 to be 2,000; it may have been still greater. *Annals of Congress,* 8th Cong., 2nd Sess., p. 1574.

[4] Antoine S. Le Page Du Pratz, *The History of Louisiana or of the Western Parts of Virginia and Carolina* (London, 1774), p. 357; Caroline M. Burson, *The Stewardship of Don Esteban Miró, 1782–1792* (New Orleans, 1940), p. 104; Gayarré, *History of Louisiana,* III, 179.

stain of illegitimacy, but many whites thought mulattoes even more dangerous than blacks. "They would like to be treated as legitimate children," warned a French visitor just before the United States gained control of the territory, "and the difference that is placed between them (and the latter) makes them hate even the authors of their being. . . ."[5] Racial discrimination increased as the free Negro caste grew. By the beginning of the nineteenth century, racial lines had been drawn so taut that free Negroes of property and rank feared to challenge the lowliest white. A visitor to New Orleans noted that quadroon naval officers might on ship "give twenty lashes with the end of a rope to white sailors, but ashore they do not even dare look them in the face."[6]

If French and Spanish creoles shared many of the racial attitudes of colonial Englishmen, they lacked the ability to do much about it. Unlike British policymakers, metropolitan authorities in France and Spain kept a tight rein on the governance of their colonies. They distinguished between free whites and Negroes by barring intermarriage, requiring manumitted slaves to respect their former masters, and punishing free Negroes more harshly than whites for certain offenses, but they generally left free Negro rights unscathed.[7] White colonists might have liked to deprive free Negroes of the basic rights of citizens, but European policymakers saw no such need. From their point of view, white colonists often posed a greater threat to metropolitan control than the free Negroes, and, as throughout Latin America, the authorities saw Negro freemen as a balance wheel against independence-minded whites. The autocratic rule of distant Continental monarchs protected free Negroes from hostile white settlers, while the developing democracy of the English colonies left freemen open to direct assault.

[5] James A. Robertson, ed., *Louisiana Under Spain, France, and the United States, 1785–1807*, 2 vols. (Cleveland, Ohio, 1911), I, 185, also I, 218–19.

[6] C. C. Robin, *Voyages dans l'intérieur de la Louisiane, de la Floride Occidentale, et dans les Isles de la Martinique et de Saint-Domingue*, 3 vols. (Paris, 1807), II, 120–1.

[7] Everett, "Free Persons of Color in Colonial Louisiana," pp. 22–4; Herbert E. Sterkx, "The Free Negro in Ante-Bellum Louisiana," unpublished doctoral dissertation, University of Alabama, 1954, pp. 4–5, 107–8; *Appendix to an Account of Louisiana*, p. 82.

The free Negro's status within the Gulf region did not rest solely on the protection of distant European monarchs or on statutory guarantees of equality. Far more important in securing the freemen's rights was their own numerical strength. By controlling the balance of power between slaves and whites, free Negroes maintained their relatively high status. While seaboard free Negroes composed but a tiny fragment of the black population of colonies that were preponderantly white, free Negroes in eighteenth-century Louisiana made up at least 10 percent of the free population of a colony that was predominantly black. In many places in the Gulf region, their numerical weight far exceeded that. In 1788, free Negroes composed more than a third of the population of the strategic port city of New Orleans, the capital of colonial Louisiana.[8] The black majority forced whites to search for additional means to protect their dominant position. Free Negroes, who shared bonds of blood as well as status with whites, provided the most natural allies.

Throughout the eighteenth century, whenever slaves, Indians, or hostile outsiders threatened the colony, whites called upon the free Negroes to protect them. As early as 1729, when there were few free Negroes in the colony, the French employed black bondsmen against the rampaging Natchez Indians. The promise of freedom transformed the slaves into fierce fighters and saved the tiny white settlement from destruction. Thereafter the French organized free Negro troops under the direction of their own officers. Negro freemen found themselves in the forefront of every engagement with the colony's enemies.

When Spain took control of Louisiana, it adopted the French policy. Indeed, the continuing loyalty of many of the white inhabitants to France forced Spanish officials to rely even more heavily on free Negro soldiers. Although the number of free Negroes was insufficient to make up a regular company, Spanish authorities assured the continued existence of the free Negro unit by placing them under the command of the captain general in Havana. In Cuba, as in all of Spanish America, free Negro militiamen were organized into *pardo,* or light-skinned,

[8] *Appendix to an Account of Louisiana,* p. 84; Burson, *Stewardship of Miró,* p. 105.

and *moreno*, or dark-skinned, units. As the number of freemen around New Orleans increased, Louisiana free Negroes were given the same somatic organization. In 1779, when Spain as an ally of the United States attempted to push the British from the lower Mississippi Valley, free Negro soldiers joined in the assault on the English forts at Baton Rouge. Later they took part in the expeditions against Mobile and the conquest of Pensacola. Between engagements against the Indians and the British, Spanish officials put free Negro militiamen to work catching fugitive slaves, crushing maroon colonies, and repairing breaks in the Mississippi levees. In the 1790s, when Americans pressed Spanish control of the Mississippi and Jacobin sympathizers plotted to reannex the colony to the French Republic, free Negro troops bolstered Spain's shaky control of Louisiana. To ward off foreign invaders and to assure domestic security, Spanish governors reorganized the two *pardo* and one *moreno* militia units and commissioned many leading freemen of color as officers.[9]

By helping to cement white colonial control of Louisiana, free Negroes protected their freedom and enhanced their claim to equality. Colonial officials appreciated the protection free Negro troops afforded them. More important, the freemen's military experience made whites respectful of free Negro liberty. When a shift in racial alliances could bring the white minority face to face with brown militiamen at the head of the black masses, whites were not about to offend free Negroes no matter how much they despised them.

The free Negro's power did not come only out of the barrel of a gun. The shortage of white men improved the economic standing of free Negroes just as it had strengthened their military position. During the eighteenth century, free Negroes moved into many of the skilled crafts and trades generally controlled by nonslaveholding whites and slaves in English mainland America. Often their white fathers aided their entry into these trades, but the absence of intense competition from middle-class whites made free Negro mobility all the easier and their success all the more certain. As whites concentrated

[9] Roland C. McConnell, *Negro Troops of Antebellum Louisiana: A History of the Battalion of Free Men of Color* (Baton Rouge, La., 1968), pp. 5–32; Klein, *Slavery in the Americas*, pp. 215–16.

their energies and invested their money in developing plantations, free Negroes, especially in the Gulf port cities, monopolized many skilled occupations. Some of the free Negro carpenters and joiners, shoemakers and tailors, coopers and painters opened their own shops. The most successful of these often purchased slaves, and a few even pushed their way into the planter class. Their powerful economic position further guaranteed their unencumbered legal status.[10]

In 1803, when the United States gained control over Louisiana, the *gens de couleur* were a small but well-placed portion of the population of the new American province. Despite their military prowess and strategic economic position, Americans might have been tempted to brush them aside and immediately assign them to the subordinate place they had devised for blacks who were free. But during the first decade of American rule, the numbers and importance of the Louisiana free Negro caste increased as colored West Indian émigrés poured into the territory. This influx compounded American problems with the anomalous Louisiana caste and made whites considerably more reluctant to act on their impulse.

The flow of West Indian free Negroes into Louisiana had begun in the 1790s and followed the lines of battle in Saint-Domingue. Spanish authorities, like Southern lawmakers, feared the black and brown refugees from Saint-Domingue and tried to stem this unwanted immigration, but with no more success. French-speaking free Negroes continued to flock to Louisiana, where the large brown creole communities welcomed them. Although the influx of mulatto émigrés waned at the end of the century, in 1803 the success of blacks in ousting the French and creating the black Republic of Haiti sparked a last wave of internecine warfare between the free people of color and the black former slaves and forced thousands of light-skinned freemen to flee the island. With free Negro immigrants barred from most seaboard slave states and the free Negro's lowly place in Southern society carefully defined, these refugees increasingly sailed for the Gulf ports.

[10] Foner, "Free People of Color in Louisiana and St. Domingue," pp. 416–17, 419–20, 423–4; Marvin Harris, *Patterns of Race in the Americas* (New York, 1964), pp. 86–9.

The new wave of free Negro immigrants revived white fears that Louisiana would follow the fate of Saint-Domingue. The black majority and the close ties many French-speaking white creoles had with Saint-Domingue gave special meaning to the rumors that insurgent leaders were circulating through the territory. The occasional discovery of free Negroes who had fought on the rebel side did nothing to assuage white anxiety. Whites shuddered "at the thought that these men with their hands still reddened with the blood of our fellow countrymen are arriving daily in great numbers" and feared "that tomorrow their smoking torches will be lighted again to set afire our peaceful homes."[11] The new American governor of Louisiana, William C. C. Claiborne, shared these fears. Early in 1804, he ordered the American-controlled forts at the mouth of the Mississippi to bar the entry of all Negroes from the Antilles. When that order, like many subsequent ones, had no effect, Claiborne broadened the proscription to include blacks "of any description whatever." Yet despite Claiborne's edicts and similar pronouncements by New Orleans officials, the flood-tide of West Indians continued.[12] A year later, the mayor of New Orleans complained that "many worthless free people of colour or persons calling themselves free arrive here daily without our being able to prevent it, or to drive them away after they had come." By 1806, the free Negro population Americans had inherited with Louisiana had almost doubled in size.[13]

If it had proved impossible to stop the steady influx of free Negroes into the territory, neither could the problem be ignored. Surrounded by a black majority and barely in control

[11] Proceedings of the New Orleans City Council, 13 March, 24 April, 30 June (quotation), 31 October 1804, typescript, NOPL.

[12] Claiborne to Mayor Boré, 19 March 1804, [20 April 1804], Claiborne to James Madison and enclosure to Boré, 12 July 1804, in Dunbar Rowland, ed., *Official Letter Books of W. C. C. Claiborne, 1801–1816,* 6 vols. (Jackson, Miss., 1917), II, 51, 113–4, 352–61; New Orleans Resolutions and Ordinances, 24 July 1805, 21 February 1806, typescript, NOPL.

[13] John Watkins to John Graham, 6 September 1805, in Clarence E. Carter, ed., *The Territorial Papers of the United States,* 26 vols. (Washington, D.C., 1934–), IX, 503, 923; Census of New Orleans in 1803 with Daniel Clark to James Madison, 17 August 1803, Orleans Territorial Papers, RG 59, NA; also *New Orleans in 1805: A Directory and a Census* (New Orleans, 1936).

of the mass of disaffected Frenchmen and Spaniards, Americans could hardly afford to introduce still another discordant and possibly explosive element. In succeeding years, the newly elected territorial legislature clamped new restrictions on free Negro immigrants and attempted to force those who entered the territory illegally to leave.[14] But it was to no avail. Not until the temper of internal warfare on Haiti cooled did the flow of refugees cease. But just when the number of immigrants was tapering off, events in Europe sparked another massive movement of Caribbean peoples and sent thousands of refugees toward the Gulf ports. In 1809, Spanish officials in Cuba, angered by the French occupation of Spain, ordered off the island the French-speaking creoles who had earlier fled there from Saint-Domingue. Between May and July, dozens of ships bulging with over six thousand refugees, including almost two thousand free Negroes, reached New Orleans. The French-speaking population of the city welcomed their creole brethren, and the City Council organized relief for the white immigrants. American officials failed to enforce the law against the free Negro, perhaps because so many were property-owning artisans. Not until months later did Claiborne halfheartedly attempt to oust the adult men and prevent others from arriving, but by then it was too late. Although some of the free Negro refugees, unable to find work or adjust to New Orleans life, left for Atlantic ports or drifted back to Saint-Domingue, most remained. They too swelled the number of Negro freemen in Louisiana. Between 1803 and 1810, the free Negro population had increased fourfold to stand at almost eight thousand. Equally important, most of the free people of color in Louisiana were natives of the West Indies.[15]

[14] François-Xavier Martin, comp., *A General Digest of the Acts of the Legislature of the Late Territory of Orleans and the State of Louisiana*, 3 vols. (New Orleans, 1816), II, 100–2. Hereafter referred to as *Orleans Law*.

[15] Hall, *Social Control in Slave Plantation Societies*, pp. 55, 126; Donald E. Everett, "Emigrés and Militiamen: Free Persons of Color in New Orleans, 1803–1815," *JNH*, XXXVIII (1953), 385–8; James Mather to Claiborne, 18 July 1809, 7 August 1809, Claiborne to Maurice Rogers, 9 August 1809, Claiborne to William Savage, 10 November 1809, in Rowland, ed., *Claiborne Letter Books*, IV, 381–2, 387–9, 405–9, 401–2, V, 3–5; ? to the Mayor, April 1809, New Orleans Municipal Papers, LSU; *Aggregate Amount of Persons Within the United States in the Year 1810*, pp. 82, 84.

Americans found the growing free Negro caste a painful and perplexing problem. In spite of the increase in whites and slaves during the first decade of American rule, free Negroes remained about one-sixth of the black population of the territory and fully a quarter of the total population of the New Orleans area. Americans thus confronted an enlarged free Negro population most unlike that of the seaboard states. Armed, skilled in military affairs, organized into regular militia units, Louisiana free Negroes were completely conversant with events on Saint-Domingue. Many had close ties with white creoles and occupied a strategic position in the economy of the territory and especially of New Orleans, a city that Americans considered the entrepôt of the trans-Allegheny West. To make matters worse, American control over the vast Louisiana territory remained uncertain. The French-speaking population, hoping for the eventual return of the territory to France, stood aloof from the new American rulers, and the Spanish creoles conspired to rejoin Louisiana with Spain's New World empire. Americans expected free Negroes to try to subvert their rule, and nowhere were freemen in a better position to do it.

The anomalous caste in Louisiana was more than an immediate insurrectionary threat. Most Americans, along with Thomas Jefferson, expected the new Western territories to be populated from the seaboard "nest" and ultimately absorbed into the growing continental empire as states the equal of others. A free Negro caste that was armed, economically secure, and well connected blocked the path of the westward march of the American people. Not only would their presence discourage white immigration, but it would also create a dual standard of free Negro behavior within the slave states. Privileged free Negroes in Louisiana might encourage those elsewhere to assert their rights more forcefully. At the very least, Claiborne feared they would be "considered as an outrage on the feeling of a part of the Union and as opposed to those principles of policy which the safety of the Southern States has necessarily established."[16] Still, if there were any doubts

[16] Claiborne to James Madison, 27 December 1803, in Robertson, ed., *Louisiana Under France, Spain, and the United States*, II, 228.

as to what American policy would be, the enmity of the white creole population, long seething under the surface, set its course. Urged on by white creoles, Americans determined to deny free Negroes the rights they had long enjoyed under French and Spanish rule. Although the wealth and power of the Louisiana free Negro caste cautioned Americans against acting precipitously, from the first they aimed to reduce free Negroes to utter subordination.

Free Negroes had ideas of their own. The treaty which transferred Louisiana to America promised that the inhabitants of the territory would enjoy "all the rights, advantages and immunities of citizens" of the United States. Free Negroes needed no help in interpreting this clause. In January 1804, while professing joy at seeing their native land united with the United States, free Negro militiamen subtly warned the new American governor that they dearly valued their liberties and fully expected Americans to honor them. "We are duly sensible that our personal and political freedom is thereby assured to us for ever," declared the free Negroes, "and we are alsc impressed with the fullest confidence in the Justice and Liberality of the Government towards every Class of Citizens which they have here taken under their Protection." To demonstrate their willingness to protect their rights, free Negro militiamen marched in force at the ceremony transferring Louisiana to the United States.[17]

During the months that followed, free Negroes pressed the Americans for a full avowal of their citizenship. In the summer of 1804, finding themselves barred from white political gatherings, free Negro leaders in New Orleans called their people together so that "they might consult together as to *their* rights." They drew up a petition demanding equal citizenship rights with whites, but a white printer refused to publish it and instead passed their sentiments on to the governor. Claiborne angrily called the city's leading free Negroes to the

[17] U.S. Department of State, *Treaties and Conventions Concluded Between the United States of America and Other Powers Since July 4, 1776* (Washington, D.C., 1889), p. 332; Carter, ed., *Territorial Papers*, IX, 174–5; Claiborne to Henry Dearborn, 22 July 1804, in Rowland, ed., *Claiborne Letter Books*, II, 217–19.

statehouse and admonished them against "publicly manifesting any disquitude *[sic]*." The freemen recanted, admitted their error, and reaffirmed their loyalty to the American regime. Although Claiborne was prepared to use "other means" to assure free Negro obedience, he happily accepted the apology. Later, when local whites demanded the names of the errant free Negroes, he refused, fearing that a dispute between whites and the rapidly increasing free Negro population would turn Louisiana into another Saint-Domingue.[18]

Although Claiborne faced down the free Negroes, the existence of the free Negro militia made him wary about using "other means." "The formidable aspect of the armed Blacks & Malattoes *[sic]*, officiered & organized" enabled free Negroes to stand up for their rights with a degree of forcefulness Americans would not tolerate elsewhere.[19] During the first years of American rule, the existence of the free Negro militia became the chief object of contention between American administrators and local whites who wanted to liquidate it and the free Negroes who desired its recognition.

Early in 1804, free Negro militiamen presented Claiborne with their demand for full and immediate recognition by the American government. They reminded him of their long record of distinguished service under the French and Spanish and declared their willingness to serve the Americans with the same fidelity. Although free Negroes carefully measured their words to strip them of the charge of intimidation, implicit in their demands was the threat that free Negro loyalty might be placed elsewhere if Americans rejected it. With brown-skinned émigrés daily pouring into the territory from Saint-Domingue, Claiborne understood that it would be dangerous to ignore the free Negroes, at least for the present. He tactfully assured them of his respect for their military abilities and his confidence in their devotion to the American government, but declared himself unable to render a final decision on the

18 Claiborne to James Madison, 5, 7, 12 July 1804, in Rowland, ed., *Claiborne Letter Books,* II, 236–40, 244–6; Proceedings of the New Orleans City Council, 7, 11 July 1804, typescript, NOPL.

19 James Wilkinson to Henry Dearborn, 21 December 1803, in Carter, ed., *Territorial Papers,* IX, 139.

status of the free Negro militia. He promised to query Washington immediately and in the meantime suggested that free Negro units continue to meet as they had been doing.

Federal officials did not like the idea of armed free Negro militiamen any more than Claiborne, but they too appreciated the delicate balance of power that existed in the new territory. Secretary of War Henry Dearborn therefore suggested that Claiborne use his own discretion as the proper means of incorporating free Negro units into American forces. In no case, however, was he to increase the size of the colored units, and if it were at all possible to diminish them without antagonizing the free Negroes, Dearborn directed him to do so.[20]

Claiborne followed his orders to the letter. He mustered former members of the free Negro companies into American service, but ignored new recruits. If freemen asked why their ranks were not being filled, the governor instructed mustering officers to deny any knowledge of a specific decision. If pressed, they might claim that another Negro company would be created later. In June 1804, Claiborne presented the free Negro militiamen with their colors, the standard of the disbanded Fourth American Regiment—revived so that whites would not have to serve under the same standard as blacks. Moreover, Claiborne placed the new free Negro company under the command of white men. This break with past policy angered free Negroes. Officers of the militia enjoyed enormous prestige within the black community, and the loss of their commissions threatened their high standing. More important, white control of the free Negro corps weakened the freemen's position in Louisiana society. Nevertheless, Claiborne persuaded the free Negroes to accept the white officers in return for recognition, a compromise that greatly undermined the free Negro's status.[21]

Claiborne's attempt to cripple the Negro militia by reducing its numbers and placing it under white direction reflected the main goals of American policy. But like the French and

[20] Free Men of Color to Claiborne, in *ibid.*, pp. 174–5; Henry Dearborn to Claiborne, 20 February 1804, in Rowland, ed., *Claiborne Letter Books*, II, 54–6; McConnell, *Negro Troops*, pp. 38–9.

[21] Claiborne to Henry Dearborn 9, 22 June 1804, Claiborne to John Wilkinson, 18 April 1804, Claiborne to Major Fortier, 22 June 1804, in Rowland, ed., *Claiborne Letter Books*, II, 199–200, 217–19, 104–5, 215–16.

Spanish governors before him, he gradually came to recognize the value of free Negro troops. While French and Spanish creoles schemed to wrest control of Louisiana from the Americans, free Negroes mounted eagles on their hats as a symbol of their allegiance to the American government. Their devotion to the United States delighted Claiborne, especially when contrasted with the sullen indifference of other Louisiana natives. General James Wilkinson, the American commander in Louisiana, was similarly impressed and concluded that free Negroes would provide the only reliable troops in case of trouble. Slowly Claiborne's opposition to the Negro militia melted away. During the summer of 1804, when whites threatened to bar a free Negro company from parading on the city square, Claiborne posted American troops to protect them; when a prominent white citizen complained about an impudent free Negro militiamen, Claiborne ignored the charge; and when whites questioned the freemen's right to their own military corps, he vigorously defended it. Claiborne emerged as the most vigorous American supporter of the free Negro militia.[22]

Local white hostility did not subside. White militiamen disliked free Negroes' occupying the same role as themselves, especially since some free Negroes enjoyed a higher rank than many whites. Claiborne's change of heart only stiffened this opposition. It seemed to confirm the fears of many white creoles that free Negro troops would be used against them in case of an attempt to rejoin the territory with France or Spain, a possibility that Claiborne himself probably entertained. In October 1804, when the legislature of the Territory of Orleans convened for the first time, local lawmakers deactivated the free Negro company by simply omitting it from the act establishing a territorial militia. The following year, the legislature repeated the omission. After only four months, the free Negro militia was again without official standing.

Free Negroes did not protest the legislative rebuke, but

[22] James Wilkinson to Henry Dearborn, 11 January 1804, in Carter, ed., *Territorial Papers,* IX, 159–61; New Orleans *Louisiana Gazette,* 29 June 1805; James Sterrett to Nathaniel Evans, 23 June 1804, Nathaniel Evans Papers, LSU; Claiborne to Andrew Jackson, 28 October 1814, in Rowland, ed., *Claiborne Letter Books,* VI, 294.

Claiborne noted that their neglect had "soured them considerably with the American government." He now doubted they could be depended upon in a moment of danger. Confirmation of the free Negroes' growing disaffection was soon at hand. Early in 1806, the governor received word that some of the leading "Creoles of color of the City of New Orleans" were plotting to return Louisiana to Spain. Claiborne, who kept a remarkably cool head in the midst of constant scheming, sifted through the evidence and discounted most of it as empty rumor. Yet even he had to admit that the free Negroes had been "tamper'd with."[23]

Fearing the growth of free Negro disloyalty, the following year Claiborne requested the legislature to recommission the free Negro militia. The governor seemed confident that the measure would pass and even asked an aide to survey the former free Negro officers in preparation for the re-establishment of their battalion. But the legislature refused to act. Instead, the attacks on Claiborne's championing of the free Negro militia grew louder and more virulent. In May 1807, the *Louisiana Gazette* reprinted a speech by congressional Representative Daniel Clark alleging that Claiborne's preference for black militiamen had alienated the native white population and greatly weakened territorial defenses. Claiborne heatedly denied the charges and later fought a duel with Clark, but Louisiana legislators remained adamant in their refusal to recommission the free Negro troops.[24]

With the destruction of the free Negro militia, whites began to whittle away at the free Negro's liberty. Slowly lawmakers enacted distinctions between the rights of black and white freemen, which, although commonplace in the seaboard states, were novel for Louisiana. In 1806, the territorial legislature barred free Negroes from carrying guns without proof of their status from a justice of the peace, authorized slaves to testify in court against free Negroes, and ordered that free Negroes be punished like slaves for certain crimes it deemed

[23] McConnell, *Negro Troops*, p. 41; Claiborne to James Madison, 8 January 1806, Statement of Stephen, [23 January 1806], in Carter, ed., *Territorial Papers*, IX, 561, 575–6; Claiborne to Madison, 24 January 1806, in Rowland, ed., *Claiborne Letter Books*, III, 248.

[24] New Orleans *Louisiana Gazette*, 23 May 1807; Claiborne to Daniel Clark, 23 May 1807, in Carter, ed., *Territorial Papers*, IX, 738.

subversive to white control. Free Negroes who tried to expand their rights were brusquely pushed into a place of subordination as whites explained that liberty did not mean equality. When several free Negroes attempted to vote in New Orleans, the City Council quickly ruled that the franchise belonged only to those who were "designated by this single phrase—*free* and *white*" and added that there was "no ambiguity in these expressions." Yet the relatively unencumbered liberty and light skin of Louisiana free Negroes created just the kind of uncertainty that made Americans most uncomfortable. Driven by the confused state of racial divisions in Louisiana, the territorial assembly went further in defining the commonplace rules of racial etiquette than the older slave states ever thought necessary. "Free people of colour ought never insult or strike white people, nor presume to conceive themselves equal to whites," declared the legislators, "but on the contrary . . . they ought to yield to them on every occasion and never speak or answer them but with respect. . . ." To prevent light-skinned freemen from eluding these carefully drawn rules of racial deportment by fading into Louisiana's swarthy French and Spanish creole population, lawmakers ordered free Negroes to be designated as such on all public documents. In the older slave states, these explicit rules of racial behavior were never written into law, because they were generally understood. Only where the free Negroes challenged the white racial ideal with special force did whites find it necessary to spell it out in fine detail and give it the force of law. After only five years of American rule, the Louisiana free Negroes' legal status had dropped dramatically. Americans had succeeded in stripping them of many rights to which they had long been entitled, and had gone far in equating their status with that of free Negroes in the seaboard slave states. Once the color line had been secured, whites moved to limit the growth of the free Negro caste. In addition to laws restricting free Negro immigration, Louisiana lawmakers prohibited masters from freeing slaves under thirty years of age except with special legislative permission.[25]

[25] Martin, comp., *Orleans Law*, I, 620, 640–2 (quotation), 648, 656, 660, II, 104, 326–32; Proceedings of the New Orleans City Council, 1 March 1805; Messages of the Mayor of New Orleans, 25 May 1808, typescript, NOPL.

As Americans prepared to further diminish free Negro liberty, new threats to the safety of the territory suddenly shifted events in favor of the free Negro. In 1811, slaves on a plantation in St. John the Baptist Parish just up the Mississippi from New Orleans rose in rebellion, wounding their master and killing his son. The insurrection spread quickly, and soon several hundred slaves were marching toward the city with frightened whites fleeing before them. Claiborne marshaled American troops and local militia and sent them against the insurrectionary blacks. In a pitched battle only eighteen miles from New Orleans, American forces defeated the rebels. Victorious, but still unsure how deep the tide of rebellion ran, Claiborne placed the territory under what amounted to martial law for two weeks. Playing their traditional role, free Negroes volunteered their services against the slave rebels. Many of these free Negroes were large slaveholders who had much to lose from a successful rebellion; others remembered that it was just such black rebels who had driven them out of Saint-Domingue. Perhaps some simply saw an opportunity to ingratiate themselves with whites. In any case, Claiborne mustered free Negroes under white officers and used them to spell the exhausted American troops. By the end of a tense two weeks, he happily reported that the free Negro militiamen had "performed with great exactitude and propriety." Indeed, their "zeal for the public safety" and his fear that next time the number of white troops might be insufficient to their task convinced Claiborne to press the legislature again to commission the free Negro corps.[26]

It was not merely restless slaves that Claiborne feared. America was fast drifting into a second war with Great Britain, and Spain, now an ally of England, was already moving troops into nearby Pensacola. While Americans looked nervously over their shoulders for signs of unrest among the slaves, they faced increasingly aggressive foreign foes. The combined internal and external threats finally convinced territorial law-

[26] Manuel Andry to Claiborne, 11 January 1811 and enclosures, Orleans Territorial Papers, RG 59, NA; Messages of the Mayor of New Orleans, 12 January 1811, typescript, NOPL; Wade Hampton to Secretary of War, 16 January 1811, in Carter, ed., *Territorial Papers,* IX, 917–19; Claiborne to Robert Smith, 14 January 1811, in Rowland, ed., *Claiborne Letter Books,* V, 100.

makers of the necessity of placing every able-bodied man under arms. In 1812, just as Louisiana became a state, the legislature acceded to Claiborne's demands and recognized the free Negro militia.

White suspicion of armed free Negroes did not dissipate with acceptance of the free Negro militia. The legislature limited the free Negro corps to four companies of sixty-four men, who would be chosen from the creoles who had paid their state taxes for the previous two years and owned land valued at more than three hundred dollars. "The Battalion of Chosen Free Men of Color," as the General Assembly denominated the free Negro militia, was an elite corps of free Negroes whose style of life ruling whites found most compatible with their own. Members of the free Negro battalion came from the first ranks of the wealthiest free Negro shopkeepers, artisans, and planters. One free Negro militiaman found physical labor such a novel experience that he wore gloves on fatigue duty. Even so, whites could not fully trust these free Negroes. Though the legislature authorized the governor to choose line officers from among their numbers, only whites could be placed in command of the free Negro battalion.[27]

Recognition of the free Negro militia came none to soon. Within months the United States declared war on England, and the war went badly. The British blockaded the Atlantic coast, burned the Capitol at Washington, and soundly defeated the American attempt to take Canada. Nevertheless, the war centered in the northeastern United States and left Louisiana largely unscathed. But in the summer of 1814, the British began to swing their main theater of operations to the Gulf region in an attempt to divide the Republic or at least cut off America's western entrepôt by capturing the lower Mississippi Valley. Crack British units, fresh from victory in Europe, flowed into the British West Indies in preparation for the assault on New Orleans. Through fall and into winter, Andrew Jackson, the roughhewn Indian fighter appointed American commander in the Southwest, prepared to defend

[27] McConnell, *Negro Troops,* pp. 50–4, 84; Claiborne to Andrew Jackson, 12 August 1814, in John S. Bassett, ed., *Correspondence of Andrew Jackson,* 7 vols. (Washington, D.C., 1926–35), VI, 436–7.

the port city. He immediately understood that free Negro soldiers would not only be a valuable addition to the American cause but a dangerous enemy if ignored. "They will not remain quiet spec[ta]tors of the interesting contest," he reminded Claiborne. "They must be for, or against us. . . ." The British too would bid for free Negro support, and in the end, "the country who extends to them equal rights and privileges with white men" would win their loyalty.[28] Determined to protect the city, Jackson did not shrink from this conclusion.

Claiborne sympathized with Jackson's analysis. He had long tried to encourage free Negro loyalty by supporting the free Negro militia. In fact, he had already called leading free Negroes to his office to urge their support "in the hour of peril." Still, most whites continued to find armed freemen not only repugnant but dangerous. Some believed that enlisting free Negroes would ultimately aid the enemy, and they urged Claiborne to disband the recently established free Negro battalion. Even those who followed Jackson's reasoning and believed that free Negro loyalty could only be purchased for full equality were unwilling to pay the price. Members of the Committee of Defense in New Orleans grudgingly accepted the use of free Negro soldiers, but urged their immediate deportation at the end of the war. The committee warned that permitting them to remain in Louisiana "with a Knowledge of the use of Arms, and *that pride of Distinction* which a soldier[']s pursuits so naturally inspires . . . would prove dangerous." But the necessities of war allowed Claiborne to override these racial fears.[29]

Free Negroes, seeing the balance of power shift in their direction, quietly began to pressure the American administration. In late August, a large number of free Negro soldiers failed to appear at militia muster. Their officers assured Claiborne that the trouble was only local in nature, but the governor worried about deeper disaffection. The migration of a

[28] Jackson to Claiborne, 21 September 1814, in Bassett, ed., *Jackson Correspondence*, I, 56–7.

[29] Claiborne to Jackson, 12 August 1814, 17 October 1814, in *ibid.*, VI, 436–7, II, 76–7; Claiborne to Jackson, 24, 28 October 1814, in Rowland, ed., *Claiborne Letter Books*, VI, 288–9, 292–5.

large number of free Negroes back to Cuba some months later confirmed Claiborne's fears that the free Negroes would not stand by the Americans.[30]

In October, worried that British agents were making inroads among the free Negroes, Jackson summoned them "to rally around the standard of the Eagle." Condemning the "mistaken policy" which deprived free Negroes "of participation in the Glorious struggle for National rights," he assured them that this "shall no longer exist." Jackson never became more specific than this in his promise of greater free Negro participation in American life, and the extravagant language of his proclamation muffled an easy interpretation as to what exactly he offered for the free Negroes' support. Still, by calling free Negroes "my brave fellow Citizens," America's "adopted sons," and "sons of freedom," Jackson strongly hinted that their support of the United States would earn them an extension of their rights if not full equality. More concretely, Jackson guaranteed free Negroes equality with white soldiers in rations, clothing, pay, and bounties. Free Negro enlistees, however, would not be accepted into American ranks, but would fight as a separate unit to prevent their exposure "to improper comparisons or unjust sarcasm." Although noncommissioned officers would be chosen from their ranks, they would be commanded by whites.[31]

Free Negroes apparently never directly questioned Jackson's offer. Perhaps they understood that the unyielding hostility of native whites made a more specific promise impossible. Doubtless they knew any attempt to squeeze more privileges from whites stood little chance of success and would only rouse white fears. Jackson, on the other hand, understood the dire state of the defenses of New Orleans and may have been susceptible to pressure from the free Negroes. At the same time, his martial policies had made him many enemies among Louisiana whites, and he had no authority to give free Negroes greater rights than the state legislature would allow. Moreover, he too had doubts about the free Negro militia, which he labeled an "experiment." Local whites remained intensely

[30] Gayarré, *History of Louisiana*, IV, 342; Claiborne to Jackson, 28 October 1814, in Rowland, ed., *Claiborne Letter Books*, VI, 292–5.

[31] Bassett, ed., *Jackson Correspondence*, II, 57–9.

suspicious. While Jackson mustered free Negro troops into federal ranks, the New Orleans City Council slapped a curfew on free Negroes, prohibiting them from traveling around the city after dark.[32]

But the experiment worked well. Within weeks Claiborne had several offers to raise new companies of free Negro soldiers. Eventually three such units were created in addition to the established free Negro battalion. Their actions during the first engagements with the British so impressed Jackson that he urged the formation of a second free Negro battalion. In late December, another unit, composed entirely of West Indian émigrés who had fought with the French in Saint-Domingue, was mustered into federal service. Both free Negro battalions distinguished themselves in the American triumph at New Orleans.[33]

Victory did not bring the promised equality. Jackson kept his word as long as the fighting lasted. When the American quartermaster questioned his policy of equal pay for all soldiers, Jackson immediately ordered payment "without inquiring whether the troops are white, black or tea."[34] But at war's end he made no attempt to redeem his pledge, and free Negroes apparently did not press their case. Louisiana whites, bolstered by a continuing stream of white settlers from the older slaveholding states and a growing slave population, remained firmly attached to white-supremacist principles.

But free Negroes did gain from participation in the American victory. Appreciation of free Negro loyalty, an understanding that their services might again be needed, and a renewed respect for their military prowess strengthened the freemen's position in Louisiana society. It arrested the sharp decline in the free Negro's status that had begun after the American occupation. Americans did not relinquish their commitment

[32] Jackson to Claiborne, 21 September 1814, in *ibid.*, II, 56–7; Proceedings of the New Orleans City Council, 17 December 1814, typescript, NOPL.

[33] Claiborne to Jackson, 20 December 1814, in Rowland, ed., *Claiborne Letter Books,* VI, 325–7; Jackson to James Monroe, 27 December 1814, 13 February 1815, in Bassett, ed., *Jackson Correspondence,* II, 127–8, 165; McConnell, *Negro Troops,* pp. 73–90.

[34] McConnell, *Negro Troops,* p. 78.

to white rule, but they no longer pressed the free Negroes with the same force. If the free Negro's status continued to erode, the rate of erosion slowed considerably. The only limitation on free Negro liberty passed between 1815 and 1830 was a proscription against free Negroes' keeping white indentured servants, a rule that was more a reflection of the freemen's continued high status than a radical deprivation of their rights.[35] Furthermore, the legislature made no attempt to disband the free Negro battalion. It continued to meet into the 1830s, when it fell victim to free Negro indifference as well as white hostility. At the same time free Negroes, along with white Louisianans, prospered from the expansion of the state's economy. The rapid growth of the port of New Orleans solidified the economic position of free Negro artisans and tradesmen. A survey of the leading members of the free Negro battalion revealed that most were self-employed shopkeepers on the busiest streets in New Orleans. In 1833, when the legislature chartered the Citizens Bank of Louisiana, the largest state bank in the United States, free Negroes were prominent among the shareholders.[36]

The valor of the free Negro battalion, together with the growing economic importance of middle-class free Negro artisans to Louisiana's prosperity, secured for freemen the same relatively high status they had achieved under French and Spanish rule. It saved the privileged position which American rule had threatened to destroy. Louisiana free Negroes could testify in court against whites, could travel freely throughout the state, and did not yet have to carry proof of their freedom or register themselves as free Negroes. American courts, following Spanish law and local custom, distinguished between light-skinned and dark-skinned freemen and presumed mulattoes to be free unless proven otherwise. Even when new laws were passed limiting free Negro liberty, lawmakers remained solicitous of the rights of creole free Negroes. When Louisiana enacted a registration code in 1830, the General Assembly specifically exempted free Negroes who

[35] *La. Laws*, 1818, pp. 186–8.

[36] McConnell, *Negro Troops*, pp. 97–102; Catterall, ed., *Judicial Cases Concerning Slavery*, III, 510.

had resided in the state before 1812.[37] Superior legal rights were only a reflection of the comparatively high social and economic standing enjoyed by Louisiana free Negroes. No other Southern state had as large a class of free Negro planters as Louisiana, and no other Southern city had as active and as educated a free Negro professional elite as New Orleans.[38]

Louisiana free Negroes maintained this privileged status throughout the antebellum years. Not until the 1830s did free Negroes face as concerted an effort to limit their legal rights as the systematic repression that demolished the liberty of seaboard free Negroes during the post-Revolutionary years. Even then, Louisiana free Negroes maintained the respect and support of much of the white community. As late as 1856, the Louisiana Supreme Court affirmed that "in the eye of Louisiana law, there is . . . all the difference between a free man of color and a slave, that there is between a white man and a slave."[39] In few other places in the South could free Negroes hope to hear a similar sentiment.

Yet the source of that sentiment, and of the difference in status between Louisiana free Negroes and those of the seaboard, remained the eighty-year head start under relatively favorable conditions, both on the mainland and on the islands of the West Indies, that Louisiana free Negroes enjoyed. While the free Negro population in the seaboard slave states had but shallow roots in the colonial years, Louisiana freemen had secured their place in the social order of the Gulf region. Americans tried to drive them from that position, and for a while it looked as though they would succeed. But the War of 1812 allowed free Negroes the opportunity to defend their long-established liberties and defeat the new white challenge.

Similar groups of free Negroes lived throughout the Gulf region, especially around the ports of Mobile and Pensacola.

[37] Catterall, ed., *Judicial Cases Concerning Slavery*, III, 447, 571; *La. Laws*, 1830, pp. 90–4.

[38] Carter G. Woodson, comp., *Free Negro Owners of Slaves in the United States in 1830* (Washington, D.C., 1924); Joseph K. Menn, *The Large Slaveowners of Louisiana* (New Orleans, 1964), pp. 92–4; J. D. B. De Bow, *Statistical View of the United States* (Washington, D.C., 1854), pp. 80–1.

[39] Catterall, ed., *Judicial Cases Concerning Slavery*, III, 649.

The cultural, demographic, and racial patterns of the French and Spanish Caribbean also predominated in the Floridas. There too, free Negroes were primarily the product of miscegenation in societies short of white women. There too, the dearth of white laborers allowed free Negroes to monopolize many of the skilled trades. There too, Spanish law and enlistment in Spanish armies gave free Negroes a measure of equality with whites. The wealth and power these free people of color had accumulated by the time the United States had wrested the Floridas from Spain forced Americans to treat them with special consideration. In 1824, when Alabama lawmakers tried to force Mobile free Negroes out of the state by burdening them with a one-hundred-dollar head tax, the governor coolly vetoed the measure as an affront to the free Negro's constitutional rights. Throughout the antebellum years, the creole free Negroes of Mobile—sometimes called the "treaty population," because the treaty that transferred West Florida to the United States guaranteed them the rights of citizens—were accorded special privileges denied to other free Negroes.[40] In the 1830s, when Alabama barred free Negroes from attending school, legislators granted "free colored creoles" in Mobile the right to create their own separate school system.[41] Similarly the colored creoles of Pensacola, unlike other Florida free Negroes, were allowed to carry firearms and occasionally even sat on juries with whites. As late as 1842, the Florida territorial council exempted free Negroes who had resided in the state before 1821 from having a white guardian supervise their affairs.[42] Nowhere else in the South

[40] U.S. Department of State, *Treaties and Conventions*, p. 1018; *Journal of the Alabama House of Representatives*, 1824, 171–2; *Ala. Laws*, 1824, pp. 122–4; *Mobile Daily Advertiser*, 15 October 1859; A. W. Bryan to ?, 16 July 1858, ACS; James B. Sellers, *Slavery in Alabama* (University, Ala., 1950), pp. 383–90; Morris Boucher, "The Free Negro in Alabama Prior to 1860," unpublished doctoral dissertation, State University of Iowa, 1950, p. 18.

[41] *Ala. Laws*, 1833, p. 68; U.S. Commissioner of Education, *Special Report*, p. 323; Horace Mann Bond, *Negro Education in Alabama, A Study in Cotton and Steel* (Washington, D.C., 1939), pp. 15, 73–4, 319 n.

[42] John P. Duval, comp., *Compilation of the Public Acts of the Legislative Council of the Territory of Florida Passed Prior to 1840* (Tallahassee, Fla., 1839), p. 218; David Y. Thomas, "The Free Negro in Florida Before 1865," *South Atlantic Quarterly*, X (1911), 335–8, 343–5; Ruth B. Barr and Modeste

did whites treat free Negro liberty with such respect. The free people of color of the Gulf ports were an exception within the South's anomalous caste.

Hargis, "The Voluntary Exile of Free Negroes of Pensacola," *Florida Historical Quarterly*, XVII (1938), 10–11; Duvon C. Corbitt, "The Last Spanish Census of Pensacola," *ibid.*, XXIV (1945), 33–7; Herbert J. Doherty, Jr., "Ante-Bellum Pensacola, 1821–1860," *ibid.*, XXXVII (1959), 352–3.

PART TWO

THE PATTERN OF FREE NEGRO LIFE

We reside among you and yet are strangers; natives, and yet not citizens; surrounded by the freest people and most republican institutions in the world, and yet enjoying none of the imunities of freedom. . . . Though we are not slaves, we are not free.

"Memorial of the Free People of Colour of Baltimore," *African Repository*, December 1826

5

New Patterns of Growth

> I concluded to set him free not only in justice to himself but that his course through life and his reward may be referred to as an example to all men of his color.
>
> Miscellaneous Petitions, 6 December 1844, VLP

THE maturation of the Southern slave system left little room for free Negroes. Slaveholders were determined to eliminate the sources of this unwanted people. The rapid growth of the free Negro population which followed the Revolution abruptly ended during the early years of the nineteenth century. Between 1810 and 1820, free Negroes increased only 20 percent, less than a third of the previous decade's growth. In the meantime, the number of whites and slaves surged upward, and by 1840, both were increasing more rapidly than free Negroes. The free Negroes' rate of growth continued to fall in the years that followed, and in some places the free Negro population suffered an absolute decline. The proportion of free Negroes in the black and the free populations slowly slipped backward. On the eve of the Civil War, Negro freemen composed slightly more than 6 percent of the black population of the South and about 3 percent of the free population. In both cases, the freemen's share of the Southern population declined markedly from 1810.[1]

Although the rate of increase dwindled, the number of free Negroes continued to grow. Some masters freed their slaves,

[1] Computed from *Population of the United States in 1860,* pp. 592–604.

TABLE 6

FREE NEGRO POPULATION, 1820–1860

	1820	*1830*	*1840*	*1850*	*1860*
United States	233,504	319,599	386,303	434,449	488,070
North	99,281	137,529	170,728	196,262	226,152
South	134,223	182,070	215,575	238,187	261,918
Upper South	114,070	151,877	174,357	203,702	224,963
Lower South	20,153	30,193	41,218	34,485	36,955
Delaware	12,958	15,855	16,919	18,073	19,829
D.C.	4,048	6,152	8,361	10,059	11,131
Kentucky	2,759	4,917	7,317	10,011	10,684
Maryland	39,730	52,938	62,078	74,723	83,942
Missouri	347	569	1,574	2,618	3,572
North Carolina	14,612	19,543	22,732	27,463	30,463
Tennessee	2,727	4,555	5,524	6,422	7,300
Virginia	36,889	47,348	49,852	54,333	58,042
Alabama	571	1,572	2,039	2,265	2,690
Arkansas	59	141	465	608	144
Florida	—	844	817	932	932
Georgia	1,763	2,486	2,753	2,931	3,500
Louisiana	10,476	16,710	25,502	17,462	18,647
Mississippi	458	519	1,366	930	773
South Carolina	6,826	7,921	8,276	8,960	9,914
Texas	—	—	—	397	355

TABLE 7

PERCENT INCREASE OF FREE NEGROES, 1810–1860

	1810–1820	*1820–1830*	*1830–1840*	*1840–1850*	*1850–1860*
United States	25.2%	36.9%	20.9%	12.5%	12.3%
North	27.0	38.5	24.1	15.0	15.2
South	24.0	35.6	18.4	10.5	10.0
Upper South	21.2	33.1	14.8	16.8	10.4
Lower South	42.1	49.8	36.5	−16.3	7.2
Delaware	−1.4	22.4	6.7	6.8	9.7
D.C.	58.1	52.0	35.1	20.3	10.7
Kentucky	61.1	78.2	48.8	36.8	6.7
Maryland	17.0	33.2	17.3	20.4	12.4
Missouri	−42.8	64.0	176.6	66.3	36.4
North Carolina	42.3	33.7	16.3	20.8	10.9
Tennessee	107.1	67.0	21.3	16.3	13.7
Virginia	20.7	28.4	5.3	9.0	6.8

TABLE 7—CONTINUED

	1810–1820	*1820–1830*	*1830–1840*	*1840–1850*	*1850–1860*
Alabama	—	175.0	29.1	11.1	18.8
Arkansas	—	139.0	229.8	30.8	−82.3
Florida	—	—	−3.2	14.1	0.0
Georgia	−2.0	41.0	10.7	6.5	19.4
Louisiana	38.1	59.1	52.6	−31.5	6.8
Mississippi	90.8	13.3	163.2	−31.9	−16.9
South Carolina	49.9	16.0	4.5	8.3	10.7
Texas	—	—	—	—	−10.6

TABLE 8

PROPORTION OF NEGROES FREE, 1820–1860

	1820	*1840*	*1860*
United States	13.2%	13.4%	11.0%
North	83.9	99.3	100.0
South	8.1	8.0	6.2
Upper South	10.6	12.5	12.8
Lower South	3.5	3.1	1.5
Delaware	74.1	86.7	91.7
D.C.	38.8	64.0	77.8
Kentucky	2.1	3.9	4.5
Maryland	27.0	40.9	49.1
Missouri	3.3	2.6	3.0
North Carolina	6.7	8.5	8.4
Tennessee	3.3	2.9	2.6
Virginia	8.0	10.0	10.6
Alabama	1.3	.8	.6
Arkansas	3.5	2.3	.1
Florida	—	3.1	1.5
Georgia	1.2	1.0	.8
Louisiana	13.2	13.1	5.3
Mississippi	1.4	.7	.2
South Carolina	2.6	2.5	2.4
Texas	—	—	.2

SOURCE FOR TABLES 6–8: *Population of the United States in 1860* (Washington, D.C., 1864), pp. 598–604.

a few slaves bought their way out of bondage, bondsmen still took their liberty by running away, and free Negroes increased by natural means. However, this growth was not everywhere the same. Economic and social changes within the South speeded the increase of the free Negro caste in some places while shutting it off entirely in others. By reinforcing the existing demographic order in some ways and countering it in others, these new patterns of growth altered the structure and the character of the free Negro caste.

MANUMISSION

The master's right to free his slaves shrank as slavery expanded. Manumission had been the primary source of free Negro increase during the post-Revolutionary decades, and Southern legislators worked to curb or abolish the practice. During the nineteenth century, lawmakers dismantled the last remnants of the liberal manumission policies of the earlier era. The older seaboard states added restrictions to their manumission statutes, and the newer states of the Southwest enacted almost prohibitory regulations, so that even the few masters who desired to liberate their slaves found it increasingly difficult. By the mid-1830s, most Southern states required slaveowners to get judicial or legislative permission to free their slaves and demanded that newly liberated bondsmen leave the state upon receiving their freedom. Those few states which still allowed slaveowners to emancipate their slaves also stipulated that manumitted blacks migrate or risk being forcibly deported or re-enslaved. Legislators further discouraged emancipation by requiring masters to remove freed Negroes and by making those manumitted liable to seizure for unpaid debts even after emancipation. By the 1850s, when many states prohibited manumission altogether, only the border states of Delaware and Missouri and newly settled Arkansas allowed masters to liberate their slaves and permitted manumitted blacks to remain in the state.[2]

[2] ALABAMA: In 1833, lawmakers, who had previously controlled the freeing of slaves, delegated that function to the courts with the provision that all emancipated slaves leave the state. The courts continued to regulate emancipation until 1860, when the legislature prohibited it entirely. *Ala. Laws,* 1833, c. 44, 1859–1860, c. 36. ARKANSAS: Until 1858, when legislators enacted a strict prohibition, slaveholders had free rein to liberate their slaves and freed

Southern courts added their muscle to this increasingly restrictive policy. Blacks who attempted to win their freedom

---

blacks could remain in the state. William McK. Ball and Sam C. Roane, comps., *Revised Statutes of the State of Arkansas* (Boston, 1838), pp. 359–60; *Ark. Laws,* 1858, c. 151. FLORIDA: Early in its territorial history, lawmakers prohibited manumission and punished slaveholders who violated the law with a two-hundred-dollar fine. Duval, comp., *Public Acts of the Territory of Florida,* p. 228. GEORGIA: After earlier restricting manumission to special legislative enactments, Georgia legislators closed various loopholes in the law (1818) and then, in 1859, forbade the freeing of slaves by will. Lamar, comp., *Laws of Ga.,* pp. 811–16; *Ga. Laws,* 1859, c. 91. KENTUCKY: Kentucky allowed masters to free their slaves, subject to varying securities, and allowed manumitted slaves to remain in the state until 1850, when blacks were forced to leave the state upon emancipation. *Ky. Laws,* 1823, c. 543, 1841, c. 92, 1842, c. 91, 1850, I, 305–8. LOUISIANA: Lawmakers shuttled responsibility for freeing slaves from one court to another until the 1850s, when it added new restrictions and then prohibited manumission entirely. In 1852, legislators provided that no slave could be freed unless he was sent outside the United States, preferably to Liberia. Three years later, drowning in petitions for special acts to allow newly freed slaves to remain in the state, the legislature again delegated authority over manumission to the courts. The emancipation of slaves became an adversary proceeding with the slaveholder arguing for freedom (and paying all costs, win or lose) and the state arguing against. In 1857, when this unique procedure was struck down by the state Supreme Court, lawmakers prohibited manumission entirely. *La. Laws,* 1827, pp. 12–14, 1830, pp. 90–4, 1852, c. 315, 1855, pp. 377–91, 1857, c. 69. MARYLAND: Lawmakers restricted manumission in 1832 by forbidding newly freed slaves to remain in the state, and then prohibited it entirely in 1860. *Md. Laws,* 1831, c. 281, c. 323, 1860, c. 322. MISSISSIPPI: After earlier restricting manumission to special legislative enactments, legislators sealed those few loopholes in the law and, in 1857, prohibited the freeing of slaves. *Miss. Law,* 1842, c. 4; *The Revised Code of the Statute Law of the State of Mississippi* (Jackson, 1857), p. 236. MISSOURI: Missouri did not disturb the master's right to free his slaves. Charles H. Hardin, comp., *The Revised Statutes of the State of Missouri,* 2 vols. (Jefferson City, 1856), II, 1478. NORTH CAROLINA: In 1831, North Carolina eased the restrictions on manumission, allowing the Superior Court to emancipate slaves provided they leave the state immediately. That act stood unamended until 1861, when the legislature prohibited the freeing of slaves by will. *N.C. Laws,* 1830, c. 9, 1860–1861, p. 69. SOUTH CAROLINA: In 1820, lawmakers made the freeing of slaves a legislative prerogative. This basic law was reinforced in 1841 and remained intact for the remainder of the period. Cooper and McCord, comps., *Statutes S.C.,* VII, 459; *S.C. Laws,* 1841, c. 2836. TENNESSEE: Legislators allowed the courts to regulate manumission with provision for the removal of emancipated blacks. *Tenn. Laws,* 1829, c. 29, 1831, c. 102, 1833, c. 81, 1849, c. 107, 1852, c. 300, 1854, c. 50. TEXAS: In 1836, the Declaration of Independence of Texas prohibited masters from freeing their slaves within the bounds of the Republic. *Laws of the Republic of Texas* (Houston, 1838), p. 19. VIRGINIA: The Virginia removal law of 1806, amended in 1815 and 1837, stood throughout the antebellum years. *Va. Laws,* 1815, c. 24, 1836–1837, c. 70.

in court met new obstacles. Hostile judges quashed many of the lenient rules for freedom suits and liberal interpretations of manumission law handed down in the earlier era. In 1820, for example, the Maryland Court of Appeals reversed its older policy of allowing hearsay evidence in freedom suits. The "general reputation" that a slave or his maternal ancestors were free, often a bondsman's only proof of freedom, was no longer admissible evidence in Maryland courts. Virginia, Georgia, and Alabama courts went even further; holding that slaves were chattel legally incapable of decision, they denied bondsmen the right to choose liberty even when their master allowed such a choice.[3] Similarly, the high courts of Virginia and Missouri, observing that slaves had no right to make contracts, invalidated agreements for freedom between master and slave.[4] Although some Southern courts were notable for their liberality in an era of increasing racial repression, judicial leniency risked legislative reversal. When the South Carolina Court of Appeals expanded the master's right to free his slaves by countenancing various forms of extralegal emancipation, lawmakers rewrote the state manumission code and slammed the doors that the court had opened.[5]

Within the bounds of this restrictive policy regional variations developed. As a general rule, manumission became increasingly difficult as one passed from the marginal slaveholding states of the border region to the cotton South. The states of the Upper South that restricted the master's right to free his slaves made manumission a judicial prerogative, while those of the Lower South usually forced would-be emancipators to go directly to the state legislature for permission to liberate their bondsmen. Slaveholders generally found it more difficult to win approval from a legislature than from a court. Between 1819 and 1829, for example, the Alabama General Assembly

[3] Catterall, ed., *Judicial Cases Concerning Slavery,* IV, 68–69, I, 243–4, III, 76–7, 166.

[4] *Ibid.,* I, 243–4, V, 213–14. Also see II, 398.

[5] A. E. Keir Nash, "Fairness and Formalism in the Trials of Blacks in the State Supreme Courts of the Old South," *Virginia Law Review,* LVI (1970), 90–3; *idem,* "Negro Rights, Unionism, and Greatness on the South Carolina Court of Appeals," *South Carolina Law Review,* XXI (1969), 141–190; S.C. *Laws,* 1841, c. 2836.

freed but slightly more than 200 blacks. On the average, a mere 20 Negroes annually passed from slavery to freedom in a state which counted almost 120,000 slaves in 1830.[6]

At the root of legislative and judicial opposition to manumission stood the growing Southern commitment to slavery. The spread of cotton culture across the Southwest and the increased demand for slaves it created throughout the South buried an earlier generation's doubts about the efficacy and morality of black bondage. Those who dared to free their slaves often faced the cold glare and angry words of their neighbors, as well as the lasting enmity of their heirs. Bitter relatives, fuming over the loss of their inheritance, often went to court and deprived slaves of their promised freedom. The sting of public rebuke intimidated many would-be manumitters. One Georgia planter, like countless other timorous slaveholders, failed to free his slaves because "he was afraid the community would think hard of him." Yet most masters needed no encouragement to keep their slaves. Slaveholding was the prerequisite for power and prestige in Southern society, and few men willingly walked away from privilege.[7]

Popular pressure and legal constraints narrowed the avenues to freedom. Despite the steady and often spectacular increase in slaves during the nineteenth century, the number of legal manumissions declined in most of the rural South. In the Southside Virginia county of Sussex, for instance, there were sixty acts of manumission between 1780 and 1800; however, in the thirty years before the Civil War less than five such deeds were recorded. The pattern was much the same elsewhere in rural Virginia. Moreover, many of the slaves freed during the nineteenth century had been willed their liberty earlier. In the newer slaveholding regions, manumission was even less frequent. In the prosperous Missouri county of Greene not a single slave was liberated between 1845 and 1860. Greene County was representative of much of the rural South.[8]

[6] Sellers, *Slavery in Alabama*, p. 364.

[7] Catterall, ed., *Judicial Cases Concerning Slavery*, III, 23; Wm. C. Fitzhugh to R. R. Gurley, 18 October 1832, ACS.

[8] Luther P. Jackson, *Free Negro Labor and Property Holding in Virginia, 1830–1860* (New York, 1942), pp. 174–5; Harrison A. Trexler, *Slavery in Missouri, 1804–1865* (Baltimore, 1914), pp. 223–5.

Although harsh laws, judicial obstructions, and hostile public opinion slowed the rate of manumission, nothing could stop a master intent on freeing his slaves. The growing commitment to slavery slowed the pace of emancipation but could not end it. Even in the Lower South, where the cotton boom sent slave prices soaring, some masters braved public censure and freed their slaves. Petitions requesting private acts of emancipation so inundated the high courts and legislatures of Louisiana and Alabama that they eventually relinquished their sole authority over manumission and turned it over to lesser jurisdictions. Local courts and police juries were much more willing to gratify the slaveholder's desire to free his slaves, especially if he was a prominent man in the community. Complaints about the ease with which these bodies granted permission to manumit slaves, long rife in the Upper South, now spread to the Lower South. "Has it not become notorious," grumbled a Louisiana slaveholder, "that . . . the policy of the police jury invariably yields to the wishes of the master, and enables him . . . to grant the emancipation?"[9]

In parts of the border South, the trickle of manumissions broadened into a stream, and in some places the stream threatened to overrun its boundaries and overwhelm slavery. During the nineteenth century, the pace of manumission quickened in the older border areas. By the 1830s, the Maryland State Colonization Society annually recorded the emancipation of over two hundred slaves, and the great majority of emancipators did not bother to notify the society when they freed their slaves. Although slaveholders in the southern part of the state screamed for new restrictions on manumission and stricter enforcement of the existing laws, the number of manumissions—most of them illegal—continued to climb. In 1850, the census reported that nearly five hundred slaves were liberated by their owners. Maryland authorities had in fact forsaken the attempt to restrain the freeing of slaves. "With all the restrictions which legislation has imposed on manumission, they still go on," observed a Baltimore politician in 1845. "It may be taken for certain that they will go on; that nothing

[9] *La. Laws*, 1827, pp. 12–14; *Ala. Laws*, 1830, p. 29; *Baton Rouge Gazette*, 16 October 1841; also see Petition from Williamson County, 1843, TLP.

can stop them."[10] The steady increase in manumission forced some Maryland whites to concede the eventual demise of slavery in their state.

Southern municipalities also bucked the general trend. While manumission declined in most of the countryside, it flourished in the cities. The difficulties of controlling urban bondsmen induced many slaveholders to relinquish their valuable property. Although most urban masters simply sold their slaves to the cotton fields of the Lower South, some allowed them to purchase their liberty or freed them outright. Petersburg slaveowners, who had manumitted 120 bondsmen between 1782 and 1806, liberated more than twice that number between 1831 and 1860. The same pattern prevailed in other Virginia cities. In Richmond, for instance, there were 90 manumissions between 1782 and 1806; however, 225 were recorded in the thirty years before the Civil War. Similarly, while rural Missourians rarely freed their slaves, a growing number of St. Louis masters liberated their bondsmen or allowed them to buy their freedom. Catching the difference between slavery in the city and in the countryside, one Virginian noted that the cities "naturally become liberalized on the subject of emancipation before the interior agricultural communities."[11]

Strict legal limitations on manumission forced many masters and slaves outside the law. Slaveholders, in league with their bondsmen, developed numerous stratagems to frustrate the often prohibitive regulations. North Carolina Quakers had pioneered in holding "slaves" who were in fact free. By the early 1820s, the Friends' nominal slavery had become notorious throughout the state, and the Quaker trustees held nearly eight hundred such "bondsmen." Thereafter the heavy administrative burden, popular opposition, and the spread of

[10] Between 1831 and 1841, the Maryland State Colonization Society recorded the manumission of 2,342 slaves, but admitted that most manumissions were not reported. *Maryland Colonization Journal*, new ser., I (June 1841), 11; De Bow, *Statistical View of the United States*, p. 64; John L. Carey, *Slavery in Maryland, Briefly Considered* (Baltimore, 1845), p. 32.

[11] Jackson, *Free Negro Labor and Property Holding*, pp. 173–4; *idem*, "Manumission in Certain Virginia Cities," pp. 278–314; Trexler, *Slavery in Missouri*, p. 244; Richard C. Wade, *Slavery in the Cities: The South, 1820–1860* (New York, 1964), pp. 264–5; Henry B. Goodwin to James Hall, 21 January 1845, Letters Received, MdSCS Papers.

colonizationist ideas caused the Friends to relinquish their trusteeship. Blacks, prodded by Quakers, migrated to the North, Haiti, and Liberia.[12] But the Quaker practice of circumventing proscriptive manumission laws by giving slaves virtual freedom spread throughout the South, greatly increasing the number of quasi-free Negroes.

Wherever legislatures or courts barred slaveholders from freeing their slaves, emancipators took matters into their own hands. Slaveowners, imitating the Quaker practice, frequently sold or willed bondsmen to a friend or a free Negro with the provision that the "slaves" be allowed to work on their own, keep their wages, and enjoy all the rights allowed free people of color. A prominent Alabama planter requested that his executor emancipate his two favorite bondsmen, but if that proved impossible they were to be left in trust to his son "for the purpose of securing to them . . . the benefits and enjoyment of their own labor. That is, they are to be free by courtesy."[13] Freedom by courtesy, or more accurately, illegal manumission, became so commonplace in some parts of the South that slaveholders boldly spelled out their design in the public record. Many South Carolina emancipators recorded their illegal deeds of manumission to assure that they would be honored. In a bill of sale typical of many registered with the secretary of state, a Charleston mistress sold her two waiting women to a friend for a nominal price of one dollar. Noting that "the Laws of this State are opposed to emancipation," she coolly stipulated that "Kitty & Mary shall enjoy full free and undisturbed liberty as if they had been regularly emancipated." In case the ban on manumission should ever be repealed, she further provided that her two "slaves" were to be legally freed. In 1841, some twenty years after South Carolina lawmakers had curbed the master's right to free his slaves and reserved that responsibility for the legislature, the state finally moved against this subterfuge. But the new law only made masters more circumspect in registering their

[12] Weeks, *Southern Quakers and Slavery*, pp. 224–9; Patrick Sowle, "The North Carolina Manumission Society," *North Carolina Historical Review*, XLII (1965), pp. 42–57; John C. Ehringhaus to R. R. Gurley, 23 June 1823, ACS; Catterall, ed., *Judicial Cases Concerning Slavery*, II, 52, 161–2; *Raleigh Register*, 30 May 1826.

[13] Sellers, *Slavery in Alabama*, p. 373. For another common subterfuge see Natchez *Mississippi Free Trader*, 13 May 1841; *Miss. Laws*, 1842, c. 4.

"deeds of sale" and did not prevent the illicit freeing of slaves. Restraining manumission, observed a South Carolina jurist in 1848, "has done more harm than good. It has caused evasions without number. These have been successful by vesting the ownership in persons legally capable of holding it, and thus substantially conferring freedom, when it was legally denied."[14]

Even when unrestricted manumission codes provided relatively easy access to freedom, many masters preferred to ignore the law. Some slaveholders found it inconvenient or expensive to free their slaves legally. Most states required that slaveowners give security so that their former bondsmen would not become public charges. In Delaware, which had a stiff security requirement, masters so flouted the law that in 1819 the legislature freed by fiat all Negroes whose masters failed to give the required bond. Elsewhere, slaveowners avoided the law to escape the responsibility for removing their slaves from the state; while others were simply too busy, too indifferent, or too lazy to bother with the legal form.[15] Blacks so freed added to the quasi-free population and enlarged the free Negro caste.

The steadfast refusal of many newly manumitted blacks to migrate after emancipation also added to the quasi-free Negro population. Most slaves, like peasantries the world over, lived in a small world. Their lives centered around the friends and relatives with whom they shared the dull oppression and small joys of the slave quarter, and they developed strong, often binding attachments to the land they worked. Uneducated, blinded by the narrow alternatives of plantation life, and fearful of being isolated in a hostile white world, they found it painful to leave the only homes they had ever known. Urban bondsmen, generally the most educated and well-traveled slaves, also shared this reluctance to leave their Southern homeland. They not only had strong family ties, but as tradesmen and artisans they had developed large clienteles

[14] Miscellaneous Records of the Secretary of State, Liber 5P, 15 July 1833, pp. 62–3, SCA; John Belton O'Neall, *The Negro Law of South Carolina* (Columbia, S.C., 1848), p. 11.

[15] *Del. Laws*, 1819, c. 224; also see Catterall, ed., *Judicial Cases Concerning Slavery*, IV, 112–13; *Richmond Whig*, 25 November 1853.

which would have been difficult to re-create in another city or town.

The large-scale emancipation of the Revolutionary era and the new opportunities that accompanied it had tended to loosen these ties and encourage manumitted blacks to venture out in search of a new life. But the repression that crushed the First Emancipation and the subsequent entrenchment of slavery undermined the optimism that had earlier accompanied freedom. During the nineteenth century, many newly freed blacks seem to have had little confidence that things could be different anywhere whites held sway. Although some Negroes were simply too poor or too tied to enslaved relatives to migrate, many more feared leaving their familiar surroundings for an unknown destination in the North or elsewhere. Charleston petitioners observed: "The Free People [of color] will never emigrate; they have so little to hope for, and so much to dread, from any change of place, that they will adhere to the spot of their nativity, under the pressure of any inconvenience. . . ." Terrified by the unknown, free blacks resigned themselves to the familiar oppressions of their homeland. Frequently they pleaded with local officials for permission to remain where they had long resided, and sometimes they simply ignored the law and settled on worthless, abandoned land near their former master's plantation. Some even refused to leave the old homestead and adamantly claimed it as their rightful home despite the stunned objections of their former owners.[16]

The freemen's persistence undermined the removal laws. Virginia had been the first state to require that newly manumitted Negroes migrate in order to enjoy their liberty. Its experience exemplifies how the reluctance of free Negroes to leave subverted attempts to prevent their increase. With the passage of the 1806 removal act, petitions from free Negroes wishing to remain in the state swamped the Virginia legislature. Unable to enforce the law and unwilling to initiate massive re-enslavement, the General Assembly gave a number of

[16] Petition from Charleston, 1822, SCLP; Petition from Richmond, 11 December 1820, VLP; John Thompson Mason to Gerrit Smith, 21 January 1850, Gerrit Smith Papers, SUL.

former slaves permission to stay. By 1815, however, emancipated blacks had sent so many petitions to the legislature that lawmakers delegated jurisdiction in this matter to the county courts, allowing them discretion to permit any Negro freed for "extraordinary merit" to remain in the Commonwealth. Although some local courts found acts of extraordinary merit in the most mundane deeds, the legislature continued to be flooded with pleas for relief from the removal law. In 1836, hard-pressed lawmakers again expanded the courts' authority by allowing them to permit any emancipated Negro who was of "good character, sober, peaceable, orderly and industrious" to reside in the state. Taking advantage of these flexible standards, hundreds of Negroes won judicial approval to stay in Virginia. By the 1840s, some sympathetic courts granted permission so regularly that their assent had become a mere formality. Occasionally, hostile judges challenged the freemen's right to remain, but most free Negroes simply ignored these rulings and applied again at the next court session, hoping that another judge might be more amenable. When sheriffs pursued these scofflaws and threatened them with forcible removal or enslavement, they appealed to white friends, armed themselves with letters of recommendation attesting to their good character, and petitioned the General Assembly. In 1836, for instance, the sheriff of Norfolk ordered Ackley White, a drayman emancipated twelve years earlier, to leave the state or be clapped into bondage. But the drayman's white customers petitioned the legislature on his behalf, praising his conduct and contending that "the drain of slave labour among us" had made his services invaluable. The legislature readily acceded to their plea.[17]

When the law failed to give way before their petitions, free Negroes generally stayed anyway, adding to the illegally freed population. Often these free Negroes, not so well connected as Ackley White, had to move quickly to stay ahead of the law. In 1836, one Virginia district attorney complained that

[17] *Va. Laws,* 1815, c. 24, 1836–1837, c. 70; Richmond Hustings Court Minutes, 1840–1845, VSL; Petition From Norfolk County, 28 December 1836, VLP; Jackson, *Free Negro Labor and Property Holding,* pp. 191–6; Jackson, "Manumission in Certain Virginia Cities," pp. 299–300.

the rule of 1806 was unenforceable because free Negroes "elude the officers of justice, by flying from neighbourhood to neighbourhood, and county to county." He redoubled his efforts and prosecuted nearly forty Negroes who had failed to leave the state as required. But whatever the outcome of these suits, few officials shared his zeal for chasing free Negroes from the Commonwealth. About ten years later, residents of the same county admitted that convictions for violating the 1806 law "have been rare occurences, & that prosecutions have, in consequence, been almost abandoned."[18]

During the nineteenth century, the growing quasi-free population came to make up an increasingly large part of the free Negro caste. Much to their surprise, Southerners continually discovered new examples of this peculiar adjunct to the South's anomalous caste. After one Virginia Negro purchased his family and agreed to migrate to Liberia, a colonization agent observed that "he has been free for some time, his master holding only pro forma ownership over him until recently when he was fully emancipated." At the death of a neighbor, a Tennessee planter found a family of nineteen "slaves" who had long been enjoying the rights of free men. "Although they are slaves," he noted, "yet they have been living to themselves for about twenty years, they have supported themselves on lands of their master and are tolerable farmers."[19] Proportionately the largest number of quasi-free Negroes resided in the Lower South, where the obstacles to manumission remained the highest. Illegally freed blacks may have composed more than half the free Negro population in some parts of the Lower South. The number of nominal slaves in Mobile had grown so large by the 1850s that court reporters regularly distinguished between bona fide free people of color and "quasi-f.p.c.'s." Southern lawmakers periodically attempted to reduce the large number of *de facto* freemen, but their efforts did little more than document the extent of the quasi-free caste. One year after Georgia slapped a $150 head tax on nominal slaves, the state comptroller admitted that only two

[18] Petitions from Loudoun County, 12 December 1836, 10 December 1847, VLP.

[19] James McDowell, Jr., to R. R. Gurley, 25 October 1831, Samuel Rhea to R. R. Gurley, 24 May 1833, ACS.

Negroes had paid the tax, "while there is little doubt that there are hundreds of nominal slaves in the State."[20]

The increase of manumission in the cities and the border area and the growth of the quasi-free Negro population did not compensate for the general decline of emancipation in the countryside. Most of the South remained untouched by the growing willingness of masters in marginal slaveholding areas to free their slaves. Even where slaveowners manumitted their slaves, few evinced the libertarian zeal that had accompanied freedom in the Revolutionary era. No longer did deeds of emancipation ring with the rhetoric of liberty and equality. Instead, slaveholders used the promise of freedom as a means of spurring productivity and assuring loyalty in areas where slavery was faltering. "The object . . . is to offer a reward to such slaves as would demean themselves correctly," frankly admitted the mayor of the French District of New Orleans. Most masters understood that freedom was the greatest gift they could give their slaves, and they consciously used it as a mechanism of control and a means of encouraging divisions among blacks. The importance of the right to manumit made many slaveowners reluctant to relinquish it, although they disliked free blacks. "We have more to dread if we close every avenue to freedom," cautioned a Tennessee lawmaker. "Let us hold out to the slave the Hope of freedom. Each master should be able to exercise the dictates of his conscience and to judge his own interests." It was with no sense of irony that South Carolina legislators freed the slaves who revealed the Vesey conspiracy.[21]

[20] *Mobile Daily Advertiser,* 10 July 1857; *Mobile Daily Register,* 5 March 1859, 24, 25 August 1859; also see *Savannah Republican,* 25 January 1847; *Ga. Laws,* 1850, pp. 376–8; "Annual Report of the Comptroller of the State of Georgia," *Georgia Legislative Documents,* 1851, p. 3, 1860, p. 13. Quasi-free slaves should be distinguished from slaves who hired their own time and as a result won a large measure of freedom, but in fact were still slaves; Wade, *Slavery in the Cities,* pp. 38–54.

The growth of a quasi-free or nominally free Negro population followed the restriction of manumission throughout the Americas. For an interesting comparison with the French Antilles, see Cohen and Greene, eds., *Neither Slave Nor Free,* pp. 144–6.

[21] Proceedings of the Council of the Third Municipality, 31 January 1848, typescript, NOPL; Nashville *National Banner,* 21 November 1833; Cooper and McCord, comps., *Statutes S.C.*, VI, 194–5.

Motivated more by cold utility than by libertarian idealism, emancipators tended to be more selective about whom they freed. Only rarely did slaveholders shed the sin of slavery at once by freeing all their slaves as did Robert Carter and George Washington in the earlier period. Instead, manumitters generally followed Thomas Jefferson's example and liberated just one or two favorites and willed their remaining slaves to a worthy relative or profitably sold them south. Slaveholders saw no contradiction in doling out liberty with one hand and tightening the chains of bondage with the other.

The slowed pace of manumission changed the character of the free Negro population as well as its size. The large, ideologically motivated emancipation of the post-Revolutionary years liberated blacks as well as browns, untutored field hands along with literate slave artisans. But when masters were selective about whom they freed, they generally emancipated only those slaves they knew best. These were not field hands but house servants, foremen, and artisans whose privileged position and skills had enabled them to develop close relationships with their owners. Typical of many emancipators, a North Carolina planter willed only one of his slaves to be freed upon his death. "The man was a leader on the farm, a kind of overseer, superintending all such operations . . . and had the full confidence of his master," reported the administrator of the estate. Moses, a Virginia bondsman, served in a similar capacity until he was freed. In addition to performing the "ordinary duties of a slave," he acted as "a Manager for his mistress having direction of the hands & charge of the plantation, stock and crops."[22] To maintain their elevated status, these privileged slaves frequently had to stand apart from the mass of plantation blacks. William and Candis Newman, the "faithful and favourite servants" of a Mississippi planter of the same name, won their owner's confidence and later their freedom by carefully keeping "their intercourse and dealing . . . entirely with white people." Similarly, Catherine Coward, a

[22] Jesse Lindsay to William McLain, 8 July 1851, ACS; Petition from Goochland County, 18 December 1822, VLP. Since domestics, skilled artisans, and tradesmen composed the majority of urban slaves, the growth of manumission in the cities increased the slaveholder's propensity to free members of slave elites.

Virginia free Negro who had enjoyed high standing as a slave, "never was the associate or companion of negro-slaves, except in the superintendence of them in the place of her mistress."[23]

When good connections were the surest passport to freedom, often blood, not service, was the basis of the special relationship that led masters to free their slaves. Of all slaves, the black concubines and children of slaveholders were most assured of emancipation. Of course, not all mulattoes who were freed descended directly from their emancipators. Many planters preferred mulatto house servants. Some slaveowners, unwilling or unable to free their light-skinned children, provided them with special training or privileged positions within the slave hierarchy; from these positions they had a chance to win their master's favor and freedom. Thus, although only a small proportion of slaves were mixed-bloods, they made up an increasingly large share of those freed. This was especially true in the Gulf ports of the Lower South, where a tradition of open relations between white men and black women had developed under French and Spanish rule. But a similar pattern of relationships could also be found in the new areas of the West, where men pioneered alone and women were in short supply. Though only a few men, like Richard M. Johnson, a leading Kentucky politician and vice-president under Martin Van Buren, lived openly with their black mistresses and provided for their mulatto children, the frequent manumission of black women and light-skinned children suggests that many more did so surreptitiously.[24]

Limiting emancipation to a few favorites also shifted the balance of the manumitted population toward women. Slave women not only made up a disproportionate number of the

[23] Petition from William and Candis Newman, MLP; Petition from Accomac County, 2 January 1838, VLP.

[24] In Richmond, a third of the 225 manumissions recorded between 1831 and 1860 indicate the color of the slaves freed. Of these, half were mulattoes. Luther P. Jackson, "Free Negro Labor and Property Holding in Virginia, 1830–1860," unpublished doctoral dissertation, University of Chicago, 1937, pp. 225–8; Charles Lyell, *A Second Visit to the United States of North America,* 2 vols. (New York, 1849), I, 208; John D. Paxton, *Letters on Slavery, Addressed to the Cumberland Congregation, Virginia* (Lexington, Ky., 1833), pp. 33–4; E. Franklin Frazier, *The Negro in the United States* (New York, 1949), pp. 53–8, 273–305; Leland W. Meyer, *The Life and Times of Colonel Richard M. Johnson* (New York, 1932), pp. 317–23.

domestic workers, but they were more apt to win the sympathy and affection of their masters. Black men, on the other hand, were more of a threat to white rule and also brought higher prices in the slave markets of the South. If a master chose but one slave for emancipation, there were many more reasons to pick a woman than a man.

Before they freed their slaves, most masters were determined to wring full value from them. Many manumitters waited until the last possible moment to liberate their bondsmen. Increasingly, slaveowners relied on wills and not deeds to free their slaves. Testamentary manumission became so prevalent during the nineteenth century that C. C. Harper, a founder of the American Colonization Society, thought it "the most powerful agent for removing slaves from Maryland." Freeing slaves after the master's death eliminated the complex financial dislocations and psychological adjustments that often accompanied emancipation, while it allowed slaveholders to enjoy the status that accrued to members of the slaveowning class. "At death," Harper tersely noted, "we can afford more than in life." Manumission by will, in short, not only protected the master's purse but relieved his conscience, and many emancipators seemed more concerned about liberating their consciences than their slaves. Apologists for slavery lashed out at "the superstitious weakness of dying men" who freed their slaves with their last breath,[25] but the latent guilt of making men into things continued to trail some slaveholders to their deathbed.

Delaying manumission, often until after the master's death, meant that many emancipated Negroes were old, decrepit, and unable to support themselves. Although manumission codes carefully prescribed the maximum age at which slaves might be freed in order to prevent worn-out bondsmen from becoming community charges, masters found it profitable to unload elderly, enfeebled slaves. Slaveholders often deposited these unwanted thralls in nearby cities, and almost every Southern

[25] C. C. Harper to R. R. Gurley, 24 April 1828, Wm. Schoolcraft to William Starr, 12 October 1853, ACS; Catterall, ed., *Judicial Cases Concerning Slavery*, II, 392–3. In Maryland, for example, 62 percent of the 4,200 manumissions executed (and reported) between 1832 and 1852 were promises of future freedom; *Debates and Proceedings of the Maryland Reform Convention to Review the State Constitution*, 2 vols. (Annapolis, 1851), II, 221.

municipality sprouted a complement of "retired" bondsmen. "There is no doubt that slaves are longer lived than free blacks," noted Hezekiah Niles in 1830, "but the larger part of the apparent disproportion of old free Negroes arises from the unpleasant and oppressive fact—that aged and infirmed and *worn-out* slaves from all parts of the state, are turned to Baltimore, to live if they can, or die if they must." Municipal officials tried desperately to force slaveowners to support their aged slaves, and some enterprising businessmen found profit in staffing their factories with elderly bondsmen, but they never seemed able to keep pace with the growing number of abandoned slaves. "Old negroes, like old horses," lamented a Richmond daily in 1858, "are often turned loose to go where they wish. . . ."[26]

Manumission was a slaveholder's prerogative, but slaves did not watch passively. Many bondsmen induced their masters to free them or allow them to purchase their liberty by pressing their owners with reminders of past services and promises of future loyalty. When that failed, some blacks tricked their owners into granting them liberty. The administrator of a Virginia estate found himself unable to employ a skilled slave profitably. The slave, who should easily have earned over $150 a year, instead returned a paltry $18 while accumulating medical bills for several times that amount. Exasperated by the steady drain on the estate, the executor offered the slave his freedom for $400, and the sum was promptly paid. Other bondsmen literally bought their master's permission. Typical of many transactions, a Maryland master freed his slave believing that "natural freedom is the right of all men . . . and also in further consideration of thirty dollars."[27] Money, even token payments, seemed to lubricate the consciences of many slaveholders.

[26] Benjamin J. Klebaner, "American Manumission Laws and the Responsibility for Supporting Slaves," *VMH&B*, LXIII (1955), 443–53; *Niles' Weekly Register*, XXVII (16 January 1830), 340; Petitions on Negroes and Slavery, 1832, DelLP; Robert S. Starobin, *Industrial Slavery in the Old South* (New York, 1970), pp. 164–5; *Louisville Daily Courier*, 12 June 1855, 13 September 1855; Richmond *Daily Dispatch*, 29 May 1858.

[27] Frederick L. Olmsted, *A Journey in the Seaboard Slave States, with Remarks on Their Economy* (New York, 1856), pp. 103–4; Anne Arundel County Manumissions, Liber C, 1816–1844, 5 September 1825, MdHR.

Slaves needed iron determination as well as cold cash to buy their way out of bondage. Slaveholders frequently thought their slaves too good to free. "No sum of Money would induce me to part with Sarah, for she is Sober, industrious & Honest so much so that my wife always finds her things in proper order without much trouble," a Tennessee slave master wrote to a free Negro anxious to buy his wife. Besides, he added, "the Price of Black people is so enormously High in this Country that I could not Replace Such a one as her I Expect for Less than Between Six & Seven Hundred dollars and such a trusty one as She is, is hard to find. . . ." But persistence occasionally paid off. An embarrassed Virginia overseer told his employer that he had no intention of selling an elderly slave to the slave's free wife, "but they were after me every day & at last I told them I would take . . . $300." Much to the overseer's surprise, the free Negro woman promptly produced the money and hired a lawyer to secure her husband's freedom papers. Fearing his employer's wrath, the overseer still tried to discourage her. "I told her that it was a great folly, because if she succeeded in obtaining his freedom, he could not enjoy it but a few years." Determined to liberate her husband, the woman retorted that "she did not mind, her wish was that he should die free."[28]

The master's permission, although crucial, was but one step toward freedom. Once it was obtained, the slave still faced enormous difficulties. When slaveholders agreed to sell slaves their liberty, they rarely took less than full price, and many masters exploited their bondsmen's desire to free themselves or their families by raising the price high above the open market rate. Moreover, slaves had no legal right to property; although a few slaveholders allowed their slaves to accumulate some personal possessions, these usually had little monetary value. To stimulate productivity, some masters permited their slaves to peddle vegetables grown on their own time, and occasionally slave hirers paid bonuses for "over work." Yet, these token payments rarely amounted to more than a dollar or two a month, and most Negroes quickly spent this pocket money to relieve the tedium of their daily life. Slaves allowed to hire

[28] James Gutherie to James Cooper, 26 February 1818, PAS; John McKean to James Dunlap, 11 December 1816, copy, McKean Letterbook, VSL.

their own time had the greatest chance of accumulatin[g] money to free themselves, but even skilled bondsmen found this difficult. In the late antebellum years, when slaves commonly sold for more than a thousand dollars, a skilled bondsman could rarely hire himself for more than two hundred dollars a year, out of which he had to pay his master and support himself. Thus even the most talented slaves found purchasing their freedom or that of a loved one a long, painful task which required immense self-discipline and years of austere living. Rising slave prices and relatively constant wages compounded their problems. A leading Richmond minister, who purchased several bondsmen to enable them to buy their freedom, concluded it was nearly impossible for slaves to free themselves. "The truth is," he noted in 1848, "[I have] given them up their time to make money as fast as they could, but found they *generally* made only about enough to pay the interest on the investment & support themselves"—and were unable to return the principle.[29]

Like manumission, self-purchase became an increasingly urban phenomenon. In the countryside, where there were few opportunities to hire out, the most skilled slaves had little chance of earning the money necessary to buy their way out of bondage even if their owner had granted permission to try. The relative closeness of city life gave urban slaves a far greater opportunity to know their masters and obtain the right to work on their own, and the diversity of the urban economy increased their chances of accumulating the necessary money. But even under the best of conditions, self-purchase was not easy. When the price of slaves nearly doubled in the 1850s, only the most industrious urban bondsmen could hope to buy their liberty.

Because of these difficulties, few blacks freed themselves without assistance. Some enterprising bondsmen appealed to the public for aid. In 1829, Henry Williams, a Baltimore slave,

29 Slaves at the Tredegar Iron Works in Richmond, for example, usually received less than one dollar a month in "over work" pay and only rarely as much as three dollars; Payroll Books, Tredegar Iron Works Papers, VSL. For some of the difficulties slaves had buying their freedom, see Anne Arundel Manumissions, Liber D, 1844–1866, 4 October 1844, MdHR; R. G. Wells to William McLain, 3 March 1855, quotation in Robert Ryland to William McLain, 11 January 1848, ACS.

bought himself by peripatetically soliciting funds between Fredericksburg and New York. George Horton peddled poems to students at the University of North Carolina to earn the price of his liberty. Others were even more ambitious. Loudoun Evans, a skilled Savannah carpenter, purchased his own freedom and then his family's with the eight thousand dollars he earned on a lecture tour of the North. Noah Davis, the minister of the Baltimore African Baptist Church, liberated his family with money earned from lecturing and from the sale of his autobiography as well as loans from benevolent whites.[30]

Many more blacks depended on their friends and relatives to extricate them from bondage. Hundreds of free Negroes used their small savings to purchase and free loved ones, especially their immediate families. In New Orleans, better than a third of the petitions for manumission between 1827 and 1851 came from Negro freemen. Sometimes relatives in the free states helped to buy enslaved brethren out of bondage. Cincinnati abolitionists found numerous blacks working to free kin south of the Ohio River. Wealthy free Negroes occasionally used their privileged position to aid bondsmen. John B. Metchum, a leader of the St. Louis free Negro community, purchased twenty blacks and allowed them to buy themselves, and Jane Minor, a Petersburg nurse, assisted nineteen bondsmen out of slavery with loans or outright gifts of liberty. At times, the black community pitched in to help one of their number. When a Liberia-bound Negro failed in her efforts to purchase her husband, Richmond friends scraped up the necessary funds so he might accompany her to Africa.[31]

[30] Henry Williams to R. R. Gurley, 19 June 1829, 23 September 1829, ACS; Sumner Eliot Matison, "Manumission by Purchase," *JNH*, XXXIII (1948), 157–8; Baltimore *Sun*, 2 July 1856; Noah Davis, *A Narrative of the Life of Rev. Noah Davis, a Colored Man* (Baltimore, 1859).

[31] Robert C. Reinders, "The Free Negro in the New Orleans Economy, 1850–1860," *Louisiana History*, VI (1965), 282; George Bain to Willis Crowell, 19 July 1858, Willis Crowell Collection in the Carter G. Woodson Papers, LC; "Report on the Condition of the People of Color in the State of Ohio," in the *Proceedings of the Ohio Anti-Slavery Convention, Held in Putnam on the 22nd, 23d, and 24th of April, 1835* (n.p., [1835]); John B. Metchum, *An Address to All the Colored Citizens of the United States* (Philadelphia, 1846), pp. 4–5; Jackson, *Free Negro Labor and Property Holding*, pp. 189–90; N. B. Clark to William McLain, 28 March 1860, ACS; Receipts for Bonds, 1840–1852, NOPL; Minutes of the First African Baptist

But the poverty of the free Negro community often forced blacks anxious to buy their freedom to depend on whites. Benevolent whites sometimes acted as secret intermediaries between bondsmen who had accumulated the necessary money and masters who were unwilling to sell them their liberty. A few whites advanced money and assisted slaves with other favors. Joseph Anderson, president of the Tredegar Iron Works in Richmond, loaned his favorite hireling, Emanuel Quivers, money at low interest to purchase his freedom and then gave him a special position in the factory to enable him to pay it back. Later Quivers made a second loan to buy his family and finally to migrate west.[32] A highly skilled, literate bondsman who worked closely with his owner in a supervisory capacity, Quivers was in no sense a typical slave. But as the doors to freedom shut, he became representative of those who could hope to obtain liberty. Like those manumitted, slaves who purchased themselves were drawn increasingly from among those who were highly skilled or well connected with whites or other free blacks.

RUNAWAYS

Seeing little chance that their owners would free them and small possibility of buying their way out of bondage, some blacks attempted to seize their liberty by running away. But as the nineteenth century went by, escaping to freedom also became increasingly difficult. Widespread manumission during the Revolutionary years had allowed fugitives to melt into a free Negro caste whose precise membership was concealed by its rapid growth. Suspicious sheriffs had difficulty distinguishing fugitives from freemen in a population that daily received new members who, like runaways, were former slaves. The sharp decline in the free Negroes' rate of increase and the new system of controls instituted by whites made it easier to identify slaves who tried to pass as free. In many crossroads

---

Church of Richmond, 5 March 1843, 16 June 1850, 8 December 1850, First African Baptist Church, Richmond; *Charleston Mercury*, 26 October 1859.

[32] Kathleen Bruce, *Virginia Iron Manufacture in the Slave Era* (New York, 1930), pp. 239–42.

towns and rural backwaters, whites knew by name the members of the small, relatively static free Negro population. Where a large number of free Negroes made personal knowledge impossible, the law required all Negro freemen to carry proof of their status and to register with local officials. Moveover, in spite of the large increase in the free Negro population after the Revolution, the presumption that all blacks were slaves remained in force in most of the South. Only Maryland and Delaware grudgingly retreated from this basic premise, and even in those states the change in the law did not alter the presumption in people's minds. In 1837, Baltimore police seized a suspected fugitive and, when he denied he was a slave, beat him "bloody as a butcher." Still, he was luckier than countless others, for the next day friends documented his free status and obtained his release. Other hapless free Negroes languished in jail and some were slapped into bondage.[33]

Still, a few slaves hurdled all these obstacles and made their way to freedom. From the Upper South, many followed the North Star to the free states, and from the Southwest some traveled to Mexico. It was difficult to reach freedom from the interior South, but some slaves created their own free soil. Runaways from Georgia and South Carolina joined with Indians in the Florida swamps and established a large maroon colony, which the United States Army continually dispersed but never quite eliminated. Fugitives established smaller maroon outposts almost everywhere that physical conditions kept whites at a distance. As late as the 1850s, slave patrols were still discovering maroon encampments in the Great Dismal Swamp of North Carolina and Virginia.[34]

As in earlier years, many fugitives attempted to pass as freemen. When they did not try to leave the South or escape to a maroon colony, they generally set out for places where they could lose themselves among a large number of free blacks.

[33] *Md. Laws*, 1817, c. 112; Catterall, ed., *Judicial Cases Concerning Slavery*, IV, 231–2; Baltimore *Sun*, 31 May 1837; St. Louis *Daily Missouri Democrat*, 14 August 1856; David White to Isaac Barton, 15 September 1824, PAS.

[34] Herbert Aptheker, "Maroons Within the Present Limits of the United States," *JNH*, XXIV (1939), 167–84; Kenneth W. Porter, "Florida Slaves and Free Negroes in the Seminole War, 1835–1842," *JSH*, XXX (1964), 427–50.

Free Negroes monopolized the boating trades on the rivers of the South, and fugitives frequently joined their friends working as sailors, fishermen, and stewards on coasting vessels and river boats. In searching for runaway slaves, masters commonly warned that their slaves would try to get aboard some steamboat. Despite the elaborate regulation of free-Negro movement, runaways continued to pass into the anomalous caste. In 1846, two North Carolina slaves escaped to a nearby Virginia county with a large free Negro population. After several years of unchallenged residence, they applied to a neighboring merchant for free papers, alleging that they had left their registers behind. The merchant obliged them, and not until five years later were they discovered to be fugitives.[35] Some slaves made good their escape for longer periods, and others were never caught.

Cities, with their large population of free Negroes, quasi-free Negroes, and slave hirelings, provided the best hiding places. Police found fugitives difficult to distinguish from the large number of unattached blacks who lived in the maze of back alleys and shanties where poverty forced freemen to congregate. In 1858, the Mobile night watch discovered two slave women who had been living as free for at least four years, and not long after, Richmond police identified a runaway who had eluded detection for twenty years. The latter case revealed the difficulty of retaking fugitives in the cities. The slave had been arrested several times previously for being in the city without papers, yet no one had ever claimed her, and after being sold into a term of servitude for court costs, she had been released. City officials could take but cold comfort in the capture of this slave, because they knew she was not an isolated case. "We have no doubt that there are many other runaways in this neighborhood who have escaped detection by misrepresenting their condition," complained the Richmond press. Police, urged on by municipal authorities, constantly redoubled their efforts to find fugitives and return them to their masters, but without notable success. Runaway slaves, lamented the mayor of New Orleans in 1834, "crowd

[35] Petition from Prince William County, 2 March 1839, VSL; Catterall, ed., *Judicial Cases Concerning Slavery*, II, 152.

in the city, hide, and make our City a den."[36] Throughout the South, blacks who escaped bondage continued to augment the free Negro population.

As a group, fugitives had always been more skilled, sophisticated, and aggressive than the mass of slaves. Even during the post-Revolutionary years, the small slave elite contributed disproportionately to those who escaped bondage for freedom. The increased obstacles that runaways faced during the nineteenth century only underscored this fact. Like those who purchased their freedom, most successful fugitives came from a small group of privileged bondsmen.

KIDNAPPING AND PASSING

The door to the free Negro caste swung out as well as in. While manumitted and fugitive slaves added to the free Negro population, manstealers dragged an indeterminate number of free blacks back into slavery. Kidnapping seems to have increased during the nineteenth century as the price of slaves soared upward. "The pecuniary advantages to be derived from this iniquitous traffick are now so great and it enlists in it so many, that they are able to evade the vigilance of the existing laws, or set them at open defiance," lamented a Delaware grand jury in 1817. Not only did the high price of slaves encourage kidnappers, but the growing belief that blacks would be happier as slaves seems to have allayed the horror in which many whites had earlier held the crime and made it more difficult to capture and convict manstealers. In some areas, they appear to have operated openly, sometimes with the tacit consent of the local officials. A Charleston grand jury found free Negroes lured into debt, then legally indentured to pay off their debt, and finally, by "a chain of inhuman proceedings," sold into bondage. Although free Negroes organized

[36] *Mobile Daily Advertiser*, 7 April 1858; Richmond *Daily Dispatch*, 24 February 1859; Minutes of the Richmond City Council, 18 July 1833, VSL; Richmond Police Day Book, 1834–1843, UVa; Proceedings of the New Orleans City Council, 14 November 1834, typescript, NOPL; also see "Report of the Visitors of the City Jail," *The Ordinances of the Mayor and City Council of Baltimore . . . to Which Is Annexed the Mayor's Communication and Reports of the City Officers.*

vigilance associations and protected their liberty with their lives, the danger persisted. "Kidnapping is the order of the day," one Richmond white sadly concluded in 1850.[37]

Some light-skinned freemen moved out of the free Negro caste in the other direction and passed into the white population. Passing, like kidnapping, was far more common than Southern whites liked to admit, although its full extent is also impossible to determine. The tawny color of some mixed-bloods so befuddled whites that they did not know quite how to categorize them. In 1850, for example, a federal census marshal in Alabama listed Jack Coon as white, but that same year the state census denoted him a mulatto freeman. Ten years later, the federal census ranked him with the Indian population. The confusion caused by light-skinned Negroes and dark-skinned whites allowed a few mulatto fugitives to pass from slavery through the free Negro caste into the white population with hardly a stop. A Charleston master warned that his wayward bondsman was so fair that "some persons would mistake him for a white man," and a New Orleans slaveowner characterized his mulatto fugitive as "light enough to pass as a Spaniard."[38]

Much to the discomfort of white people, the boundaries between the races never seemed firm enough. Mixed-bloods of various proportions continually scooted under the color line and blended into the white population. Most crossed the barrier between black and white silently, leaving no trace of their passage. But a few tried to win legal sanction for their higher status. In most Southern states, one black ancestor in the previous two or three generations legally made a person a Negro.[39] Mixed-bloods who were further removed from a

[37] Petitions on Negroes and Slavery, 1817, DelLP; R. W. Bailey to William McLain, 11 February 1850, ACS; Charleston Grand Jury Presentment, Spring 1816, SCA. The best sources of information on kidnapping are the records of the Pennsylvania Abolition Society in HSP and the various *Minutes of the American Convention of Abolition Societies*.

[38] Boucher, "The Free Negro in Alabama Prior to 1860," pp. 96–7; Charleston *Southern Patriot and Commercial Advertiser*, 24 February 1820; New Orleans *Daily Picayune*, 31 October 1856.

[39] Virginia, Kentucky, Missouri, North Carolina (except for marriage to a white person), Arkansas, Florida, and Mississippi legally defined the Negro as a person with one black ancestor in the previous two generations. Georgia, Alabama, North Carolina (in case of marriage to a white person), Tennessee, and Texas legally defined the Negro as a person with one black ancestor in the

black progenitor than the legal requirement sometimes petitioned legislatures for relief from their disabilities or took their case to court to prove that they were "white." Virginia provided the most detailed procedure for legal passing. In 1832, after loading new weights on the free Negro's liberty, lawmakers allowed light-skinned freemen to escape the new disabilities by applying to the county courts "with satisfacory evidence of a white person" that they were not black. If the courts concurred, such mixed-bloods escaped the free Negro's proscribed status. Since the law did not provide for positive rights, only those light enough to pass could move into the superior caste; others remained attached to the free Negro population although legally distinct from it.[40]

No other state passed a similar law, but it appears that passing was much more common in the Lower South, where

---

previous three generations. Maryland, South Carolina, and Louisiana never prescribed a legal definition for the Negro. Hening, comp., *Statutes Va.*, XII, 184; Littell and Swigert, eds., *Digest of Statute Law of Kentucky*, II, 1164; Evans Casselberry, ed., *The Revised Statutes of the State of Missouri* (St. Louis, 1845), p. 392; *N.C. Laws*, 1826, c. 21; E. H. English, ed., *A Digest of the Statutes of the State of Arkansas* (Little Rock, 1846), p. 546; Duval, comp., *Public Acts of the Territory of Florida*, p. 218; *Miss. Laws*, 1822, p. 183; *Ga. Laws*, 1840, pp. 32–3; John J. Ormond *et al.*, comps., *The Code of Alabama* (Montgomery, 1852), pp. 58, 424; *N.C. Laws*, 1838, c. 24, and to the fourth generation, Catterall, ed., *Judicial Cases Concerning Slavery*, II, 102–3; Return J. Meigs and William Cooper, comps., *The Code of Tennessee Enacted by the General Assembly of 1857–'8* (Nashville, 1858), p. 687; William S. Oldham and George S. White, eds. *A Digest of the General Statute Laws of the State of Texas* (Austin, 1859), p. 669.

40 Petition from Davidson County, 7 October 1815; TLP; Petition from Enoch Perrill, 13 November 1833, Petition from Malachi Hagins, Petition from Andrew Barland, n.d., MLP; *Miss. Laws*, 1833, c. 39; O'Neall, *Negro Law of South Carolina*, pp. 5–7; *Va. Laws*, 1832, c. 80. The Virginia law was probably an outgrowth of a private act allowing several former slaves who "are not negroes or mulattoes although descended from a coloured woman" to remain in the state; *Va. Laws*, 1832, c. 243. Until a survey of county court records is made, precisely how many free Negroes used the Virginia law to pass into the white caste will be a moot question. However, there can be no doubt that many mixed-bloods took advantage of the law. In 1854, when some whites demanded its repeal, "A Friend to Humanity" wrote that "the law has been in force for many years and the Courts have been constantly acting under it; and so far as the writer of this is advised, there never has been by any person, any objection to it, until the last twelve months"; *Richmond Enquirer*, 24 February 1854, and pp. 365–6 below. Not all states made provision, legal or judicial, for light-skinned free Negroes to "pass" legally; *African Repository*, IX (January 1834), 321–2.

a large mixed-blood population blended imperceptibly into the white. The confusion engendered by the largely mulatto caste induced some Lower South states to take additional precautions against the incursion of light-skinned freemen into the white caste. Georgia lawmakers provided the legal means for whites suspicious of a neighbor's ancestry to take persons enjoying "the rights and privileges of free white citizens" to court and, if they were shown to be of more than one-eighth Negro "blood," to push them into the free Negro caste.[41] No other state enacted a similar skeleton-rattling measure, but many Lower South states followed Georgia's lead and raised the color line a notch. While most Upper South states followed Negro ancestry back two generations in distinguishing blacks from whites, persons with one African ancestor three generations removed were legally deemed black in much of the Lower South. It was a fine distinction usually without much practical importance; whites generally lumped mulattoes and Negroes together and treated anyone who looked remotely like a Negro as black. But the legal distinction accurately reflected regional differences in the composition of the free Negro caste, a greater sensitivity to questions of color in the Lower South, and probably the greater possibilities for passing in that region.

Southerners liked the genetic precision inherent in their legal definitions of the Negro. But in distinguishing between black and white, they incorporated their own social standards as well. Wealthy, well-connected mixed-bloods clearly had a better chance of hurdling the color line than those with just a fair skin. The process of elite passing can best be viewed in South Carolina. Fearful of pushing too many persons of both colors to the wrong sides of the color line, the South Carolina legislature never legally defined the Negro and left the problem of distinguishing between mixed-bloods and whites up to the courts. South Carolina jurists generally drew the line between white and black at somewhere between a quarter and an eighth Negro ancestry, but they also made legal passing contingent on social acceptability as well. "Whenever the African taint is so far removed, that upon inspection a party may be

[41] *Ga. Laws*, 1840, pp. 32–3.

fairly pronounced to be white, and such has been his or her previous reception into society, and [they enjoy] . . . the privileges usually enjoyed by whites," declared one low-country judge, "the Jury may rate . . . them as white." Allowing the question of whiteness to turn on public acceptance as well as genealogy enabled many well-placed whites to free their mulatto children from their proscribed status. In addition, a few successful South Carolina free Negroes wriggled out of the free Negro caste by claiming Indian ancestry. "Every day," complained a leading Charleston newspaper, "persons of color, whose blood on their mothers [*sic*] side is Indian, are exempted from the state tax imposed upon persons of color, and allowed other privileges of white men." Of course, some of these elite free Negroes, like the Dereef family of Charleston, may well have had both Indian and black ancestors, but the fact that they were allowed to take refuge in their Indian status suggests that money could bleach, especially in parts of the Lower South.[42]

Although whites might sympathize and occasionally even connive with light-skinned free Negroes anxious to improve their status, it was the persistence and ingenuity of Negro freemen that made passing possible. Free Negroes continually found new ways to escape the oppression that bound them. Fair-skinned freemen in New Orleans, for example, facilitated the movement of their descendants into the white caste and simultaneously erased the record of their black ancestry by having their children baptized as whites. Officials railed against the "mischievous consequences" of this practice and ordered doctors to designate the color of the mother and father on all birth certificates, but a steady stream of litigation suggests it was to no avail.[43] Numerous light-skinned free

[42] O'Neall, *Negro Law of South Carolina,* pp. 5–7; *Charleston Mercury,* 16 August 1823; David Gavin Diary, 9 November 1855, typescript, SHC; *List of the Tax Payers of the City of Charleston for 1860* (Charleston, 1861), pp. 319, 315–34.

[43] Perry S. Warfield, ed., *Digest of the Acts of the Legislature . . . Together with the Ordinances and Resolutions of the City of New Orleans . . . 1848* (New Orleans, 1848), pp. 80–1; New Orleans *Bee,* 9 February 1856; *New Orleans Daily Delta,* 12 April 1858; James H. Johnston, *Race Relations in Virginia and Miscegenation in the South* (Amherst, Mass., 1970), pp. 165–216.

Negroes simply walked away from their proscribed status, shrinking the free Negro caste.

IMMIGRATION AND EMIGRATION

Migratory patterns affected the growth of the free Negro population, the distribution of free Negroes within the South, and the character of the free Negro caste. Nineteenth-century Americans were on the move, pushing their way across the continent, building towns and cities at every junction. Free Negroes too shared this urge to travel, but immigration restrictions often stood in their way. Whites, unwilling to live near free Negroes and ever fearful of mobile free-Negro revolutionaries, had early passed laws to restrict or prohibit free-Negro movement. Soon after being admitted to the Union, new states, following the lead of the old, barred the entry of free Negroes into their borders. Yet the law alone could not stop a determined black emigrant, any more than it could force manumitted slaves to leave. Far more than restrictive regulations, the free Negroes' precarious, often impoverished situation anchored them to their homes and made them reluctant to emigrate. Ties of home and kin, their reputation with white customers or employers, their familiar daily routine, and their knowledge of the countryside often provided the only security poor free Negroes had in a society that was hostile to their very existence. Fear that these ties might be sundered frightened many blacks; for them, any change could only be for the worse. The friends of one Tennessee free Negro who had been threatened with expulsion from the state vividly depicted the web of relationship that bound free Negroes to the communities in which they lived. He had resided in Nashville "from the time of his youth; there he has toiled with his hands, day after day & year after year; and there are all his associations and feeling—his preferences are *there*—his attachments are *there*—he could not live and enjoy life *anywhere* else." The trauma of breaking these lifelong ties induced some black emigrants to return to the South after they had left. "So marked was the difference in manner and habits of the people of Ohio," observed one returning Virginia free Negro, that she could not remain "in the least happiness or contentment."[44] Ties of blood and friendship were strong, sometimes too strong.

Skilled black tradesmen and artisans may have felt none of these anxieties. The self-esteem generated by their success countered the dismal fear of change, while it magnified the felt oppression of their daily lives. The belief that things could be different and better often encouraged them to seek a better life elsewhere; from this class came a disproportionate share of the free Negro emigrants. But their very success also bound elite free Negroes to the communities in which they resided. Many worked at trades which provided a healthy living in the South, but which white workingmen monopolized in the North and which simply did not exist in Africa or elsewhere. For such skilled free Negroes, migration often meant a sure loss of economic status. Some Southern blacks who went north, like Frederick Douglass, had difficulty finding work at the trades they had practiced in the slaveholding states. Even if they recovered their economic position, the prestige that had accrued to it in their old home might not be forthcoming to an outsider. Although they smarted under the lash of oppressive white rule, they too felt a deep love for their Southern home. "I feel this is my country and leaving it will come hard," a wealthy Charleston free Negro told an English visitor.[45]

Despite the pain and expense of cutting Southern ties, many free Negroes did leave, some gladly. Pulled by the promise of

[44] Petition from Davidson County, 1883, TLP; Petition from Albemarle County, 14 February 1839, VLP. The census indicates free Negroes were less mobile than whites. In 1850, 17 percent of the nation's freemen lived outside the state of their birth, while almost a quarter of the native-born white population had so moved. This disparity is balanced by the fact that migration was illegal throughout the South and in parts of the North, so that free Negro immigrants had reason to disguise their place of birth. On the other hand, many free Negro immigrants moved from their native states as slaves and later obtained their liberty. J. Potter, "The Growth of Population in America, 1700–1860," in D. V. Glass and D. E. C. Eversley, eds., *Population in History: Essays in Historical Demography* (London, 1965), p. 635.

[45] Theodore Hershberg, "Free Blacks in Antebellum Philadelphia: A Study of Ex-Slaves, Freeborn and Socio-economic Decline," *Journal of Social History*, V (1972), 183–209, documents the ability of ex-slaves, many from the South, to succeed in a Northern city. J. Benwell, *An Englishman's Travels in America* (London, [1853]), p. 198.

new opportunities and driven by the desire to escape the oppressive presence of slavery, a steady stream of free Negroes migrated north. Generally, poverty forced them to stop at the first free state. Although the New England states allowed free Negroes the largest measure of freedom, the border states received the bulk of the free Negro immigrants. In 1850, nearly half the free Negroes in Indiana had been born in the South. Within the North, the cities attracted most of the black émigrés. By 1860, Negroes born in the South made up more than half of the blacks in Chicago, almost a third of those in Philadelphia, and more than a quarter of those in Boston. Some more venturesome blacks traveled to the new Pacific territories. Following the discovery of gold, a Virginia colonization agent found free Negroes throughout that state suffering from "California fever." Black emigrants to the West, like countless other Americans, soon urged their friends to join them. "This is the best place for black folks in the globe," wrote an enthusiastic black to a Missouri friend. "All a man has to do is to work, and he will make money. [It has the] best climate in the world and a healthy country to live in." By 1860, over four thousand free Negroes had moved to California.[46]

The steady flow of Negroes into the "free states" brought the familiar cries for restriction. The border states, partly because of their large Southern-born population and partly because of their propinquity to the South, were most fearful of a massive black influx. During the antebellum years, Ohio, Indiana, Illinois, and Iowa limited free Negro entry. Although Ohio, under pressure from abolitionists, eventually repealed its restriction, Illinois and Indiana went on to write the ban on free Negro immigrants into their state constitutions.[47] But Northern laws fared no better than Southern ones, and a stream of Southern-born blacks continued to move north.

[46] Emma Lou Thornborough, *The Negro in Indiana: A Study of a Minority* ([Indianapolis], 1957), p. 32; *Population of the United States in 1860*, pp. 608, 610, 613; T. Johnson to William McLain, 5 February 1849, ACS; P. Brown to Alley Brown, 1 December 1851, California-Oregon Papers, MoHS.

[47] Eugene H. Berwanger, *The Frontier Against Slavery: Western Anti-Negro Prejudice and the Slavery Extension Controversy* (Urbana, Ill., 1967), pp. 43–51; Frank U. Quillin, *The Colorline in Ohio* (Ann Arbor, Mich., 1913), p. 22; Thornborough, *Negro in Indiana*, pp. 37–8.

In the North, blacks were despised and degraded as in the South. Whites usually proscribed them from political rights, barred them from most public institutions, segregated them in others, and limited them to the most menial jobs and the worst housing. Still, free Negroes enjoyed a degree of liberty and self-expression unknown in the slaveholding states. The host of black newspapers, the activities of black abolitionists, organized churches, schools, and conventions, all spoke to the differences between North and South. No matter how successful a black tradesman might be in the South, he never dared raise his voice against racial oppression. Although omnipresent racism made a mockery of many of the legal rights of Northern blacks, Southern free Negroes who moved north generally found a measure of liberty altogether absent in the slave states.

But many blacks saw little to distinguish the racism of the North from that of the South. Wealthy blacks who sent their children north for an education often discovered that their well-qualified offspring could not find employment in the free states. Without steady work, the benefits of Northern freedom dissolved into empty bitterness. "[The only] advantage I can see by living in Philadelphia is that if my family is sick, I can send for the doctor at any time of night without a ticket," charged a Charleston-born free Negro. Disillusioned by the barren promise of the free states, some blacks looked elsewhere. After having seen "the legal slavery of the South and the *social slavery* of the North," observed a Liberia-bound black, he knew he could "never be a *free man* in this country."[48]

Although most free Negroes bitterly opposed colonization, they were of two minds about Africa. They adamantly proclaimed their American nationality, but the motherland had undeniable pull. Free Negroes—of all denominations—called their churches "African churches," their schools "African schools," and their benevolent societies "African benevolent societies." In a sense, their ambivalence toward Africa mir-

[48] Leon F. Litwack, *North of Slavery: The Negro in the Free States, 1790–1860* (Chicago, 1961); *African Repository,* XV (June 1839), 178–80; James M. Bland to William McLain, 3 July 1848; J. W. Hall to William McLain, 19 May 1845, ACS.

rored white attitudes toward Europe. No matter how vehemently whites denounced Europe as a land of decadent monarchies and haughty aristocrats, they could not escape common cultural ties. In like fashion, black Americans were drawn to Africa in search of their own identity.[49]

Much of the Pan-Africanism was involuntary. Some emancipators forced their slaves to migrate by giving them a choice between Liberia and bondage.[50] But blacks often jumped at the chance to sail for Africa. A North Carolina free Negro declared that the desire to go back to Africa had been "abirdon [a burden] on my mind ever since I was a boy of fourteen years old hearing my mother tell aBought [about] her grandfather being kidnaped and brought from His mother country." The memory of Africa, however dim, reinforced the desire to escape white rule and form a strong black nation. "I believe that a man of color must seek and obtain a home [,] a peace [*sic*] of earth that he could call his own, and water it with the sweat of his brow, he must plant the trees of liberty and build a temple sacred to Religion and Justice" pronounced a St. Louis free Negro.[51]

While most free Negro emigrants saw Africa as a haven from white oppression, others had grander plans and hoped to enrich themselves by serving the commercial needs of the new colony. Louis Sheridan, a wealthy North Carolina merchant, migrated along with twenty-five thousand board feet of lumber and thirty-five tons of merchandise which he hoped to sell in Liberia. Hezekiah Grice, an ambitious Baltimore freeman and founder of the Negro Convention Movement, wanted to establish an association to trade with Liberia. Assuring colonizers that he could raise the necessary capital among wealthy free Negroes in Baltimore, Philadelphia, and New York, he proposed to send a schooner with about

[49] Hollis R. Lynch, "Pan-Negro Nationalism in the New World, Before 1862," *Boston University Papers on Africa*, II (1966), 147–79.

[50] R. W. Bailey to William McLain, 25 October 1850, 31 October 1850; A. G. Hubbard to R. R. Gurley, 19 March 1858, ACS.

[51] John Moore to [William McLain], 14 June 1853; N. D. Artist to William McLain, ? July 1855, ACS; S. W. Jones to ACS, 29 December 1851, Carter G. Woodson, ed., *The Mind of the Negro as Reflected in Letters Written During the Crisis, 1800–1860* (Washington, D.C., 1926), p. 69.

two thousand dollars worth of "suitable merchandise" immediately and later establish regular packet service. In 1845, perhaps at Grice's behest, the Maryland legislature incorporated the Chesapeake and Liberia Trading Company, although it was "*a nigger concern* altogether."[52] William N. Colston and John Jenkins Roberts, two prominent Petersburg free Negroes, founded another successful trading company. In 1829, Roberts migrated to the new colony as an agent of Colston, Roberts & Company and later became the first president of the Republic of Liberia. Colston remained in the United States, sending goods from Petersburg, Philadelphia, and New York via the company-owned trading vessel. By 1834, he announced his interest in investing another ten thousand dollars in the African trade.[53]

Missionary zeal to Christianize Africa and convert heathens also motivated some of the black emigrants. White ministers, who were the backbone of the colonization movement, encouraged Negroes to follow in their footsteps. Although many blacks desirous of getting to Africa simply told these men what they wanted to hear, other emigrants believed themselves messengers of the gospel. Certainly there can be no doubt that Lott Cary and Daniel Coker, two of the first emigrants, were at least partially motivated by the desire to evangelize, and others followed their lead. "I have a burning desire to go to Africa to preach the word of God to the natives . . . ," wrote a black Virginian. Another free Negro emigrant wanted to convert the African "people from Ignorance [,] Superstition[,] barbarism & Paganism to the true religion & civilization that characterises the United States." Missionary zeal mixed freely with other hopes and desires. Peter Butler, a Virginia free Negro, wished to "teach Sinners the way of salvation and also Educate his children and enjoy the rights of a man." Even William N. Colston combined his intense commercial ambitions with a desire to carry back "the

[52] Francis Bacon to Joseph Gales, 21 December 1831, C. C. Harper to R. R. Gurley, 9 April 1829, James Hall to William McLain, 10 March 1845, ACS; *African Repository*, XXIX (January 1853), 19–22; New York *Colored American*, 4 August 1838, 8 December 1838.

[53] Jackson, *Free Negro Labor and Property Holding*, pp. 147–9; William N. Colston to Joseph Gales, 24 July 1834, 16 September 1834, William N. Colston to Philip Fendall, 20 January 1835, ACS.

glorious Gospel of the Son of God, and the consequent light of Civilization."[54]

But most Negro emigrants neither sought riches nor desired to spread the Word; they simply wanted a place where they might be truly free. "[I] am not going to Liberia with expectations of getting rich or anything of that kind," declared a Tennessee free Negro. "But i am going to injoy that Liberty that i Beleave that god has Designed for all mankind." "I just want to get some place where I can live at," observed another freeman, "and make a living for myself and family. . . ." In Liberia, he continued, "I suppose I will be at Liberty . . . to Locate where I like providing the first place I mite stop did not suit me." These men did not leave their homes easily, but only after investigating every alternative. Samuel Sharp, a Maryland free Negro, migrated first to New Jersey, where he "found himself much oppressed"; he moved on to Canada, and later considered going to Texas with Benjamin Lundy before he finally sailed for Liberia. A Virginia free Negro had much the same experience. "I have tried a great many placies in these unites states," he wrote, "and find that none of them is the home for a culerd man and So I . . . wish to be and Emigrant for the land of my auntsesters."[55]

The exodus to the North and Africa as well as smaller migrations to Canada, the West Indies, and Europe slowed the growth of the Southern free Negro population. During the nineteenth century, the proportion of American free Negroes living in the South shrank steadily, and the center of the free Negro population slowly moved northward. More important, this outward migration stripped the Southern free Negro caste of some of its most talented, ambitious, and aggressive members. Among the blacks born free in the South who later rose to prominence in the North were Martin Delany, Daniel Payne, Robert Purvis, and David Walker. Many of the leaders of the

[54] Jery McHung Farles to William McLain, 16 August 1856, Peter Bolling to William McLain, 13 March 1848, William N. Colston to Joseph Gales, 24 July 1834, ACS.

[55] John A. Ford to William McLain, 1 September 1854; Joseph A. Preacher to William McLain, 29 July 1858, ACS; *African Repository,* XXXI (1835), 367–8; Eli Stokes to James Hall, 26 September 1843, Letters Received. MdSCS Papers.

African Methodist Episcopal Church, a largely Northern organization, first achieved freedom in the slaveholding states. Southern free Negroes also left their mark on the black settlements around Wilberforce and Buxton in Canada and dominated the government of the Republic of Liberia. Thus the departure of free Negroes from the South, although not equal in numbers or importance to later migrations, drained the free Negro caste of many potential leaders.[56]

Offsetting this outmigration, a small number of Northern and West Indian blacks moved into the South. Many came to visit friends and relatives, others to find work when ice blocked ports, closed roads, and made employment difficult to get in the North. Despite the presence of slavery, steady work, newly made friends, and perhaps the salubrious climate induced some to stay. New Orleans, a bustling port, attracted many such emigrants. "In open violation of the law and every maxim of good policy, hundreds of free Negroes, from the Northern States, are now to be found residing in New Orleans," grumbled one editor in 1823. The legislature eventually added new restrictions on free Negro entry, but the need for labor prevented their enforcement. During the 1850s, when Southern fear of free Negro subversion reached a fever pitch, the practice of allowing Northern and West Indian free Negroes easy access to the city again came to the fore. According to one newspaper, "the law was so rarely enforced that our free colored population actually in the State in contravention of the law became unaware of the fact. Having lived so long here unmolested, they never dreamed a sword hung by a hair over their heads." The governor fumed, lawmakers piled new restrictions on the old, and the police enforced them with a vengeance. Within a few months, the crisis had passed, leaving free Negroes ruffled but largely undisturbed.[57] The pattern was a familiar one throughout the South. Legislatures, in-

[56] Richard Bardolph, *The Negro Vanguard* (New York, 1959), pp. 19–131; Robin W. Winks, *The Blacks in Canada* (Montreal, 1971), pp. 114–241; J. Gus Liebenow, *Liberia: The Evolution of Privilege* (Ithaca, N.Y., 1969).

[57] New Orleans *Louisiana Gazette*, 5 February 1823; *La. Laws*, 1830, pp. 90–4, 1841–1842, c. 123, 1859, c. 87; *Journal of the Louisiana House of Representatives*, 1857, p. 7, 1860, p. 8; New Orleans *Daily Picayune*, 4 September 1859. Also see *Charleston Mercury*, 3 September 1823; *Natchez Daily Courier*, 8 November 1859.

furiated at their inability to control free Negro movement, continually added new injunctions and stiffened penalties against free Negro immigration, but the largely redundant legislation only reveals a continuing problem, not its ultimate solution. The trickle of blacks into the South continued down to the Civil War, although it never fully compensated for the growing outmigration.

Whatever the lure of Africa and the North, most migrating free Negroes did not leave the South. Like whites, they generally moved along parallel lines of latitude in searching for new opportunities. Free Negroes from Virginia and North Carolina tended to migrate to Kentucky and Tennessee, and those from South Carolina and Georgia moved to Alabama and Mississippi. But unlike that of white emigrants, the movement of free blacks within the South had a distinct northward thrust. Free Negroes avoided the rich belt of loamy black soil that stretched across Georgia, Alabama, and Mississippi, which became the heartland of the plantation South. The Lower South, except for its cities, attracted few blacks. Free Negroes who bucked the general trend and moved from the Upper to the Lower South often found opposition so intense that they beat a hasty retreat. As in the northward migrations, free Negro emigrants generally stopped at the border of the first neighboring state. Border counties in almost every Southern state sported a disproportionately large free Negro population. Free Negroes found these borderlines a strategic boon in their endless battle with the law. When one state threatened them, they simply slipped across the state line and waited for the furor to pass.[58]

Cities were the chief harbors for the free Negro migrants. In the cities, free Negroes found a greater range of economic opportunities and enjoyed a richer social life. Almost every Southern city had an African church that functioned openly and sometimes free from white control. Schools and benevolent societies where free Negroes could provide for their

[58] James M. England, "The Free Negro in Antebellum Tennessee," unpublished doctoral dissertation, Vanderbilt University, 1941, pp. 21–2; Edward F. Sweat, "The Free Negro in Antebellum Georgia," unpublished doctoral dissertation, Indiana University, 1957, pp. 7–8; Wikramanayake, *A World in Shadow*, pp. 27–9; G. B. Milligian to Katherine Milligan, 25 June 1822, Milligan-McClaure Papers, HSD.

own advancement and security were usually forced to meet clandestinely, but everywhere strengthened black life. Besides these institutions, grocery stores and tippling shops provided places where blacks could gather by themselves, far from the watchful, proprietary eye of the slave master.

The steady influx of rural free Negroes spurred the growth of the urban free Negro population. By 1860, over a third of the Negro freemen in St. Louis were natives of other Southern states, as were over five hundred free Negro residents of New Orleans and Baltimore. The number of urban freemen grew more rapidly than the total free Negro population. For example, although the free Negro population of Virginia increased more than 60 percent between 1820 and 1860, that of Richmond more than doubled and Petersburg's increased almost threefold. The same was generally true throughout the South. Although the rapid growth of urban free Negroes reflected, in part, a higher rate of manumission in the cities, it was primarily the result of migration from the countryside.[59]

THE RESULTING DEMOGRAPHIC PATTERNS

The peculiar pattern of growth resulting from manumissions, successful escapes, and natural increase, from kidnapping and passing, and from in- and outmigration gave the free Negro caste a unique demographic profile. Unlike whites or slaves, free Negroes shunned the rich agricultural interior and lived on the periphery of the South. Wherever the plantation culture held sway, few free Negroes could be found.[60]

[59] *Population of the United States in 1860;* Wade, *Slavery in the Cities,* pp. 325–30; Richmond *Daily Dispatch,* 26 May 1859; also see New Orleans *Daily Picayune,* 8 March 1856.

[60] Unless otherwise noted, this demographic profile has been computed from the published United States censuses, 1820–60.

The census figures cited in the text and the accompanying tables, despite their apparent specificity, should be taken as estimates only. The census has historically underestimated the number of blacks, and the free Negro caste posed special problems for even the most sophisticated enumerations, which the antebellum censuses certainly were not. In addition to the difficulties caused by confused racial identifications of a racially mixed group and the general reluctance of census marshals to visit the black alleys where many free

The cities that ringed the South were centers of free Negro population. The propensity of urban masters to free their slaves, the ability of fugitives to find freedom within municipal limits, the steady influx of rural free Negroes, and the abandonment of enfeebled bondsmen in the cities swelled the number of urban free Negroes. Although the majority of free Negroes, like the vast majority of Southern people, resided in the countryside, free Negroes were the most urban caste in the South. In 1860, better than a third of the Southern free Negro population dwelled in cities or towns, while barely 15 percent of the whites and about 5 percent of the slaves lived in urban centers. Free Negroes were more than twice as urban as whites and seven times as urban as slaves. Urban freemen also tended to congregate in the larger cities for the same reasons they preferred urban to rural life. More than two-thirds of the urban free Negroes lived in cities of ten thousand or more.

Negro freemen were also generally older than slaves or whites. Delays in manumission and the difficulties of self-purchase or escape meant that many blacks did not achieve their liberty until maturity. This, combined with the dumping of elderly slaves and the comparatively low rate of natural increase among free Negroes,[61] resulted in an older free Negro

---

Negroes lived, many Negro freemen saw little reason to have themselves recorded in the census. Some—notably fugitive and quasi-free Negroes who had no legal standing as free persons—avoided enumerators at all cost. Although it is probable that the undercount of free Negroes was fairly constant during the antebellum years, it is my belief that the census underestimates the Southern free Negro population by at least 20 percent.

[61] Little is known about the birth and death rates of antebellum whites and even less about those of slaves and free Negroes. Southern law provided that children should follow the status of their mother, and any match between a free Negro woman and a white, black, or Indian man or between a white woman and a black man, no matter what his status, added to the free Negro population. Yet despite the numerous possible combinations for free Negro increase, the caste did not grow as rapidly as either whites or slaves. In 1860, there were 1,156 free Negro children under ten years of age for each 1,000 free Negro women of childbearing age (16–44), while there were 1,410 white and 1,427 slave children under ten years of age for each 1,000 white and slave women, respectively. Although the census figures are not always directly comparable, they also suggest that the freemen's rate of natural increase was slowly declining during the antebellum years (computed from the published United States censuses, 1820–60). I have followed Yasukichi Yasuba's method of computing refined birth ratios; *Birth Rates of the White Population in the*

TABLE 9

PROPORTION OF FREE NEGROES, WHITES, AND SLAVES URBAN,* 1860

	Free Negroes	Whites	Slaves
United States	47.3%	32.9%	—
North	61.4	40.6	—
South	35.2	14.8	5.0%
Upper South	32.3	16.7	6.2
Lower South	53.2	11.4	4.3

* All places, incorporated and unincorporated, greater than 2,500 in population.

TABLE 10

PROPORTION OF URBAN POPULATIONS RESIDING IN LARGE CITIES,* 1860

	Free Negroes	Whites	Slaves
United States	62.5%	51.2%	—
North	55.7	48.5	—
South	72.7	68.7	46.8%
Upper South	69.2	69.4	41.8
Lower South	85.5	66.7	51.4

* All places, incorporated and unincorporated, greater than 10,000 in population.

SOURCE FOR TABLES 9–10: *Population of the United States in 1860* (Washington, D.C., 1864).

population. In 1860, about 28 percent of the free Negro caste was under ten years of age, while slave and white children of the same age composed over 30 percent of their respective populations. On the other hand, better than 20 percent of the free Negroes were over forty years old, while about 15 percent of the slaves and whites had reached that age. Compared

United States, 1800–1860: An Economic Study (Baltimore, 1962) p. 60. The most sophisticated studies of black fertility and mortality during the antebellum years unfortunately fail to distinguish between free and slave blacks; Reynolds Farley, *Growth of the Black Population: A Study of Demographic Trends* (Chicago, 1970), pp. 31–5, and "The Demographic Rates and Social Institutions of the Nineteenth-Century Negro Population: A Stable Population Analysis," *Demography,* II (1965), 386–98; Jack E. Eblen, "Growth of the Black Population in *antebellum* America, 1820–1860," *Population Studies,* XXVI (1972), 273–89.

with whites and other blacks, there were fewer free Negro youngsters and many more old folks. The free Negro caste was a top-heavy group.

In contrast to the white and slave populations, there were many more free Negro women than men in the South. The great preponderance of free Negro women was confined almost entirely to the cities. There the combined effects of manumission and migratory patterns played havoc with the sexual balance. Urban emancipators tended to bestow favors on women, partly because slave women outnumbered slave men in the cities and partly because close intermingling encouraged sexual liaisons which sometimes led to manumission. While emancipated women increased the urban free Negro population, the greater mobility of free Negro men allowed a disproportionate number of them to leave the South. Although the slaveholding states had an excess of free Negro women, the Northern border states had a surplus of free Negro men. But the sexual imbalance generally stopped at the city line. In most settled rural areas, the number of free Negro men and women was roughly the same. On the frontier, where free Negro men, like white men, pioneered alone and later brought their families, the sexual balance usually favored men.

As a general rule, freemen were lighter in color than slaves. Although some of the fairest free Negroes passed out of the caste, the manumission of the children of slaveholders and

TABLE 11

PROPORTION OF FREE NEGROES, WHITES, AND SLAVES FEMALE, 1860

	Free Negroes	*Whites*	*Slaves*
United States	52.0%	48.6%	—
North	51.4	48.7	—
South	52.6	48.5	49.9%
Upper South	52.3	48.9	49.7
Lower South	54.5	47.9	49.9
Urban South[a]	56.9	48.4	52.2
Large Southern Cities[b]	58.5	49.1	53.5
Rural South	50.3	48.5	49.7

[a] Places greater than 2,500 in population.
[b] Places greater than 10,000 in population.

SOURCE: *Population of the United States in 1860* (Washington, D.C., 1864).

other privileged bondsmen and the free status accorded the offspring of white and Indian women by black men made free Negroes a disproportionately mulatto caste. In 1860 fully 40 percent of the Southern free Negro population were classified as mulattoes, while only one slave in ten had some white ancestry. Urban free Negroes, as usual, were an exception to the rule. The intermingling of whites and blacks in Southern cities produced a free Negro population that was generally lighter that that of the countryside. But throughout the South, a light skin was the freeman's distinguishing characteristic.[62]

TABLE 12

PROPORTION OF FREE NEGROES AND SLAVES OF MIXED RACIAL ANCESTRY, 1860

	Free Negroes	*Slaves*
United States	36.2%	—
North	30.9	—
South	40.8	10.4%
Upper South	35.0	13.4
Lower South	75.8	8.5
Delaware	14.6	4.6
D.C.	40.4	4.9
Kentucky	38.1	19.2
Maryland	19.1	10.2
Missouri	46.9	19.1
North Carolina	71.6	6.9
Tennessee	58.7	13.6
Virginia	40.5	14.3
Alabama	78.0	7.9
Arkansas	60.4	12.6
Florida	69.0	8.5
Georgia	57.2	8.0
Louisiana	81.3	9.8
Mississippi	77.7	8.4
South Carolina	72.0	5.3
Texas	76.9	13.7

SOURCE: U.S. Bureau of the Census, *Negro Population of the United States, 1790–1915* (Washington, D.C., 1918), p. 220.

[62] In 1850 and 1860, the census distinguished between "mulatto" and "black" members of the free Negro and slave populations. However, census marshals were not given any criterion for distinguishing mulattoes from blacks or even whites. Presumably, all those who were not full-blooded blacks yet

The tawny color of many free Negroes suggests other characteristics which distinguished Negro freemen from the mass of slaves. The slaveholder's increasingly selective liberation of favored bondsmen and the difficulties slaves had running away or purchasing their liberty meant that free Negroes were generally more skilled, literate, and well connected with whites than the mass of slaves. Even before they were emancipated, most free Negroes had enjoyed a privileged position within the slave hierarchy.

The distinctions between whites and slaves and free Negroes hid the major cleavage within the Southern free Negro caste. The great mass of Negro freemen lived in the tidewater of the Upper South between Delaware and North Carolina, where the post-Revolutionary manumission movement had flourished. Better than half the free Negroes in the South resided in Delaware, Maryland, and Virginia. To the south and the west, the free Negro population thinned. Proportional to total population, Maryland had more free Negroes than Virginia, Virginia than North Carolina or Kentucky, Kentucky than Tennessee or Missouri. By 1860, more than 85 percent of the Southern free Negro caste resided in the Upper South.

A second but considerably smaller group of free Negroes lived in the Lower South. As in the Upper South, the greatest proportion of free Negroes dwelled on the periphery in the port cities that stretched from Charleston on the Atlantic to New Orleans on the Gulf of Mexico and up the Mississippi River past Natchez to Memphis. The older states of the Lower South had resisted the post-Revolutionary manumission movement, and the newer states had either been unsettled or under foreign domination during the Revolutionary era. From the first, the free Negro population of the Lower South was largely the product of illicit sexual relations between black slave women and white men which led directly to manumission or to privileged positions from which elite slaves could buy their way out of bondage.

The distinctly different origins of free Negroes in the Upper

---

were unable to pass for whites were listed as "mulattoes." Naturally, census figures on the color of both the free Negro and slave populations must be viewed with even more than usual skepticism. *Negro Population, 1790–1915* (Washington, D.C., 1918), pp. 207, 220–1.

and Lower South were reflected in other characteristics as well. The free Negro population of the Lower South was much lighter than that of the Upper South. While the post-Revolutionary manumission movement and the continued decline of slavery in the border states encouraged slaveholders to emancipate black as well as mulatto slaves, miscegenation and selective emancipation produced a light-skinned population in the Lower South. The influx of brown émigrés from Saint-Domingue and elsewhere in the West Indies into the ports of the Lower South further widened the somatic gap between Lower and Upper South free Negroes. Ideological emancipation waned in the Upper South during the nineteenth century, and emancipators (except in the border states) adopted the pattern of manumission that had always been present in the Lower South. But a large free black—as opposed to mulatto—population had already established itself, and the comparatively small increment of mixed-bloods lightened the free Negro caste of the Upper South but did not alter its black majority. On the eve of the Civil War, mixed-bloods composed only a third of the free Negro population in the Upper South, while fully three-quarters of Lower South free Negroes had some white ancestry. In some of the port cities of the Lower South, mulattoes made up nearly 90 percent of the free Negro caste. Whites, recognizing the distinction between these light-skinned freemen and those of a darker hue, designated them "free people of color," a term used frequently in the Lower South but rarely in the Upper South.[63]

[63] "The term 'person of color' is a term of as settled significance and import as any to be found in our laws, or in common parlance. It is a term in general use all over the West Indies, and is never applied to any persons but those of *mixed blood* and who are *descended from negroes*"; *Charleston Mercury*, 16 August 1823. Also see O'Neall, *Negro Law of South Carolina*, p. 16; Dorothea O. McCants, ed., *They Came to Louisiana: Letters of a Catholic Mission, 1854–1882* (Baton Rouge, La., 1970), p. 28. In New Orleans, the term "quadroon" was also widely applied to all those of mixed ancestry, notwithstanding its specific allusion; Isaac Holmes, *An Account of the United States* (London, 1823), pp. 332–3; Christian Schultz, *Travels on an Inland Voyage . . . 1807 and 1808*, 2 vols. (New York, 1810), II, 195. But since the distinction between free mulattoes and blacks was never formally recognized by law, confusion remained. Sometimes whites in the Upper South applied "free people of color" to their dark-skinned free Negro caste, and even in the Lower South whites commonly used it to refer to all free Negroes, black and mulatto.

The free people of color of the Lower South were also more urban than those of the Upper South. Ideologically inspired manumission by the Revolutionary generation had created a large free black peasantry throughout the Upper South, and most stayed in the countryside. In 1860, barely a third of Upper South free Negroes lived in cities. Even Baltimore, which had the largest urban black population in the nation, contained less than a third of Maryland's free Negro population. On the other hand, better than half the free Negroes in the Lower South resided in urban areas.

Free Negroes were an even more anomalous group than their name suggests. Drawn from the slave elite, they were generally older and more urban than whites or slaves. A largely mulatto caste with ties of blood and kinship with black and white, they were clearly distinct from both. But the characteristics that distinguished free Negroes from whites and slaves were magnified in the free people of color of the Lower South. As a general rule, Lower South free Negroes were not only more urban and light-skinned, but better educated, more skilled, and more closely connected with whites than those of the Upper South. The South, in short, spawned two distinct groups of free Negroes. Their differences as well as their similarities reflected and influenced white racial attitudes. Those attitudes determined, in large measure, the free Negro's place in Southern society. The South was, after all, a white man's country.

6

A White Man's Country: White Racial Attitudes and Policies

> You may manumit a slave but you cannot make him into a white man.
>
> Robert G. Harper, *Letter to E. B. Caldwell* (1818)

THE desire to keep the South a white man's country governed white racial thought and policies throughout the antebellum years. Southerners could not conceive of a society in which whites and blacks lived as equals. They tolerated, even welcomed, large numbers of blacks so long as they were slaves who, however grudgingly, did their masters' bidding. But free Negroes, like unruly slaves, were out of "their place." By sharing the white man's proudest possession, free Negroes undermined the distinctions between white and black, free and slave, and challenged white racial ideals. To combat this threat, whites pushed free Negroes into "a social dungeon" and constantly rendered that dungeon "more dismal, damp, and gloomy."[1]

It took but scant provocation for whites to chip off another

[1] Ulrich B. Phillips, "The Central Theme of Southern History," *American Historical Review,* XXXIV (1928), 30–43; "Report of the Committee on Colored Population," *Maryland Legislative Documents,* 1843, doc. M, p. 47.

piece of the freemen's ever-shrinking liberty. In 1822, for instance, when Virginia legislators found the state penitentiary crowded and the treasury low, they ordered free Negro felons to be whipped and sold into slavery. Enthusiasm for the new penal system quickly spread to nearby Maryland and Delaware, both of which barred free Negro convicts from the state penitentiary and local jails and subjected them to the lash or to sale for a term of years out of the state.[2] Cries of inhumanity forced Virginia and Maryland to revoke these penal codes, although not before many free Negroes had been enslaved. But in repealing these bone-chilling enactments, lawmakers stiffened the penalties for free Negro criminals. In Virginia free Negro convicts served a minimum term of five years, and Maryland ordered criminal freemen banished upon pain of enslavement when their confinement was complete. Significantly, these Draconian measures were not a response to any real or imagined threat to white dominance.[3] A minor fiscal crisis was enough to encourage some whites to drive free Negroes into permanent bondage.

Although Southern whites almost uniformly feared and despised free Negroes, the nature of white racism differed greatly in the Upper and Lower South. The regional division which had appeared earlier over the African slave trade and was embodied in the diverse character of the free Negro caste widened during the antebellum years. Ideological lines never rigidly followed geographic boundaries, but each region developed its own views on race and slavery, which were reflected in its attitudes toward the free Negro. Inevitably some regional overlap of racial ideologies existed, and of course each section had its share of dissenters; yet within the context of the slave society, regional distinctiveness generally prevailed. At the bottom, these ideological differences reflected a divergence between a society of planters and a society of middling farmers, each of which was undergoing profoundly different demo-

2 "Report of the Committee to Examine the Penitentiary," *Journal of the House of Delegates of Virginia*, 1822–1823, app., pp. 18, 20–1; *ibid.*, 1823, p. 7; *Va. Laws*, 1822, c. 32; *Md. Laws*, 1825, c. 93; *Del. Laws*, 1826, c. 352, 1827, c. 50.

3 *Journal of the House of Delegates of Virginia*, 1824, pp. 6–7; *Journal of the Proceedings of the House of Delegates of Maryland*, 1826, pp. 47–8; *Va. Laws*, 1824, c. 45; *Md. Laws*, 1826, c. 229.

graphic, economic, and racial changes. But like all ideologies, they eventually took on a life of their own, separate and distinct from their material base. Taken together, the differences between the Upper and Lower South deeply affected the free Negro's place in Southern society.

The nagging belief that slavery was somehow wrong lingered in the Upper South and tempered the development of racial thought and policies. Few whites doubted that slavery was an essential means of controlling a culturally inferior race, but fewer still thought it was the best system for either blacks or whites. A continuing belief in the unity of creation and the universality of liberty impugned the idea of the happy slave. Although whites valued the benefits they wrung from slave labor and showed little disposition to relinquish them, they commonly lamented the ill effects of bondage on whites. Competition with black bondsmen devalued labor in the white man's eyes, deterred immigrants from settling in the South, drove off ambitious youth, and discouraged industry among those who remained. Casting a jealous eye on the rapid growth of population and wealth in the North, many Upper South whites openly denounced slavery as a drag on the economic development of the region. "Slavery is no longer compatible with progress," moaned one Marylander in 1845, "it is a dead weight and worse; it has become a wasting disease, weakening the vital power—a leprous distillment into the life blood of the commonwealth." Similar sentiments were echoed by Cassius Clay in Kentucky and others in northern Virginia. Yet, the old idea that slavery sapped white society of its vitality enjoyed its greatest popularity along the tidewater, where much of the land lay depleted from overuse and young men and women left for the West as soon as they came of age. Many whites believed that if slavery were gone, the "half-cultivated fields, dilapidated negro log huts, a dirty, slovenly negro population . . . whose happiness depends on their humility and ignorance" would disappear too. In their place would appear "neat farmhouses and well cultivated fields, such as delight the eye of the traveler in almost every free state." Land values would rise, taxes would fall, "our credit would be as high as our honor deserves," and sons and daughters would stay home.[4] Many Upper South whites longed to rid themselves of all Negroes and of slavery with them.

The desire to be free of Negroes was strengthened by the possibility that someday they would be gone. For generations, coffles of slaves had been trudging from the region to the rice swamps and cotton fields of the Lower South. The steady migration weakened slavery and stimulated manumission. Masters who believed slavery was a fetter on white industry often did not want to encumber their children with a legacy of slaveholding. Besides, the promise of future freedom might spur slave productivity and enable marginal farmers to turn a profit for at least a few more years. Although natural increase kept the number of slaves high in the Upper South, by the 1830s parts of Virginia and North Carolina were feeling the combined effects of migration and manumission. Already the governor of Delaware had conceded that manumission would eradicate bondage in that state within a generation, and Maryland slavery had begun a decline from which it would never recover.[5] If the process of Negro removal would not be completed in anyone's lifetime, at least some whites could conceive of a society without slaves, something that was impossible in the Lower South.

Toleration—not celebration—of slavery dominated racial thought in the Upper South. It allowed the Southern emancipation movement to stage a modest revival in the 1820s, so that by the end of that decade there were more antislavery societies in the Upper South than in the North.[6] It gave antislavery

[4] Carey, *Slavery in Maryland,* p. 33; R. S. Steuart, *Letter to John L. Carey on the Subject of Slavery* (Baltimore, 1845), pp. 6–7; also see debates over slavery in the Virginia legislature January to April 1832 in the *Richmond Enquirer,* especially 14 February 1832; *Richmond Whig,* 25 July 1845; Horace Greeley, ed., *The Writings of Cassius Marcellus Clay* (New York, 1848), pp. 224–6, 268–9; David L. Smiley, *The Lion of White Hall: The Life of Cassius M. Clay* (Madison, Wis., 1962); Reuben Dawson *et al., Address to the People of Kentucky, on the Subject of Emancipation* (n.p., [1849]).

[5] *Delaware Senate Journal,* 1823, p. 9.

[6] The history of the Southern antislavery movement is yet to be written. The standard work, Alice D. Adams, *The Neglected Period of Antislavery in America, 1808–1831* (Boston, 1908), is outdated in conception as well as available evidence. More useful are Gordon E. Finnie, "The Antislavery Movement in the Upper South Before 1840," *JSH,* XXXV (1969), 319–42; Merton L. Dillon, *Benjamin Lundy and the Struggle for Negro Freedom* (Urbana, Ill., 1966); Weeks, *Southern Quakers and Slavery;* Chase C. Mooney, *Slavery in Tennessee*

whites enough strength to launch major assaults on slavery in Virginia in 1831 and Kentucky in 1849 that shook the peculiar institution in those key states.[7] Still, no matter how intense their hatred of slavery, whites feared free Negroes even more. Southerners who willingly conceded the antislavery argument and bemoaned the detrimental effects of slavery on whites stood paralyzed by the thought of emancipation. However abhorrent, slavery was a necessity as long as blacks remained in the South.

The idea that slavery was a necessary evil bounded the white man's view of the free Negro in the Upper South. Free Negroes, he believed, were inveterate idlers and potential incendiaries who contaminated slaves and threatened white rule, but they were not natural slaves. The dangers inherent in allowing some blacks to be free induced lawmakers to strip Negro freemen of their rights, force them to work, and even pack them off to Africa, but few thought they should be reduced to slavery. The charges of inhumanity that forced Virginia and Maryland to repudiate enslavement as a punishment for criminal free Negroes suggest the continuing respect for liberty—even a black man's liberty. Although whites commonly boasted that bondsmen were better fed, clothed, and housed than free Negroes, hardly any yet felt the need to follow that idea to its logical conclusion.

For most Upper South whites, Negroes were rational if culturally inferior beings capable of improvement and desirous of liberty. Whites did not need to invent a theory of innate inferiority to show why many free Negroes were poor, shiftless, and criminal. Cut off from education, deprived of many of the possibilities for economic advancement, and denied recognition by the larger society, they naturally fell to the base of the social order. A disproportionate number of the state's crim-

---

(Bloomington, Ind., 1957), chap. 3; J. Winston Coleman, Jr., *Slavery Times in Kentucky* (Chapel Hill, N.C., 1940), pp. 270–325; Patrick Sowle, "The North Carolina Manumission Society," *North Carolina Historical Review*, XLII (1965), 47–69.

[7] Joseph C. Robert, *The Road from Monticello: A Study of the Debate of 1832* (Durham, N.C., 1941). There is no adequate study of the Kentucky Debates in 1849, although the record of the Constitutional Convention is full; *Report of the Debates and Proceedings of the Convention for the Revision of the Constitution of the State of Kentucky* (Frankfort, 1849).

inals were free Negroes, admitted a writer to a leading Richmond newspaper, but what else could be expected of a people barred from the benefits of "civilization"? Crime was ever the poor man's lot, and the same charges leveled against free Negroes were hurled at the poor in Europe: "Here color marks that scale; and we attribute to race that which belongs to class."[8] With the proper incentives, whites had no doubt free Negroes could improve themselves. Indeed, this was precisely what made them so dangerous. Offered the chance, admitted a Maryland lawmaker, "coloured freedmen will become men of like passions with white men. These passions will gather a strength with time. They will desire to add house to house, field to field." The struggle for liberty would not stop at the countinghouse; it would lead to the statehouse and eventually to the bedroom. "The moment a free mulatto obtains a little property, and is favored by being admitted to vote, he will . . . soon connect himself with a white woman," intoned a North Carolina lawmaker.[9] The black man's "passion" for liberty exposed the white man's deepest fears.

White prejudice, not natural law, barred free Negroes from full participation in Southern society. Whites in the Upper South frankly admitted this. The Founding Fathers wrote the principles of white rule into the Constitution, observed a representative to the Tennessee Constitutional Convention in 1834. By " 'We, the people of the United States,' they meant we the *free white* people . . . and the free white people only." The Negro was an unassimilable alien who had to be nailed to the lowest rung of the social ladder. Neither freedom nor good work could force whites to recognize him as an equal. "Be their industry ever so great and their conduct ever so correct, whatever property they may acquire or whatever respect we may feel for their character," declared a Maryland Federalist in 1818, "we could never consent, and they could never hope to see . . . free blacks or their descendants visit our houses, form part of our circle of acquaintances, marry

[8] Richmond *Daily Dispatch*, 9 March 1853; also see *African Repository*, IX (January, 1834), 324–5; George M. Fredrickson, *The Black Image in the White Mind: The Debate on Afro-American Character and Destiny, 1817–1914* (New York, 1971), chap. 1, especially pp. 6–21.

[9] *Maryland Colonization Journal*, I (August 1838), 77, (September 1838), 82; *Proceedings and Debates of the Convention of North-Carolina*, p. 71.

into our families, or participate in public honours or employment."[10]

Republican government, from the American view, depended on an interested and virtuous citizenry. Barred from respectable society, excluded from public office, and prevented from fulfilling their natural desire to better themselves, free Negroes could have no interest in the good order of Southern society, for they would fare as well under any other system. With little attachment to the government, naturally they would be the first to try to undermine it. In any dispute between whites and their slaves, free Negroes could be expected to stand with those in bondage. The fact that Upper South freemen, like slaves, were overwhelmingly black in color and rural in residence reinforced the long-standing belief that free blacks were more black than free. "Their interests and associations," observed a Tennessee lawyer, "are identified and blended with the slave, and what is for the benefit of one is for the benefit of the other—both adverse and hostile to the interest of the white man."[11] True to the memory of the Revolution, whites in the Upper South could not escape the belief that oppressed men were incorrigible subversives.

In the white mind, the free Negro was considerably more dangerous than the slave. Although free Negroes, with the exception of Denmark Vesey, rarely had anything to do with slave insurrections, whites uniformly identified them as the most rebellious. Following the Nat Turner rebellion of 1831, whites directed their frenzied outrage not so much against slaves as against free Negroes. In Southside Virginia, near the scene of the rebellion, white mobs roamed the countryside, assaulting free Negroes and forcing them to take refuge in the woods for months after. Townspeople in Raleigh, North Carolina, fearing that the rebellion would spread, clapped every free Negro into jail. Perhaps that was for the best, for in a nearby county a gang of white toughs kicked down the door to one free Negro's home and murdered the entire family.

[10] *Nashville Republican,* 15 July 1834; Robert G. Harper, *Letter to E. B. Caldwell, Secretary of the American Society for Colonizing Free People of Color of the United States* (Baltimore, 1818), p. 7.

[11] *Proceedings and Debates of the Convention of North-Carolina,* p. 78; *Nashville Republican,* 5 July 1834.

Officials captured one of the killers, but there seemed little chance that he would be brought to justice. "The mere imprisonment of this man has already aroused considerable excitement among the nonslaveholding population," observed a local white.[12] These assaults were more than outrages by poor whites. From all over Virginia and Maryland poured demands for the physical removal of free Negroes. In isolated Northampton County on the Eastern Shore of Virginia, leading citizens met and decided it was "absolutely necessary" to rid the county of Negro freemen. They agreed not to employ free Negroes or rent them land or houses, and eventually borrowed $15,000 from the state to facilitate deportation.[13] Yet only a handful of free Negroes were implicated in the Nat Turner rebellion, and after the postinsurrection hysteria subsided, most of the free Negroes arrested in Southampton County were quietly released.[14]

As far as free Negroes were concerned, Southampton was no isolated incident. Whenever the South felt threatened, free Negroes suffered hard times. The success of Toussaint L'Ouverture, the Missouri Crisis, the Vesey conspiracy, the advent of Garrisonian abolition, all stimulated assaults on the free Negroes' liberty and often their persons. In part, free Negroes simply provided the handiest scapegoats. It made no sense to cripple valuable slave property or to limit the liberty of those who had none. The slaves' position, which sheltered them from white vigilantism, seemed to intensify the abuse heaped on the free Negroes. Their presence reminded a people who professed, above all, to value liberty and despise tyranny that they themselves were tyrants. And it told them that the Negro—however fawning and servile in appearance—would ever be a foe. The free Negro, in short, personified the dangers and guilt inherent in owning slaves.

[12] *African Repository,* VII (October 1831), 245–7; John McPhail to R. R. Gurley, 23 September 1831, John C. Ehringhaus to R. R. Gurley, 29 September 1831, ACS.

[13] Annapolis *Maryland Gazette,* 12 January 1832; *Richmond Enquirer,* 11 November 1831; Petition from Northampton County, 6 December 1831, VLP; *Va. Laws,* 1831, c. 23.

[14] Henry I. Tragle, ed., *The Southampton Slave Revolt of 1831: A Compilation of Source Material* (Amherst, Mass., 1971), pp. 61, 97, 180–1, 209 n., 229–45.

Given these beliefs, whites did not need to degrade free Negroes on the scale of being to deprive them of their rights. Characteristically, the 1834 Tennessee and the 1835 North Carolina constitutional conventions disfranchised the free Negro without discussing the nature of the Negro at all. Questions of "*policy and expediency*," as one Tennessee delegate emphasized, provided reason enough to take away the freemen's suffrage in states where property-holding free Negroes had long voted according to the same requirements as whites. When the opponents of Negro disfranchisement suggested that suffrage was the natural right of all free men, restrictionists did not feel compelled to counter, as many later would, that Negroes were not men. They denied free Negroes the right to vote for the same reason they barred women from the polls: it contradicted the "manners and habits" of the country.[15] Circumstances and beliefs, not divine strictures or natural law, made disfranchisement necessary.

Because whites believed free Negroes to be men and women like themselves, they could not trust them to be a buffer class between whites and slaves who would ally themselves with slaveholders and serve as a safety valve for black discontent. This role, common in Latin America and to a lesser extent in the Lower South, was unacceptable in the Upper South precisely because whites could not conceive of free people permanently accepting limited liberty. When the opponents of disfranchisement in North Carolina suggested that free Negro loyalty might be purchased by allowing a few wealthy free Negroes token privileges, they met stormy resistance. Although such a policy aimed to use free Negroes as a tool of white domination and only incidentally raised the freemen's status, it frightened most delegates. One representative warned that these token rights would bring swarms of free Negroes from all parts of the United States into North Carolina; eventually they might preponderate and threaten white dominance. Admitting any Negro to a degree of equality with whites in-

[15] For the Tennessee and North Carolina debates on Negro disfranchisement see *Nashville Republican*, 1–15 July 1834 and *The Proceedings and Debates of the Convention of North-Carolina*, pp. 60–82, 351–8. Quotations in *Nashville Republican*, 15 July 1834. An exception may be the speech of W. H. Loving at the Tennessee Convention, *ibid.*, 5 July 1834.

evitably shook the entire system of white control. "If they are to be placed in the situation of free men, and to be our equals," noted another delegate, "why not admit our slaves to the same equality?" The predictable answer to that rhetorical question was not long in coming: "This is, to my mind, a *nation of white people*. . . ."[16] In the end, North Carolina, like Tennessee, disfranchised wealthy free Negroes while allowing all white men to vote.

Nevertheless, many whites felt uncomfortable in the tyrant's role. Occasionally, their lingering attachment to the equalitarianism of the Revolutionary era broke through the encrusted racism. One delegate to the North Carolina convention bridled at taking the freemen's suffrage because "he always felt extremely reluctant to deprive any human being of a right." Another adamant opponent of disfranchisement affirmed that "if he could not render the situation of a human being more eligible, he would not make it more ineligible." As long as expediency and not natural or divine law governed white racial policy, the opponents of free Negro restriction could argue from the same premises as those who favored it. At the Tennessee and North Carolina conventions, supporters of the free Negro's right to vote put expediency behind black suffrage. Reminding the convention that the Saint-Domingue rebellion began when the French deprived free Negroes of long-cherished liberties, some delegates denounced disfranchisement as impolitic.[17] Such arguments did not win out, but the powerful opposition to disfranchising free Negroes revealed their strength. In Tennessee, free Negroes were deprived of the vote by a 33 to 23 margin, and in North Carolina, where free Negroes enjoyed some electoral power, a change of three votes out of over one hundred would have reversed the outcome.[18] The arguments used to oppose disfranchisement, although clearly a secondary theme, provided thin but

[16] *Proceedings and Debates of the Convention of North-Carolina*, pp. 62, 356.

[17] *Ibid.*, p. 352.

[18] *Journal of the Convention of the State of Tennessee* (Nashville, 1834), pp. 208–9; *Proceedings and Debates of the Convention of North-Carolina*, pp. 80–1. A second attempt at the North Carolina convention to allow some wealthy freemen to vote was defeated 64 to 55; *ibid.*, pp. 357–8. For an analysis of the disfranchisement vote in the North Carolina convention, see Franklin, *Free Negro in North Carolina*, pp. 109–16.

nonetheless important protection against white racial oppression.

Free Negroes did not have to depend on white liberality alone for defense against rampant racism. The reluctance of whites to work at trades identified with blacks and the continual drain of slaves from the Upper South made free Negro labor increasingly important during the antebellum years. Throughout the Upper South, but especially along the tidewater and in the cities, free Negroes were an important and often an indispensable part of the labor force. "It is unquestionable," noted a Maryland lawmaker, "that quite a large part of our soil would not be tilled without their aid." Even where free Negroes were not numerous enough to be indispensable, their presence gave a flexibility otherwise unobtainable to the labor-starved economy of the Upper South. In many places, free Negroes did seasonal or occasional work, harvested crops, fished, and manned the boats that traversed the rivers of the region. The availability of free Negro workers often permitted yeomen farmers who were unable to purchase slaves, or enough slaves, to turn a profit. There are "many families in the state," observed a Virginia newspaper, "whose condition is such that they cannot afford the luxury of a servant, at the present high rate of hire, but who are in the habit of hiring free Negroes, for one or two days a week, to perform those offices for which a slave is indispensable."[19] The freemen's labor not only allowed nonslaveholders fuller participation in the Southern economy but also permitted them to lord it over black workers and vicariously to enjoy the privileges of a planter. In giving nonslaveholders a chance to flaunt their white skin, the free Negro indirectly strengthened the slave regime. But the belief that free Negroes were "necessary adjuncts" to the slave society who did useful and even indispensable work also acted as the most important bulwark against white repression in the Upper South.

In the Lower South, this antidote to white racism was considerably less potent. Only in the cities and in parts of rural Louisiana did free Negroes compose a substantial portion of

[19] *Baltimore American,* 9 June 1859; clipping from the *Richmond Whig,* n.d., with W. H. S[tarr] to ? , February 1858, ACS; Petition from Westmoreland County, 9 March 1838, VSL.

the work force. A rapidly growing slave population served the needs of planters and was the basis of the prosperity of the region. Lower South whites denied that slavery was an unfortunate expedient which either disrupted the economy or drove off their children. Instead, they saw it as the source of all wealth and the foundation of white unity. Increasingly, but by no means universally, they celebrated slavery as the best system for blacks as well as whites. "The African negro is destined by Providence to occupy this condition of servile dependence . . . ," exclaimed George McDuffie, the governor of South Carolina, in 1835. "They have all the qualities which fit them to be slaves, and not one of those that would fit them to be free men." It was not merely the benefits of liberty that distinguished blacks from whites. No incentive could raise the African above the mudsill of civilization, for God had placed them a step below whites. The Negro was a lesser human being than the white, perhaps even a different species. "Personal observation must convince every candid man," declared William Drayton of Charleston, "that the negro is constitutionally indolent, voluptuous, and prone to vice; that his mind is heavy, dull, and unambitious; and that the doom which made the African in all ages and countries, a slave—is the natural consequence of the inferiority of his character."[20]

The belief that Negroes were natural slaves did not come easily even in the Lower South. Although the positive-good argument had deep roots in the racial thought of the region, whites were slow in systematizing that defense of slavery. Probably most whites found such a powerful argument superfluous as long as slavery went unchallenged. Perhaps those prescient enough to peek into the corners of the positive-good logic saw that it necessitated a denial of the ideas of the Declaration of Independence and a rewriting of the Biblical

[20] *Journal of the General Assembly of the State of South Carolina,* 1835, p. 6; [William Drayton], *The South Vindicated from the Treason and Fanaticism of the Northern Abolitionists* (Philadelphia, 1836), pp. 232–3. For the development of positive-good argument in the Lower South, see William W. Freehling, *Prelude to Civil War: The Nullification Crisis in South Carolina, 1816–1836* (New York, 1966), chap. 3; Fredrickson, *Black Image in the White Mind,* pp. 46–70. Such sentiment could be heard in the Upper South, but, as Fredrickson points out in his analysis of the racial ideas of Thomas R. Dew, the so-called positive-good theorist, it was ambiguous and still confused with the necessary-evil arguments; *ibid.,* 44–6.

story of creation. Many were unwilling to make that leap. Into the 1840s, many, perhaps most, Lower South whites continued to talk of the Negro as subject to the same "operations of human nature" as themselves. Even in South Carolina, the heartland of positive-good thought, opposition to this more assertive defense of slavery survived. "Negroes are not what some would make them out to be," warned a prominent Charleston minister in 1845; "they are capable of . . . being influenced by good principles."[21] Nevertheless, promoted by powerful men like Drayton, McDuffie, and Calhoun and spurred on by Northern attacks on the sin of slaveholding, the positive-good argument gave the racial thought of the Lower South a distinctive tone.

Positive-good theory left little place for the free Negro. If slavery was the natural state for blacks, freedom was an impossible anomaly. "Emancipation would be a positive curse," asserted McDuffie, "depriving them of a guardianship essential to their happiness. . . ."[22] The poverty, indolence, and criminality that whites identified with the free Negro were not the legacy of slavery or the result of white prejudice, but simply the product of the Negro's innately limited abilities. Only bondage allowed blacks to lead a normal, useful life. Although positive-good ideologues rarely pressed their case, the logic of their argument held inherent dangers to the free Negro's liberty.

Paradoxically, positive-good thought also provided free Negroes with a modicum of protection against white racism. For once whites accepted the logic of the positive-good argument, free Negroes seemed less threatening. No longer was the free Negro an incorrigible subversive, longing for liberty and locked in a mortal struggle with the white oppressor. Nature had so debased blacks that they hardly endangered whites. Some positive-good theorists maintained that blacks had neither the will nor the ability to overthrow white rule.[23] To

[21] *Proceedings of a Meeting in Charleston, S.C., May 13–15, 1845, on the Religious Instruction of the Negroes* (Charleston, 1845), p. 42; Natchez *Mississippi Free Trader*, 12 August 1841.

[22] *Journal of the General Assembly of the State of South Carolina*, 1835, pp. 6–7.

[23] [Drayton], *The South Vindicated*, p. 300.

the extent that the belief that Negroes were natural slaves made whites more secure, free Negroes benefitted. Of all the Southern states, South Carolina had one of the mildest free Negro codes. Its measured reaction of the Vesey conspiracy contrasted markedly with the wild hysteria that gripped Virginia in the wake of the Nat Turner rebellion. During the 1840s and 1850s, while other states tightened the clamps on the freemen's liberty, South Carolina lawmakers hardly took notice of the free Negro caste. When they did, legislators did not blast free Negroes with their pent-up fears and anxieties as was commonly the case in the Upper South. Instead, they often expressed sympathy for the free Negro who floundered hopelessly in the white world. In 1858, the Committee on Colored Population of the South Carolina legislature brushed aside demands for new restrictions on the free Negro's rights by declaring them "unjust and inhuman . . . to a class . . . whose disabilities should entitle them to our protection & sympathy."[24] The easy confidence of Lower South whites in their superiority over a comparatively small free Negro population bred a willingness to tolerate the anomalous caste.

The patriarchal ideology of the plantation regime reinforced this acceptance of the free Negro. The planters of the Lower South liked to view their plantations not merely as money-making enterprises but as families, and they preferred to see their slaves, not as employees, but as "their people" or even "their children." Slaveholders adopted the symbolic role of father to their slaves to legitimize their rule and reinforce the slave's dependence. With stern justice, they meted out rewards and punishments and demanded the deference due their position.[25] This paternalism had special meaning when applied to the light-skinned free people of color of the Lower South, who very often were the planters' children; ideology and

[24] "Report of Committee on Colored Population," 6 December 1858, with Fairfield County Grand Jury Presentment, Spring 1858, Grand Jury Presentments, SCA.

[25] Eugene D. Genovese, *The Political Economy of Slavery: Studies in the Economy and Society of the Slave South* (New York, 1965), and *The World the Slaveholders Made: Two Essays in Interpretation* (New York, 1969); Eric R. Wolf, "Specific Aspects of Plantation Systems in the New World: Community Sub-Cultures and Social Classes," in Michael M. Horowitz, ed., *People and Cultures of the Caribbean* (New York, 1971), especially pp. 167–9.

reality blended in the white view of the free Negro caste. If the presence of a largely black and rural free Negro population in the Upper South tended to identify the free Negro with the slave, the overwhelmingly mulatto population of the Lower South suggested a different kind of alliance.

Lower South whites treated mixed-bloods with special consideration. Although many whites despised mulattoes as haughty bastards whose arrogance made them more dangerous than the blacks, the close connections between mulattoes and whites and the general sympathy for a people who looked so much like themselves generally shifted the balance of opinion. Not only was it easier for light-skinned freemen to pass for white in the Lower South, but once they were accepted as "white," few questions were asked. A South Carolina judge saw nothing strange in the fact that many mixed-bloods who had passed for white "now enjoy all the rights of citizens; [and] some who have lost that distinctive mark, hold offices, as well as lands, and even seats in the legislature." Similarly, when an Alabama prosecutor tried to charge one light-skinned rapist under the free Negro code, a Supreme Court justice abruptly dismissed the case, declaring: "If the statute against mulattoes is by construction to include quadroons, then where are we to stop? . . . are we not bound to pursue the line of descendants, as long as there is a drop of negro blood remaining?"[26] The Lower South's relatively porous color line made whites wary about pressing the distinction between white and black too far.

The somatic similarities between whites and light-skinned freemen also encouraged whites to share their prized attributes with mixed-bloods. Some Lower South whites, following the logic of positive-good thought, speculated that the mulatto was a race distinct from the Negro. The product of "two distinct species—as the mule from the horse and the ass," the mulatto was more intelligent than blacks although naturally not as bright as whites. In short, to the extent that "white blood" coursed through their veins, mixed-bloods were whites. Richard Arnold, a Savannah physician and politician, stated the principle explicitly: "I know that the greater the mixture of Cau-

[26] Catterall, ed., *Judicial Cases Concerning Slavery,* II, 334–5, III, 176.

casian Blood the more liable the subjects to be affected simularly [*sic*] to the white. The Mulatto is almost useless as a field hand, not being able to bear the rays of the sun with the same impunity as his sable brother." Reasoning from the same premises, a Georgia newspaper warned light-skinned free Negroes not to migrate to Africa. Not only would they have to war with full-blooded Africans as they had in Saint-Domingue, but mixed-bloods could not survive the hot African sun.[27]

The nature of slavery in the Lower South supported the idea that free people of color were a separate caste distinct from both whites and slaves. Beginning late in the eighteenth century, changes in the economy and society steadily ameliorated the lot of the slave in the Upper South. In the Lower South, no such improvement took place. Instead, the pressures for ever higher productivity debased the conditions of plantation slavery. Although slavery was slavery, the fear in which Upper South bondsmen held being "sold down the river" suggests the extent of the regional differences in bondage. The degradation of slave life in the Lower South elevated the free Negro caste. The greater the distinction whites were able to make between slaves and free Negroes, the greater their willingness to accept Negro freemen as a distinct part of the social order. While the improvement of slave conditions in the Upper South shrank the differences between slaves and free Negroes, the debasement of slave life in the Lower South magnified them. Lower South whites, unlike those of the Upper South, could conceive of free Negroes standing apart from the slaves.

The close connections with whites, light skin, urban residence, comparatively high occupational status, and the very name "free people of color" distinguished Lower South free

[27] Josiah C. Nott, "The Mulatto a Hybrid—Probable Extermination of the Two Races If the Whites and Blacks Are Allowed to Intermarry," *American Journal of the Medical Sciences,* VI (1843), 254; Richard H. Shryock, ed., *Letters of Richard D. Arnold, M.D., 1808–1876* (Durham, N.C., 1929), pp. 33, 66–7; *Savannah Morning News,* 20 February 1851; also see Stanton, *The Leopard's Spots,* pp. 66–8. The image of the mulatto in the Lower South again illustrates the influence of the West Indies on the Lower South. Like Arnold, one Jamaican planter believed that "on the sugar estates one black is considered as more than equal to two mulattoes"; Edward Braithwaithe, *The Development of Creole Society in Jamaica, 1770–1820* (London, 1971), p. 177; also Goveia, *Slave Society in the British Leeward Islands,* 231–2.

Negroes from the overwhelmingly black, rural slaves and raised the free Negro's standing in Southern society. Whenever the specter of Negroes—free and slave, brown and black—united against whites was posed, there were whites aplenty to deny the possibility of such an alliance. Whites in the Lower South displayed a remarkable ability to resist the Upper South tendency to jumble all Negroes together. Edwin C. Holland, one of the few South Carolinians to urge the forcible expulsion of free blacks in the aftermath of the Vesey conspiracy, made it clear that he aimed his demands at full-blooded free Negroes only. While he attacked free blacks as "an idle, lazy, insolent set of vagabonds, who lived by theft or gambling," he lavished praise on free mulattoes as "industrious, sober, hard-working mechanics, who have large families and considerable property." Warning authorities that failure to expel free blacks would lead to endless rounds of rebellion, he suggested that free mulattoes would play a very different role. "They are in our estimation . . . a barrier between our own color and that of the black—and in case of *insurrection*, are more likely to enlist themselves under the banner of the whites."[28] Holland singled out successful free mulattoes as worthy of trust, but since most Lower South free Negroes were of mixed racial origins his ideas reflected white attitudes toward the entire caste. "The relation of the free colored people and the slave is not one which gives any apprehension as to the quiet and contentment of the latter," declared a leading New Orleans daily. "Those who are free and in good circumstances regard the slave with more disdain and antagonism than the white man. . . ."[29] Ties of blood and a shared life-style cut across the color line to nurture a belief that some free Negroes might be more free than Negro. The elevated status of the free people of color and the lowly condition of slaves in the Lower South allowed a three-caste system much like that of the West Indies to develop wherever free Negroes were numerous. The idea that the free people of color were dependable and useful allies who offered

[28] [Edwin C. Holland], *A Refutation of the Calumnies Circulated Against the Southern and Western States, Respecting the Institution of Slavery* (Charleston, 1822), pp. 83–5. For the importance of "somatic distance" in determining patterns of race relations, see Harmannus Hoetink, *Caribbean Race Relations: A Study of Two Variants* (London, 1967), pp. 120–90, especially pp. 153–60.
[29] *New Orleans Daily Delta*, 17 July 1852.

whites an ear in the enemy camp guarded the free Negro's existence in the Lower South.

Although all white Southerners shared the desire to subordinate free Negroes, the different racial attitudes of Upper and Lower South whites spawned two distinctive approaches to controlling the anomalous caste. In part, these differences in racial policy reflected the diverse character of the free Negro caste. The large, rural free black population of the Upper South posed very different problems of control than the small number of urban free people of color in the Lower South. But again, regional variations in economy, in social structure, and most important, in the direction of development accentuated these differences. More than anything else, the white man's vision of the future of the South shaped his racial policies toward the free Negro. Upper South whites lived in a declining slave society whose edges already showed signs of fraying and whose future was uncertain. The steady drain of slaves from the border regions by sale and manumission forced Upper South whites to wonder where their society was going and what life would be like for their posterity. In the Lower South, whites had no such doubts. Riding the crest of the great cotton boom, they were confident of their future, certain that their children would live as they had. The diversity of racial policies thus measured not only the regional differences in the character of the free Negro caste, but the diverging hopes and fears of Southern whites.

The desire to be rid of free Negroes, perhaps all Negroes, stood at the heart of the racial policies of the Upper South. Believing that blacks were a people yearning for liberty but forever barred from enjoying it in America, Upper South whites saw only three alternatives: amalgamation, race war, or physical separation. Amalgamation was too repulsive even to consider. Any man would gladly consign "his daughter to a silent tomb," intoned one Maryland legislator, "than see her led to the hymenial altar by the hand of a colored man." Race war was equally frightening. Although whites boasted of their confidence in the outcome of such a conflict—not a single Negro "would be left to tell the tale of his sorrows"—they despaired of the bloody and inhuman results. By reduction, the solution became obvious: "Amalgamation is futile in the extreme, extermination we all would avoid, and the only rational and Christian alternative is colonization."[30]

Colonization was more than the last desperate alternative. Southern emancipationists who had been stymied by the stony logic of the necessary-evil argument believed that colonization would neutralize the most potent objection to gradual abolition. Since whites were most fearful of blacks who were free, removing manumitted Negroes would disarm popular opposition to emancipation and make masters more willing to liberate their slaves.[31] In fact, colonizationists tried to avoid the term "emancipation" and talked instead of extirpation, implying that blacks would be pushed out of the region with slavery. Their grand design was to nibble away at slavery in the border regions by manumission and deportation. As slavery declined, white workers would replace black and naturally provide more efficient—hence cheaper—labor, which in turn would further speed the eradication of bondage. Emancipation in Maryland, argued John H. B. Latrobe, a leading colonizationist, in 1833, would influence other border states and would eventually place the states to the south under pressure to do the same. Ultimately, it would "thrust the dividing line between the free states and the slave states southward, and having given a free neighbor to Virginia," the process would begin anew until slavery was cleared from the land.[32]

Of inestimable value to whites, colonization would also be a blessing to blacks. Freed of the weight of white prejudice, free Negroes could enjoy the liberty with which God endowed all men. Transportation to Africa, wrote Virginia colonization-

[30] *Maryland Colonization Journal,* I (August 1838), 77; new ser., I (June 1841), 1–15.

[31] Benjamin Swain to Isaac Barton, 13 June 1827, PAS; for growing colonization sentiment within the Southern antislavery movement, see H. M. Wagstaff, ed., *Minutes of the N.C. Manumission Society, 1816–1834* (Chapel Hill, 1934), pp. 20, 35–38, 42–5, 56–8, 61–8; Fredrickson, *Black Image in the White Mind,* pp. 9–10.

[32] Latrobe to R. R. Gurley, 27 January 1827, Latrobe to ACS Board of Managers, 29 December 1834, also James Birney to R. R. Gurley, 24 September 1833, ACS; Latrobe to William McKinney, 24 June 1833, Latrobe to Cortland Van Rensselaer, 10 July 1833, quotation in Latrobe to B. B. Thatcher, 23 July 1833, Corresponding Secretary's Letterbook, MdSCS Papers.

ists, "wipes from his character, the obloquy which here rests upon it, and opens before his vision a bright prospect of usefulness and happiness, and freedom. In a word, it translates him from 'darkness into light.'" While the free Negro in the United States was condemned as hopelessly degraded, once in Africa he became a superman capable of converting the "dark continent" to republicanism, Christianity, and the commercial economy. "It is not altogether illogical," colonizationists assured themselves, ". . . that because free black men do not thrive in the United States . . . free blacks cannot thrive anywhere."[33]

Whatever the leadership of the colonization movement desired, many of their strongest supporters wanted only to be rid of free Negroes. Some clearly hoped that deportation would strengthen slavery by freeing the region of a caste they deemed subversive. After one stormy meeting, Latrobe admitted that although many "looked to colonization as a means of *extirpating* slavery," others saw it only "as a means of *perpetuating* it." Bidding for legislative support, leading colonizationists frequently discovered they had little in common with many of their warmest friends. The great supporters of deportation in the Maryland legislature, reported one chagrined lobbyist, backed it from "views more circumscribed. They are in favor of getting clear of *free blacks,* and *there they stop.*" Gradual emancipation made them "wince," and they opposed colonization "in its amplified features."[34]

The vehement opposition to any proposal that smacked of emancipation forced colonizationists to cater to the anti–free Negro element of their constituency. Increasingly, the emancipationist impulse which early characterized the colonization movement was buried under the demands that free blacks be shipped off to Africa. To win slaveholder approval, some colonization societies warned their agents "to avoid everything relating to the question of slavery." Instead, they emphasized the degraded condition of the freemen and the benefits that

33 *African Repository,* V (March 1829), 18, XXIV (May 1848), 143, XXVII (July 1851), 204–6.

34 Latrobe to Cortland Van Rensselaer, 10 July 1833, Corresponding Secretary's Letterbook, MdSCS Papers; William McKinney to Thomas Emory, 24 January 1832, Agent's Letterbook, MdSCS Papers; also see St. Louis *Missouri Gazette,* 23 March 1817, and St. Louis *Missouri Republican,* 9 March 1827.

would accrue to whites once free blacks were gone. They reiterated their reverence for the rights of the master and lauded colonization as a bulwark against fanatical Northern abolitionism. Although many colonizationists saw these genuflections to the slaveholder as tactical concessions that did not alter the goal of eventual emancipation, they gave away too much. In yielding to the slaveholder, colonization lost its moral authority as an antislavery movement and alienated the only people who could assure its success—the free blacks.[35]

Nevertheless, propelled by the often contradictory support of would-be emancipationists and confirmed slaveholders, colonization sentiment flourished in the Upper South. In 1817, leading statesmen and clergy from the region joined with conservative Northern reformers to found the American Colonization Society. Agents of the society swarmed over the region, enlisting members, peddling the *African Repository*, and founding auxiliary societies. Soon the groundswell of support was felt in Upper South legislatures. In 1826, Maryland appropriated a thousand dollars annually for the support of the state auxiliary. The following year, Delaware, Kentucky, and Tennessee endorsed colonization, and Virginia, which had reaffirmed its support in 1816, seemed on the verge of giving the society financial aid.[36]

Virginia legislators rejected the society's plea for funds, but colonizationist strength surged again in the 1830s. Nat Turner's rebellion sparked new demands to be rid of the free Negro. In 1831, during its debate on the restriction of manumission, the Maryland General Assembly considered Virginia's policy of re-enslaving emancipated Negroes who failed to leave the

[35] J. H. B. Latrobe to William Handy, 20 October 1837, Latrobe Letterbook, MdSCS Papers; for the abolitionist critique of colonization, see William Lloyd Garrison, *Thoughts on African Colonization* (Boston, 1832); [William Lloyd Garrison], *The Maryland Scheme of Expatriation Examined* (Boston, 1834). This, however, does not detract from the fact that many colonizationists remained opposed to slavery. The point is well made by Fredrickson, *Black Image in the White Mind*, pp. 9–10.

[36] Staudenraus, *African Colonization Movement*, pp. 69–116, 169–84; *Md. Laws*, 1826, c. 172; *African Repository*, V (November 1829), 302–5; *Va. Laws*, 1816, Resolution 1; Benjamin Brand to R. R. Gurley, 11 December 1827, ACS; "Report of the Committee [on Colonization]," *Journal of the House of Delegates of Virginia*, 1827.

state. The proposal aroused a flurry of opposition, and the combination of humane pressure and the knowledge of Virginia's inability to enforce the removal requirement defeated the proposed restriction. But Maryland legislators balked at the continued growth of the state's free Negro population. To assure the removal of emancipated slaves and perhaps many already free Negroes, lawmakers appropriated $200,000 to be spent over twenty years to colonize emancipated slaves and consenting freemen in Africa.

The Maryland plan was the most ambitious Negro-removal scheme yet formulated. The legislature ordered county clerks to report all manumissions to a state-appointed Board of Managers for the Removal of Colored People, which instructed the rechartered Maryland State Colonization Society to remove the emancipated slaves to Africa or wherever else the society deemed suitable. Newly freed Negroes who wanted to remain in the state could choose re-enslavement or appeal to a county orphan's court to remain. Emancipated Negroes who rejected slavery and migration to Africa but were unable to obtain court permission to stay in the state might be forcibly deported.[37]

Virginia soon adopted a similar policy. In the aftermath of the great debate over slavery, Virginia lawmakers agreed to a five-year annual appropriation of $18,000 to transport newly emancipated slaves and free Negroes to Africa. Although larger than the Maryland grant, the Virginia appropriation was considerably more cautious. While Maryland authorized the State Colonization Society to spend public funds to publicize emigration and to develop an African colony, Virginia lawmakers agreed to pay only a maximum of $30 for each adult sent to Africa. Tennessee appropriated funds for colonization the following year, but was even more miserly. Its legislature granted the State Colonization Society $10 for each Negro sent to Liberia and fixed the maximum annual appropriation at $500.[38] Such niggardly appropriations doomed colonization, but still

[37] Penelope Campbell, *Maryland in Africa: The Maryland State Colonization Society, 1831–1857* (Urbana, Ill., 1971), pp. 30–8; *Md. Laws,* c. 281, c. 323.

[38] Robert, *Road from Monticello,* p. 34; *Va. Laws,* 1832, c. 13; *Tenn. Laws,* 1833, c. 44.

three Southern states had committed themselves to the idea of deporting free Negroes. Colonization was fast becoming the official policy of the Upper South.

The white man's increased interest in Negro removal only estranged blacks. The colonizationists' blatantly racist appeal brought immediate opposition from the supposed beneficiaries of white benevolence. In 1817, soon after the formation of the American Colonization Society, Richmond free Negroes cautiously attacked the removal policy. They agreed that many blacks might benefit from emigration, but declared their preference to be "colonized in the most remote corner of the land of our nativity, than to be exiled to a foreign country." To the north, free Negroes were even more determined not to be ousted from America. "Why should we abandon our firesides and everything associated with the dear name of *home*," asked Baltimore schoolmaster William Watkins in 1829, "undergo the fatigues of a perilous voyage, and expose ourselves, our wives, and our little ones, to the deleterious influences of an inconsequential sun, for the enjoyment of liberty divested of its usual accomplishments, surrounded with circumstances which diminish its intrinsic values . . . ?"[39] Watkins's views quickly spread. At a mass meeting in 1831, Baltimore free Negroes served notice that they had no intention of leaving. "We consider that land in which we were born our only 'true and appropriate home' and when we desire to remove we will apprise the public of the same, in due season."[40]

Free Negroes had little use for colonizationists who emphasized their degraded condition. What seemed to incense blacks most was the fact that colonizationists admitted blacks were people the equal of others and still refused to allow them to participate in American society. Free Negroes believed that if colonizationists were sincerely concerned with the welfare of blacks, they should attack slavery openly and work to improve the lot of the free Negro in America. In 1826, Jacob Greener, "a very clever black man," interrupted a Baltimore

[39] Garrison, *Thoughts on African Colonization*, app., pp. 62–5; "A Colored American," *Genius of Universal Emancipation*, 29 November 1829. "A Colored American" is identified as Watkins in Wendell Phillips Garrison and Francis Garrison, *William Lloyd Garrison, 1805–1879*, 4 vols. (Boston, 1885–9), I, 145 n.

[40] Garrison, *Thoughts on African Colonization*, app., pp. 21–2.

colonization meeting and demanded that "the first object of the colonization society should be to educate the coloured children." Like other Negro freemen, Greener complained that colonization aggravated their deprived condition and inflamed white prejudice by emphasizing their lowly status. Only by eliminating white prejudice and washing "from the 'stars and stripes' one of the blackest spots that ever cursed the globe" could colonizationists prove their friendship.[41] The white lecturer struggled uncomfortably under Greener's rapid-fire questioning and left the meeting without making a single convert.

Free Negroes did more than protest the deportation policy; they organized opposition so tightly that few emigrants could be found. Cities, with their large free Negro populations, became beehives of anticolonizationist activity. "The prejudices of the coloured people in Baltimore and other large Towns, against African Colonization, are so strong that distributing literature among them would be to throw it away," observed a Maryland colonizationist in 1832. The opposition of urban free Negroes demoralized the colonizationists, and they designed their pamphlets "principally for those who live in the Country and in the Villages."[42]

But urban freemen were soon out in the countryside stiffening rural resistance. Some colonization agents claimed free Negroes trailed them from village to village. After persuading a free Negro to migrate to Africa, one agent discovered, "in a day or two after, that someone had been after him, filling the mind of the emigrant . . . with alarming & false statements, and changing him from his purpose." Some of these anticolonization emissaries tried to frighten the rural free Negroes with stories of sale to the south or the West Indies. Colonization agents often found themselves welcomed by free Negroes one day and attacked the next as slave traders and kidnappers. When these tales failed to scare rural folk, urban free Negroes denounced would-be emigrants as "traitors to their race," arguing that "every emigrant to Africa diminished by one the numerical force upon which they had relied for extorting from

[41] *Ibid.*, pp. 39, 54; C. C. Harper to R. R. Gurley, 13 December 1826, ACS.

[42] C. C. Harper to R. R. Gurley, 1 August 1832, State Manager's Letterbook, MdSCS Papers; E. Minor Atkinson to William McLain, 7 March 1846, ACS.

the fears [of whites that] which they could not obtain by justice of the whites—political and social equality—called among the colored people in common parlance 'their rights.' . . ."[43]

Many rural free Negroes needed no prompting to stir their opposition to deportation. As soon as they heard whites were for it, they were against it. Free Negroes refused to believe "a white man would aid them," reported a Maryland agent in 1837. "The more you urge them," observed a Virginia minister, "the more they won't go. We must hold up emigration as a favor & a privilege granted them, for they will not do it to oblige us." Colonizationists sometimes tried to win black support by enlisting the aid of sympathetic blacks. In 1838, a white agent traveled through Maryland with Alexander Hance, a free Negro who had returned from Liberia to purchase his family. It was to no avail. "*I am represented as a negro trader*," the agent reported. "Hance subsidized by me. And both in league to secure the Confidence of the free blacks, that they may be sold into perpetual salvery."[44] Although whites doubtless exaggerated the conspiratorial scheming of urban freemen and underestimated the reluctance of a rural Negro peasantry to leave their homes, the universal opposition of free Negroes to colonization was undeniable.

Once potential emigrants reached the cities of embarkation, free Negroes administered final warnings about the dangers of emigration. Repeatedly, colonization agents found potential emigrants mysteriously vanishing. "Our slaves ought not to remain in Norfolk more than a few days," warned a Virginia agent in 1827, "for although they may consent to go to Africa, yet most of them would rather make their escape to New York or Phila. and would embrace any opportunity for doing it." Despite close supervision, few vessels left for Africa with a

[43] J. H. B. Latrobe to William Handy, 20 October 1837, Latrobe Letterbook, MdSCS Papers; John Kennard to J. H. B. Latrobe, 30 April 1838, Letters Received, MdSCS Papers; quotations in *Communication from the Board of Managers of the Maryland State Colonization Society to the President and Members of the Convention Now Assembled in Baltimore* (Baltimore, 1841), pp. 7–8, 12–13.

[44] John L. Hawkins to J. H. B. Latrobe, 4 April 1837, Letters Received, MdSCS Papers; D. I. Burr to R. R. Gurley, 5 November 1823, ACS; John H. Kennard to J. H. B. Latrobe, 30 April 1838, Letters Received, MdSCS Papers.

full contingent. Although many blacks needed no invitation to escape, everywhere free Negroes worked busily to convince them to remain in America. In 1831, Baltimore freemen visited potential emigrants and harangued them "not only in private houses, but in public meetings," until more than half refused to go. Still displeased that the ships would leave at all, free Negroes invaded departing vessels and recited their opposition to colonization one last time.[45] The free Negro's persistence undermined the white man's most durable racial desire.

While free Negroes disrupted removal plans, the meager appropriations and outright hostility of some whites doomed them. Farmers and fishermen who depended on free Negroes to harvest their corps and work their nets were reluctant to see them leave. Although many tidewater farmers joined the clamor against the evils of a large free Negro population, others viewed colonization as a scheme to rob them of their labor force. One Maryland yeoman frankly admitted that he opposed the colonization society because it would "make Labouring men scarce." In seeking potential emigrants, colonization agents had to contend not only with militant free Negroes but with angry farmers and fishermen as well. According to one North Carolina colonizationist, some of the free Negroes willing to leave for Africa were "prevented from Emigrating by the more wealthy who are in the habit of employing them to work on their farms."[46]

Driving free Negroes from the country did not solve the problems of the tidewater farmer. In 1838, when demands for the forcible expulsion of emancipated Negroes who had ignored the colonization law resounded in the Maryland legislature, lawmakers brushed them aside, noting that removal would be "productive of an immense loss to *land renters* . . .

[45] Benjamin Brand to R. R. Gurley, 8 January 1827, Charles Howard to R. R. Gurley, 18 November 1831, also see Benjamin Brand to R. R. Gurley, 20 August 1827, 3 November 1827, ACS.

[46] F. Henderson to Moses Sheppard, 29 October 1832, Letters Received, MdSCS Papers; J. W. Lugenbeel to William McLain, 18 October 1852, ACS; also see John L. Hawkins to J. H. B. Latrobe, Letters Received, MdSCS Papers; and Petitions from Fairfax County, 8 June 1839, Prince William County, 2 March 1839, VLP.

who work their land by hired labor." Forcing large numbers of free Negroes out of the state, the Committee on Colored Population admitted, would inflate wages and cause farmers to abandon their fields. Already besieged by the problems of a deepening depression, legislators refused to tamper with the state's dwindling labor supply.[47]

Reluctant to expel free Negro workers, farmers still needed some means of controlling their labor force. The steady increase of free Negroes and the decline of slavery during the 1830s pointed the direction of Upper South development and stimulated demands for a system of controlling free Negro workers. But at the source, these demands were more than a product of the need for the freemen's muscle. Southern racial ideology depicted whites as independent and self-reliant and blacks as dependent and servile. The realization that they were dependent on "lazy, irresponsible, lawless, and miserable free Negroes" to cultivate their fields angered whites.[48] They seemed to sense that the free Negroes' disregard for their carefully drawn contracts, sudden disappearance during harvest time, and refusal to work under the same conditions as slaves indicated more than natural indolence or even the lingering effects of slavery. Reliance on black workers gave free Negroes a measure of power which whites found intolerable.

Tidewater whites searched for some means to strip free Negroes of the power that accrued to them by virtue of control over their own labor. Delaware planters urged lawmakers to empower "our farmers and housekeepers to *compel* such as otherwise would be idle and worthless to enter into engagements for the month or the year, at the customary wage." Similar demands resounded throughout the tidewater during the late 1830s, and legislation to translate those pleas into law was soon wending its way through the Maryland General Assembly. In 1840, an Eastern Shore representative amended a free Negro bill to allow county sheriffs to hire out all unmarried free Negro men who failed to provide themselves a "home" by the first day of the year. The local sheriff would supervise the free Negroes' employment to assure them of a

[47] *Maryland Colonization Journal,* I (April 1838), 16.
[48] Petitions on Negroes and Slavery, 1841, DelLP.

"fair price" for their labor and good treatment throughout their service. Necessary clothing and food would be deducted from the freemen's wages, which would be paid at the end of the year less the sheriff's fee of 6 percent. Attempts to postpone debate failed as pressure for what would later be called black codes pushed the bill into law with but one change. The new law embodied all of the proposals to extort free Negro labor, but applied only to free Negroes without visible means of support and industrious habits. But since whites determined who had industrious habits, the caveat provided little protection. Furthermore, a free Negro who was still unemployed ten days after completing his or her services could again be sold "as a slave" to the highest bidder for the following year. In 1847, Delaware passed a similar enactment permitting justices of the peace to hire out all free Negroes lacking good and industrious habits, and giving their employers "all the rights of a master."[49]

The new black codes may have comforted some tidewater farmers, but they left unresolved the larger problems confronting the Upper South. Colonization, as the enactment of black laws conceded, had failed to stem the growth of the free Negro caste. The steady, seemingly unstoppable increase of freemen continued as if the strictures against emancipated blacks remaining in the South did not exist. The Panic of 1837 broke many marginal slaveholders and forced them to sell their slaves south, speeding the exodus of slaves and whites from the region. But the free Negroes remained and increased. The colonizationist dream that slavery might someday be chased from the Upper South by a combination of manumission and sale turned into a nightmare as the free Negro population ballooned ever larger. Some whites began to worry that in time free Negroes would preponderate. They compulsively examined the census and computed the proportions of whites, slaves, and free Negroes and their increase and decrease, compared these proportions with past censuses, and projected their counts into the future. What would Maryland be like in a hundred years? asked one state legislator. Our children

[49] *Ibid.*, 1847; *Journal of Proceedings of the House of Delegates of the State of Maryland*, 1839, pp. 210–11; *Md. Laws*, 1839, c. 38; *Del. Laws*, 1847, c. 334, c. 412.

would be living then, "if there was any space unoccupied by the free negro race."[50]

Nowhere was the sense of crisis greater than in Maryland. Maryland whites had watched slavery wither in neighboring Delaware until it barely qualified as a slave state. As slaves streamed out of Maryland, the number of manumissions increased and fugitives grew more audacious; the signs of decline and decay became more apparent. Slaveholders complained that already men were bidding for public office who had no direct attachment to their peculiar institution and cared little about the special needs of the masters. Even more frightening was the growth of the free Negro caste. Although they differed among themselves as to the desirability of emancipation or even extirpation, nonslaveholders and slaveholders dreaded the continued growth of the state's free Negro caste, already the largest in the nation. Between 1830 and 1840, despite new repressive legislation and an enormous investment in African colonization, Maryland free Negroes had again increased by nearly a fifth while slaves had decreased by almost as much. Called to account for the failure to remove emancipated blacks, the leaders of the colonization society conceded that they had invested their time and the state's money in developing an African colony around Cape Palmas and that the removal laws of 1831 were a "dead letter." Many whites worried that if the present trend continued Maryland was "destined to be a free negro state."[51]

The specter of a free Negro majority haunted Maryland whites. Accepting the failure of colonization and recognizing their dependence on black workers, they searched for a solution to the vexing free Negro problem. In 1842, southern Maryland slaveholders, anxious to secure new protection for slavery, held a convention which proposed new restrictions on manumission and restraints to prevent runaways. But slavery

[50] See for example, *Maryland Colonization Journal;* "Reports of the Committee on Coloured Population," *Maryland Legislative Documents; Communication from the Board of Managers of the Maryland Colonization Society; American Farmer,* 3rd ser., I (1839), 107; Baltimore *Sun,* 14, 15 January 1842; *Baltimore American,* 4 March 1842.

[51] *Communication from the Board of Managers of the Maryland Colonization Society,* p. 11; James Price to James Hall, 2 June 1841, Letters Received, MdSCS Papers; quotation in *Baltimore American,* 4 March 1842.

would never be secure so long as free Negroes flaunted their liberty. To eliminate the free Negro's subversive influence, slaveholders suggested new enactments to lock Negro freemen into a system of peonage barely removed from chattel bondage. Free Negroes, under the proposed legislation, would be barred from holding land, except under short-term leases, and prevented from traveling freely and controlling their own family or religious life. Appalled by the severity of these measures and fearful that they would drive free Negroes out of Maryland and wreck the state's economy, nonslaveholders rallied to defeat these proposals.[52] But the attacks on the free Negro continued. Three years later, when some hundred slaves made a mass escape from southern Maryland, slaveholders stormed back into the legislature with similar demands. Again, they were beaten back, but the regularity of their assaults was becoming obvious to all.[53] More frightening still, slaveholders seemed to be accomplishing piecemeal what they were unable to do all at once. Maryland and Delaware tightened their black codes, and demands for free Negro removal and discipline spread to other Upper South states. North Carolina farmers urged the passage of legislation to hire out indolent free blacks, and William Smith, the popular governor of Virginia, began his campaign to sweep free Negroes from the state. "The nearer [free Negroes] approach numerical, social or political equality," observed one Maryland colonizationist, "the nearer they approach that crisis which must drive one

[52] For the 1842 Slaveholder's Convention, see *Niles' National Register,* LXI (25 September 1841), 58, (22 January 1841), 322–3, (5 February 1842), 356–8; *Baltimore American,* 14, 15, 19 January 1842; Baltimore *Sun,* 14, 15, 18 January 1842. Baltimore was the center of opposition to the slaveholder's proposals; see "Report of the Committee on Coloured Population," *Maryland Legislative Documents,* 1841, doc. H; *Baltimore American* and Baltimore *Sun,* February–March 1842; *Journal of the Proceedings of the House of Delegates of the State of Maryland,* 1841 (December), p. 414.

[53] *Baltimore American,* 20 December 1845. Most of the runaways were captured entering the District of Columbia, but some made it to freedom in Canada. Baltimore *Sun,* 9, 10, 14 (quoting the Port Tobacco *Times*), 18, 22, 30 July 1845; *Journal of Proceedings of the House of Delegates of the State of Maryland,* 1845, pp. 242–87, 295, 351, 365–6; "Report of the Select Committee of Delegates of Charles County, Relative to the Removal of the Free People of Color of Charles County," *Maryland Legislative Documents,* 1845, doc. G; for the usual opposition in Baltimore and the northern counties, Baltimore *Sun,* 26 February 1846, 4 March 1846.

race from the field. It is the universal impression that something must be done."[54]

The urge to solve the free Negro problem did not yet infect the Lower South. To be sure, Lower South lawmakers rarely missed an opportunity to widen the social distance between free Negroes and whites by further degrading the free Negro. Occasionally, they went beyond the bounds of the proscriptions enacted in the Upper South, but nowhere in the Lower South did whites dwell upon the free Negro problem with the same intensity as whites in the Upper South. No Lower South state ever considered the kinds of comprehensive black codes demanded in Virginia and North Carolina and enacted in Delaware and Maryland. The free people of color were simply too few in number or too closely aligned with whites, and Lower South whites were too confident about their own future to be much bothered by the anomalous caste.

Differences in racial policy between the two regions crystallized over colonization. If militant Northern abolitionists denounced colonization as a front for slavery, the planters of the Lower South took the colonizationists' professed opposition to slavery in dead earnest. Morbidly sensitive to any talk of emancipation now or in the most distant future, they viewed deportation of those slaves to be freed as an opening wedge that would encourage manumission and soften the South for eventual abolition. In the plantation heartland, slaveholders were especially suspicious of colonization intent. The tremendous effort to clear the Black Belt of a handful of free Negroes made no sense. They wondered who the *real* targets of deportation were. In areas where there were few free Negroes, colonizationists had to be abolitionists. Besides, a change of country could no more improve the African than any other change of circumstance. "If American slaves could be colonized," declared the governor of Alabama, "they would descend to the condition of natives, instead of imparting the benefits of their limited information and civilization to them." Since

[54] Petition from Parquotank County, [1846–1847], NCLP; *Journal of the House of Delegates of Virginia,* 1846–1847, pp. 9–10, 1847–1848, pp. 19, 21–2, 1848–1849, pp. 21–3; *Maryland Colonization Journal,* new ser., II (February 1844), 122.

blacks could not care for themselves without the aid of a white master, deportation would subject them "only to a lingering death, by famine, by disease, and other accumulated miseries."[55] Within the framework of the positive-good argument, colonization made no sense.

During the 1820s, when Upper South lawmakers were warming to colonization with resolutions of praise and occasional donations of funds, the Georgia legislature fired off a searing condemnation, denouncing deportation as a scheme to impoverish and depopulate the South and "diminish the welfare of the negroes themselves." South Carolina soon joined the fray. Fearful that Congress would appropriate funds for the American Colonization Society, low-country planters roasted colonization leaders as abolitionists who wanted to wreak havoc on the South. A colonization agent who visited Charleston in 1829 found opposition intense. After a week of canvassing, he uncovered only one contributor, who turned out be be a Northern man. Opposition to colonization grew during the 1830s. Following the Nat Turner insurrection, when the states of the Upper South opened their treasuries to state colonization societies, the Lower South fumed with indignation. Those few agents who strayed from their regular routes and dipped down into the Lower South almost always came away with their pockets empty. Sometimes, they were chased out with threats of violence. Although a few auxiliary societies were eventually established, colonization had few friends in the Lower South.[56]

The planters of the Lower South opposed colonization chiefly because of its emancipationist implications. But, significantly, they did not try to distinguish between the antislavery and the anti-free Negro elements in colonization and to im-

[55] *Journal of the Alabama House of Representatives,* 1840, p. 17; [Drayton], *The South Vindicated,* p. 241.

[56] *Ga. Laws,* 1827, pp. 197–8; *African Repository,* VI (September 1830), pp. 195–209; Freehling, *Prelude to Civil War,* pp. 122–6; B. N. Pals to R. R. Gurley, 23 May 1829, John Caldwell to John Douglass, 14 April 1842, A. E. Thom to William McLain, 27 August 1849, ACS; *Baton Rouge Gazette,* 14 November 1840; Franklin L. Riley, "A Contribution to the History of the Colonization Movement in Mississippi," *Publications of the Mississippi Historical Society,* IX (1906), 337–414; Charles S. Sydnor, *Slavery in Mississippi* (New York, 1933), pp. 203–38.

plement the latter. Believing free Negroes to be useful intermediaries between whites and slaves, they had no reason to ship them off to Africa.

Lower South racial policy centered around the delicate task of building the free Negroes' middle position, allowing them just enough latitude to assure their loyalty but not so much as to encourage them to challenge white dominance. The three-caste system inherited from French and Spanish rule in the Gulf ports and introduced into South Atlantic cities like Charleston and Savannah by West Indian émigrés flourished in the ports of the Lower South and to a lesser degree in the hinterland. Although it was only rarely powerful enough to receive explicit legal sanction, whites supported the development of a loyal middle caste by patronizing free Negro tradesmen, lending them money, selling them land, and protecting them at moments of danger. Occasionally, whites granted the most successful free people of color additional rights and quietly allowed them to vote, to testify in court, and ultimately to pass into the white caste. Freemen responded to their special status by drawing away from slaves and developing numerous exclusive organizations such as the creole schools, volunteer fire companies, and fraternal organizations which flourished in many Lower South cities. Although it was not as overt as the West Indian system, the three-caste social order of the Lower South was apparent to all who cared to look. At times, it could hardly be missed. Many of the theaters of the Lower South set aside special seats for free people of color. Located above the white loge and below the black balcony, the "quadroon boxes" were a physical embodiment of the free Negro's place in the social order of the Lower South.[57] But, as with all essentially informal social practices, the extent of the three-caste system did not become fully manifest until it was challenged. When some

[57] *Ala. Laws,* 1833, p. 68; *Report of James P. Screven, Mayor of Savannah, for the Year Ending September 30th, 1857* (Savannah, 1857), pp. 29–31; Proceedings of the New Orleans City Council, 31 October 1812, Messages of the Mayor of New Orleans, 20 May 1820, 14 June 1820, typescript, NOPL; *New Orleans Crescent,* August–December 1857; New Orleans *Daily Picayune,* 8 January 1853, 5 June 1856, 4, 19 November 1856; David Grimsted, *Melodrama Unveiled: American Theater and Culture, 1800–1850* (Chicago, 1968), p. 53; George W. Pierson, *Tocqueville and Beaumont in America* (New York, 1938), pp. 628, 631.

whites threatened the long-established prerogatives of the free people of color, commonplace notions that there was "nothing to single them out as the universal enemy of the white" were rushed to the fore, often with good effect. Fear that pushing free Negroes too hard would break down "the barrier which now separates the free colored man from the slave and assigns him an intermediary *caste* between the slave and his master" not only restrained white racism but allowed the free people of color to wring additional concessions from whites.[58]

Bolstering the free Negro's middle position increased the risk that freemen might become too independent and forget "their place." To make every free Negro, no matter how light-skinned or wealthy, directly beholden to some white, most of the states of the Lower South required free Negroes to take guardians to supervise their legal affairs and to act as their agents in any dealing with the law.[59] The guardianship codes shrank the freeman's liberty dangerously close to that of the slave, but they were not simply a crude surrogate for slavery. Instead, they allowed free Negroes to prosper as their industry dictated—thus to continue to serve the white community—and to keep a foot (and an ear) in the slave camp, while they remained distinct from bondsmen. The guardianship system delicately placed free Negroes above slaves while securely locking them below whites in the kind of paternalistic relationship that planters idealized.

The foundation of the three-caste system of the Lower South was a small free Negro population closely connected to whites by ties of blood, friendship, or, in the case of guardianships, the law. While whites allowed these free Negroes to prosper, those who stood outside these relations with whites were viewed with intense hostility. None of these outsiders seemed more dangerous than the well-traveled black

[58] *Journal of the Louisiana House of Representatives,* 1846 (adjourned session), p. 71; *Charleston Courier,* 9 December 1835.

[59] Clayton, comp., *Laws of Ga.,* pp. 655–6; *Ga. Laws,* 1826, pp. 161–3, 1833, pp. 226–9, 1840, c. 139, 1851, c. 60; Cooper and McCord, comps., *Statutes S.C.,* VII, 461–2, VIII, 547–8; *Fla. Laws,* 1842, pp. 34–6, 1843, p. 50, 1848, p. 27; *Ala. Laws,* 1851, c. 75, 1853, c. 52. Tennessee briefly flirted with enacting a guardianship law, but repealed the code before it was to go into effect; *Tenn. Laws,* 1851, c. 300, 1853, c. 50.

sailors who mixed promiscuously with free Negroes and slaves in every Southern port. To prevent them from contaminating free Negroes with abolitionist doctrine and upsetting the fine balance of the three-caste system, nearly every Lower South state prohibited black sailors from walking its streets by quarantining them on their ships or locking them in jail as soon as they came ashore. The states of the Upper South, on the other hand, viewed black sailors as no more dangerous than their own free Negro populations and never saw any need for such laws. Only where the fragile three-caste system needed protection from outsiders unfamiliar with its subtle privileges and restrictions was it necessary to draw a firm line against black seamen.[60]

By definition, the three-caste system elevated the free Negro above the slave. It allowed free Negroes to achieve a modicum of wealth and respectability, although it strengthened the larger system of race oppression. Like the importance of free Negro labor in the Upper South, the freemen's middle position in the Lower South allowed them just enough room to create their own life under the hateful glare of whites and within the slave society.

[60] Cooper and McCord, comps., *Statutes S.C.*, VII, 461–7; *Ga. Laws*, 1826, pp. 161–3, 1829, pp. 167–71, 1854–1855, c. 94; *Fla. Laws*, 1832, pp. 143–4; *Ala. Laws*, 1839, pp. 134–6, 1841, pp. 11–12; *La. Laws*, 1841–1842, pp. 308–14, 1852, c. 279, 1859, c. 87; Warfield, ed., *Digest of Acts of the Legislature*, p. 80; H. P. N. Gammel, comp., *Laws of Texas*, 10 vols. (Austin, 1898), IV, 466. Philip M. Hamer, "Great Britain, the United States, and the Negro Seamen Acts, 1822–1848," *JSH*, I (1935), 3–28, and "British Consuls and the Negro Seamen Acts, 1850–1860," *ibid.*, pp. 138–68. Of the states of the Upper South only North Carolina passed seamen acts, and it quickly retreated from its position; Franklin, *Free Negro in North Carolina*, pp. 69–70, 141.

7

The Economics of Marginality

Whenever the avenues of employment are crowded—whenever the price of labour is brought low by competition—whenever it is a favour to be employed . . . then the colored man will know that the time . . . is at hand. *In the struggle for bread the colored man will go to the wall.*

Maryland Colonization Journal, October 1846

The free negro performs many menial offices to which the white man of the South is adverse. They are hackmen, draymen, our messengers, and barbers; always ready to do many necessary services; if they are driven from the Southern States who will supply their place?

Nashville Republican Banner, 15 January 1860

JUST as most free Negroes lived on the periphery of the South, so they worked on the margins of the Southern economy. The great source of Southern wealth was the plantation, and only a few free Negroes had anything directly to do with that institution. Yet the plantation needed supplies and services to feed itself and market its products. On the farms that grew food for slaves and nonslaveholders, on the riverboats and drays that carried goods to and from plantations, and in the cities that mediated between the plantation heartland and the outside world, most free Negroes earned their livelihood. Taking advantage of the peculiar needs of the Southern economy and utilizing skills they carried out of bondage, a growing number of free Negroes prospered, accumulated property, and displayed symbols of middle-class respectability. But even in the marginal occupations allowed Negro freemen, they met racial proscription and increasing competition from white and slave workers. While many free Negroes made a comfortable living, most were pushed into dismal poverty, forced to live and work under conditions barely distinguishable from those of the mass of slaves. Thus the motion of the Southern economy cut the free Negro caste sharply along class lines, often dividing the free Negro caste against itself.

Most free Negroes, like most Southerners, lived in the countryside and earned their living working the land. Throughout the rural South, free Negroes worked as farmhands and casual laborers. The occupations of free Negroes in North Carolina, an overwhelmingly rural state with no large urban center, typified those of most rural freemen. In 1860, fully 75 percent of North Carolina free Negroes worked as farmers, common laborers, ditchers, and woodchoppers. Most of the remainder did similar work as turpentine hands, tanners, and weavers. Women generally worked as laundresses, housekeepers, and seamstresses, although doubtless they too spent considerable time in the fields. Only a fraction of the rural free Negro population engaged in skilled trades. Among the 7,000 free Negroes whose occupations were listed by the census, there were about 250 carpenters, 150 blacksmiths, 100 coopers, and a smattering of masons, shoemakers, and mechanics. Even then, census enumerations probably underestimated the number of free Negro farm workers and exaggerated the proportion of skilled freemen. The occupations of many free Negroes were unspecified, and often census marshals merely denoted "free nigger."[1]

Along the coast and on the rivers of the South, free Negroes served as boatsmen and fishermen. Slaves had long monopo-

[1] Franklin, *Free Negro in North Carolina,* pp. 134–5; Luther P. Jackson, "The Virginia Free Negro Farmer and Property Owner, 1830–1860," *JNH,* XXIV (1939), 394–8; Jackson, *Free Negro Labor and Property Holding,* pp. 75–82; England, "Free Negro in Ante-Bellum Tennessee," pp. 223–5; Sweat, "Free Negro in Antebellum Georgia," pp. 146–53; Ulrich B. Phillips, ed., *Plantation and Frontier,* 2 vols. (Cleveland, Ohio, 1910), II, 143–7.

lized boating trades, and free Negroes moved easily into these occupations. The ease with which slave boatsmen escaped made many masters chary about hiring them and gave free Negroes an added advantage. Every ship that touched Southern shores had a contingent of free black sailors, observed a Virginia newspaper in 1860. "Besides those having entirely colored crews nearly all the larger vessels and some of the smaller ones, (schooners, &c.,) have colored cooks and stewards."[2]

The hard life in the countryside drove free Negroes to the cities. Urban freemen generally did much better than rural folk. The diversity of city life enabled them to practice a wider variety of trades and frequently to earn higher wages. Although free Negroes were challenged by an influx of immigrant workers and an increase of slave hirelings, the steady exodus of slaves to the cotton fields of the Lower South and of native white workers to the Northwest continually created new opportunities. The rising price of slaves and the desire of white artisans to escape the invidious comparison with blacks drove wages up and made urban businessmen grateful for the free Negro's presence. But, as in the countryside, free Negroes usually labored at occupations that offered little status or remuneration.

The occupations practiced by urban free Negroes varied from city to city and depended on the nature of the economy, its prosperity, and the number of competitors they faced, as well as on the skill and acumen of the freemen themselves. In the Upper South, urban free Negroes generally worked as factory hands, teamsters, common laborers, washerwomen, and domestics. In Richmond, for example, fully half the adult free Negro men labored in tobacco factories, paper mills, and iron foundries, which made up the industrial core of the city in 1860. Almost another 20 percent worked as waiters, white washers, and stevedores or did a variety of menial jobs as day laborers. Only a third of Richmond's free Negroes could claim a skilled trade. This was a high proportion by rural standards, but compared with other urban workers, free

[2] Jackson, *Free Negro Labor and Property Holding*, p. 107; *Harper's New Monthly Magazine*, XIV (1856–7), 442; New Orleans *Daily Picayune*, 6 February, 1841; Petersburg *Press*, 6 January 1860.

TABLE 13

SKILL LEVEL OF MAJOR ETHNIC AND RACIAL GROUPS OF FREE ADULT* MALE WORKERS IN RICHMOND, 1860

	Skilled[a]		*Unskilled*[b]	
	Number	*Percentage*	*Number*	*Percentage*
Free Negroes	174	32%	362	68%
Southern-born whites	1,419	88	210	12
Northern-born whites	286	88	39	12
British	187	92	18	8
Germans	515	92	43	8
Irish	318	39	507	61
Totals	2,899	70	1,179	30

* Fifteen years and older.

[a] Includes bakers, barbers, blacksmiths, bookbinders, bricklayers, brickmakers, cabinetmakers, carpenters, coopers, gunsmiths, iron molders, jewelers, lithographers, locksmiths, machinists, millwrights, musicians, painters, plasterers, printers, shoemakers, stonemasons, tailors, tinsmiths, watchmakers, wheelwrights.

[b] Includes cooks, ditchers, factory hands, gardeners, laborers, sailors, servants, teamsters, waiters, whitewashers.

SOURCE: Richmond manuscript census, 1860, NA.

Negroes fared poorly. Nearly 90 percent of the native white men worked in a skilled craft, and German-born and British-born workers were even more successful in achieving high occupational status. Even Irish immigrants, who occupied the bottom of the white occupational hierarchy, stood above the free Negroes. Almost 40 percent of the Irish men in the city practiced a skilled trade.[3]

Black women also worked at menial, servile occupations. Southern cities allowed few opportunities for lucrative employment to women of any color. Like poor white women, most free Negro women worked as cooks, laundresses, house-

[3] Richmond manuscript census 1860, NA. I would like to thank Herbert G. Gutman for sharing with me his pioneering studies of the social order of Richmond and Charleston. These occupational reconstructions were done by Professor Gutman from data collected by Elizabeth Uwen, Ursula Linguies, and Mark Sosower.

For other Upper South cities see Jackson, *Free Negro Labor and Property Holding,* pp. 98–9; Franklin, *Free Negro in North Carolina,* pp. 98–9; Dorothy S. Provine, "The Free Negro in the District of Columbia, 1800–1860," unpublished M.A. thesis, Louisiana State University, 1963, pp. 166–7; Free Negro Bonds and Lists of St. Louis Free Negroes, Tiffany Collection, MoHS.

keepers, and peddlers. But many more free Negro than white women were forced to work. The sexual imbalance of the free Negro caste in the cities placed many black women at the head of their household, and even when a man was present, his income was often insufficient to support the family. The large number of black women who worked further diluted the proportion of free Negroes who practiced skilled trades.

The free people of color of the Lower South ports were considerably more successful than Upper South free Negroes. In Charleston, a declining city which could boast neither the new industry nor the booming commerce of Richmond, three-quarters of the free Negro men worked at skilled trades in 1860. Indeed, free Negro artisans controlled a large share of the work in some prominent trades and dominated others outright. Fully a quarter of the city's carpenters, nearly 40 percent of the tailors, and three-quarters of the millwrights were free Negroes, although Negro freemen composed only 15 percent of the free male work force. Unlike those in Richmond, free Negroes in Charleston enjoyed a level of occupational skill which surpassed that of most whites. Except for German immigrants and Southern-born whites, free Negroes were the most skilled group in the city.[4]

TABLE 14

SKILL LEVEL OF MAJOR ETHNIC AND RACIAL GROUPS OF FREE ADULT* MALE WORKERS IN CHARLESTON, 1860

	Skilled[a]		*Unskilled*[b]	
	Number	*Percentage*	*Number*	*Percentage*
Free Negroes	404	76%	130	24%
Southern-born whites	610	80	177	20
Northern-born whites	103	61	66	39
British	99	63	57	37
Germans	347	77	105	23
Irish	402	36	725	64
Totals	1,965	61	1,260	39

* Fifteen years and older.
[a, b] See table 13.

SOURCE: Charleston manuscript census, 1860, NA.

[4] Charleston manuscript census, 1860, NA. For other Lower South cities see John W. Blassingame, "A Social and Economic Study of the Negro in New Or-

The comparatively lofty occupational status of Lower South free Negroes was but another manifestation of their high social standing. It reflected, in part, their entrenched position and their close ties with upper-class whites who patronized their shops and protected them from competitors. In the cities of the Upper South, free Negroes did not enjoy the benefits of these relations. Thus, the differences in occupational status of the free Negroes of the Upper and Lower South were rooted in the diverse patterns of manumission that created the free Negro caste. The large-scale ideological manumission which had spurred the growth of the free Negro caste in the Upper South, particularly in the years following the Revolution, had made little provision for the freemen's future. Since the motive to emancipate was abstract principle and that principle required nothing but the bestowal of freedom to be satisfied, manumitters rarely concerned themselves with the ability of slaves to support themselves after liberation. It was enough that the slave was free and the sin washed from the master's conscience. The selective, personal, often paternal emancipation that characterized manumission in the Lower South and the West Indies (from where many freemen had migrated) had little to do with abstract principle. Most manumitters freed only a favorite bondsman and continued to hold slaves, their faith in the institution of slavery unshaken. But the personal concerns that motivated them did not end with the emancipation of their slaves. Manumitters frequently prepared their slaves for freedom by teaching them a trade or providing for their support after slavery. The close relations between masters and former slaves gave new freemen a ready market, and prominent slaveholders also encouraged their friends to patronize their former trusted bondservants. Once free Negroes had secured their economic position, they proved difficult to dislodge.

Although many free Negroes, especially in the port cities of the Lower South, did strikingly well, the great majority remained unskilled laborers. Poverty forced many of them to

---

leans, 1860–1880," unpublished doctoral dissertation, Yale University, 1970, p. 132, app., table 5; De Bow, *Statistical View of the United States*, pp. 80–1; Boucher, "Free Negro in Alabama," pp. 368–71, 397–424, 438–42, 486–93.

accept whatever pay they were offered, to work at two or three jobs to earn a living, and to send their wives and children out to work to make ends meet. Even then grim necessity pressured free Negroes to relinquish much of their liberty, and terms of service sometimes became indistinguishable from slavery itself. Some free Negroes signed long-term contracts for nominal wages or maintenance and literally became wage slaves. For no more than the promise of food, clothing, and shelter, hundreds of free Negroes in the Northern Neck of Virginia sold their services for terms of twenty years. In Westmoreland County, for example, about 250, a quarter of the county's free Negroes, lived in this state of near-slavery.[5]

Free Negroes usually avoided long-term servitude, but many labored under yearly contracts which left little to set them apart from bond slaves. These contracts, similar to those given to slave hirelings, ran from Christmas to Christmas and often specified that the free Negroes work according to the rules governing slave hands. Like many free Negro workers, Aaron Griggs hired himself to a Louisiana planter "to work as one of the hands of the plantation." He pledged not to leave the plantation during his term of service, "to go out to the fields at the *same hours* with the people of the plantation & to work with Mr. Wm. Droughon (overseer of the plantation)." In addition to these arrangements, employers often furnished periodic allotments of food and clothing similar to those which slaves received, and deducted expenses monthly or at a final Christmas accounting. Once expenses were deducted there was little left, and free Negro workers frequently found themselves in debt to their employers. Sometimes they were obliged to sign on for another term under the same hard conditions. Free Negroes struggled to escape their perennial indebtedness, but, as one South Carolina minister noted, "when the *Squaring off* day comes I fear they will find more outstanding debts against them, and fewer in their favour than they calculate on finding."[6]

[5] Jackson, *Free Negro Labor and Property Holding,* pp. 72–4.

[6] Wright, *Free Negro in Maryland,* pp. 158–65; Jourdon Woolfolk Account Book, 1854–1865, VHS; Aaron Griggs Contract, 1823, A. P. Walsh Papers, LSU; Ben Brown Contracts, 27 December 1837, 11 January 1840, John Martin Contract, 3 January 1839, Willie Jones Contract, 31 December 1841, Robert Leslie Papers, Duke; *Richmond Enquirer,* 18 December 1845; "Free Soloman"

Wary of year-long contracts, free blacks generally preferred to hire themselves on a short-term basis for cash wages. Several North Carolina free Negroes signed on with a road gang only on condition that they would be paid by the month. "They say," reported the foreman of the crew, "that they think by their conduct &c they will be enabled to increase their wages."[7] But not all free Negroes could win such favorable terms of employment. Their poor bargaining position pushed many of them outside the cash economy. Some employers paid free Negro workers in kind and not in cash. Farmers and merchants treasured this variant of the barter system because they profited from the merchandise with which free Negroes were paid as well as from the freemen's labor. Occasionally, they opened stores and encouraged sales by allowing freemen to pay with future wages or crops. The practice of paying free Negroes with merchandise allowed shrewd businessmen to cheat unsuspecting black workers out of a fair return on their labor. Free Negroes who exchanged their labor directly for goods generally received less than the usual dollar-per-day wage.[8] More important, increasing indebtedness bound free Negroes to the farmer-merchants who employed them, further limiting their ability to escape their impoverished lot. Like many blacks in the postbellum years, some free Negroes found themselves entrapped in the sticky web of debt peonage.

Searching for some way out of the vicious cycle of debt and *de facto* servitude, free Negroes generally tried to avoid direct employment by whites and instead rented land which they farmed on their own. Many black tenants did well and accumulated property in the form of household furnishings, tools, and farm animals. But most fared little better than the mass of free Negro farmhands. Some fell into debt to white landlords and were forced to pledge their crops to remain solvent. Between 1850 and 1854, one Virginia free Negro annually sold his stock, farm equipment, and crops "now stand-

---

account in Davis Richardson Ledger, 1825–1827, Duke; W. R. Hemphill to William McLain, ? January 1845, ACS.

[7] W. D. Moreley to E. B. Dudley, 27 January 1837, Letters Received, Executive Papers, NCA.

[8] Vansant Ledger, Bloomsburg Mills Ledger, Gittings Account Book, MdHS; Davis Richardson Ledger, Duke; Ebenezer Blakiston to Henry Ridgely, 22 March 1824, Ridgely Family Papers, DelHR.

ing in the field" in order to satisfy his creditors. Other tenants found themselves similarly burdened by debts for which they had to pledge their future produce.[9] The perennial pledge of crops not yet harvested or even sown, like the postbellum crop-lien system, operated to restrict free Negro mobility and tie them to the land.

Free Negroes did not stand alone in poverty. Without savings to fall back upon, many poor whites were also forced to take the first job that came their way and sign contracts that were less than fair. Frequently they too found themselves perennially in debt to their employers, ensnared by unfavorable tenancy agreements, and paying inflated prices at the company store. But if whites shared the penalties of poverty, blacks carried the burden of race by themselves.

Unlike whites, free Negroes could be forced into long terms of servitude for failure to pay fines, taxes, or jail fees. These delinquencies were often small, but free Negroes were usually hired at such low rates that they had to serve long terms. In 1819, for instance, Virginia lawmakers prescribed sixteen cents per day as the minimum rate for hiring delinquent free Negroes, and later they dropped the legal rate to ten cents. Although sales were public and labor usually in demand, whites conspired to prevent the maximum rate from exceeding the legal minimum. By the 1840s, debt-ridden Virginia free Negroes were rarely hired out for more than ten cents per day. Thus a fine of ten dollars could lead to forced labor for more than three months. Although no state regulated the rate of delinquent-hire as closely as Virginia, the rush to purchase these free Negroes suggests similar practices in other states.[10]

Free Negroes were sold into terms of servitude for failing to pay private debts as well. Although workingmen toppled the old system of imprisoning and hiring out debtors in many states, free Negroes were often excluded from these reforms. Delaware, for example, had allowed debtors to be hired out in

[9] Jackson, *Free Negro Labor and Property Holding*, pp. 108–9; Jackson, "Free Negro Farmer," pp. 398–406, 428–35.

[10] *Revised Code of Laws of Virginia*, 2 vols. (Richmond, 1819), I, 434–5; *Va. Laws*, 1852, c. 15; Hustings Court Records of Richmond and Petersburg, 1845–1860, VSL; Baltimore *Sun*, 18 January 1842; *N.C. Laws*, 1831, c. 13; South Carolina Grand Jury Presentments, 1816, SCA; *S.C. Laws*, 1843, c. 2243, 1844, c. 2285; *Miss. Laws*, 1822, p. 183.

lieu of imprisonment since colonial times. In 1827, a new law provided that women and white men had to give their consent before they could be sold. But the status of free Negro men was left unchanged and they continued to be auctioned into terms of servitude for their unpaid debts. During the 1840s, the threat of sale for private and public debts was compounded in Delaware and Maryland by harsh black codes which allowed officials to hire free Negro "vagrants" into yearlong terms of servitude.[11]

Apprenticeship laws provided still another means of locking free Negroes into virtual slavery. Ideally, apprenticeship allowed young men and women a chance to learn a trade and support themselves, but when applied to free blacks it increasingly became an unadorned system of labor extortion. During the nineteenth century, while legislatures and courts improved the condition of white apprentices, free Negroes lost many of their rights to maintenance and training. Many states eliminated the requirement that masters teach apprenticed free Negroes how to read and write. Even where this requirement remained in force, local courts tended to ignore it. More damaging still, judges commonly bound free Negro children to the lowly occupations they deemed proper for blacks. In Maryland, for instance, most free Negroes were apprenticed to farmers, boys as farmhands and girls to learn the "mysteries of housewifery." Occasionally, even girls were put into field work. With no provision for education or special training, free Negro apprentices were little better off than slaves. Farmers bid for the labor of free Negro apprentices and demanded that the children of indigent freemen be bound out, even without their parents' approval. Georgia lawmakers, responding to such pleas, ordered free Negro children apprenticed until age twenty-one if it was shown that they were "not being raised in a becoming and proper manner." In some places, the advantages of holding black apprentices

[11] Richard B. Morris, "The Course of Peonage in a Slave State," *Political Science Quarterly*, LXV (1950), 241–3; *Del. Laws*, 1826, c. 57, c. 362, 1827, c. 50; *Md. Laws*, 1831, c. 58; *N.C. Laws*, 1831, c. 13; also *Md. Laws*, 1825, c. 161, 1839, c. 38, 1854, c. 273; *Va. Laws*, 1814, c. 103; *N.C. Laws*, 1826, c. 21; *Ga. Laws*, 1833, pp. 226–8; Duval, comp., *Public Acts of the Territory of Florida*, pp. 229–30.

became so great that authorities had difficulty binding out white children.[12]

The law only reflected the larger pattern of discrimination. All else being equal, white employers generally hired whites over free Negroes. When they did condescend to employ free Negroes, many whites could not conceive of entrusting them with responsible positions. Some whites doubted that free Negroes could perform any but the simplest tasks. "A negro can never be a competent mechanic, because he is intellectually and mentally incapable of such elevation," declared a Tennessee newspaper. "He is unfit for everything save plantation and menial services." Racial prejudice relegated many free Negro workers to the meanest drudgery at the lowest pay. Characteristic of many Southern enterprises, the Frederick and Valley Turnpike of Virginia employed a mixed force of whites, slaves, and free Negroes to keep its right of way in good repair. But free Negroes, along with slaves, were uniformly assigned to the rank of axeman, the worst-paying job on the road. The Petersburg and Norfolk Railroad also employed free Negro axemen for about $150 a year. Again, there were no white axemen. Rodmen, the next highest-paid workers above axemen, received $40 a month. All the rodmen were white. At times, the shortage of hands or a freeman's skill forced employers to ease their discriminatory policies, but these changes usually came at the lowest level of employment. Free Negroes worked alongside white laborers on the stations and sections of the North Carolina Railroad, but no free Negroes served as stationmasters, agents, engineers, conductors, or watchmen. Even at these low levels of employment, free Negroes were often paid less than whites. The standard wage for day laborers in the Norfolk shipyards was one dollar, but free Negro workers rarely earned more than seventy-five cents a day.[13]

[12] *Va. Laws,* 1804, c. 11, 1808, c. 60; *Md. Laws,* 1808, c. 54; *N.C. Laws,* 1838, c. 38; *Ky. Laws,* 1842, c. 112; Casselberry, comp., *Revised Statutes of the State of Missouri,* p. 392; Morris, "Course of Peonage in a Slave State," p. 240; Wright, *Free Negro in Maryland,* pp. 136–48, 154; Franklin, *Free Negro in North Carolina,* pp. 122–30; James H. Boykin, *The Negro in North Carolina Prior to 1861* (New York, 1958), pp. 19–23; Report of the Overseer of the Poor, York County, VSL; *Ga. Laws,* 1854–1855, c. 93.

[13] *Nashville Republican Banner,* 12 June 1858; "Report of the Board of Public Works," *Virginia Legislative Documents,* 1853–1854, doc. XVII, 133–4,

Whites felt comfortable employing free Negroes at jobs nominally designated for slaves. It assured them that freedom did not significantly alter the black's status and seemed to guarantee that free Negroes would not challenge their rule. Not surprisingly, whites treated free Negro and slave workers much the same. Some white employers boasted that their "free colored workers hire themselves annually upon the same terms and conditions as slaves and are subject to the same discipline." Like slaves, free Negro hands were called by a single name occasionally prefaced by the word "free." Indeed, whites seemed to go out of their way to degrade free Negroes by employing them at jobs they considered too dangerous for their valuable slave property.[14] Yet free Negroes were not slaves, and ironically that sometimes redounded to their misfortune.

Since free Negroes and slaves generally hired out on the same terms, many employers preferred slaves to free Negroes because they afforded them greater control of their work force. Advertisements which littered the columns of Southern newspapers gave evidence of this choice. In Baltimore, where free Negroes greatly outnumbered slaves, employers were most explicit in their preference. A commonplace advertisement for a "colored man to act as a porter in a grocery store" carefully noted that "a slave would be preferred." Although slaves won a large measure of freedom in the cities, the distinction between free and bond Negroes was never entirely lost. Notices for waiters, cooks, house servants, and even day laborers carried the same proscriptive amendment. Some employers eschewed hiring bondsmen who had been promised freedom in the future. A Baltimore housekeeper advertised for servants to wash, cook, and iron, but emphatically added "they must be SLAVES FOR LIFE." Free Negroes thus had the disadvantages both of being black and of being free in a white

---

1855–1856, doc. XVII, 974; "Report to the Stockholders of the North Carolina Railroad," *North Carolina Legislative Documents,* doc. XIII, 17; Payroll Ledgers, Norfolk Naval Yards, 1844, 1846–1848, RG 71, NA.

[14] *Richmond Enquirer,* 18 December 1845; William S. Pettigrew to Moses, 12 June 1857, typescript, Pettigrew Family Papers, SHC; clipping from the *Richmond Whig,* n.d., with W. H. S[tarr] to ?, February 1858, ACS. For the general denomination of free Negroes by a single name, see Richardson Davis Ledger, Duke; Bloomsburg Mills Ledger, Gittings Account Book, MdHS.

society dominated by slave labor. Their color disqualified them from many jobs; their status excluded them from others. This dual proscription operated on even the lowest levels of employment to limit the free Negro's economic opportunities. "Wanted TWO BOYS for setting up TEN PINS," read a notice in a leading Baltimore journal; "German boys or slaves preferred."[15]

The preference of employers for white or slave labor forced free Negroes to underbid whites and work on the same terms as slaves. By accepting lower wages and longer hours, many free Negroes found employment, but they aroused the ire of white workingmen, who complained that free Negroes depressed their standard of living. "We consider the free negro mechanic a curse on our working interest," exclaimed white workingmen in Petersburg, "inasmuch as they nearly monopolize work at reduced prices." North Carolina mechanics reiterated that it was impossible to compete with free Negroes because they lived under conditions whites would not tolerate. Even more galling, white artisans found themselves equated with blacks because they worked at the same trades. "I despise working by the side of a negro," hissed a St. Louis workingman. "They are the worst class on the levee . . . a slur on our employment."[16]

White mechanics demanded that blacks, both slave and free, be restricted to domestic or menial jobs, which "by common consent are admitted to be their appropriate avocations." But planter-dominated legislatures saw the limitation on the use of slave labor as a threat to the value of their property and even as the first step toward abolition. Although some states excluded blacks, especially free Negroes, from certain jobs, these were usually occupations with especially high status or subversive potential such as preaching, making drugs, selling liquor, printing, or piloting ships. These proscriptions hampered the development of a black middle class,

[15] Baltimore *Sun*, 30 July 1840, 23 February 1838, 8 April 1851.

[16] *Richmond Enquirer*, 27 August 1857; "A Memorial to Encourage the Mechanics of North Carolina," *North Carolina Legislative Documents*, 1850–1851, doc. CVI, 687–8; St. Louis *Daily Missouri Democrat*, 27 July 1858. For a discussion of the opposition of white workers to black competition and its antislavery implications, see Ronald T. Takaki, *A Pro-Slavery Crusade: The Agitation to Reopen the African Slave Trade* (New York, 1971), pp. 44–54.

but they did not ease the competitive challenge white workingmen feared. Municipalities proved somewhat more responsive to the pleas of white workers. Yet even in the cities, solicitude for the rights of the master throttled attempts to curb the use of blacks, while the general shortage of workers made even minor restrictions difficult to enforce.[17] Thwarted in their attempts to limit black competition by the power of the slave-owning class, workingmen increasingly turned their pent-up anger upon the free Negro.

With increased frequency, militant white workingmen petitioned legislatures and organized workingmen's associations to exclude free Negroes from certain trades. Although a growing sense of class consciousness occasionally cut across racial lines, many unions were organized for the specific purpose of eliminating free Negro competition. Even the most class-conscious Southern workers seemed to believe the right to organize belonged to whites only. "Craftsmen and other laborers have an undoubted right to 'strike for higher wages,'" declared a prolabor St. Louis newspaper, "that is when they are white men. Color of course gives a different complexion to these rights." Occasionally, the festering hostility of white workers broke out in violent clashes with blacks.[18]

Proscriptive laws, pressure on white employers, and sporadic violence slowly drove free Negroes from many trades. The proscriptive process advanced at an uneven pace as freemen in different occupations and in various cities came under attack, but everywhere it operated in much the same manner. In many places, free Negroes suddenly found legal obstacles to employment in trades they had long practiced. Free Negro mechanics had to pay high licensing fees to work in Charleston and Savannah, free Negro butchers were barred from the city market in Memphis, and free Negro masons in Georgia had to have their work approved by whites. When white workingmen failed to push through such discriminatory legislation, in-

[17] Petition from Charleston, 1826, SCLP; Takaki, *Pro-Slavery Crusade*, pp. 44–51.

[18] St. Louis *Daily Missouri Democrat*, 30 April 1859; *Niles' Weekly Register*, XL (27 August 1831), 452–3; Washington *National Intelligencier*, 27–28 August 1835. But when Louisville draymen went on strike in 1853, the caravan of wagons was neatly divided between black and white carters; *Louisville Daily Democrat*, 11 March 1853.

formal pressure often proved just as effective in excluding free Negroes. In 1827, Baltimore draymen petitioned the state assembly to prohibit free Negroes from being licensed as carters. To assure their case a hearing, they hired a lawyer to carry their petitions to Annapolis and offered him a two-hundred-dollar bounty if he was successful. Free Negroes, fearful of the proscriptive precedent, rallied opposition among Baltimore's leading merchants and sent a counterpetition. Although the legislature sidestepped the entire controversy by tabling the question, more direct pressure on employers not to hire black wagoners drove many free Negroes from the trade. The same combination of legal and extralegal pressures later squeezed free Negroes from this profitable business in St. Louis and New Orleans.[19]

The influx of Irish and German workers into Southern cities speeded the exclusion of Negro freemen from many occupations. The competition free Negro workers faced from newly arrived immigrants in Baltimore was a typical example of how white immigrant workers limited the free Negro's opportunities in every Southern city. During the 1830s, visitors to Baltimore first noted that "Irish and other foreigners are, to a considerable extent, taking the place of colored laborers and other domestic servants." With white workers available in growing numbers, white employers exercised their racial preference in many trades traditionally dominated by blacks. Advertisements for white house servants, for example, appeared with increased regularity. Wealthy whites seemed to garner added status by keeping white maids and coachmen. One merchant boasted that his household contained six servants, "*all white.*" "This," he added pointedly, "makes it more pleasant." White businessmen frequently exercised the same preferences on the docks and in the warehouses and factories that they did in their homes. Immigrants replaced free Negroes

[19] Cooper and McCord, comps., *Statutes S.C.*, VI, 177–8; Edward G. Wilson, comp., *A Digest of All the Ordinances of the City of Savannah* (Savannah, 1858), pp. 7, 173–4; L. J. Dupree, comp., *A Digest of the Ordinances of the City Council of Memphis for the Years 1826 to 1857* (Memphis, 1857), p. 146; *Ga. Laws*, 1845, p. 49; *Journal of Proceedings of the House of Delegates of the State of Maryland*, 1827, pp. 119, 125, 410; *Genius of Universal Emancipation*, 12 January 1828; St. Louis *Daily Missouri Democrat*, 29 December 1853; Reinders, "Free Negro in the New Orleans Economy," pp. 276–7.

as stevedores and hod carriers, moved into the coalyards, and even took over much of the farm labor in the surrounding countryside. Previously, free Negroes had controlled all of these jobs, reported a Maryland colonizationist in 1851. "Now all this is changed. The white man stands in the black man's shoes, or else is fast getting into them."[20]

Heightening competition from immigrant workers was only one of the challenges free Negroes faced as Southern entrepreneurs sought to stretch their labor supply. In the 1830s, white women were introduced into Virginia tobacco factories. Contact between white women and black men, however, raised hackles, and many manufacturers retreated to the more traditional work force. But the rising price of slave labor forced businessmen to reconsider this decision. During the 1850s, employers again hired white women, usually taking care to separate them from black men.[21] This new competition further undermined the sagging economic position of the free Negro worker.

Weighed down by racial proscriptions, many free Negroes sank into abject poverty. The absence of steady employment prevented them from saving anything from their meager wages, and the preferences of white employers meant they were usually the first to be fired when the economy turned sour. The Panic of 1837, like many lesser fluctuations in the economy, forced thousands of free Negroes to plead for public relief. Baltimore blacks, who composed about 17 percent of the population of the poorhouse (and a like proportion of the population of the city) in 1835, made up almost a quarter of the inmates five years later as the depression set in. Many more free Negroes, perhaps too proud to accept relief, wandered the streets, and the police herded many into jail for petty crimes. The police blotter revealed the depth of the

[20] Ethan A. Andrews, *Slavery and the Domestic Slave Trade in the United States* (Boston, 1826), p. 73; James Nicols to Nicholas Ridgely, 22 March 1847, Ridgely Family Papers, DelHR; *Maryland Colonization Journal*, new ser., VI (October 1851), 71. Earl F. Niehaus documents the same process in New Orleans; *The Irish in New Orleans, 1800–1860* (Baton Rouge, La., 1965), pp. 49–52.

[21] *Farmer's Register*, III (1836), 575; *Richmond Enquirer*, 1 August 1855; *Petersburg Daily Express*, 1 June 1858, 18 August 1858, 19 March 1859, 4 May 1859.

free Negro's desperation. In 1838, one free Negro, arrested for stealing some sausage, pleaded "he was hungry, and he merely took a small piece to eat." At the same court session, several more free Negroes were jailed for taking coarse clothing, and the press reported that a free Negro woman attempted to commit suicide because "she had not sufficient clothing to shelter her from the cold."[22]

Confronted with these harsh realities, many free Negroes retreated from the competitive economy. Some chose a meager living of subsistence farming, and occasional labor in preference to the difficult task of trying to succeed in a society that worked to prevent their success. Others, pushed off good lands and deprived of the right to work regularly, were overwhelmed by the cycle of poverty; after several generations of dirt farming and sporadic employment, they knew no other life. But for many of these free Negroes, the refusal to work was a conscious attempt to assert their independence and remind whites of their reliance on black labor. When one Maryland aristocrat asked a free Negro to help him with his garden, the free Negro smugly refused. "I soon perceived that he wished me to be an importunate suitor," observed the gardener. "At this my nature revolted and I soon left him. I resolved to let him and his class see, that a white man, even one who has been tenderly brought up, *need* not be so dependent on the blacks, as they seemed to think."[23]

Although free Negroes frequently asserted their independence by refusing to work, most found this a Pyrrhic victory. Ultimately, the right to collect their own wages, accumulate property, and control their own family life distinguished them from the slaves. Free Negroes, like whites, needed meaningful work not merely to support themselves and their families but to bolster their self-esteem. Its absence often drained free blacks of self-respect and robbed them of a sense of purpose. Most free Negroes thus tried to find the independence they craved, not by refusing to work, but by working harder and

[22] Wright, *Free Negro in Maryland*, pp. 248–9; Baltimore *Sun*, 10, 22 February 1838, 11 June 1838. Also *Petersburg Daily Southside Democrat*, 7 July 1855.

[23] James Nicols to Nicholas Ridgely, 25 May 1841, Ridgely Family Papers, DelHR.

parlaying skills and connections with white employers into a better life. Despite growing proscriptive pressure, a good many succeeded.

The nature of the Southern work force and Southern attitudes toward blacks and work often allowed many free Negroes to turn their status and their color to their advantage in seeking employment. Farmers and merchants who desired to employ free workers but were unwilling to pay the wages whites demanded often hired free Negroes. Charleston merchants admitted that in spite of the Negro seaman laws free Negroes continued to dominate the maritime trades for the "obvious reason that the services of coloured seamen, as cooks and stewards, can be more cheaply and readily procured than those of whites." Businessmen also found advantages in the free Negro's legal disabilities. Many preferred to contract with free Negro workers because freemen could not testify against them in court. On the other hand, employers who believed blacks to be more tractable than whites and had been accustomed to being served by slaves found free Negroes the closest substitute. This preference for black workers, especially in the service trades, assured free Negroes of jobs wherever slaves were in short supply. In many places, free Negroes monopolized work as caterers, stable owners, bathhouse keepers, and tailors as well as lesser jobs as carters, butchers, coachmen, and delivery boys. Whites generally did not challenge the free Negroes' pre-eminence because of the stigma attached to working at the same trades as blacks. A Virginia farmer told Frederick Law Olmsted that "no white man would ever do certain kinds of work . . . and if you should ask a white man . . . he would get mad and tell you he wasn't a nigger."[24] Many of the jobs deemed "nigger work" were drudgery deserving of that epithet, but others provided steady work and lucrative wages. Some were skilled trades that demanded craftsmanship of the highest order.

The stigma of "nigger work" greatly enlarged the free

[24] Petition from Charleston, 1830, SCLP; *Easton* (Md.) *Star*, 21 February 1860; *African Repository*, VIII (October 1832), 240; Olmsted, *Journey in the Seaboard Slave States*, pp. 91–2. An interesting discussion of Southern attitudes toward work from a different perspective is David Bertelson, *The Lazy South* (New York, 1967); also see C. Vann Woodward, *American Counterpoint: Slavery and Racism in the North-South Dialogue* (Boston, 1971), pp. 13–46.

Negro's economic opportunities. Southern society identified labor with blacks, and whites disdained jobs at which blacks worked. The more closely blacks were connected with a trade, the greater the scorn of whites. To work at the same job as blacks was not only to acquire the characteristics whites imputed to blacks, but also to violate one of the primary tenets of the proslavery argument. The promise of Southern life was that slavery would free all whites from the drudgery that normally fell to the poor and created class divisions. Slavery thus eased class distinctions and established a general equality among whites that would be impossible in a free society. Whites doing "nigger work" degraded whites, elevated blacks, and made a shambles of the proslavery argument. Slaveholders disliked hiring whites for jobs normally done by blacks almost as much as white workers disliked the jobs. Opposition to whites doing "nigger work" was naturally strongest in the Lower South, where slavery was most deeply entrenched and the defense of slavery most explicit. Highly attuned to the positive-good argument, Edward Laurens, a leader of the South Carolina nullification movement, clearly saw the connection between the refusal of whites to work and the high occupational status of the free people of color in Charleston. He vigorously denied the common cant that the pleasures of urban life dissipated the city's best young men. "The true state of the case is," Laurens insisted, "that we first degrade the occupation by employing colored persons, and are then surprised that our young men, (whose spirit and highmindedness we endeavor almost daily to excite,) will not enter the arena with them."[25]

The most important "nigger work" was barbering. Free Negro barbers could be found in every Southern city, and despite the proscriptive pressures free Negroes faced in other trades, the number of black barbers grew steadily during the antebellum years. By the eve of the Civil War, the trade had become so closely identified with free Negroes that an English visitor proclaimed it their "birthright." In many ways, barbering typified the kind of work in which free Negroes had the best chance of success. The servile nature of the job drove

[25] Edward Laurens, *A Letter to the Hon. Whitemarsh B. Seabrook* (Charleston, S.C., 1835), pp. 9–10.

away white competitors, while it encouraged the patronage of white customers who felt they should be served by blacks. Opening a barbershop did not take a great deal of capital, and success depended mainly on the ability to please a white clientele—a talent many free Negroes carried out of slavery. Moreover, unlike many of the trades at which free Negroes worked, barbering was not physically burdensome. The diversity of the trade and the moderate physical demands allowed hard-working free Negroes to give full rein to their ambition. Free Negro barbers rented carriages, ran bathhouses, sold clothing, and pulled teeth. In addition to all of these, William Johnson, a successful Natchez barber, invested his profits in real estate and made loans to the city's leading white businessmen.[26]

The occupations that were designated "nigger work" varied from place to place. Trades from which free Negroes were barred in one city were dominated by them in others. Thus, while white workingmen dislodged free Negroes from the draying trade in Baltimore and St. Louis, freemen controlled that work in other cities. In 1836, Norfolk whites, complaining of the growing shortage of slave labor, petitioned the Virginia Assembly to allow a free Negro carter to remain in the state because draying was "a negro job." Similarly, although there was not a single free Negro tailor in Richmond in 1860, free Negroes made up almost 40 percent of the membership of that craft in Charleston.

If the specific occupations varied, the character of "nigger work" was everywhere the same. These occupations were almost always service trades that required little capital and generally depended on white customers. Usually, they were more closely identified with the plantation, where free Negroes had originally learned them, than with the industrializing sector of the economy. While some of these trades were servile in nature, they generally required considerable skill. Indeed, skill was an essential element in many of the jobs

[26] William Russell, *My Diary, North and South,* 2 vols. (London, 1863), I, 73–4; Wright, *Free Negro in Maryland,* p. 155; *Nashville Republican,* 21 April 1836, 9 April 1841; *Nashville Republican Banner,* 28 December 1856; William R. Hogan and Edwin A. Davis, eds., *William Johnson's Natchez,* 2 vols. (Baton Rouge, La., 1951). Barbering was also a prominent free Negro occupation in colonial Brazil; Cohen and Greene, eds., *Neither Slave Nor Free,* p. 103.

TABLE 15

MAJOR FREE NEGRO* CRAFTS, RICHMOND, 1860

	Number of skilled free Negroes	*Proportion of skilled free Negroes*	*Proportion of all skilled workers free Negroes*
Total free Negro skilled workers	174	100%	6%[a]
Barbers	33	19	54
Plasterers	27	16	50
Carpenters	27	16	6
Blacksmiths	22	13	16
Shoemakers	17	10	7
Bricklayers	16	9	17

* Men over fifteen years of age.
[a] Computed from major free ethnic and racial groups: native whites, British, Germans, Irish, and free Negroes.

SOURCE: Richmond manuscript census, 1860, NA.

TABLE 16

MAJOR FREE NEGRO* CRAFTS, CHARLESTON, 1860

	Number of skilled free Negroes	*Proportion of skilled free Negroes*	*Proportion of all skilled workers free Negroes*
Total free Negro skilled workers	404	100%	20%[a]
Carpenters	133	33	27
Tailors	48	12	38
Bricklayers and brickmasons	27	7	26
Painters	24	6	18
Butchers	22	5	41
Barbers	20	5	80
Shoemakers	19	5	15
Millwrights	15	4	75

* Men over fifteen years of age.
[a] Computed from major free ethnic and racial groups: native whites, British, Germans, Irish, and free Negroes.

SOURCE: Charleston manuscript census, 1860, NA.

deemed "nigger work." Without it, these trades would have been open to the lowest portion of the white work force, who might not have cared what they were called so long as they could enjoy steady employment. The skills free Negroes acquired because of the stigma of "nigger work" protected their jobs from the least skilled white workers, while fear of being identified with blacks guarded freemen from more accomplished white competitors.

Skilled free Negro artisans and tradesmen clustered in these stigmatized occupations. In 1860, over 80 percent of Richmond's skilled free Negro men worked at six trades: barbering, carpentering, plastering, blacksmithing, bricklaying, and shoemaking. The remaining free Negro artisans and tradesmen were limited to another dozen crafts, although more than fifty other occupations were practiced in the city. Many prominent trades had no free Negro members. A free Negro cabinetmaker, tinsmith, machinist, or iron molder could not be found in Richmond. Of the city's sixty-four stone masons, only one was a free black. The refusal of whites to employ or work alongside blacks limited the free Negro's occupational opportunities even where free Negroes did comparatively well. Charleston free Negroes, despite their considerably higher level of skill, were also confined to a small number of trades. In 1860, 45 percent of the skilled free Negro men were carpenters and tailors. Six other occupations—painting, bricklaying, butchering, barbering, shoemaking, and lumber milling—made up another 30 percent of the skilled free Negro work force.[27] Thus, while the opprobrium whites attached to "nigger work" helped protect free Negro craftsmen from destructive competition, it also reflected the fragility of their place in the Southern economy. Isolated in a few crafts, Negro freemen were vulnerable to any revision in the definition of "nigger work." Competition from whites or a shift in the economy which eliminated free Negroes from only a handful of trades could be disastrous.

Disaster never struck, in large measure, because of a general shortage of skilled workers. The steady expansion of the Southern economy made employers careful to conserve their work force. They might have wished to replace free Negroes with white or slave workers, but these substitutes were becoming increasingly expensive and even at higher rates they were not always available. Attempts to enthrall free Negro workers and opposition to free Negro removal wherever free-

[27] Petition from Norfolk, 18 December 1836; VLP; Richmond and Charleston manuscript censuses, 1860, NA.

men were numerous suggest the growing importance of the free Negro's labor. Hard-pressed farmers and merchants frequently petitioned to exempt free Negroes whose "skills were much required" or who were "regularly engaged to white persons" from laws that might remove them from the South.[28]

The growing complexity of the Southern economy also protected the freemen's jobs and enlarged their opportunities. The South was industrializing more slowly than the North, but it was industrializing. Southern industries, usually primary processing, grew rapidly during the antebellum years. As these industries expanded, the need for transportation, warehouses, and allied service trades also increased. Slave labor proved very adaptable and slaves, especially hirelings, filled many of the jobs in the new industries.[29] But the supply of slaves was short, and free Negroes, able to set their own terms of employment, took up much of the slack in the expanding sectors of the Southern economy.

Economic changes in the South strengthened the free Negro's bargaining position. Free Negro craftsmen generally earned good wages, and many achieved modest wealth. Thomas Day, a North Carolina free Negro known as the finest furniture maker in the state, usually received the premium his work deserved. In 1847, the president of the University of North Carolina accepted Day's bid for library shelving although it was a hundred dollars higher than "a very respectable" Chapel Hill firm's. "For my justification," the president wrote Day, "I must rely upon the superior manner in which I expect you to execute the work." However, he carefully warned the black craftsman "not to mention to anyone the amount you are to receive." Day's work, in a heavy Empire style often embossed with American eagles, won him many

28 Petition from Essex County, December 1842, Petition from Accomac County, 14 December 1838, VLP; Petition from Hawkins County, 6 September 1832, TLP; Petition from Richard Sanders, 7 December 1833, Miscellaneous Petitions, 1860, box 107, MLP.

29 Starobin, *Industrial Slavery in the Old South*, especially pp. 3–34; also Charles B. Dew, *Ironmaker to the Confederacy: Joseph R. Anderson and the Tredegar Iron Works* (New Haven, Conn., 1966); Bruce, *Virginia Iron Manufacture;* James F. Hopkins, *A History of the Hemp Industry in Kentucky* (Lexington, Ky., 1951); Joseph C. Robert, *Tobacco Kingdom* (Durham, N.C., 1938); and J. C. Sitterson, *Sugar Country: The Sugar Industry in the South, 1753–1950* (Lexington, Ky., 1953).

similar commissions. By 1860, he held property valued at more than four thousand dollars, owned several slaves, and employed a white journeyman. Although only a few free Negroes could match the extraordinary talent of Thomas Day, the ideological and economic forces that pushed Day to prominence helped many freemen. Visitors from the North, where labor was highly valued and blacks did not enjoy protection from the "nigger work" stigma, marveled that "some of the best [Southern] mechanics . . . are colored men and among them are several master workingmen, who employ considerable numbers of colored laborers."[30]

With labor scarce, the occupational shelters created by the stigma of "nigger work" were easily defended by the freemen's skill. White workingmen failed to dislodge free Negro mechanics and artisans from many trades because their talents were too much in demand. If whites objected to working alongside blacks, there were many blacks to take their place. Indeed, the free Negro's high level of skill often made him the indispensable element in the work force. When white laborers refused to work under the direction of a free Negro foreman on one New Orleans construction project, the owners agreed to remove him if one of the whites would take his place. The job proved to be beyond their abilities, and when no one came forward, the free Negro continued as before.[31]

Fierce competition sometimes forced black craftsmen to exchange their saws for shovels and occasionally drove free Negroes completely out of certain occupations, but they did not give up their places easily. Their strategic position within

[30] Thomas Day to David L. Swain, 17 November 1847, quotation in David L. Swain to Thomas Day, 24 November 1847, University of North Carolina Papers, UNC; Franklin, *Free Negro in North Carolina,* pp. 45, 142, 144, 160; Andrews, *Slavery and the Domestic Slave Trade,* p. 162. The relationship between Northern attitudes toward work and the "free labor" or Republican ideology is discussed in Eric Foner, *Free Soil, Free Labor, Free Men: The Ideology of the Republican Party Before the Civil War* (New York, 1970), pp. 11–39. The proportion of Negroes who worked in skilled trades was generally lower in the North than in the South. In New York City, for example, only 13 percent of the blacks were engaged in a skill craft in 1855; Robert Ernst, "The Economic Status of New York City Negroes, 1850–1863," *Negro History Bulletin,* XII (1949), 139–43; also Litwack, *North of Slavery,* pp. 113–86.

[31] Ambrose C. Fulton, *A Life's Voyage, A Diary of a Sailor on Sea and Land, Jotted Down During a Seventy Years' Voyage* (New York, 1898), pp. 107, 239.

the Southern economy allowed them to defend themselves, and even to turn the tables on whites. When white shipworkers tried to exclude free Negro caulkers from the Baltimore docks, free Negroes organized their own workingmen's association and eventually monopolized the trade. Up until the 1830s, slaves, free Negroes, and whites worked side by side in the shipyards of Baltimore. But whites grew increasingly restive laboring alongside men they deemed inferiors and grumbled that "free colored mechanics were eating the bread which should be eaten by American freemen." The depression that followed the Panic of 1837 increased competition between white and black workers and further stirred racial antagonism. When the demand for ships caused by the Mexican War strengthened their bargaining position, whites used their new power to push many black workers from the docks. In the shipyard where Frederick Douglass worked, white carpenters threatened to strike unless blacks were dismissed, and when some employers balked at the threat, they forcibly removed free Negroes and slave hirelings from the docks. Their success encouraged other white workingmen to try and dislodge free Negro and slave competitors. To counter this threat, free Negro caulkers organized their own union, excluded whites, and, according to one account, set wages and insisted on black foremen. Some years later, when a white caulker was brought into one shipyard, free Negroes "threw down their tools and refused to work until he was discharged from the vessel."[32] Blacks, so long proscribed by whites, had learned their lesson well.

While most successful freemen earned their living serving whites, the increasing number of free Negro and slave hirelings, especially in the cities, provided a small but growing market for black entrepreneurs. In every Southern city, free Negroes ran boardinghouses for free Negroes and slaves whose owners allowed them to live on their own. African churches and schools supported black ministers and teachers, and a few Negro merchants profited from trade with Liberia and Haiti. But the most common black enterprises were small cookshops and groceries, which usually doubled as saloons and gambling

[32] Frederick Douglass, *My Bondage and My Freedom* (New York, 1855), pp. 310–15; *Baltimore American*, 8 July 1858.

houses where free Negroes, slaves, and occasionally whites gathered. Although white officials viewed "the numerous Tippling Shops erected on the highways and in our Towns by free negroes" as a source of disorder that encouraged thievery and worse, they flourished throughout the South.[33] The attempts of the Richmond authorities to dislodge free Negroes from that business suggests the pervasiveness of the black-owned groceries.

"The Mayor has set out with the determination of breaking up as far as possible, these haunts of misery and degradation," announced a leading daily in 1853.[34] Determination might be applauded, but stopping the extensive trade was quite another thing. Free Negroes tucked their shops away in alleys, basements, and other places that made them difficult to detect. Sometimes there were secret passwords, hidden doorways, and long, mazelike tunnels to prevent discovery. When the police raided one suspected confectionery shop, they found no evidence of foul play. But just as they were leaving the shop, one suspicious officer "detected a secret door in the partition, and opening it, found it led to a narrow passage. Passing through it for some distance, he came upon a large bar room, handsomely fitted up, in which one man was indulging to his heart's content." Even after discovery, customers often made their escape through specially prepared exits, leaving no evidence of wrongdoing. Legally licensed grocers might be dragged into court and fined for not paying taxes and other violations of the city code, but much to the mayor's distress they soon reopened their shops. Unlicensed free Negro shopkeepers were not so fortunate. The mayor systematically closed their stores and the City Council refused to issue new licenses to black shopkeepers. But the trade was too profitable for free Negroes to abandon. Clinton James, like other free Negro saloon keepers, quietly relocated his shop, and when it was rediscovered he confidently paid his fine and began again in still another location. When the exasperated mayor ordered James whipped, he hired a lawyer and took the case to a higher court. The judge disqualified the prohibition of free Negro cookshops, but the mayor appealed the case and

[33] Petition from Davidson County, 8 October 1813, TLP.
[34] Richmond *Daily Dispatch*, 20, 31 August 1853.

it wended its way to the Virginia Supreme Court. Although the high court upheld the ban, still the trade did not abate. "Cook shops, kept by Negroes, are forbidden by law, as is the sale of ardent spirits," observed the Richmond *Dispatch* in 1860, "and yet there are scores of the colored continually engaging in these lawless callings."[35]

Despite the harassment, many free Negro cookshops thrived. Some groggeries were lavishly fitted out. The all-purpose store run by Clinton James comprised the entire floor of a large building. "The house has four rooms on the first floor," noted a police reporter; "the first was used as a grocery, the second as a bar room, the third as a snack room, and the fourth as a kitchen." Richard Taylor, "a fine mustached mulatto," ran the "Taylor Hotel" in an alley behind the palatial Richmond Exchange Hotel. Customers dropped in day and night, some drank "juleps, some port-wine sangarees, some whiskey punches, some lemonpops," some played cards, dominoes, and dice on marble tables, and some occasionally enjoyed the company of "ladies (of a certain class) rustling in silks and odoriferous as pinks and honeysuckles." These enterprises not only were extremely profitable, but they gave their owners a sense of pride, self-respect, and most important, independence from whites. It was from this class of black-supported businessmen as well as those artisans whose skill gave them a sense of independence that much of the leadership of the free Negro caste derived. Small wonder that whites were anxious to crush these groggeries and cookshops and that the Richmond press grumbled uncomfortably when they discovered that the customers "all spoke in the most respectful terms of '*Mr.* Taylor,' the proprietor of the opposition Exchange."[36]

By serving the growing black community, doing jobs white workers found distasteful, and accepting lower wages, free Negroes found work on the margins of the Southern economy. Although whites kept pushing on these marginal jobs, limiting them by law and informal agreements, and excluding free

[35] *Richmond Enquirer,* 1, 10 December 1853; Richmond *Daily Dispatch,* 7 May 1853, 11, 13 November 1854, 13, 14 February 1855, 11 October 1855, 9 May 1860; Catterall, ed., *Judicial Cases Concerning Slavery,* I, 233.

[36] Richmond *Daily Dispatch,* 22 January 1855, 1 December 1853; *Richmond Enquirer,* 23 September 1853.

Negroes when they found out how profitable such work might be, free Negroes had become such an integral part of the Southern economy that they proved impossible to dislodge. Despite all whites could do, some free Negroes prospered. Their success was reflected in the growth of free Negro property holding. Although some of the most successful freemen drained their savings to purchase the liberty of friends and relatives, and others migrated from the South, the number of landowning free Negroes grew. In Nansemond County in tidewater Virginia, the number of free Negro farmers increased steadily between 1830 and 1860, although the free Negro population remained relatively constant. In 1830, there were 18 Negro freemen who owned their own land, 45 in 1840, 66 in 1850, and 86 in 1860. The growth of a black landowning class in Nansemond County mirrored that of the state generally. In 1830, there were fewer than 700 free Negro farmers who owned their own land in Virginia. Although the state's free Negro population increased only 21 percent during the next thirty years and many of the most prosperous black farmers migrated North, by 1860, 1,200 rural free Negroes controlled over sixty thousand acres of land worth about $370,000.[37]

The growth of free Negro property holding followed a similar pattern throughout the South. Although the full extent of the development of black landownership awaits close analysis of census and tax records on the county and ward level, fragmentary evidence from several states confirms the steady and pervasive growth of free Negro wealth. Between 1850 and 1860, the value of Negro-owned real estate in thirty-three Tennessee counties—for which comparable data are available—more than tripled, while their free Negro population increased less than 20 percent. By the eve of the Civil War, free Negroes in these Tennessee counties held land worth about $435,000 and a quarter of a million dollars in personal property. Georgia census records reveal much the same pattern of growth in the decade before the war. The value of black landownership in fifteen selected counties from various parts of the state containing almost half the free Negroes in

[37] Jackson, "Free Negro Farmers," pp. 406–8.

Georgia increased from $55,000 in 1850 to $90,00 in 1860, while the free Negro population grew by less than a fifth. A similar analysis of Alabama and Florida census returns and Maryland tax records shows the same steady and occasionally spectacular increase in free Negro property ownership.[38]

The general shortage of workers in the cities and the wider range of available trades enabled urban free Negroes to enjoy an even richer prosperity than their rural counterparts. Free Negro property holding generally increased more rapidly in the cities than in the countryside. In rural Virginia, the value of free-Negro-owned land more than doubled between 1830 and 1860, but it grew more than sixfold in the cities. Urban free Negroes also increased more rapidly than those in the countryside, but the growth of property holding among city blacks outstripped the difference in the numerical increase of urban and rural population. Only a third of Virginia's free Negroes lived in urban areas in 1860, but they controlled land valued at 30 percent more than that of rural free Negroes. In the same year, Davidson County (Nashville) free Negroes held almost half the black-owned real estate in Tennessee, although that county contained less than 10 percent of the free Negro population of the state. In the upper reaches of free Negro society the urban bias became more pronounced. Eleven out of twelve Maryland free Negroes worth more than a thousand dollars lived in Baltimore or its suburbs. As free Negro immigrants understood well, cities were the gateways to prosperity.[39]

Yet, landowning free Negroes remained a very select group. Both in the countryside and in the cities, wealth was distributed extremely unevenly within the free black community. While most free Negroes were propertyless, a relatively small number of blacks owned land worth several thousand dollars.

[38] England, "Free Negro in Tennessee," pp. 225–33; Sweat, "Free Negro in Georgia," pp. 154, 158; Russell Garvin, "The Free Negro in Florida Before the Civil War," *Florida Historical Quarterly,* XLVI (1967), 12; Boucher, "Free Negro in Alabama," pp. 368–507; Wright, *Free Negro in Maryland,* p. 184.

[39] Jackson, *Free Negro Labor and Property Holding,* p. 138; Wright, *Free Negro in Maryland,* pp. 186–7; England, "Free Negro in Tennessee," pp. 232–3; Sweat, "Free Negro in Georgia," pp. 154, 158; Boucher, "Free Negro in Alabama," pp. 368–71, 397–424, 438–92, 466–93; Dorothy Provine, "The Economic Position of Free Blacks in the District of Columbia, 1800–1860," *JNH,* LVIII (1973), 67–72.

The same unequal distribution of wealth characterized the free Negro property-holding class. In Chatham County (Savannah), 7 slaveholding free Negroes held more than half the real estate owned by free Negroes in 1850. Similarly, 26 Shelby County (Memphis) free Negroes worth more than a thousand dollars controlled two-thirds of the free-Negro-owned real estate in that county and city in 1860. Even in Petersburg, where property ownership was fairly widespread among Negro freemen, 29 free Negroes, about 10 percent of the property-holding blacks and less than 4 percent of the free Negro heads of households in 1860, controlled almost a third of the city's free-Negro-owned land. Although careful study is still needed to delineate fully the structure of free Negro communities (and to compare it with that of the white community), almost all of these successful free Negroes were tradesmen or skilled mechanics serving white customers. Only 12 of the nearly 250 free Negroes who owned property in Petersburg worked in the tobacco factories. Most of these free Negroes held only small parcels acquired late in the 1850s. On the other hand, almost all free Negro barbers, draymen, liverymen, confectioners, and restaurateurs held some real estate.[40] Although these men were not representative of the free Negro caste generally, they were typical of the free Negro elite throughout the cities of the South.

Besides providing income and adding a measure of comfort, property ownership had immense symbolic importance to free Negroes. In a society where their legal status was steadily degenerating, the ownership of property held out hope that improvement was possible. Free Negroes, like many other ethnic groups, seemed to use property mobility as a means of compensating for the barriers to the traditional routes of occupational mobility.[41] Real estate holdings also provided unimpeachable evidence of the free Negroes' ability. Whites might deny their business acumen or skill, but land, houses, and other material possessions were impossible to ignore. These

[40] Sweat, "Free Negro in Georgia," pp. 154, 171; England, "Free Negro in Tennessee," pp. 227–8, 233; Jackson, *Free Negro Labor and Property Holding*, pp. 151–9, 240–1.

[41] Stephan Thernstrom, *Poverty and Progress: Social Mobility in a Nineteenth-Century City* (Cambridge, Mass., 1964), pp. 155–7, 200–1.

possessions not only countered the white stereotype but also served as the mark of distinction between elite freemen and the mass of blacks who lived in desperate poverty. Wealthy free Negroes hoped they would offer some protection against capricious whites who wanted to push them into slavery. Finally, they proved some blacks could excel some whites. Thus free Negroes were continually adding to their property, trading up to a bigger lot or a larger house, and carefully passing their property on to their children, hopeful that proof of their prosperity would induce whites to ease their oppression. Property ownership was the most important symbol of the free Negroes' success in a society which allowed them few such symbols.

Elite free Negroes worked hard to achieve their privileged positions, but once at the top of black society they did not fully escape white rule. No matter what its symbolic value, property ownership did not provide independence for most successful freemen. The alliances necessary for climbing the ladder of success may have increased their dependence on whites. Many owed their privileged status directly to connections with white merchants and planters. Although most landowning free Negroes seem to have purchased their property without aid, the free Negro elite generally had help from white parents and benefactors. Significantly, the largest slaveholding free Negro planters were almost uniformly mixed-bloods.[42] Economic dominance allowed whites to regulate the membership of the free Negro elite by determining who could buy land, open shops, or engage in certain trades. For example, a leading colonizationist reported it was impossible for most free Negroes to work in the carting trade between Virginia and North Carolina. "The case of John Morris," he added, "was different—Morris had been for years a Hack Driver between Elizabeth City, N.C., and Norfolk, and was intimately and favourably known to every principal man and business man in Norfolk and Portsmouth."[43] Leading men in

[42] Jackson, *Free Negro Labor and Property Holding*, pp. 125–7; Joseph K. Menn, "The Large Slaveholders of the Deep South, 1860," unpublished doctoral dissertation, University of Texas, 1964, pp. 208–10.

[43] William H. Starr to J. W. Lugenbeel, 5 June 1852, ACS; J. Prentis to James Henderson, 28 September 1817, Dismal Swamp Papers, Duke; Petition from Northampton County, 6 December 1831, VLP.

Norfolk let John Morris earn a living and perform a valuable service, but only at a price. He had to conform to their standards of a "good Negro." Thus, ambitious free Negroes needed not only ready cash, good credit, and quick wits to achieve economic success, but also the concurrence and active support of whites. Through the impersonal operation of the economy, and more important, through personal and sometimes familial relations, the free Negro's economic advancement came to depend on white support. By pursuing success in the white economy, free Negroes tied themselves to the white standard of values.

The full extent of the free Negroes' dependence on the white-controlled economy is suggested by a comparison of the growth of free Negro property holding in Richmond and Norfolk. In the years after the Revolution both cities expanded rapidly. Richmond, a new town established on the fall line of the James River, was named state capital in 1779. As it grew, it became a major center of tobacco manufacturing and canal and rail transportation. Later, the Tredegar Iron Works, the largest in the South, located in the city and brought with it allied industries. Norfolk, on the other hand, fell upon hard times during the 1790s and never recovered its former prosperity. The growth of the ports of New York and Baltimore robbed Norfolk of the growing commerce with Europe and reduced it to a minor stop on the coastal trade. Meanwhile, internecine rivalries between Virginia cities and canal and railroad interests prevented Norfolk from developing a hinterland market which might have stimulated local enterprises. Isolated from the mainstream of trade and unable to develop new industries, the city stagnated. Disaster was avoided when the federal government located a naval yard in the city, but prosperity never fully returned.[44]

The stagnation of Norfolk's economy stifled the growth of a class of property-holding free Negroes. Although the municipal black code enacted by Richmond authorities was considerably harsher than that of Norfolk, Richmond free Negroes prospered while those in Norfolk languished. By 1830, five

[44] H. J. Eckenrode, ed., *Richmond, Capital of Virginia* (Richmond, 1938), pp. 14–18, 69–71; Thomas J. Wertenbaker, *Norfolk, Historic Southern Port* (Durham, N.C., 1931), pp. 158–205.

times as many free Negroes owned real estate in Richmond as in Norfolk. During the next thirty years, while the value of Negro-owned real estate increased tenfold in Richmond, it declined in Norfolk. The depressed economy heightened competition between white and black workers. White workingmen replaced free Negroes in most of the skilled trades and even moved into barbering, a free Negro monopoly in most of the South. Young free Negro men left the city in droves looking for new opportunities. In 1860, women composed 65 percent of the city's free Negro population.[45] Free Negroes who sought independence by working within the Southern economy often found themselves deeper in the white man's grip.

Free Negroes, both urban and rural, divided sharply along class lines, and developments during the antebellum years seemed to be driving them farther and farther apart. Whites pushed many free Negroes closer to slavery by forcing them to work under the same conditions as slaves and depriving them of all but the most menial jobs. Some freemen slipped through this fine web of discrimination and proscription, practiced lucrative trades, accumulated property, and grew in wealth. Part of this class, because of the independence their skills afforded or because of the support of black customers, stood aloof from whites. Their independence nurtured a strong sense of race consciousness, which pushed them into a leadership position within the free Negro caste. But most of the free Negro elite was intricately involved in the white economy. While these elite free Negroes curried favor with white employers and customers, they absorbed white values and ideals. Close ties of friendship and sometimes of blood reinforced their solicitude for white opinion and the distance they felt between themselves and the mass of poorer blacks. Slowly their way of life and their way of thinking diverged from that of the mass of free Negroes.

[45] Jackson, *Free Negro Labor and Property Holding*, pp. 138, 92.

8

The Sources of Free Negro Identity

Even whilst walking through the streets in company with another, he [Denmark Vesey] was not idle; for if his companion bowed to a white person he would rebuke him, and observe that all men were born equal. . . .

An Official Report of the Trials of Sundry Negroes, Charged with an Attempt to Raise an Insurrection in the State of South Carolina (1822)

I think society is made up of two distinct parts, on one hand, wolves and foxes and, on the other hand, lambs and chickens to provide food for the former.

Andrew Durnford to John McDonogh, 27 January 1844

The agent observed, that it was a happy thing for the expedition that I had come on; that I served as a kind of middle link between the white and colored, and that if they had not confidence in them, (the agents,) yet they had in me; and as I was in the cabin with the agents, I was in all their councils, &c.

Journal of Daniel Coker, a Descendant of Africa (1820)

WHITES and slaves stood at the extremes of Southern society. According to law and custom, white citizens enjoyed nearly total freedom and black slaves almost none. Neither citizen nor slave, free Negroes dangled awkwardly in the middle of the Southern caste system. They shared some of the privileges of whites and were burdened with many of the liabilities of slaves, yet they stood apart from both. Their social identity was further obscured by class divisions within the caste, and the fissures along class lines were complicated by color, ethnic, and denominational differences. Origin and interest often divided rich and poor, mulattoes and blacks, Episcopalians and Baptists, creoles and "Yankees" as much from each other as from whites or slaves. Still, within this matrix of whites and slaves, rich and poor, mulattoes and blacks, free Negroes tried to define their role as privileged, if oppressed, blacks.

The search for the freemen's identity begins with the diverse conditions of free Negro life. Most free Negroes lived in the countryside, where they squatted in shanties on scraps of land that no one else seemed to want. Tucked away well off the main road, these isolated cottages and shacks occasionally grew in number until they composed a small village whose general location was familiar to whites but whose fluctuating membership remained shrouded in mystery. A South Carolina sheriff trying to collect back taxes from delinquent free Negroes in one piedmont county despaired of "the difficulties in finding them, on account of the peculiar situation of their place of residence."[1]

These black villages, however ramshackle, allowed free Negroes a degree of autonomy and a chance to escape the pressures of the white-dominated world. Many poor freemen did not enjoy even these small privileges. Thousands of free blacks had no independent residence and lived under the supervision of whites. In 1830, at least a quarter of the free Negroes in thirty-one Virginia counties lived with their white employers. In some parts of the state the proportion was much higher, and in a few areas a majority of the free Negroes lived in white households. These Virginia counties were probably typical of much of the rural South. Adams County, Mississippi, with the largest free Negro population in that state, had an almost identical proportion of freemen—one out of four—residing with whites who probably were their employers. In North Carolina, so many free Negroes dwelled with their white employers that the state made white householders responsible for collecting the freemen's taxes.[2]

[1] Deed of Execution, n.d., Richland County, SCLP.

[2] Jackson, *Free Labor and Property Holding*, pp. 70–1; Hogan and Davis, eds., *William Johnson's Natchez*, p. 11; *N.C. Laws*, 1828, c. 34.

White employers, who were frequently slaveowners, usually quartered free Negro hands with slaves. Some slave housing was clean and well maintained; most was not. In any case, the houses of most rural free Negroes differed little from those of bondsmen. A German nobleman traveling between Washington and Baltimore noticed a scattering of tiny, ill-constructed houses unlike any he had seen in the North. The majority of "these small houses," he observed, "are inhabited by negroes who generally had a very tattered appearance."[3]

For the mass of urban freemen, the conditions of life were much the same. Most lived in the poorer neighborhoods located on the outskirts of cities or in the low-lying areas around rivers and railroad yards. Although these localities were unattractive and often unhealthy, low land valuations and cheap rents drew free Negroes. The Oglethorpe ward of Savannah, which contained almost half the city's free Negroes, was typical of the neighborhoods in which most freemen lived. Located between the railroad tracks and the river, it was the industrial and commercial heart of the city. It included, among its hundreds of workshops and warehouses, the depot and yards of the Georgia Central Railroad and the terminus of the Savannah and Ogeechee Canal. Of its nearly five hundred buildings only five were brick, and unlike almost every other ward, it contained no public square.[4]

Within these crowded neighborhoods, free Negroes lived in back alleys, dank cellars, factory lofts, and the corners of abandoned industrial sites. They frequently carved respectable dwellings out of these crude conditions. Two Baltimore free Negroes remodeled a house in a brickyard to provide apartments for their families. When they squabbled over the property, the press gave a detailed description. The house "had two separate and distinct apartments, with a door to each, and they separately occupied those apartments. There was a yard before each portion of the house, and a gate for entrance into each. These yards were about 2½ yards wide." Such quarters were cramped and their location was hardly ideal, but they were

[3] Karl Bernhard, Duke of Saxe-Weimar Eisenach, *Travels Through North America, During the Years 1825 and 1826*, 2 vols. (Philadelphia, 1828), I, 169.

[4] Joseph Bancroft, *Census of the City of Savannah*, 2nd ed. (Savannah, 1848), pp. 8–9, 13–14; *Savannah Daily Republican*, 24 March 1855.

better than the cheerless dwellings where many free Negroes lived. After visiting a free Negro family, a sympathetic Southern woman described their home as a "tottering hovel, situated in the heart of Norfolk. It is a miserable apology for a human habitation, containing but two apartments, one above the other." Inside, conditions were even worse. "On one side of the first or ground floor," she reported, "is a wretched bed supported by some boards, and broken chairs"; on the other side of the room lay a free Negro child, slowly dying, probably of tuberculosis. Observers in other cities found free Negroes living in the same grim conditions. "The lowly dwellings occupied by the lower class of coloured people," noted a visitor to Richmond, "are of a miserable kind, resembling the worst brickhouses in the back lanes of English manufacturing towns."[5]

Yet no unitary black ghetto developed. The absence of urban transportation and the need for blacks to live near their place of work scattered free Negroes throughout Southern cities. Even with the advent of omnibuses in the 1830s, whites were reluctant to create a single community which might unite blacks and serve as a breeding ground for insurrection. Free Negroes usually could be found in almost every section of Southern cities, living close to whites of every nationality. Although the poorer districts of most cities contained an occasional all-Negro block—or more frequently, all-black rooming houses—working-class neighborhoods usually were a mélange of whites and blacks. Surveying one such district in Baltimore, a city physician observed "rows of houses occupied by Germans, Irish, and free blacks." Freemen and whites mixed at the other end of the social scale as well. Wealthy free Negroes had little trouble escaping the dreary lower-class neighborhoods and finding homes in the better parts of Southern cities. William Johnson, a successful free Negro barber, land speculator, and moneylender, built a commodious brick house on one of the finest streets in Natchez, far from the tawdry "Under-the-Hill" area where the poor of all colors

[5] Baltimore *Sun*, 7 November 1838; Margaret Douglass, *Educational Laws of Virginia, the Personal Narrative of Mrs. Margaret Douglass, a Southern Woman, Who was Imprisoned . . . for the Crime of Teaching Free Colored Children to Read* (Boston, 1854), p. 12; William Chambers, *Things As They Are in America* (Philadelphia, 1854), pp. 271–2.

congregated.[6] In many Southern cities, free Negroes owned homes in the finest residential neighborhoods. Often their houses were larger and better constructed than those of their white neighbors.

A close inspection of residential patterns in Charleston on the eve of the Civil War suggests the full extent of the intermingling of free Negroes and whites. Although the proportion of free Negroes living in the back alleys of the Neck was higher than that in the airy streets near the bay, Negro freemen resided on every major thoroughfare and most of the minor ones. Measured by the index of dissimilarity, racial segregation was only slightly higher than ethnic segregation and considerably lower than class segregation.[7] At times, the indiscriminate dis-

[6] Thomas H. Buckler, *A History of Epidemic Cholera as it Appeared at Baltimore City and County Almshouse . . . 1849* (Baltimore, 1851), pp. 5, 12; Hogan and Davis, eds., *William Johnson's Natchez*, p. 34.

[7] INDEX OF DISSIMILARITY—CHARLESTON, 1861

Free Negroes/whites	23.2
Free Negroes/South Carolina–born whites	20.1
Free Negroes/Irish*	34.9
Free Negroes/British (England, Scotland, Wales)	34.8
Free Negroes/Northern-born whites†	28.2
Free Negroes/Germans	22.9
South Carolina–born whites/Irish	21.8
South Carolina–born whites/British	15.3
South Carolina–born whites/Northern-born whites	12.9
South Carolina–born whites/Germans	10.4
British/Irish	19.0
Germans/Irish	18.9
Germans/British	13.1

* Refers to place of birth.

† States remaining in the Union.

One index of class is the division of the city into those living in brick and wooden houses, on the assumption that the more substantial brick houses would generally be preferred. The index of dissimilarity of brick and wooden houses is 51.

The index is computed from Frederick A. Ford, comp., *Census of the City of Charleston, South Carolina for the Year 1861*, pp. 8–9, 11, 15–20; Karl E. and Alma Tauber, *Negroes in Cities: Residential Segregation and Neighborhood Change* (Chicago, 1965), p. 46.

The index of dissimilarity is one measure of segregation. It assumes that if the choice of residence were not influenced by race or some other factor (wealth, occupation, or ethnicity, for example) blacks and whites would be scattered throughout a city according to their share of the city's population. No neighborhood, ward, or block (depending on the unit of measurement) would be all black or all white. Each race would be represented in every neighborhood in the same proportion as in the city as a whole. Thus in a city which

tribution of free Negro and white residences threw the two castes together in striking combinations; wealthy whites and impoverished freemen, elite free Negroes and poor whites, frequently found themselves neighbors.

However, people of equal rank generally clustered together regardless of race. The changing residential patterns of Meeting Street, a prominent boulevard that stretched the length of the city, reveal that within the web of class and caste, class determined residence more often than race. Near the Bay, Meeting Street was home to the leading low-country families. Nearly all their houses were brick, and homeownership was almost universal. No Charleston free Negro could match the wealth of the Gourdins, De Saussures, and Grimballs, and few Negro freemen made their homes at this end of the street. Those who did were overwhelmingly women in the employ of these first families. Midway through the city, after passing through the commercial district, the character of Meeting Street changed. The stately brick homes of South Carolina's gentry yielded to a mixture of clean, well-tended brick and wooden houses. Here the city's successful merchants, upward-mobile tradesmen, and white-collar workers made their homes. On a two-block strip between John and Mary streets, nearly all the householders worked at these occupations. Among the most prominent residents of this portion of Meeting Street were James Tupper, a white South Carolina–born insurance executive; Albert Bischoff, a wealthy grocer from Germany; Otis Chaffee, a Rhode Island–born wine merchant; Allston Seabrook, a planter who bore two of the proudest names in the state; and Francis St. Marks, a free Negro barber who practiced at the luxurious Charleston House. Like his prominent white neighbors, St. Marks owned his own home—his was brick, while theirs were wood—considerable real estate, and a handful of slaves. Not all the free Negroes on these blocks equaled

---

was one-third black, approximately one in every three households in every neighborhood could be expected to be black. In such a situation, the index of dissimilarity would be zero. If, on the other hand, all blacks lived in one neighborhood and all whites in another, the index of dissimilarity would be a hundred. In short: the higher the value of the index, the greater the degree of segregation; the lower the value, the greater the intermixture.

For a fuller explanation of the index of dissimilarity see Tauber and Tauber, *Negroes in Cities*, pp. 28–31, 202–44.

St. Marks in wealth, but then, neither did many whites. His nearest white neighbors, Dr. Edward C. Keckeley, a customs inspector, and Christian Hilken, a grocer, owned less property than the barber, and neither held slaves. As Meeting Street pushed toward the city line, the houses again became smaller and the scattering of brick residences was replaced by solid rows of wooden structures. Meeting Street now became home to Charleston's artisans, day laborers, newly arrived immigrants, and slaves who were living away from their masters. But here too, free Negroes and whites mixed easily. Martha Evans, a sixty-year-old free Negro greengrocer, owned her own home near Reid Street and rented the adjacent property to Charles Huston, a white engineer from New York. Farther down the block lived Henry Hicks, a propertyless white Kentucky-born stablekeeper. Across the street resided Owen Gahagen, a white man who was probably new in the city, as he was yet to be listed in either the city directory or the federal census. Next door to Gahagen was a row of houses occupied by slaves. Free and slave, white and black, native and foreign-born, the unbroken mixture continued as Meeting Street proceeded toward the city boundary.[8]

Still, many whites did not like living near blacks, especially free ones. In New Orleans, real estate developers anxious to widen Bourbon Street and transform that winding alley into a busy thoroughfare fumed when they discovered that some of the choicest lots were owned by free Negroes. "Capitalists are willing to embark on such projects," noted one daily, "but . . . they are reluctant to erect elegant edifices for respectable tenants, in the immediate vicinity of negro hovels."[9] Yet it was not the free Negroes who lived in hovels who most angered whites. Often the burning embarrassment whites felt living near free Negroes obviously more successful than themselves proved far more disturbing than the presence of a handful of Negro shanties in a nearby alley. While few whites

[8] Meeting Street was reconstructed from Ford, comp., *Census of Charleston;* Charleston manuscript census, 1860, NA; Means and Turnbull, comps., *The Charleston Directory* (Charleston, 1859); *Directory of the City of Charleston* (Savannah, Ga., 1860); *List of the Tax Payers of the City of Charleston for 1859* (Charleston, 1860); *List of the Tax Payers of the City of Charleston for 1860* (Charleston, 1861).

[9] New Orleans *Bee,* 13 May 1836.

objected to living in close quarters with slaves over whom their dominance was secure, living near free Negroes who displayed the trappings of success and symbols of affluence disturbed them. At the same time, many freemen disliked residing near whites. The white man's proprietary attitudes and constant demands for deference galled them, and some sought succor by physically withdrawing and living among blacks. By the eve of the Civil War, these complementary pushes and pulls were creating the beginnings of black ghettos. Even within the context of the limited residential segregation of Southern cities, free Negroes were living farther apart from whites than were slaves. In Charleston, for example, the index of dissimilarity between whites and free Negroes was more than twice that between whites and slaves.[10] During the 1850s some builders had begun to cater to this growing residential segregation by slapping together "rows of buildings constructed expressly for . . . negroes or persons of color." Still, most blacks remained untouched by this growing residential separation, and it remained relatively minor compared with contemporary Northern standards.[11]

[10] Index of Dissimilarity—Charleston, 1861

White/slave	11.4
White/free Negro	23.2
Slave/free Negro	25.3

This index is computed from Ford, comp., *Census of the City of Charleston*, pp. 15–20. See also Charleston Grand Jury Presentation, Spring 1856, SCA; *Charleston Courier*, 15 December 1859.

[11] The development of residential segregation in the South lagged far behind that in the North. No Southern city had a "Nigger Hill" as did Boston, a "Hayti" as did Pittsburgh, or a "Little Africa" as did Cincinnati. In general, the indexes of dissimilarity between whites and free Negroes—that is, the proportion of the population that would have to move to create a random racial distribution—were lower in Southern cities than in those of the North. Confident of their racial hegemony, Southerners did not feel as strong a need to seal blacks off in separate neighborhoods.

Index of Dissimilarity—Free Negro/White, 1860

Boston	61.3
Chicago	50.0
Cincinnati	47.9
Indianapolis	47.2
Philadelphia	47.1
Nashville	43.1
New York City	40.6
St. Louis	39.1

Dilapidated housing was only one of the consequences of the freemen's poverty. Like other poor people, most free Negroes also lacked nourishing food, good water, proper clothing, and adequate sanitation. This grim combination made them especially susceptible to the diseases that stalked their overcrowded neighborhoods. The all too common results of the conditions of free Negro life were noted by the health officers in the Spring Garden section of Baltimore. Despite its bucolic name, the district was a grimy industrial subdivision packed with immigrant "mechanics, labourers, and coloured population." Most of Baltimore, the physicians noted, was well drained and safe from epidemics. "The Spring Garden district, on the contrary, is level and low . . . and is liable . . . to remittent and intermittent diseases."[12]

"The Cholera has made its appearance in Portsmouth," a colonization agent ominously noted in 1832, "and is particularly destructive to the blacks." As the plague moved inland, slaveholders removed themselves and their valuable property from the cities where the disease left its most devastating mark. Most free Negroes had no such option, and they died by the hundreds. During the epidemic, almost five hundred persons died in Baltimore. The victims, as one journalist quaintly put it,

---

New Orleans	35.7
Brooklyn	35.5
San Francisco	34.6
Mobile	29.8
Wilmington	26.1
Charleston	23.2
Baltimore	22.1
Louisville	20.0

These figures are not directly comparable, since ward structures differed from city to city and contained varying degrees of intraward segregation. The existence of an undetermined amount of intraward segregation tends to obscure the total degree of segregation. Although only suggestive, the general pattern reflected in the rank order of Southern and Northern cities tends to confirm that Southern cities were less segregated than their Northern counterparts. And of course, all nineteenth-century cities were considerably less segregated than the cities of contemporary America, where the indexes of dissimilarity (computed from block-by-block comparisons) are well over 90.

The index is computed from *Population of the United States in 1860;* also see Litwack, *North of Slavery,* pp. 168–70; Tauber and Tauber, *Negroes in Cities,* pp. 29–62, 203–4.

[12] "Sanitary Report of Baltimore," *Ordinances of the Mayor and City Council of Baltimore,* 1850, app., pp. 208–9.

were "chiefly persons little known." But even within this lower-class group, a disproportionate number of the dead were free Negroes. In the first week of September, for example, 254 persons died. Of these, 104 were Negro and 92 were free. Free Negroes made up only 14 percent of the population of the city, but over one-third of the victims. In subsequent epidemics, this pattern persisted.[13]

Even during good times, free Negroes apparently had a higher mortality rate than whites or slaves. "The chances for life . . . among the slaves in Baltimore," estimated one visitor, "appear to be considerably greater than that of free blacks, the deaths among the slaves being only about two thirds as great as among the free people of color." The city's mortality records, though woefully inadequate, generally bear out this sad estimate. Apologists for slavery made much of this fact, and some whites used it to support the most frivolous stereotypes. "If any cause shall operate to prolong the stay of cholera among us," announced a Richmond newspaper in 1854, "it will be excessive indulgence in watermelons by negroes." Occasionally some saw through the shibboleth of race to other causes. Surveying the carnage in 1832, Hezekiah Niles argued that free Negroes were "less cautious than white persons," but he also observed they were "less carefully attended." Niles was only nudging the truth. Malnutrition and the lack of proper clothing weakened the free Negro's resistance. Filthy living conditions and poor medical care made the slaughter inevitable whenever disease struck.[14]

But again, wealthy free Negroes had little trouble escaping the havoc which deadly epidemics wreaked on poorer folk. When yellow fever struck Natchez in 1839, William Johnson followed the city's leading citizens and moved himself and his family to his farm. Many died that summer from the fever, but Johnson boasted, "I am in the Country Sound as a Dollar."[15]

[13] William McKinney to Charles Howard, 30 July 1832, Letters Received, MdSCS Papers; *Richmond Enquirer,* 23 October 1832; *Niles' Weekly Register,* XLIII (8, 22 September 1832), 24, 52; Buckler, *History of Cholera,* pp. 17–18.

[14] Andrews, *Slavery and the Slave Trade,* pp. 44–5; the mortality statistics for Baltimore were listed annually in the *Ordinances of the Mayor and City Council of Baltimore; Richmond Whig,* 1 August 1854; *Niles' Weekly Register,* XLIII (15 September 1832), 44.

[15] Hogan and Davis, eds., *William Johnson's Natchez,* p. 267.

Like other elite free Negroes, Johnson used his wealth to protect himself from the burdens of both class and race.

Class standing influenced the freemen's relations with whites, slaves, and other free Negroes just as it affected their choice of residence and their life-chances. Despite the dense wall of racial antagonism and the intense economic competition which divided whites and blacks, close living conditions and the common pattern of their daily lives frequently pushed the races together. Men and women who lived and worked together often ignored the stigma attached to racial mixing, and occasionally close, even intimate friendship flowered. In isolated rural backwaters, whites and free blacks alike turned away from the hard life of scratching at the soil and hunted and fished together. After a long day in the woods, they might share a jug of sour mash and laugh at the aristocratic pretensions of local nabobs. An upcountry South Carolina patrol, drawn by the sound of loud music and raucous laughter, discovered "a collection of free blacks, slaves and some white folks, fiddling and frolicing generally" in a secluded free Negro settlement. Such racial intermingling offended and frightened white leaders, but close relations between poor free Negroes and whites continued to surface in the most offhand fashion. Late in the 1840s, Jasper Hunt, a North Carolina free Negro, migrated to the barren, sandy region along the Virginia coast. Like local whites, Hunt eked out a meager living fishing and scavenging the wrecked ships that periodically drifted ashore. Common interests and the tedium of daily life drew Hunt and his white neighbors together. "It seems that this fellow was treated with much respect by whites," one official observed, ". . . all sitting at the same table, & they (the whites) calling him Mr. Hunt." Later Hunt had a falling out with his white friends, but their earlier intimacy was a matter of common knowledge. "I think much if not all of this affair grew out of too much familiarity," chimed in another local leader, "not keeping the negro at a distance & in his place together with the Devil's agent, ardent spirits, of which all seemed to have freely taken that morning."[16]

[16] *Charleston Courier,* 8 May 1857; Jasper Hunt Pardon Papers and Related Documents, September 1851, especially J. J. Burroughs to Robert E. Taylor, 9 July 1851, Executive Papers, VSL.

Under the pressure of common conditions, poor blacks and whites became one. They lived together, worked together, and inevitably slept together, hopelessly blurring the color line. A Florida census taker found that most of the free Negroes in his neighborhood were "mixed blooded almost white and have intermarried with a low class of whites—have no trade, occupation or profession. They live in a Settlement or Town of their own, their personal property consists of cattle and hogs. They make no produce except Corn Peas and Potatoes and very little of that. They are a lazy, indolent smooth ass race."[17]

The cramped working-class districts of Southern cities promoted the same easy intimacy between free Negroes and whites. Children of both races often grew up and played together on the same city streets. "We daily meet white boys hand and glove with free negroes of the lowest grade," grumbled a Petersburg newspaper in 1857. In time, whites generally outgrew their childhood intimacy with blacks and accepted the racial mores of Southern society, but the closeness of urban quarters allowed some friendships to continue into later life. When a Baltimore judge asked one freeman if he wanted to call any witnesses for his defense, the free Negro sang out, " 'Here Betsy!' Obedient to the summons, a white woman came up who stated her name to be Elizabeth Cook. 'Do you allow him to call you Betsy?' inquired the state's attorney. 'Yes,' she pertly replied, and went on with the same warmth to vindicate the conduct of her sable friend and neighbor." The police blotters of every Southern city turned up similar instances of racial friendships. When the Richmond city guard arrested a free Negro woman for striking a white, one observer testified that the "parties reside in the neighborhood of the Old Court House Tavern, are associates, and have heretofore been on terms of intimacy."[18]

Fraternization between whites and free Negroes extended to all corners of working-class life. Poor whites and blacks often patronized the same tippling shops, gambling houses, and other places of entertainment. In a typical haul, Richmond

[17] Garvin, "Free Negro in Florida Before the Civil War," p. 12.

[18] *Petersburg Daily Democrat,* 8 July 1857; Baltimore *Sun,* 28 September 1837; Richmond *Daily Dispatch,* 29 September 1854.

police arrested "a very interesting kettle of fish, at a negro den . . . where white, yellow and black congregate to eat, drink and be merry," and the Nashville guard broke into "a cockpit on Front Street, where a large crowd of negroes and white men had congregated to fight chickens and carouse." Some places became notorious for their racial mixing. In New Orleans, the intersection of Bourbon and Orleans Streets was "distinguished for the equality which reigns between black and white—all was hail fellow well met, no matter what the complexion."[19]

Free Negroes and whites profited from the close relations between the races. Many cookshops and gaming houses where whites and blacks congregated were jointly owned by integrated partnerships of underground entrepreneurs. A raid on a Baltimore gambling den in 1854 revealed that it was run by three white men and a free Negro; somewhat later, Nashville police discovered that a wealthy freeman had an interest "in a contraband business in wet groceries, in the management of which Mrs. Nancy Walker, a white woman, is the ostensible representative."[20]

Even more common than these integrated enterprises were gangs of white and black thieves that operated in every part of the South. White criminals found free Negroes ideal collaborators because most were desperately poor and generally unable to testify against their white partners. In the larger cities, some white thieves encouraged black criminality by establishing depots or "night cribs" where blacks might bring stolen merchandise, find protection, or simply spend the night.[21] Free Negroes generally welcomed these criminal alliances with whites. Although whites cheated blacks by giving them nominal prices for valuable merchandise, white henchmen also hid them from suspicious police, wrote them passes, and even forged freedom papers. Only a few whites took the risks necessary to aid Negro freemen, but they were numerous enough to keep police busy in every Southern city.

[19] Richmond *Daily Dispatch*, 1 December 1853; *Nashville Republican Banner*, 16 February 1859; New Orleans *Louisiana Gazette*, 20 May 1810.

[20] Baltimore *Sun*, 3 January 1854; *Nashville Republican Banner*, 30 January 1858.

[21] *Journal of the Virginia House of Delegates*, 1848–9, p. 22; *Richmond Whig*, 1 November 1853; Richmond *Daily Dispatch*, 18 December 1856.

The bonds of friendship sealed by common conditions moved some whites to aid free blacks in preserving their liberty. Many whites, like one Richmond Irishman, assumed "ownership of the colored folk with whom he was in the habit of communing, that they may evade the cognizance of the City Watch." The intimate relations that developed between whites and blacks also induced some whites to help their enslaved friends evade the law. "The extent to which female runaway slaves (especially if they happen to be paled by amalgamation) are harbored in this city, is truly a matter of surprise," groaned a New Orleans editor. "Almost every day it is noted on the police records, that May, Jean, Jenette, Lucy, Susan, or some other refugee from service is caught in the premises of Mr. so and so, and that Mr. so and so had been arrested for harboring and concealing her." While some whites found pleasure in aiding blacks, others found profit. Illegally freed and fugitive blacks often paid whites well for playing the role of master while allowing them full freedom. Every Southern city had a few white men who appeared to hold the papers of every free Negro arrested without them in his possession. These "Negro agents," usually struggling lawyers or saloon keepers who catered to blacks, were not the only whites to whom free Negroes might look for help. A growing number of immigrant workingmen, fired with opposition to slavery, welcomed the opportunity to strike a blow at the peculiar institution while at the same time making a few dollars. "Not only free Negroes," observed a Richmond editor in 1860, "but low white people can be found, who will secret a slave from his master in order to get his services, satisfied in their minds that if detected, they can excuse themselves by declaring their ignorance of this status."[22]

Warm friendships between free Negroes and whites also flourished at the other end of the social spectrum. As with relations between poor whites and free blacks, class interests and shared styles of life pierced the walls of racial suspicion in the upper reaches of Southern society. Planters, secure in their social position, occasionally found they had much in common with the successful, literate freemen with whom

[22] *Richmond Whig*, 1 November 1853; New Orleans *Daily True Delta*, 20 October 1855; Natchez *Mississippi Free Trader*, 21 August 1841; Richmond *Daily Dispatch*, 21 December 1860.

they swapped property and traded slaves. Sometimes whites took a close personal interest in these exceptional free Negroes, acting as their business advisers and protectors. Often, of course, there was good reason for these paternal concerns. In many Southern communities, especially those of the Lower South, ties of blood bound free Negroes to the most prominent white families. Among the largest free Negro taxpayers in Charleston, for example, were Hugers, Legares, Poinsetts, and Trescotts. Blood relations aside, similar interests and mutual respect also helped bridge the color line. William Johnson maintained strong ties with Adam Bingaman, a wealthy Mississippi planter and prominent Whig politician who lived with a free Negro woman. The close friendship between Mrs. Johnson and Bingaman's mistress brought the families together on many social occasions. Bingaman no doubt felt a special closeness to Johnson, for he understood it was Johnson's status, not his own, that his children would inherit. But beyond this, Bingaman found he had a good deal to share with the wealthy barber. They compared notes on hunting and the latest race-track sensation—a passionate interest of both men. Bingaman later moved to New Orleans with his mistress, but the families continued to stay in touch, and after Johnson's death, Bingaman helped his widow manage the family estate. A similar friendship existed between Andrew Durnford, a successful free Negro sugar planter, and John McDonogh, a wealthy New Orleans merchant and philanthropist. Although McDonogh liked to play the sage father to the younger Durnford and Durnford was usually in his debt, their personal relationship was that of equals. When McDonogh abused their friendship by using the planter's land without compensation, Durnford felt no qualms about rebuking him. Still, these relations were maintained only on a private level, and publicly both whites and blacks trimmed their friendships to fit the demands of Southern racial mores.[23]

[23] *List of the Tax Payers of the City of Charleston for 1860,* pp. 315–34; Hogan and Davis, eds., *William Johnson's Natchez, passim;* William Johnson Papers, LSU, especially M. E. Bingaman to Mrs. Johnson, 21 April 1860; Durnford Letters in John McDonogh Papers, TUL, especially Andrew Durnford to John McDonogh, 23 March 1844, 16 August 1844; also see Noisette Family Papers, SCHS; Alfred Huger to Governor Manning, 5 May 1853, Huger Letterbooks, Alfred Huger Papers, Duke.

The pattern of interracial sexual unions reveals the full range of relationships between whites and blacks. Although these illicit sexual liaisons bespoke exploitation as well as intimacy, their circumstances sometimes suggest the close, friendly ties between whites and blacks. Perhaps nowhere were these relations more frequent than in the working-class districts of Southern cities. Although the taboo on interracial sex was the strictest rule of the Southern racial code, and laws forbidding sexual relations between whites and blacks littered the statute books, violations were commonplace. The Mobile city guard found "Eliza Crowe, the widow of a once very respectable tailor . . . with two negro men in her house, each occupying beds and the door locked." On a tip, Louisville police followed a white man to the home of a free Negro woman. After waiting a few minutes, they broke in and found them "snugly ensconced between the straw and feather bed." Similarly, the Petersburg night watch happened upon "a den of male and female reprobates . . . composed of George Addington and Susan Evans, white; and George Bartley, Susan Smith, and Sarah Smith, mulattoes; all of whom were found lying together promiscuously, upon a bunk redolent with fumes of whiskey."[24]

Brothels were perhaps the most integrated places in the South. After the death of Aunt Henny, the Negro madam of one of the most luxurious houses in St. Louis, litigation revealed that "Catherine Flynn, a white girl, lived in this nigger den for seven or eight years as a public prostitute." In a typical raid, Richmond police closed another house of ill fame where "men and women of diverse colors, at different periods, do congregate for most unhallowed purposes." But police vigilance was never a match for the profits and pleasures whites and blacks found in the illicit trade. In the wake of a New Orleans crackdown, the press noted the usual quota of "busy lawyers and interested landlords" scurrying to secure the release of their clients and trying to reverse the new stiff regulations.[25]

[24] *Mobile Daily Advertiser,* 10 November 1859; *Louisville Daily Democrat,* 10 March 1857; Richmond *Daily Dispatch,* 27 July 1857.

[25] St. Louis *Daily Missouri Democrat,* 9 June 1860; Richmond *Daily Dispatch,* 27 April 1853; New Orleans *Daily Picayune,* 3 May 1857.

Southern sexual mores, following the traditional Western pattern, incorporated a double standard. Sexual relations between white men and black women were politely reproved, but unions of white women and black men were vehemently and often violently condemned. Yet many Southern white women did not feel quite so strongly, and some took part in interracial sexual relations as fully as men. New Orleans police found a "flaxen-haired German girl" and a "good looking mulatto . . . in a closer intimacy than the law allows." The Louisville guard arrested several "southern ladies of northern principles" for "amalgamation," and Richmond police discovered "two youthful white girls, not of uncomely figures of shape . . . pandering for lucre's sake to the passions of negroes." A few white women openly rejected the primary tenet of Southern racial morality. Confronted with the evidence of her illicit relation with one of the leading black musicians in New Orleans, one white woman boldly resolved to stay with him. With equal candor, a Virginia white woman told her husband "that she had not been the first nor would she be the last guilty of such conduct, and that she saw no more harm in a white woman having a black child than a white man's having one, although the latter was more frequent."[26]

Lower-class whites were probably most likely to reject Southern sexual standards, but the white elite did so as well. Some wealthy planters and merchants took black mistresses. Most doubtless kept these relations discreetly out of view, but some flaunted their illicit conduct. "There are large numbers of our young men and several of our merchants," wrote a North Carolina planter from New Bern, "who have negro wives or 'misses' and keep them openly, raising up families of mulattoes." Such mixed racial unions were even more commonplace in the Lower South. Mobile authorities complained bitterly that white men hired handsome fair-skinned slaves and free women of color by the year and set up housekeeping in the better residential neighborhoods.[27]

[26] New Orleans *Bee*, 30 June 1855; *Louisville Daily Democrat*, 7 May 1851; *Richmond Enquirer*, 17 August 1859; *New Orleans Crescent*, 26 June 1860; Petition from Powhatan County, 6 December 1815, VLP; Johnston, *Race Relations in Virginia*, pp. 250–68.

[27] Franklin, *Free Negro in North Carolina*, pp. 190–1; *Mobile Daily Advertiser*, 25 May 1850.

In New Orleans, the century-old tradition of mixed racial unions hardened into an informal but relatively stable extra-marital institution known as *plaçage,* which provided a degree of security for black women while maximizing the sexual freedom of white men. Around *plaçage* there grew up a number of subsidiary institutions, the most famous of which were the masked balls given for free women of color and white men and frequently attended by white women and black men.[28]

Sometimes strong bonds of affection steeled whites and blacks to challenge racial standards and establish open, stable relationships. A white Tennessee schoolteacher, deeply in love with his free Negro wife, pleaded with the American Colonization Society for permission to migrate to Liberia. "My wife is a Quadroon of New Orleans," he declared; "we have been married five years and have two children, who being only ⅛ African, are blue-eyed, and flaxen haired; and nearly as 'pale-faced' as myself. Still, they are *coloured* and that is a word of tremendous import in North America!" Although comfortable and respected, he was constantly reminded of his "transgression against National feeling" and feared "bequeathing to my children a hopeless degradation! I will go *anywhere,*" he concluded, "to avoid so hateful an alternative." Although rare, such relationships could be found in every part of the South, as the anonymous notation "white wife" or "white mother" in the census and the steady manumission of light-skinned children indicated.[29]

The strength and persistence of these liaisons were demonstrated whenever officials challenged them. An attempt to pre-

[28] Thomas Ashe, *Travels in America* (London, 1809), pp. 314–15; Schultz, *Travels on an Inland Voyage,* II, 193–4; James Stuart, *Three Years in North America,* 2 vols. (Edinburgh, 1833), II, 237–9; Harriet Martineau, *Society in America,* 2 vols. (New York, 1837), II, 116–17; G. W. Featherstonhaugh, *Excursion Through the Slave States,* 2 vols. (London, 1844), II, 267–70; Olmsted, *Journey in the Seaboard Slave States,* pp. 594–8; Philo Tower, *Slavery Unmasked* (Rochester, N.Y., 1856), pp. 326–7; for masked balls, see New Orleans *Bee,* 21, 28, 30 November 1835, 1 January 1857; New Orleans *Daily Picayune,* 27 October 1837, 25 December 1855, 22 February 1857; Joseph G. Tregle, Jr., "Early New Orleans Society: A Reappraisal," *JSH,* XVIII (1952), 34–6.

[29] James Richardson to Henry Clay, 28 April 1832, also James Richardson to R. R. Gurley, 5, 10 May 1832, ACS; Johnston, *Race Relations in Virginia,* pp. 263–5.

vent black women from inheriting a portion of their white lovers' estates brought howls of protest in the Louisiana legislature. One representative assured the assembly that "a black woman who lived with a white man might be as virtuous as if she were his wife," and doubtless more virtuous than a white woman who lived in similar circumstances since she was prohibited from marrying her paramour. Even on the eve of the Civil War, when the pressures of the sectional conflict were driving Southerners to make their social practices consonant with their racial ideology, the South Carolina General Assembly quietly buried a petition lamenting that whites were "frequently found living in open connection with negro and mulatto women" by simply declaring "the evil complained of cannot be prevented by legislation."[30]

Yet Southern leaders despised these illicit combinations of whites and free Negroes. They worried not only about goods stolen, slaves run off, and the growing number of mixed-bloods, but also about the implicit challenge posed by such relationships to the Southern social order. Whites maintained their dominance by differentiating themselves from blacks and monopolizing the symbols of superiority. This not only allowed whites to control blacks but permitted a small group of slaveowners to dominate Southern society. Friendly relations between whites and blacks based on rough equality of condition blurred the color line and threatened the slaveholders' hegemony. Against these ties, Southern leaders arrayed an ideology and a social system which asserted the supremacy of all whites over all blacks. Even the meanest white benefitted from this arrangement by standing above the most prosperous free Negro. The ideology of white unity was reinforced by giving poor whites part of the responsibility for enforcing racial mores. All whites were liable to participate in slave patrols, and most free Negro laws provided special payments for informers. These petty inducements helped to cement white unity, but the psychological benefits poor men and women received from their alliances with wealthy planters were doubtless even more important. When whites per-

[30] New Orleans *Daily Picayune*, 7 February 1840; Petition from Barnwell County, 1860, with "Report of Committee on Colored Population," 29 November 1860, SCLP.

sisted in violating the tenets of racial unity, Southern leaders brusquely stripped them of their caste benefits. "Nigger lovers" had trouble finding work, receiving protection from the law, or even being believed. Having allied themselves with blacks, they were treated like blacks. When a Richmond white woman claimed she had been raped by a free Negro, the police simply ignored her charge. Since she associated with "none other than the lowest and most debased free Negroes in the Valley," sneered one observer, "it will be difficult to induce them to believe a single sentence uttered by her."[31] The rewards dispensed to loyal whites and the punishments rained on the disloyal destroyed many of the fragile ties of common condition which united some whites and blacks, and prevented most interracial friendships from spreading beyond their narrow bounds. Although friendly, even equalitarian relations between whites and blacks continued to exist on the margins of Southern society, they never threatened white supremacy.

If racial ideology effectively united whites and separated them from most blacks, it also sealed the bonds of racial unity between the mass of free Negroes and slaves. Similar living conditions, common origins, and family ties further cemented these relations. Free Negroes and slaves commonly joined together as man and wife. Slaveholders disliked these matches, fearing that free Negroes would help their spouses to abscond, upset slave discipline, and, if the free partner was a woman, deprive them of valuable offspring. Nevertheless, Negro freemen and slaves continually joined together and often confirmed the slaveowners' dread prophecies.

Family relations were only one measure of the close ties between free Negroes and slaves. Freemen and bondsmen labored in the same fields and workshops, often attended the same African churches, and spent their spare moments in the same groggeries and groceries. Masters bemoaned this intermingling and complained that it rendered their slaves valueless. Yet a raid on almost any black grocery was sure to yield a mixed catch of free and slave Negroes. After arresting one free Negro for entertaining slaves, a Nashville officer grumbled

[31] Richmond *Daily Dispatch,* 27 April 1854; also see Benwell, *Englishman's Travels in America,* p. 208.

that it was "a practice . . . all too common among the free darkies."[32]

Friendships sparked in the workshops, churches, and groceries where free Negroes and slaves rubbed elbows reinforced race loyalties and encouraged free Negroes to help slaves to freedom with forged passes, with loans of money, or simply by standing as their masters. Free Negroes commonly employed slave hirelings, acted as intermediaries for slave-stolen goods, and gave bondsmen a place to stay far from their master's watchful eye. Although the freemen's privileged status enabled them to aid slaves, bondsmen found ways of reciprocating. Besides patronizing free Negro cookshops and boardinghouses, they sometimes warned freemen of lurking slave patrols, fed them out of their master's kitchen, and during hard times supported them with stolen food and clothing. "In the neighborhood of almost every mill," lamented Virginia slaveholders, "there are located squads of free Negroes who it is believed are sustained almost entirely by [slave] millers with their unlawful gains taken from their customers. And these slave millers are a sort of link of communication between our slaves and the free persons of colour, by which we believe much injury done to our best interests."[33]

Many free Negroes helped individual slaves to ease the burden of bondage or to escape it altogether, but few went beyond this. Although their existence implicitly challenged slavery, free Negroes were not a revolutionary caste. With the exception of Denmark Vesey, free Negroes were notably absent from slave rebellions.[34] Indeed, George Pencil, the freeman who helped expose the Vesey plot, was more rep-

[32] *Nashville Republican Banner*, 21 June 1857.

[33] Petition from Charles City County, 27 December 1831, VLP.

[34] The debate over the Vesey conspiracy is reviewed in Robert S. Starobin, ed., *Denmark Vesey: The Slave Conspiracy of 1822* (Englewood Cliffs, N.J., 1970), and in Starobin's essay "Denmark Vesey's Slave Conspiracy of 1822: A Study in Rebellion and Repression," in John H. Bracey, Jr., *et al.*, eds., *American Slavery: The Question of Resistance* (Belmont, Calif., 1971), pp. 142–57. Also useful is John O. Killens, ed., *The Trial Record of Denmark Vesey* (Boston, 1970), although for a full account of George Pencil's role one must turn to the manuscript record of the trial in SCA. The absence of free Negroes from slave rebellions generally is suggested in a negative way by Herbert Aptheker, *American Negro Slave Revolts* (New York, 1943), who, despite a wide-ranging approach, gives little evidence of free Negro participation.

resentative of the free Negro's role in slave rebellions than Vesey himself. Standing a step above the slave, free Negroes simply had too much to lose to take the lead in breaking the bonds of servitude. They too suffered the pains of white oppression, but free Negroes could look down to slavery as well as up to complete freedom. They could see how their status might degenerate, and they knew that whites needed only the flimsiest excuse to take their liberty. Having learned to squeeze a few precious benefits from their caste status, they were not about to surrender them without a guarantee of something better. Freedom within the context of slavery gave free Negroes something to protect and transformed them into a conservative caste. The general insecurity of free Negro life, the sure knowledge that free Negroes suffered whenever whites felt threatened, and their growing material prosperity reinforced that conservatism.

Unless they were willing to challenge the slave system directly, free Negroes found that their social advancement hinged on their ability to distinguish themselves from the mass of slaves. The closer free Negroes could approximate the white ideal, the greater their chances of acceptance. The difference in status between Upper and Lower South free Negroes fully illustrates this principle, although the principle itself held for the entire South. Acceptance, of course, was not equality, but as in the Lower South, it could markedly improve the freemen's standard of living. Thus the central paradox of free Negro life was that while full equality depended on the unity of all blacks, free and slave, and the abolition of slavery, substantial gains could more realistically be obtained within the existing society by standing apart from the slaves. Consciously or unconsciously, upward-striving free Negroes understood this and acted on it. There were many more George Pencils than Denmark Veseys.

Status differences continually eroded the bonds of racial unity and turned free Negroes and slaves against each other. In the eyes of some free Negroes, the degradation of the slave elevated their status just as the degradation of all blacks elevated the status of all whites. These free Negroes held slaves in contempt and disparaged them as "slave niggers." Anxious to ingratiate themselves with white patrons and protectors, they vigorously defended slavery as the proper status for the majority of blacks. John Chavis, a free Negro preacher and schoolmaster, opposed emancipation and urged his white friends to resist the abolitionist onslaught. He denied that Congress had the authority to legislate against slavery because "the Laws of the Country have had slaves the property of the holder equal to his cow or his horse and that he has a perfect right to dispose of them as he pleases." The sting of such rebukes angered slaves, and many withdrew from association with free Negroes. This was especially true in the Lower South, where somatic, ethnic, and religious differences widened the gap between freemen and bondsmen. "It is seldom that slaves and free negroes agree," noted the New Orleans *Picayune*. "Our Southern darkies think that the 'gemman ob color' put on too many airs, and he scoffs at him and hates him accordingly." A Charleston minister found much the same kind of tension between free Negroes and slaves when he tried to join the two in a single congregation. The slaves, he reported, "seemed as reluctant to attend meetings frequented by people of color, as those of the white."[35]

Although status differences between free and slave blacks cut through the free and slave populations at all levels, they tended to be greater at the top than the bottom. The common conditions under which poor free Negroes and unskilled slaves lived rendered the question of status meaningless. Among elite blacks things were considerably different. Wealthy freemen wanted little part of slaves, except as property. But the contempt that sometimes characterized relations between free Negroes and slaves did not always emanate from free Negroes. Privileged bondsmen, especially house servants, often looked down upon the lowly free Negroes who lived in grinding poverty. When one Kentucky free Negro moved his family to Virginia, he complained that he "suffer[ed] more abuse from

[35] Petersburg *Express*, 2 February 1858; Chavis to Willie P. Mangum, 4 April 1836, in Henry T. Shanks, ed., *The Papers of Willie P. Mangum*, 5 vols. (Raleigh, N.C., 1950–6), II, 418–20. Chavis also opposed recognition of Haiti; Chavis to Mangum, 20 November 1825, *ibid.*, I, 203–4. New Orleans *Daily Picayune*, 30 June 1860; *Public Proceedings Relating to Calvary Church and the Religious Instruction of Slaves* (Charleston, 1845), p. 53; also Lambert, *Travels Through Lower Canada and the United States*, II, 414–16.

the slaves here than we ever did from white people where we came from [,] Which is indeed extremely disagreeable."[36]

Whites promoted these differences between free Negroes and slaves, just as they tried to divide field hands and house servants, unskilled bondsmen and slave artisans. They gladly rewarded free Negroes who informed on slaves, just as they almost always freed slaves who revealed impending insurrections. But it was the structure of the slave society, far more than conscious policy, which drove the deepest wedge between free and bond blacks. Economic success in the South depended largely on the ownership of slaves, and free Negroes were no more exempt from this than whites. Although most free Negro slaveholders were truly benevolent despots, owning only their families and friends to prevent their enslavement or forcible deportation, a small minority of wealthy freemen exploited slaves for commercial purposes. This small group of free Negroes were generally the wealthiest and best-connected members of their caste.[37]

The same lines of class and color that separated free Negroes from slaves also created divisions within the free Negro caste. Wealthy free Negroes often looked with disdain upon their poorer brethren who caroused with slaves and lowly whites. William Johnson despised the promiscuous nightly revelry that characterized black life "Under-the-Hill" in Natchez. Although as a young man Johnson had expended considerable sums for "Sensuality" (and then carefully listed those expenditures in his account book), he set rigid moral standards for his slaves and free Negro apprentices. When he caught several of them flirting with a handsome black girl at the door of his shop, he sharply dressed them down: "Oh what Puppys, Fondling—beneath a Levell, Low minded Creatures. I look upon them as Soft." The raucous doings of poor blacks offended

[36] George Erskine to R. R. Gurley, 30 July 1829, ACS; also James Roberts to Willis Roberts, [February 1830], Roberts Family Papers, LC.

[37] Woodson, comp., *Free Negro Owners of Slaves;* Calvin D. Wilson, "Negroes Who Owned Slaves," *Popular Science Monthly,* LXXXI (1912), 483–94; Jackson, *Free Negro Labor and Property Holding,* pp. 205–29; Franklin, *Free Negro in North Carolina,* pp. 159–61; Menn, "Large Slaveholders of the Deep South," pp. 208–10; Wikramanayake, *A World in Shadow,* pp. 31–2, 73, 105–6, 109.

and threatened Johnson. Eventually he withdrew even from casual association with them rather than risk being associated with their misdeeds. After a near-riot in the balcony of a Natchez playhouse, he curbed his attendance though he dearly loved the theater. While he dissociated himself from poor blacks, Johnson carefuly cultivated the habits of white gentility. He bred racehorses, hunted, gave his daughters music lessons, lined his study with books, subscribed to several New York journals, and gambled inveterately. Johnson treasured his friendship with the white elite who embodied the values he most admired. When John A. Quitman, the fiery Mississippi politician and future governor, hand-delivered a letter to Johnson, the barber swelled: "He did me proud. He did me proud." Eventually Johnson tired of scraping for these small honors, but he remained deeply immersed in the ideals of the Southern elite. Like most successful Southern entrepreneurs, Johnson found fulfillment in the countryside, not the city. Toward the end of his life, he purchased a sprawling farm outside Natchez which he called "Hard Scrabble," hired a white overseer, and worked it with his slaves, free Negro apprentices, and white tenant laborers. The man who had made his way up as a barber and moneylender concluded that landownership was "the key to happiness."[38]

Slaveholding free Negro planters identified even more closely with the Southern ideal. Andrew Durnford, who owned a Louisiana plantation which he worked with some seventy-five slaves, was finely attuned to the planter ideology and considered himself a patriarchal master in the best tradition. Although he railed endlessly against the seeming incompetence and indolence of his "rascally negroes," he took pride in his role as their protector as well as their owner. When Norbert Rillieux, a French-trained free Negro engineer who had invented a new method of refining sugar, offered Durnford $50,000 for use of his plantation to test the vacuum process, the planter turned him down, noting that he could not "give up control of his people." Durnford's "people" of course were slaves, and he treated them as such despite their similar complexion. With the exception of his personal body servant, he

[38] Hogan and Davis, eds., *William Johnson's Natchez, passim;* William Johnson Papers, LSU.

never showed any interest in releasing them from bondage. In 1835, Durnford traveled north to Virginia to purchase additional hands for himself and his white mentor, John McDonogh. During his trip, he confronted, perhaps for the first time, the Southern distaste for slave traders, as opposed to those who bought and used slaves, and he consciously manipulated that idea to obtain lower prices. Yet, throughout his lengthy discussion with McDonogh on what he called "Negro traders," he showed not the slightest understanding that that term when applied to him might have two additional meanings, for Durnford literally was a Negro trader and some blacks might consider his actions treasonable.[39] These possibilities were lost on Durnford because he fully identified with the white slaveowning elite. Many wealthy freemen, like Durnford, considered themselves more white than black, no matter what their precise racial heritage. They showed little sympathy for the slave and had few qualms about the morality of slavery. Durnford's Northern-educated son, who urged amelioration of slave conditions—not emancipation—had no greater sense of identification with blacks than his father. He supported African colonization for slaves—but not for himself—spoke of colonization as repatriation, and lauded the plan to return blacks to "the land of *their* fathers."[40]

The lofty status of elite freemen rested largely on wealth. They saw themselves not merely as men the equal of others but as men better than most. If they scorned poor free Negroes and slaves for fear of being identified with the black masses, they hated poor whites all the more, because Southern ideology, despite its three-caste aspects, allowed even the lowest whites to threaten free Negroes like William Johnson with "a good nigger beating." Yet the tension between wealthy free Negroes and poor whites transcended Southern racial etiquette. Well-

[39] St. Rosalie Plantation Journal, TUL; Durnford Letters in John McDonogh Papers, especially 30 January 1843, 9 June 1835; also see David O. Whitten, ed., "Slave Buying in 1835 Virginia as Revealed by Letters of a Louisiana Negro Sugar Planter," *Louisiana History,* XI (1970), 231–44. An analysis of Durnford's record as a middle-sized sugar planter indicates he earned more raising slaves than selling sugar; David O. Whitten, "A Black Entrepreneur in Antebellum Louisiana," *Business History Review,* XLV (1971), 201–19.

[40] Thomas McDonogh Durnford to John McDonogh, 5 January 1842, also 24 March 1845, typescript, John McDonogh Papers, TUL.

placed free Negroes found the poor white's way of life as alien and distasteful as that of the poor black and viewed the easy congeniality between lower-class whites and slaves with extreme distrust. Indeed, one of the many ironies of William Johnson's life is that the only slave to escape his service was helped to freedom by a man Johnson denounced as a "white scoundrel." Such ironies were not lost on the free Negro elite. More than anything else, they yearned to live in a class society where they could escape the stigma of race. Their social views tended to be very conservative, even somewhat anachronistic in the post-Jacksonian South. John Chavis shared the general pessimism about human nature of his Federalist and Whig patrons. "I do not believe," he wrote to Willie P. Mangum, a conservative North Carolina senator, "that mankind are capable of living under, either a Democratic, or a Republican Government. The bonds of such a Government are not sufficient to restrain the corruptions of human nature. The volcano will burst & the lava spread far and wide its destructive ruin." Similarly, Andrew Durnford thought society was "made up of two distinctive parts, on one hand, wolves and foxes and, on the other hand, lambs and chickens to provide food for the former. In the forest," he added wistfully, "a lion recognizes another lion, a tiger does not make another tiger its prey. . . ."[41] As a lion in his own right, Durnford wished for recognition from the other lions; he could take care of the lambs.

In striving to identify with the white upper class, the free Negro elite became imbued with the very racial attitudes that prevented them from fully enjoying the benefits of their elevated class position. Most of the members of the upper crust of free Negro society were mixed-bloods, whose close connection with whites enabled them partially to overcome the burdens of race. "Many of them," observed the free Negro chronicler of the "Colored Aristocracy" of St. Louis, "are separated from the white race by a line of division so faint that it can be traced only by the keen eye of prejudice. . . ."

[41] Hogan and Davis, eds., *William Johnson's Natchez*, pp. 184–5; William Johnson to O. L. Bemis, 24 July 1837, copy, William Johnson Papers, LSU; Chavis to Willie P. Mangum, 8 August 1832, in Shanks, ed., *Papers of Mangum*, I, 565–9; Andrew Durnford to John McDonogh, 24 January 1844, John McDonogh Papers, TUL.

Some of these wealthy, light-skinned free Negroes not only mimicked white values but accepted "whiteness" as the standard of superiority and looked down on all blacks, free and slave. Their racist attitudes were reflected in what one free Negro called "the great ambition" of free Negro women: "to marry a man [as] nearly white as possible." Occasionally, their unspoken beliefs were blurted out in the taunts of young children. In Louisville, school officials discovered a light-skinned girl passing as white when she boasted that she was smarter than her brother although "he *was* whiter than she."[42] Some light-skinned free Negroes, following the logic of one line of white racial thought, seemed to regard themselves as physically distinct from blacks. Several potential immigrants to Liberia wondered if mixed-bloods could tolerate the African sun; and a few, fearing they could not, refused to go. William Kellogg, a North Carolina mulatto, went beyond this reasoning and denounced Liberian colonization for mixed-bloods. Fearful that "the prejudice that exists between Blacks and Mulattoes in the United States" would continue in Africa, he decided to remain in "the hands of my superiors" rather than fall "into the hands of my inferiors." Kellogg pleaded with the American Colonization Society to sponsor a separate refuge for mixed-bloods, reminding them that there were "a great many mulattoes within these United State[s] who are stronger allied to the white man than they are to the Blacks."[43]

The color line between brown and black never rigidly followed class divisions. There were many poor mulattoes and a few wealthy blacks. In addition, denominational differences, distinctions between free Negroes who had enjoyed freedom for generations and those *nouveaux* who had but recently won their liberty, crisscrossed class and caste distinctions. Commonplace differences between city and rural folk added still greater complexity and made easy generalizations about free Negro social structure impossible.

[42] Cyprian Clamogan, *The Colored Aristocracy of St. Louis* (St. Louis, Mo., 1858), pp. 3–4. Clamogan is identified as a free Negro in R. V. Kennedy, comp., *St. Louis Directory, 1859* (St. Louis, 1859). *Louisville Daily Courier,* 26 December 1854.

[43] James Winn to William McLain, 6 September 1850, E. Douglas Taylor to John Lugenbeel, 22 October 1850, N. D. Artist to John Lugenbeel, 8 November 1850, William Kellogg to [William McLain], 6 October 1852, ACS.

In the Lower South, these differences were further complicated by a large number of free people of color of French and Spanish ancestry and Catholic religion who remained aloof from the "Yankee" blacks who had migrated to the Gulf ports or were manumitted by late-arriving Protestant masters. In some places, French- and Spanish-speaking creole Catholic freemen established separate communities apart from whites as well as blacks.[44] In cities like Pensacola, Mobile, and especially New Orleans, they strove to keep their creole heritage alive through French- and Spanish-language schools and by educating their children in Europe or the West Indies. The efforts of French-speaking New Orleans free Negroes were rewarded in the 1840s when creole culture enjoyed a brief renaissance. In 1843, the French-educated free Negro intelligentsia established a short-lived literary review entitled *L'Album Littéraire* in which they published poetry, short stories, and a few articles subtly attacking caste discrimination. Two years later, Armand Lanusse, the headmaster of the city's leading free Negro academy, edited *Les Cenelles*, an anthology of poems by leading creole freemen. Steeped in romantic sentimentality, the bitter-sweet tone of many of these poems suggested at once the free Negroes' growing disenchantment with life in New Orleans and their close ties with French culture. American racism and respect for French life induced many of the best-educated free Negroes to return to France, where some achieved considerable success. Victor Séjour, the son of an émigré from Saint-Domingue, became a moderately successful Paris playwright and later secretary to Louis Napoleon. Edmund Dédé, a musician trained in both New Orleans and Paris, rose to the directorship of the Bordeaux Symphony, and Norbert Rillieux became headmaster of the Ecole Centrale of Paris. But many more of these creole intellectuals remained in New Orleans, performing professional services of various kinds for wealthy whites as well as free Negroes.[45] The wealth, education, and continental polish of

[44] *Mobile Tribune*, quoted in *Clark County* (Ala.) *Democrat*, 29 July 1858. Also see "A Romance of Little Wassaw," typescript, UGa.

[45] R. L. Desdunes, *Nos Hommes et Notre Histoire* (Montreal, 1911); Charles Barthélemy Roussève, *The Negro in Louisiana, Aspects of His History and His Literature* (New Orleans, 1837); Edward M. Coleman, ed., *Creole*

these men and women suggest the range of the free Negro class system even within one ethnic subdivision.

In spite of the complexity of free Negro class and caste structure, of its regional, color, religious, and ethnic subdivisions, wealth and a light skin remained the most common prerequisites for membership in the upper crust of free Negro society. Tied tightly to whites by blood and business connections, elite freemen came to venerate economic success and to idealize the style of life of the white upper class. "Wealth makes the man," boasted one successful St. Louis free Negro, "the want of it the fellow." Some wealthy free Negroes used their elite status as a means of escaping their caste, culturally and sometimes physically. Even in the Upper South, where the social and somatic distance between slave and free, rich and poor Negroes was comparatively small, a Baltimore minister reported that successful free mulattoes tended to "look upwards, not downwards . . . constantly seeking, and acquiring too, the privileges of whites." Like the white aristocracy they idealized, these free Negroes had a flair for high living. They lived in fine houses, rode in elegant carriages, and wore fashionable clothes. The difference between their way of life and that of most free Negroes is aptly illustrated by the wardrobe James Colston packed on his trip to Liberia. While most free Negroes were hard pressed to feed their families, Colston packed "two boxes segars, Two boxes Wine, Port & Carett, [and] One Basket with [?] preserves & ham with three jars current [*sic*] Jelly." While most free Negroes were poorly clothed, Colston packed "Thirteen new shirts nine linnen & four cotton, Two flannel shirts, Four inside new cotton shirts, Two cotton night shirts, Seventeen white cravats . . .Six Pocket Handkerchiefs . . . Eleven pair Pantaloons . . . Five coats . . . Sixteen pair Hose . . . Ivory Head cane, [and an] Umbrella." While most free Negroes were illiterate, Colston packed "Clarkes Commentary on the New Testament in two vols., Watsons Theological Dictionary, Watson Theological Institutes . . . , Four vols of Wesleys Work . . . , Usebious Ecclessastical History, Sturms Reflections . . . , Authentic Key

---

Voices: Poems in French by Free Men of Color First Published in 1845 (Washington, D.C., 1945); T. A. Daley, "Victor Séjour," *Phylon*, IV (1943), 5–16.

to the Door of F[ree] Masonry, [and] Eulogy on Wilberforce." With the good wine and fine cigars often came slaveownership, travel, and the Southern code of chivalry. Like the white gentry, free Negroes took their disputes to the field of honor—pistols at twenty paces.[46]

Aping the white elite did not gain wealthy freemen entry into white society, and even the most sumptuous personal luxuries could not fully ease the pain of white oppression. Indeed, success made white proscription and discrimination all the more galling. Having climbed to the top of free Negro society, the elite could see, perhaps as poorer freemen could not, the full extent of the world that whites kept from them. Many successful free Negroes despised the lucrative but demeaning service trades that provided the economic basis of their elevated positions. They yearned to be teachers, lawyers, and doctors, while whites forced them to work as barbers and barmen. "I hate the name barber," one successful Alabama free Negro told his son; "there are so many superior occupations."[47] Although elite free Negroes served cheerfully and acquiesced to "their place" in Southern society with hardly a murmur, they never forgave whites. A wealthy barber whom whites patronized as "Uncle John" privately noted that he liked "the Southern people individually but collectively and politically 'Dam em.' "[48]

Thus elite free Negroes were suspended uncomfortably between slave and free, black and white. The ambiguity of their social position was often embodied in their mixed racial origins and tawny color, but it clearly went beyond these physical attributes. Wealthy, literate, enjoying a style of life more like whites than slaves, they felt the tug of racial loyalty coming from both directions; yet they were barred from full acceptance in white society and often viewed with suspicion by blacks. Some, like John Chavis and Andrew Durnford, threw in their lot wholeheartedly with whites, although even they

[46] Clamogan, *Colored Aristocracy of St. Louis*, p. 7; *African Repository*, IX (January 1834), 322; Luther P. Jackson, "Free Negroes of Petersburg, Virginia," *JNH*, XIII (1927), 376; *New Orleans Crescent*, 14 July 1853.

[47] John Rapier to John Rapier, Jr., 17 March 1857, Rapier Papers, HUL.

[48] Loren Schweninger, "James Rapier and Reconstruction," unpublished doctoral dissertation, University of Chicago, 1972, chap. 1; Miscellaneous Papers of John Rapier, HUL.

remained extremely sensitive about their position. Others moved in the opposite direction and became black leaders of the first rank. Still, they could not escape the ambiguity of living with a foot in both the white and the black worlds. The insecurity that sprang from their inability to find a place among either whites or blacks sometimes gnawed at their self-esteem and bred a corrosive self-hatred. Daniel Coker, a leading Baltimore minister and schoolman, was tormented his entire life by his middle position as a free Negro and a person of mixed racial heritage. Elected in 1816 to be the first bishop of the African Methodist Episcopal Church, he was deposed in favor of Richard Allen, apparently because a full-blooded black was wanted for that position. He continued as minister of the largest African church in Baltimore, but he met opposition from both blacks and whites and eventually was excommunicated by Allen. Coker's troubles within the African Methodist organization seemed to aggravate long-festering doubts about his own identity. His mixed racial origins clearly disturbed him. The son of a white woman and a black man, he condemned racial amalgamation as "truly disgraceful to both colours" and declared that black men with white wives "are generally of the lowest class, and are despised by their own people." Coker later recovered his position within the church, but by then he had tired of the internal warfare of the AME and decided to migrate to Africa on a ship sponsored by the American Colonization Society. Even then his ambiguous position haunted him. On board, he roomed with the white colonization agents and not the black colonists, and he thought himself "a kind of middle link" between white and black on the ship.[49]

[49] For biographical information about Coker, I have relied on Handy, *Scraps of AME History;* Payne, *Recollections of Seventy Years* and *History of the AME Church;* and Smith, *Biography of David Smith.* Invaluable in any assessment of Coker are three pamphlets by him: *Dialogue Between a Virginian and an African Minister* (1810); *Sermon Delivered Extempore in the African Bethel Church in the City of Baltimore on the 21st January, 1816 . . . on Account of the Coloured People Gaining Their Church (Bethel) in Pennsylvania* (n.p., [1816]); *Journal of Daniel Coker* (1820). Clues to some of Coker's problems with the Methodist Church can be found in D. Coker to ?, 3 June 1817, MdDL. Coker, whom Smith described as "nearly white," did not escape his color problem by migrating to Africa. After being appointed justice of the peace, his right to sit in judgment on blacks was challenged because of his mixed

Migration offered an escape for Coker, but Africa provided no haven for other elite free Negroes afflicted with similar problems and self-doubts. Rather than leave the country, they often walled themselves off in their own genteel society—a small, limited, but comfortable world where they were the unchallenged masters of their own fate. Behind the walls of these elite communities, they soothed their bruised egos by flaunting their position at the top of Negro society. Their exclusive balls and parties asserted their elevated status and distinguished them from the mass of poor free Negroes and slaves whose crude lives, emotional religion, and strange dialect so horrified them. The security of these communities allowed elite freemen to prosper and to transfer their high status to their children, thereby compensating in some measure for the white man's rebuff. But during the antebellum years, these upper-class refuges became increasingly isolated and inbred. On the one hand, the threat of whites envious of the freemen's wealth and standing, and on the other, the fear of sliding into the dismal poverty that characterized the lives of the mass of blacks pushed this brown elite farther and farther from either world. Elite free Negro communities became closed corporations of closely knit families, and status within these communities came to depend on skin color and ancestry as well as wealth. These freemen married among themselves, and it often seemed that their purpose was to breed themselves closer to the white ideal, perhaps with the hope of someday winning the full acceptance they craved.[50]

The elite communities varied in size from place to place, but they rarely amounted to more than 10 percent of the free Negro caste, and usually not even that. In some places a handful of families constituted the entire free Negro upper class.[51]

---

origins; Smith, *Biography of David Smith,* p. 33; *Journal of Daniel Coker,* pp. 36–7.

[50] E. Horace Fitchett, "The Traditions of the Free Negro in Charleston, South Carolina," *JNH,* XXV (1940), 139–53, and Wikramanayake, *A World in Shadow,* give a graphic picture of one such elite free Negro community. Glimpses into the lives of upper-class freemen in New Orleans, Natchez, St. Louis, and Florence, Alabama, can be found in Desdunes, *Nos Hommes et Notre Histoire;* Hogan and Davis, eds., *William Johnson's Natchez;* Clamogan, *Colored Aristocracy of St. Louis;* James Rapier Papers, HUL.

[51] Brown Fellowship Society Papers, SCHS; D. Clayton James, *Antebellum Natchez* (Baton Rouge, La., 1968), p. 178.

Nevertheless, as the wealthiest, best-educated, and best-connected portion of the free Negro caste, they were disproportionately important. Their celebration of white values and disdain for the black masses had a powerful influence on all free Negroes. Their self-imposed isolation deprived the free Negro caste of many potential leaders.

Yet the free Negro elite never entirely abandoned the larger black population. If they stood at arm's length from the mass of blacks, elite freemen were also at the head of the line. Brandishing a finely honed sense of *noblesse oblige*, they occasionally reached out to poorer free Negroes and took the lead in establishing African churches, schools, and fraternal organizations. But even those members of the free Negro elite who dedicated their lives to serving their people often did so with an air of condescension. Sometimes their attitudes toward poor freemen were but an imitation of the shabby paternalism with which whites treated them. Sensing this, less successful free Negroes often viewed the elite with suspicion if not overt hostility. Daniel Payne, a light-skinned free Negro schoolteacher who was forced to leave Charleston in the 1830s and later became a bishop of the AME Church, felt the sting of this distrust when he was denied the pastorate of a Baltimore congregation. Church members, he was informed, "[say you have] too fine a carpet on your floor, and you won't let them sing the cornfield ditties, and if one of them should invite you to dine, or take tea with him, you are too proud to do it."[52] Having isolated themselves from the black masses and identified with the values of white society, the elite could never fully win the confidence of the majority of free Negroes. In securing their own class position, they became leaders without a following, isolated and impotent at the top of black society, estranged from their potential constituents. Attempts to unify the free Negro caste would be made, but they would emanate from men of different rank and social background with nowhere near the resources of the elite. Class and caste tension within the free Negro caste thus often divided free Negroes from one another as much as it divided them from whites.

[52] Payne, *History of the AME Church*, pp. iv–v.

9

The Free Negro Community

> As among our people generally, the Church is the Alpha and Omega of all things.
>
> Martin Delany to Frederick Douglass, 16 February 1849

WHILE some free Negroes tried to escape their caste by walling themselves off from the mass of blacks or by attempting to melt into the white population, others worked to pull free Negroes and slaves together to create a united black caste. These black leaders, usually not so well off as the elite, were often excluded from the upper crust of free Negro society by their dark skin or their recent passage from slavery to freedom. Unlike the elite, they generally maintained close ties with friends still in bondage and never held slaves for commercial purposes. Frequently, they earned their living serving black customers in cookshops and groceries or were skilled artisans whose abilities allowed them a large measure of independence from whites. Denmark Vesey, a representative of this group, won his liberty by chance in a Charleston lottery and did not owe it to the benevolence of a white master. Although a successful carpenter, Vesey had few ties with the city's light-skinned elite who joined together at the monthly meetings of the Brown Fellowship Society. Instead, he made his home among the poorer free Negroes and slaves of Charleston's Neck and chose a slave woman for his wife. Because of his recent escape from slavery and his continued close relations with slaves, Vesey could forget neither the pain of his own enslavement nor the fact that his children had inherited their mother's status. His discontent led him to bring Negro freemen and slaves together in what was probably the largest black conspiracy during the antebellum years.[1] No other free Negro leader went as far as Vesey in organizing free Negroes and slaves to demand liberty and equality for all blacks, but many took the lead in forming institutions where free Negroes and slaves might gather to improve and protect themselves. The most important of these was the African church, with its subsidiary schools, fraternal organizations, and benevolent societies. By providing succor for the oppressed, educating the young, aiding the aged, and burying the dead, these institutions became the center of free Negro community life.

From the time the free Negro caste formed in the years following the Revolution, whites feared the black church. They detested the independence it offered free Negroes and slaves, and they worried that it would breed insurrection. Even during their first years, African churches were harassed by hurriedly enacted legal restrictions and attacked by angry mobs which disbanded many of the most promising black institutions and forced black leaders to flee from the South.

White opposition to independent black institutions intensified during the antebellum years. White clergymen no longer sanctioned separate black churches, and white officials did little to protect black schools from the public hostility they frequently faced. Public opposition to African churches and schools increasingly led to harsh legislative restrictions. During the 1820s, Southern lawmakers picked away at the free Negroes' right to form their own institutions or meet anywhere without direct white supervision. The fears aroused by Nat Turner's rebellion speeded the slow, fitful pace of restriction and turned the trickle of proscriptive enactments into a flood. Angry whites shut black churches or severely limited their independence, ousted black preachers, and prescribed white

[1] Starobin, ed., *Denmark Vesey;* John M. Lofton, *Insurrection in South Carolina: The Turbulent World of Denmark Vesey* (Yellow Springs, Ohio, 1964).

supervision for all black gatherings. In addition, several states forbade free Negroes to attend schools, and a few even legislated against freemen learning to read and write.[2]

The new laws again disrupted the development of independent black institutions. African churches and schools throughout the South were forced to close their doors or meet clandestinely. Even the established African Methodist Episcopal Church felt the pinch of the harsh regulations. Between 1818 and 1826, the membership of the Baltimore conference of the AME Church doubled. During the next ten years, as congregations disbanded and conventions lagged, the number of members declined. The prohibition of black ministers in many states had an equally devastating effect. In North Carolina, John Chavis and Ralph Freeman, who had long preached to mixed congregations, were barred from their pulpits. Chavis and Freeman, both old men, protested but quietly surrendered to the new rule. Younger and more energetic black ministers, however, fled the South. The migration of many leaders, declining membership, and pressure from white churchmen forced some African churches to surrender their highly prized autonomy.[3]

But as in years past, legal and extralegal restraints could not repress the desire of blacks to control their own religious life. Even within white organizations, free Negroes frequently managed to win some small degree of autonomy. Black laymen were sometimes allowed to exhort their brethren, and occasionally black boards of deacons were appointed to discipline the Negro membership. Although such privileges did

[2] *Minutes of the Portsmouth Baptist Association,* 1826, p. 4, 1827, pp. 4–5, 1828, pp. 5–6, 1829, p. 4; *The Emancipator (Complete), Published by Elihu Embree, Jonesborough, Tennessee, 1820* (Nashville, Tenn., 1932), pp. 82, 90; *Md. Laws,* 1828, c. 151; *Va. Laws,* 1830, c. 39; *N.C. Laws,* 1830, c. 6; *Miss. Laws,* 1822, p. 183; *Va. Laws,* 1831, c. 22; *N.C. Laws,* 1831, c. 4; *Md. Laws,* 1831, c. 323; *Del. Laws,* 1832, c. 176; *Ala. Laws,* 1832, pp. 12–18; *Ga. Laws,* 1833, pp. 34–5; *Mo. Laws,* 1846, act of 16 February 1847. South Carolina had earlier restricted independent black worship; Cooper and McCord, comps., *Statutes S.C.,* VII, 440–3, 448–9. The strictures against Negro education are summarized in Woodson, *Education of the Negro,* pp. 159–69.

[3] *Minutes of the Dover Baptist Association,* 1832, p. 19, 1833, p. 13, 1834, p. 7; Wright, *Free Negro in Maryland,* p. 227; Franklin, *Free Negro in North Carolina,* pp. 180–2; Minutes of the Orange Presbytery (copy) in Papers Relating to Chavis, Ruffner Papers, HFPRC; *Minutes of the Portsmouth Baptist Association,* 1834, p. 8, 1835, pp. 6, 10.

not automatically upset the power of white ministers and laity, many black leaders transformed these modest grants of authority into almost total independence. In 1845, one rural Baptist church replaced their entire board of deacons when they found the blacks had "so far transcended the power vested in them as to take the whole discipline of the coloured members into their own hands." Similarly, the appointment of a few Negro exhorters by the First Baptist Church of Richmond encouraged many blacks to preach in groups of their own. Before long, white churchmen were deluged with complaints about "the irregular and improper conduct of coloured persons" who declared themselves authorized to preach and exhort. Unable to determine how many blacks had been so authorized, the white minister recalled the licenses of all black preachers and issued them anew with greater care. Selective relicensing failed to prevent blacks from preaching, and a year later a special meeting of the Negro deacons had to admonish all blacks "who have been exercising a public gift contrary to the rules of the church."[4]

No matter how much authority blacks usurped within the white churches, they still preferred their own independent organizations. Despite fears of white retaliation, free Negroes occasionally joined by slaves continued to press for separate African churches. In 1823, complaining that they were excluded from most of the city's churches, over a hundred Richmond freemen and slaves petitioned the Virginia General Assembly for the right to build their own meetinghouse. They promised to submit to any restrictions the legislature deemed necessary for the "preservation of peace and good order," but tactfully added that "it would be most pleasing to them to have a voice in the choice of their teacher." Ignored by the General Assembly, Richmond blacks took their demands to the local Baptist church, where they met the same cold reception.[5]

[4] Minutes of the First Baptist Church of Raleigh, 25 January 1823, 1 February 1823, NCA; Minutes of Fork Baptist Church, 1825–1873, June 1845; Minutes of the First Baptist Church of Richmond, copy, 3 July 1829, 7 July 1829, 30 June 1830, 16 September 1830; Minutes of Long Branch Baptist Church, 1807–1841, 26 October 1839, VaBHS.

[5] Petition from Richmond, 3 December 1823, VLP; Minutes of the First Baptist Church of Richmond, copy, 30 June 1830, VaBHS; Petition from Richmond, 17 December 1834, also from Petersburg, 8 January 1839, VLP.

Receiving little satisfaction in answer to their carefully drawn petitions, some blacks quietly formed their own organizations and took their meetings to empty fields, back alleys, and private homes. Whites worried about these illicit assemblies and tried to eliminate them, but with little success. Petersburg authorities, pestered throughout the antebellum years by an active black church movement, shared the frustrations of municipal officials throughout the South. In 1847, "a citizen" of Petersburg complained that free Negroes were meeting regularly without white supervision. He hinted that the police were ignoring the law and reminded them that "some very good people agree with this legislation and think these acts worthy of support." Nine years later, however, the same complaints were still ringing through the press. Although the police broke up several unauthorized prayer meetings, a leading daily lamented that "there are many gatherings . . . without the interference of the citizens."[6]

In many places, black persistence simply overwhelmed white vigilance. After the initial crackdown, the repressive laws fell into disrepair and African churches quietly resumed their steady growth. Black churches in the border states generally recovered first from the repression that followed the Nat Turner rebellion. Between 1836 and 1856, the membership of the Baltimore conference of the AME Church more than doubled. It was not long before whites in other parts of the South were complaining that the restrictions on black churches had become "virtually obsolete." Late in the 1830s, African churches again began sprouting all along the urban periphery of the South. By 1840, Louisville and Lexington each had two new black churches and St. Louis had one. A few new African churches were also organized in the Gulf port cities, although most creole freemen remained within the Catholic Church.[7]

[6] *Petersburg Republican,* 21 July 1847; *Petersburg Daily Democrat,* 2 October 1856.

[7] Wright, *Free Negro in Maryland,* p. 227; Petition from Charleston, 1834, SCLP; *Louisville Directory for the Year 1832* (Louisville, Ky., 1832), p. 142; *Directory of the City of Lexington and the County of Fayette for 1838 & 1839* (Lexington, Ky., 1838), pp. 13, 85; Charleston Keemble, comp., *The St. Louis Directory for the Years, 1836–7* (St. Louis, Mo., 1836), p. 42; Bancroft, *Census of Savannah,* p. 45.

New black churches were formed in a variety of ways. Some were the product of the growth and division of established organizations. The Bethel AME of Baltimore, for example, fathered several other churches. The Little Bethel was formed by the overflow from the larger church, and the Ebenezer AME was created as a result of doctrinal and personal conflict within the older body. Occasionally, itinerant black preachers found congenial congregations and put down permanent roots. Sometimes, pious whites lent a hand. William Crane, a wealthy Baptist layman, funded the construction of the First African Baptist Church of Baltimore and helped Moses Clayton and Noah Davis buy their freedom so they might take the pulpit of the newly established church.[8] But, as in earlier years, most African churches were formed when blacks withdrew from white congregations.

The attempt of Charleston free Negroes to break away from the Methodist Church and establish their own organization exemplifies how the diverse but complementary pressures of white racism and the desire of blacks for autonomy stimulated the establishment of African churches in many communities. The Charleston Methodist Church, like many formed in the heat of the evangelical enthusiasm of the post-Revolutionary era, had long welcomed both black and white members. But during the early years of the nineteenth century, as the black membership multiplied and evangelical ardor cooled, many white members withdrew from the mixed congregation and few other whites joined to take their place. Although whites remained in control of the church, the power of the black membership increased with its numbers. The black majority won the right to control its own finances, discipline its members, and elect officers to special quarterly conferences. Suddenly, in 1815, whites reasserted their control over the quarterly conferences. Claiming that the black officers were corrupt, they disfranchised them and took over governance of the institution.

[8] George F. Bragg, *The First Negro Priest on Southern Soil* (Baltimore, 1909), pp. 9–14; Edward S. Abdy, *Journal of a Residence and Tour in the United States of North America, from April, 1833, to October, 1834,* 3 vols. (London, 1835), I, 155–6, II, 53–4; Azzie B. Kroger, *Negro Baptists in Maryland* (Baltimore, 1946), pp. 5–8; Davis, *Life of Noah Davis,* pp. 35–59; George E. Adams, *Life and Character of William Crane* (Baltimore, 1868), pp. 11–14, 26–9.

Blacks did not immediately protest against this revolution in church affairs, but quietly prepared to win back their rights within the regular Methodist organization or, if necessary, outside it. Morris Brown, a wealthy free Negro, a member of the Brown Fellowship Society, and a leader within the Methodist Church, traveled to Philadelphia to consult with Richard Allen and obtain a charter for the new organization. In 1818, following a dispute over the use of the Negro burial ground, Brown and a majority of the black membership seceded from the old church *en masse* and established the Charleston AME Church. "The galleries, hitherto crowded," recalled one white clergyman, "were almost completely deserted, and it was a vacancy that could be felt." Although harassed by whites, Charleston blacks soon purchased a lot, built a hall, and met regularly for the next four years. Not until the storm of opposition that followed the Vesey conspiracy was their church dismantled and Brown forced to leave the state.[9]

The destruction of the Charleston AME suggests the vehement opposition independent black churches faced during the antebellum years, but behind that intense hostility pressure was slowly building to allow free Negroes and slaves their own separate places of worship. The number of black church members was rapidly increasing throughout the South. In many churches, Negro members greatly outnumbered whites. By 1838, for example, fifty-seven churches in the Dover Baptist Association of Virginia had more blacks than whites, and over 60 percent of the association's members were black. One church reported over eight hundred members, of whom only forty-one were white.[10] A large portion of these were slaves perfunctorily enrolled by their masters. Yet if even a fraction of the black membership had attended services, there would have been little room for whites.

[9] Mood, *Methodism in Charleston,* pp. 129–33; Petition from Charleston, 1820, SCLP; Charleston *City Gazette,* 4 December 1817, 10 August 1822; *Charleston Courier,* 9 June 1818; Wikramanayake, *A World in Shadow,* pp. 121–8, 130–1, 142–3. For other African churches established in a like fashion, see Luther P. Jackson, "Religious Development of the Negro in Virginia from 1760 to 1860," *JNH,* XVI (1931), 189–91; Minutes of the 14th Street Presbyterian Church, Washington, D.C., Woodson Papers, LC.

[10] George B. Taylor, *Virginia Baptist Ministers, Third Series* (Lynchburg, Va., 1912), pp. 314–15; Ryland, *Baptists of Virginia,* pp. 281–2; Richmond *Religious Herald,* 26 November 1840.

The expansion of black church membership vexed white churchmen. Free Negroes and slaves swelled the rolls of white churches, necessitating larger meetinghouses, inflating maintenance costs, and disturbing whites. Although Negroes were segregated, some intermingling was unavoidable. Much to their disgust, white members were often jostled by crowds of blacks who blocked church entrances, and sedate services were occasionally interrupted by emotional outbursts from the galleries. The inconveniences that accompanied the growth of Negro church attendance made whites increasingly willing to have blacks out of the way.[11]

But Negroes could not be left without the Word of God and a chance for salvation. While many whites were bothered by the growing black enrollment in their churches, others worried about the black souls that went unsaved. The legislation depriving free Negroes and slaves of their own churches merely heightened the sense of responsibility some white clergymen felt for Christianizing blacks. In 1832, soon after Virginia passed its restrictive laws, one Baptist churchman lashed out against his fellow ministers for failing to convert heathen blacks in their midst. He denounced the argument that Negroes were not suitable subjects for Christianity. "What real minister of Christ," he asked, "without emotions of regret, without sighs and tears of sympathy, and without forming a judgment of a just and judicious God, can attend some of our houses of worship, and behold multitudes of immortal beings entirely excluded from there and deprived of the means of religious instruction, because they were born with a black or yellow skin, and in a state of bondage?" Scolding fellow ministers for paying more attention to distant Africans than to native blacks, other churchmen suggested that the failure to give proper religious instruction to slaves and free Negroes left them susceptible to the appeals of untutored black preachers like Nat Turner.[12]

The rise of the abolition movement and the division of the

[11] Jeremiah Bell Jeter, *The Recollections of a Long Life* (Richmond, Va., 1891), p. 209; [Robert Ryland], "Reminiscences of the First African Baptist Church," *American Baptist Memorial,* XIV (1855), 262–3.

[12] *Minutes of the Appomattox Baptist Association,* 1832, p. 12; Richmond *Religious Herald,* 13 February 1835.

leading denominations along sectional lines intensified the missionary zeal of Southern ministers. Abolitionist charges that slavery denied Negroes the benefits of salvation stung Southern clergy into action. By the 1840s most churches had accepted the goal of converting Negroes to Christianity as not only necessary but desirable. "[We do not propose to] enter into any argument to prove it is the duty of our churches and of Christian masters to provide for the religious instruction of our slaves and free people of color," declared one Baptist association in 1859 with an air of finality. "That question, we think, has been settled by reports of former years."[13]

As pressure for Negro religious instruction mounted, white ministers composed treatises on how blacks might best be converted, churches set up committees on the religious instruction of slaves, and some of the larger denominations commissioned missionaries to proselytize slaves.[14] These itinerant missionary efforts absorbed most of the money and energy of interested Southern clergy, but some ministers moved in a different direction and tried to organize separate churches where blacks, both free and slave, might worship under white supervision and control. Unlike the evangelical ministers who had made earlier efforts to convert blacks, these churchmen were not driven by the equalitarian zeal or the great revivalist enthusiasm of the late eighteenth century. Almost uniformly they accepted slavery, and many had been among the most ardent defenders of the peculiar institution. Instead, they were motivated by a paternal concern for the black man's soul, a belief that religion would make it easier to control blacks, and a clear knowledge that their white parishioners

[13] Luther P. Jackson, "Religious Instruction of Negroes, 1830–1860, with Special Reference to South Carolina," *JNH*, XV (1930), 78–9; *Minutes of the Albemarle Baptist Association*, 1859, p. 19.

[14] For the missionary efforts of Southern clergy, see Charles C. Jones, *The Religious Instruction of Negroes in the United States* (Savannah, Ga., 1842); Woodson, *History of the Negro Church*, pp. 148–66; Jackson, "Religious Instruction of Negroes," pp. 278–314; Haven P. Perkins, "Religion for Slaves: Difficulties and Methods," *Church History*, X (1941), 228–45; Stiles B. Lines, "Slaves and Churchmen: The Work of the Episcopal Church Among Southern Negroes, 1830–1860," unpublished doctoral thesis, Columbia University, 1960; Thomas L. Williams, "The Methodist Mission to the Slaves," unpublished doctoral thesis, Yale University, 1943.

had no desire to add to the already swollen Negro membership of their churches.

At the center of the movement to allow blacks their own churches was an understanding that blacks cared little for white-sponsored religion. Southern clergy admitted that the style of preaching demanded by white congregations did little to arouse blacks. When forced to attend services in white churches, observed one Baptist, "the usual African resort is a loud, comfortable snoring nap."[15] Frequently, blacks used church attendance as a pretext for their own gatherings. After joining in the white services, they would meet in the woods for their own worship. Whites worried that independent, unsupervised black religion fostered all kinds of subversion. "Too many of them indulge and cherish the idea that God instructs them in some direct and miraculous manner," complained one Virginia proponent of separate religious instruction. Their belief in direct communication with God was wrong and dangerous. It not only usurped the minister's role but it did away with the need for any white intermediary. Without whites to interpret the Lord's words, there was no telling how they might be understood. Rather than discouraging these subversive tendencies, allowing blacks to attend white services often encouraged them. Sermons prepared for white congregations might take on entirely different meanings when they fell on black ears. Separate religious instruction would allow whites the opportunity to purge blacks of these ideas as well as of the emotionalism that attended their worship. White ministers would save blacks "from appeals which madden rather than instruct—from a religion which puffs up but does not edify."[16]

Still, the proposals to give Negroes separate instruction or churches of their own encountered stiff opposition. Fearful that any change in the Negro's regimen would excite new

[15] *Minutes of the Rappahannock Baptist Association,* 1850, p. 11; [John T. Watkins] to Editor of the *Farmville Journal,* [16 October 1856], John Hubbard Papers, SHC.

[16] *Minutes of the Rappahannock Baptist Association,* 1850, p. 12; Richmond *Religious Herald,* 17 February 1832; James H. Thornwell, *A Review of Rev. J. G. Adger's Sermon on the Instruction of the Colored Population* (Charleston, S.C., 1847), p. 13.

expectations, arouse unrest, and spark a revolt, many whites opposed the missionary efforts of the clergy. To meet these objections, churchmen had to tailor their programs to inculcate submission and obedience. "It is not proposed to indoctrinate them in Locke or Sidney or to make the bill of rights the foundation of a course of lectures for them, or even to teach them their A.B.C.," declared one supporter of separate religious instruction, "but simply, that they should not lye, that they should not steal, that their own interest and welfare are identified with their master, and that therefore it behooves them to be faithful, industrious, obedient, and diligent. . . ." Ministers assured their opponents that "negroes who have from childhood enjoyed the stated ministry of the gospel seem to assimilate themselves more to whites, not only in their manner of speaking, but of thinking and acting."[17] These promises did not satisfy all hostile whites, but the proposals for the separate religious instruction of free Negroes and slaves nevertheless gained growing public support.

The formation of African churches during the antebellum years was thus both a response to the desires of blacks and a reflection of the attitudes of whites. Most whites, despite their repressive laws, believed that all men, no matter what their status, had the right to salvation and that salvation could be secured through organized religion. Although they were suspicious of black churches and black ministers in particular, whites found it increasingly difficult to resist black demands for their own institutions, especially when they took a form that so resembled their own. Besides, many thought religion would provide another means for controlling restless slaves and free Negroes. Blacks, for their part, played on white religious ideals as well as the desire of many whites to get the growing number of Negro converts out of white churches. Although blacks would have preferred to have their own preachers and total control of their own institutions, they accepted the white man's terms, confident they could outwit and outlast the white ministers and laymen who supervised their affairs. In opting for separate institutions, blacks reiterated the

17 [John T. Watkins] to the Editor of the *Farmville Journal*, [16 October 1856], Hubbard Papers, SHC; *Public Proceedings Relating to Calvary Church*, pp. 27–8.

belief that they could create a better life if only the whites would leave them alone.

By the 1840s, pressure from blacks desiring their own churches and the belief of many whites that Negroes could better be served within separate institutions were coalescing to establish African churches in areas long opposed to those institutions. With the successful founding of one African church, opposition to others dropped away and dozens of black meetinghouses opened their doors. Soon after the establishment of the First African Church of Richmond in 1841, white members of the Second Baptist Church sponsored a Second African. Before long, the two African churches produced their own progeny, so that by 1860 there were four African Baptist meetinghouses in Richmond. Not to be outdone, other denominations followed the Baptists' lead. In 1856, Richmond Methodists established an African church, and four years later the Committee on Religious Instruction of the local Episcopal church recommended placing "people of color into separate and distinct congregations."[18]

New African churches soon appeared in other Virginia cities. In 1843, the Portsmouth Baptist Association again reversed its policy and recognized the Third Colored Church of Petersburg. Three years later the Manchester African and the Midlothian African were organized in Chesterfield County, which adjoins Richmond. In 1855 and 1856, African churches were established in Alexandria and Fredericksburg. In all, between the formation of the First African Baptist Church of Richmond and the Civil War, fourteen new black Baptist churches were established in Virginia.[19]

Meanwhile, the movement to Christianize blacks by allowing them separate churches spread beyond Virginia. In 1845, leading South Carolina ministers and laymen met in Charleston, surveyed the development of separate African churches

[18] Richmond *Religious Herald*, 7 September 1838; [Ryland], "Reminiscences of the First African Baptist Church," pp. 262–5, 289–92, 321–7, 353–6; Robert Ryland, "Origins and History of the First African Baptist Church," in *The First Century of the First Baptist Church of Richmond, Virginia, 1780–1880* (Richmond, 1880); Ryland, *Baptists of Virginia*, pp. 284–5; Richmond *Daily Dispatch*, 18 August 1856; *Diocese of Virginia, Sixty-Fifth Annual Convention, 1860* (Richmond, 1860), pp. 63–70, quotation on p. 69.

[19] Ryland, *Baptists of Virginia*, pp. 285–6.

throughout the South, and announced that the religious instruction of Negroes was "THE GREAT DUTY, and in the truest and best sense, THE FIXED, THE SETTLED POLICY OF THE SOUTH." Encouraged by those bold words, Charleston Episcopalians set to work organizing the first black church in Charleston since an angry mob had demolished the AME meetinghouse after the Vesey conspiracy. In 1849, the Calvary Church opened to Negro freemen and slaves.[20]

Pushed by blacks and paternalistic white clergy of various denominations, the number of African churches in the South increased rapidly during the 1840s and 1850s. By the eve of the Civil War, Baltimore had fifteen African churches representing five different denominations. Although Baltimore naturally had the largest number and variety of black churches, every Southern city had some. Louisville had nine African churches, Savannah five, Nashville and St. Louis four, Memphis and Mobile two, and Raleigh one.[21] The membership of these churches comprised both free Negroes and slaves, but freemen, because of their status, quickly became the dominant figures in their operations.

African churches, for the most part, remained confined to the cities. In rural areas, independent black churches continued to be viewed with intense suspicion. While planters might be convinced to build a small "praise-house" for their slaves or to allow a missionary churchman to baptize them, they never considered granting even the limited independence blacks obtained within urban churches. Black ministers who ventured into the countryside to carry the Word to rural free Negroes and slaves often did so at the risk of their lives, and even whites had trouble organizing black churches in the country-

[20] *Proceedings of a Meeting in Charleston*, p. 72; Robert F. Durden, "The Establishment of Calvary Protestant Episcopal Church for Negroes in Charleston," *South Carolina Historical Magazine*, LXV (1964), 63–84.

[21] *Woods' Baltimore Directory for 1858–'59* (Baltimore, n.d.), pp. 538–40; Henry Tanner, comp., *The Louisville Directory and Business Advertiser for 1859–1860* (Louisville, Ky., 1860), pp. 310–12; *Directory for the City of Savannah . . . 1860* (Savannah, Ga., 1860), no pagination; *Nashville City and Business Directory for 1860–61* (Nashville, Tenn., 1860), p. 80; *Kennedy's St. Louis Directory* (St. Louis, Mo., 1860), pp. 8–10; *Memphis City Directory for 1854–'5* (Memphis, Tenn., 1854), p. 74; [Henry] Farrow and [W. B.] Dennett, comps., *Directory for the City of Mobile* (Mobile, Ala., 1859); Franklin, *Free Negro in North Carolina*, pp. 176–7.

side. "Separate services for colored people may work well in the towns and cities," observed one Baptist association on the eve of the Civil War, "but experience shows objections to be against this plan in country churches."[22]

Wherever they were established, African churches quickly became the centers of black religious life. In spite of watchful white supervisors and meddling white trustees, blacks flocked to the new churches. In 1842, the first full year of operation of the First African Church of Richmond, over 600 black members were enrolled. During the next decade the growth of membership slackened, but only slightly. By 1852, the First African boasted over 2,000 members. That same year, African Baptist churches in Lexington and Louisville enrolled almost 3,000 members and St. Louis over 800. Baptists failed to attract a large black following in Maryland, but the Baltimore conference of the AME Church counted over 5,000 members in 1855. These churches were usually the largest in the area. Visitors rarely reported an empty seat in African churches, and black congregations were constantly outgrowing their meetinghouses. Although precise figures are not available, it is probable that a higher percentage of Negroes than whites were regular churchgoers. "Among the *white* population," noted one Baltimore missionary in 1837, "the proportion of professors of religion is not quite one to every two families; while among the *blacks* the proportion is nearly one to each family." This survey was admittedly crude, but the large size of the African churches lends credence to the idea that Negroes had a higher rate of church membership than whites.[23]

In escaping from whites, blacks did not always elude the divisions within the black community. Instead of healing the breaches between free Negroes and slaves, rich and poor, mulattoes and blacks, many African churches merely embodied them. Upper-class freemen often stood apart from the indepen-

[22] Autobiography of Hiram Revels, Carter Woodson Papers, LC; Minutes of Long Branch Baptist Church, 1807–1841, 6 June 1840; Minutes of Walnut Grove Baptist Churches, 1841–1859, 7 October 1849, 20 October 1849, VaBHS; quotation in *Minutes of the Concord Baptist Association*, 1860, p. 5.

[23] J. Lansing Burrows, ed., *American Baptist Register for 1852* (Philadelphia, 1853), pp. 360, 362, 364, 368, 116, 120, 197; Richmond *Daily Dispatch*, 27 July 1857; "Statisticks on Destitution in Baltimore," *Baltimore Literary and Religious Magazine*, III (1837), 279.

dent African churches. Many feared their white patrons and customers would be offended if they became too closely identified with the mass of free Negroes and slaves who attended these institutions. Others simply wanted nothing to do with the poor blacks, whose style of life was so alien to their own. Where they could, elite free Negroes joined white churches, sometimes the church of their former master, or attended churches composed exclusively of free Negroes of like status. Often these were Episcopal or Presbyterian meetinghouses, whose sedate services were in striking contrast to those of the African Baptist and Methodist churches.[24] In eschewing the black church and joining elite congregations, wealthy free Negroes not only divorced themselves from the mass of free Negroes but also engaged in the traditional form of denominational mobility familiar to generations of successful Americans.

In the Lower South, where somatic and cultural differences between free and slave, mulatto and black, were comparatively large, the alienation of the free Negro elite from the black church was especially evident. In some places, wealthy free people of color quietly purchased pews within white churches, and in the Gulf port cities the mass of colored creoles worshipped in the large cathedrals whose spires dominated those cities. Indeed, rather than form their own religious institutions many Protestant freemen married and baptized their children in Catholic churches, in part because of their availability and in part because certificates of marriage or baptism might serve as added proof of freedom in case of trouble.[25] The ability of elite free Negroes to enter these white institutions hindered the development of their racial consciousness and slowed the establishment of African churches in the Lower South. In many cities with sizable free Negro populations, free people of color failed to create an independent black church. While Lower South free Negroes were

[24] Jackson, "Religious Development of the Negro in Virginia," p. 192; Minutes of the Gillfield Baptist Church, Petersburg, 17 May 1857; Simms, *First Colored Baptist Church,* p. 58; quotation in Franklin, *Free Negro in North Carolina,* p. 190; John P. Green, *Fact Stranger Than Fiction* (Cleveland, Ohio, 1920), p. 13.

[25] Fitchett, "Traditions of the Free Negro in South Carolina," p. 149; Baptismal Certificates in William Johnson Papers, LSU; Meullion Papers, LSU.

generally better off economically than those of the Upper South, the African church remained comparatively underdeveloped in that region.

Occasionally, there were attempts to cut across the barriers of class and caste and unite all blacks in one church. The efforts of Morris Brown to plant a branch of the AME Church in Charleston may have been one such broadly based movement. It attracted members of the Brown Fellowship Society, including Brown himself, as well as many of the slave leaders who later joined with Denmark Vesey. But few men had Brown's charisma or ability to keep the fragmented black community together, especially in the face of intense white opposition.

The free Negro membership of the African churches was generally drawn from the poor and middling free Negroes, who may have practiced a skilled trade or owned some property but were in no position to imitate the white elite. Their daily lives were closely intertwined with those of the slaves, and many had slave husbands or wives. Thus, the membership of the African church, while embodying class differences within the free Negro caste, also reflected caste unity between poor and middle-class freemen and bondsmen.

The overwhelming majority of these blacks, like most lower-class whites, preferred the evangelical style of the Baptist and Methodist denominations. While the few African Episcopal and Presbyterian churches stood almost empty, blacks packed the churches of these other denominations.[26] In copying the denominational forms of white institutions, the African churches did not become merely a dark reflection of the white churches. Instead, blacks used the forms whites allowed them to blend the heritage of Africa with their American experience and create their own unique religious style, theology, and polity. Differences in religious style were most apparent. Long after the evangelical enthusiasm of the eighteenth-century revivals had run its course within most white churches, it remained central to black religious life. The "loud singing and praying and sometimes loud shouting," the rhythmic "Amen! or Glory be to thy name! or Truth, Lord!" and

[26] Abdy, *Journal of a Residence*, II, 54–5.

the fiery sermons that seemed to act "like spiritual Spanish flies" gave black religion a distinctive style. Nearly every white visitor to an African church commented on the "tornado" of emotions that accompanied the services, and not a few suddenly found themselves swept up in it. "The meeting commences with singing, through the whole congregation," noted one staid New England visitor to a Louisville African church; "loud and louder still were their devotions—and oh! what music, what devotion, what streaming eyes, and throbbing hearts; my blood ran quick in my veins, and quicker still. . . . It seems as though the roof would rise from the walls, and some of them would go up, soul and body both."[27]

The emotional gospel preached in African churches suggests that many Negroes used religion as a means to escape the oppression of their daily lives and to compensate for their crushed ambitions.[28] Whites encouraged this escapism and tried to use the church as a mechanism for controlling blacks. Robert Ryland, the white minister of the First African Church of Richmond, gave divine sanction to white rule in his sermons. "God has given this country to the white people," he bluntly told the black congregation. "They are the lawmakers—the masters—the superiors. The people of color are the subjects—the servants—and even when not in bondage, the inferiors. In this state of things, God enjoins you to your submission." Not all white clergymen were as heavyhanded as Ryland, but most felt it "a duty to teach *obedience* and *subordination* to *their Masters* as well as *piety* to *God*." By urging their people to turn from the meager rewards of this world to those of an-

[27] Jefferson Hamilton to the Mayor, 11 April 1840, Interesting Transcriptions from the City Documents of Mobile, 1815–1859, typescript, MCH; George Lewis, *Impressions of America and the American Churches* (Edinburgh, 1845), pp. 167–70; Frederick von Raumer, *America and the American People*, (New York, 1846), pp. 434–5; Fredrika Bremer, *The Homes of the New World*, 2 vols. (New York, 1853), II, 234–8; Tower, *Slavery Unmasked*, p. 252.

[28] This theme is emphasized in Benjamin E. Mays, *The Negro's God as Reflected in His Literature* (Boston, 1938), and E. Franklin Frazier, *The Negro Church* (New York, 1963). For a healthy corrective to this view see Joseph Washington, *Black Religion* (Boston, 1964), and Vincent Harding, "Religion and Resistance Among Antebellum Negroes, 1800–1860," in August Meier and Elliott Rudwick, eds., *The Making of Black America*, 2 vols. (New York, 1969), I, 179–97.

other, black ministers often sounded the same themes as white. Andrew Marshall, the popular free Negro minister of the First African Church of Savannah, admonished his congregation with "some good practical maxims of morality, and told them they were to look to a future state of rewards and punishments in which God would deal impartially with 'the poor and the rich, the black man and the white.'" Some Negroes seem to have internalized this idea of submission to worldly authority with expectations of some heavenly equality. Frederick Douglass found that many religious blacks were "under the delusion that God required them to submit to slavery and to wear their chains with meekness and humility." Many more blacks identified with a different Biblical tradition. Some may have seen themselves as chosen deliverers of their people, and others compared their plight to that of the peoples of the Old Testament whose oppressors suffered earthly retribution. When one visitor to a Richmond church asked a little girl who Joseph's brothers sold him to, she blurted out, "The *Nigger traders*, ma'm!"[29]

White churchmen had hoped that the separate instruction of blacks would allow them to purge black religion of its distinctive style and content. Committees on the religious instruction of Negroes were forever reminding ministers that blacks were prone to "groan and shout under inflammatory appeals" and cautioning them to use "didactic address." But the independence afforded by separate African churches allowed blacks greater freedom of expression, and the fervor of black congregations seemed to grow despite the best efforts of white clergymen. In 1855, Robert Ryland confidently announced that he had tempered the zealous enthusiasm of his congregation: "They are learning to avoid the habits of whining, snuffing, grunting, drawling, repeating, hicouphing [*sic*] and other vulgarities of prayer. . . ." Yet four years later, when an Episcopal minister exchanged pulpits with Ryland, his sermon was greeted with shouts of "'Amen,' 'Glory,' 'That's

[29] Richmond *Daily Dispatch*, 6 August 1852; Lyell, *Second Visit*, II, 14; also Bremer, *Homes in the New World*, I, 352–4; Frederick Douglass, *The Life and Times of Frederick Douglass* (Hartford, Conn., 1881), p. 85; Loveland Journal, 14 April 1855, Duke.

so,' &c., with a vehemence unparalleled." The emotional fervor and the élan bred in these separate black institutions reinforced the distinctive style of black religion. Rather than fostering reliance on white ministers and forms, separate black organizations seemed to spur the development of an independent spirit. White ministers frequently found blacks contemptuous of white religious forms. They looked upon whites as merely taught by the Book, observed one Virginia churchman, while they considered themselves "instructed by the inspiration of the Spirit."[30]

Black religion was thus a source of both accommodation and resistance to white authority. While some black ministers mouthed the white man's words, others used the church as a refuge from white oppression. Throughout the South, black life revolved around the church. Many freemen were baptized, married, and buried in the same church.[31] African churches strengthened the black family by insisting that marriages be solemnized by religious services, punishing adulterers, and occasionally reuniting separated couples. The church was more than a source of discipline; it was a center for education, a provider of social insurance, and a place where blacks might relax and organize community entertainment. African churches supported schools and fraternal associations; church choirs gave concerts; church auxiliaries sponsored fairs, picnics, and banquets. The church expressed the community's social conscience by aiding the poor, supporting missionary activities, and helping other free Negro communities establish like institutions. In allowing blacks to govern their own affairs, the church fed the ambitions and bolstered the confidence of

[30] [Ryland], "Reminiscences of the First African Baptist Church," pp. 264–5, quotation at 289–90; Richmond *Daily Dispatch*, 25 October 1859; Richmond *Religious Herald*, 17 February 1832.

[31] The nature of the federal census makes it impossible to reconstruct the free Negro family with any degree of accuracy. Studies by E. Franklin Frazier (*The Free Negro Family* [Nashville, Tenn., 1932] and *The Negro Family in the United States* [Chicago, 1939]), however, confirm my own impression that it was a strong, durable institution. Indeed, it is impossible to conceive of the free Negro community, as outlined in this chapter, without a strong family at the core. Further study is needed, however, to determine precisely the character of the free Negro family and its relation to free Negro class structure, and to compare it with the white and the slave family.

black leaders.[32] Not surprisingly, ministers became the most important element in the black leadership class. More than this, the church gave free Negro communities a sense of unity and common purpose. Belonging to a larger social group strengthened free Negroes against the hostile white world which tried to render them impotent. It bred a sense of group identity and solidarity, which in turn fostered pride and self-respect and nurtured the belief that free Negroes could control their own destiny.

Next to the church, the African school was the most important institution in the free Negro community. Free Negroes were anxious to educate themselves and their children. Given the opportunity, black parents pushed to have their children attend school. At the insistence of one church member, Daniel Payne, then an AME minister in Baltimore, agreed to tutor her child. "As soon as this became known," Payne found himself "besieged by other parishioners, and was finally constrained to yield to their request, so that within twelve months I found myself at the head of a school of about fifty." A visiting white clergyman also noted the free Negro's enthusiasm for education. Touring one lower-class district of Baltimore, he found an equal proportion of Negro and white children attending school. The blacks, he concluded, "appear to be more desirous of instruction than the whites; for when it is gratuitous to both, the same portion of each is found at the school, although the physical condition of the blacks, has been shown to be worse than that of the whites, and the obstacles to attendance of schools, therefore comparatively greater to them."[33]

Like whites, free Negroes believed education was a means of bettering themselves. Fredericksburg freemen, petitioning

[32] Minutes of the First African Baptist Church, Richmond; Minutes of the Gillfield Baptist Church, Petersburg; St. Louis *Daily Missouri Democrat,* 29 December 1853, 7 January 1854; Baltimore *Sun,* 10 March 1854, 1 January 1857, 11, 12 May 1859, 17 February 1860; *New Orleans Crescent,* 7 April 1856; Petersburg *Daily Express,* 27 April 1859, 14 June 1859; *Charleston Courier,* 29 November 1859; Petersburg *Press,* 2 March 1860, 4 April 1860; Frederick Law Olmsted, *The Cotton Kingdom,* 2 vols. (New York, 1861), I, 260.

[33] Payne, *Recollections of Seventy Years,* pp. 78–9; "Statisticks on Destitution in Baltimore," pp. 278–9.

the Virginia General Assembly for permission to establish a school, gave voice to the desires of free Negroes throughout the South. "So general has become the diffusion of knowledge," they declared, "that those persons who are so unfortunate as not to be in some degree educated are cut off from the ordinary means of self-advancement & find the greatest difficulty in gaining an honest livelihood." When the legislature rejected their petition and spitefully passed a new law forbidding free Negroes who left the state for an education to return, the city's leading free Negroes migrated north. Other Southern freemen moved to Canada, Europe, and Liberia for much the same reason. Education, however, was more than a means of self-improvement. A "good education," declared William Watkins, a leading Baltimore schoolmaster, "is the *sine qua non* as regards the elevation of our people."[34]

As the center-pole of the free Negro community, the African church carried much of the burden for educating black people. Every African church had a Sunday school, and most supported day schools where black children attended classes free or at a minimal charge. In the cities of the border states, schools were first established in the years immediately following the Revolution and expanded with the free Negro population. In Baltimore, for example, Daniel Coker's school, attached to the Saratoga Street AME Church, grew rapidly during the first two decades of the nineteenth century. Other ministers followed his lead, so that by the 1840s over six hundred black students were enrolled in African schools. The expansion of the African church during the 1840s and 1850s boosted school enrollments still higher. New church buildings generally included schoolrooms, and church laymen were generous in supporting teachers. In addition to the usual Sabbath and primary schools, a few of the larger denominations sponsored secondary schools. In 1855, Baltimore Baptists

[34] Petition from Spotsylvania County, 16 March 1838, VLP; *Va. Laws*, 1838, c. 99; W. B. Hartgrove, "The Story of Maria Louise Moore and Fannie M. Richards," *JNH*, I (1916), 25–7; Jesse Rankin to William McLain, 21 August 1850, ACS; Ira Easter to J. H. B. Latrobe, 10 May 1836, Letters Received, MdSCS Papers; William Watkins, *An Address Delivered Before the Moral Reform Society, in Philadelphia, August 8, 1836* (Philadelphia, 1836), pp. 13–14; Marshall Hall, *The Two-Fold Slavery of the United States* (London, 1854), p. 136.

launched a high school with a four-year course of study including all "the usual branches taught in our best Academies." Not to be outdone, the bishops of the AME Church established a secondary school of their own. By 1860, Baltimore's fifteen African schools had enrolled over 2,600 black students.[35]

Patterns of church-sponsored education were much the same throughout the cities of the Upper South, although on a smaller scale. In the Lower South, where African churches were not nearly as numerous, schools tended to be independent organizations supported by wealthy freemen. In Charleston, Thomas Bonneau, a prominent slaveowning free Negro, sponsored a school for free Negro children. Creole free people of color in the Gulf port cities generally educated their children in French-language academies and sent them abroad to finish their schooling. And throughout the South, wealthy free Negroes employed private tutors for their offspring.[36]

The freemen's interest in education seemed only to harden white opposition to an educated black population. When whites established public school systems for their own children, they generally barred free Negroes from participating or even from having a fair share of the public funds to support separate black academies. In 1860, Baltimore freemen paid five hundred dollars in taxes to support schools they could not attend. In many places, public hostility to educating Negroes and proscriptive laws prevented blacks from organizing schools even if they financed them on their own. Nevertheless, blacks risked imprisonment and the lash to keep their schools open. After Georgia prohibited the education of free Negroes, Julian Troumontaine, a free Negro instructor of the Savannah African School, took his academy into hiding and continued to teach free Negro children until he was caught fifteen years later.

[35] Wright, *Free Negro in Maryland,* pp. 204–32; *Maryland Colonization Journal,* I (April 1838), 68; Richmond *Religious Herald,* 6 December 1855; Davis, *Life of Noah Davis,* pp. 83–4.

[36] C. W. Birnie, "The Education of the Negro in Charleston, South Carolina, Before the Civil War," *JNH,* XII (1927), 13–21; Boucher, "Free Negro in Alabama," pp. 124–5, 312–17; *Mobile Daily Advertiser,* 2 May 1850; Nathan Wiley, "Education of the Colored Population of Louisiana," *Harper's New Monthly Magazine,* XXXIII (1866), 244–50; Betty Porter, "The History of Negro Education in Louisiana," *Louisiana Historical Quarterly,* XXV (1942), 730–7; Desdunes, *Nos Hommes et Notre Histoire,* pp. 18–21, 28–31.

Such clandestine schools could be found in almost every community that legally prohibited them. When a Richmond newspaper complained that black children were seen every Sunday morning marching to church with books in their hands, the police raided one African meetinghouse and found their worst suspicions confirmed. "The officers, on entering the basement, found the negroes alone, some with some without books—the pastor Rev. T. Lindsay, and perhaps other white persons, being in the room above. . . ." As with the formation of the African church, black persistence seemed to wear whites down until the proscriptive laws fell into disuse.[37]

The inability or refusal of whites to shut these schools pointed to a growing ambiguity in white thought about educating blacks. Quakers, emancipationists, and churchmen of all denominations quietly ran schools for free Negroes and sometimes slaves as well. Since they valued education highly, these Southerners found it difficult to equate schooling with subversion. Few Southern churches lacked a Sunday school for Negroes, free and slave. In 1853, when Norfolk officials prosecuted one Southern white woman for keeping a school for freemen, she embarrassed local clergymen by demonstrating that blacks were taught to read and write in the basements of the leading white churches. Some years later, a Richmond newspaper reprinted the strictures against Negro schools, angrily noting that there was "good reason to believe that there are schools in this city in which negroes are taught by white persons to read and write."[38] Yet these whites were a small minority, and the black church carried most of the burden of educating black folks.

African churches not only celebrated life but also dignified death. Even in death, blacks could not escape systematic

[37] Woodson, *Education of the Negro,* p. 307 n.; Richard R. Wright, *A Brief Historical Sketch of Negro Education in Georgia* (Savannah, 1894), pp. 17–20; *Richmond Whig,* 9 September 1856; Richmond *Daily Dispatch,* 24 August 1858; William Ferguson, *America by River and Rail* (London, 1856), p. 123.

[38] Woodson, *Education of the Negro,* pp. 205–8; Dunlap, *Quaker Education, passim;* U.S. Commissioner of Education, *Special Report,* pp. 199–222; Wagstaff, ed., *Minutes of the N.C. Manumission Society,* pp. 59–61; Minutes of the African and the Africana School Societies, HSD; *Proceedings of a Meeting in Charleston,* p. 38; M. Douglass, *Educational Laws of Virginia,* pp. 9, 29–32; Richmond *Daily Dispatch,* 25 October 1855.

racial proscription. Whites no more wanted to be buried near black people than they wanted to mix with them in the same church or ride with them in the same coach. The equality that death brought pushed whites to find some means to distinguish themselves from blacks for eternity. Cemeteries, which were designed to mirror the social order of the living, universally placed blacks in some obscure corner. Raleigh officials, following the common practice, divided the town burial ground into three parts: one for citizens and their friends; another for white paupers, criminals, and strangers; and a third for blacks.[39] In so dividing public burial grounds, whites both reiterated their disdain for blacks and admitted to a belief that no man should depart this world without some degree of dignity. Still, they had no desire to tend a black corpse. Even where legally required to supervise black funerals or direct the services, few whites intruded into black people's privacy during a moment they too held sacred. Besides, white ministers and morticians could rarely be obtained for the piddling fees blacks could afford to pay. A Richmond churchman reported that although the law prohibited blacks from being left alone at the graveyard, "the city authorities connive at them, as it seems hard for colored people to be buried like brutes without any religious respect; and white ministers cannot be found."[40]

Once again the needs of blacks and the attitudes of whites conspired to provide another place where black people might be on their own. Left to themselves, blacks contrived to linger a little longer where they could at last escape the white man's prying eyes. They embellished their funeral services with long eulogies, hymns, and songs. Occasionally some brought instruments to accompany the singers, and sometimes it seemed as if every black person in the community was marching to the burial site. "Three or Four, sometimes every evening in the week, there are Funerals of Negroes, accompanied by processions of 3, 4, and 5 hundred Negroes and a tumultous crowd of other slaves who disturb all the inhabitants around the burying Ground," complained a citizen of Charleston. The funeral became one of the most important occasions in the

[39] *Ordinances and By-Laws of the Board of Commissioners for the Government of the City of Raleigh, from 1803 to 1854* (Raleigh, N.C., 1854), p. 75.
[40] *Public Proceedings Relating to Calvary Church,* pp. 48–9.

social life of many black communities. Blacks preened themselves and donned their best clothes to mark these important events. Rather than a somber occasion, the funeral became a joyous event. Not only was the deceased escaping the oppression of this world, but he was providing another opportunity for blacks to gather away from whites. Whites could not help but notice the striking difference between these ceremonies and their own somber memorials. When the deacon of the Third African Baptist Church of Savannah died, the pageantry amazed the local press. "We noticed in the procession, three uniformed [black] fire companies, and another joined them on the South Commons. The Porter's Association, of which he was a member, turned out, and wore black scarfs with white rosettes. We also noticed in the procession two or three benevolent associations, distinguished by suitable dress. A spectator counted thirty-five carriages, well filled, besides a number of other conveyances, and many on horse back following the hearse. It is estimated between 2,000 and 5,000 colored persons were in the procession."[41] Whites ridiculed the attachment blacks had to the lively burial of the dead. But the amusement with which whites viewed these ceremonies only increased the Negro's latitude in transforming the funeral into a central event in black life.

To provide for their burial, blacks organized fraternal associations to purchase burial plots and headstones and, when the moment came, to rent a hearse to carry a fallen member to his final resting place. Some societies dressed their members in special uniforms, and a few hired bands for the occasion. Having once provided for the dead, these organizations turned their attention back to the living. Fraternal organizations, often affiliated with African churches, supplied nearly every conceivable service to the black community. Disabled members were furnished with weekly "sick dues" to assure them an income while they could not work; the elderly were given pensions, as were the widows and children of dead members.

[41] *Charleston Patriot,* 19 September 1835; *Savannah News,* quoted in *Louisville Daily Courier,* 6 March 1855; Lillian Foster, *Way-Side Glimpses, North and South* (New York, 1860), p. 109; George H. Clark to Mary E. Clark, 9 May 1847, George Clark Papers, TSA; *Public Proceedings Relating to Calvary Church,* p. 42.

A few societies also insured the wives of members and provided for payment upon their death, perhaps so a housekeeper might be hired and family life not be disrupted. To assure that the sudden death of a member would not permanently lower the family's economic and social status, some of the wealthier associations ran schools for orphan children or apprenticed the children of deceased members to successful free Negro tradesmen. In addition to these financial benefits, the benevolent societies also furnished companionship for the sick and disabled by ordering all members to spend some time with incapacitated members. Those who failed to fulfill these responsibilities could be fined or expelled. In providing companionship for the disabled and giving pensions and annuities to elderly members or their survivors, these primitive insurance organizations helped free Negroes cushion the shock of the periodic epidemics, fluctuations of the economy, and vicious racism which touched every black community.[42]

In addition to insuring their members against disaster, fraternal societies took on a variety of jobs. Since kidnapping was an ever-present danger, most black communities probably had at least one association like Baltimore's Society for Relief in Case of Seizure to guard against manstealers. Many societies were organized along occupational lines and, like white workingmen's associations, tried to secure better wages or a degree of job security in an era when free Negroes were being pushed out of a number of trades. Still other benevolent associations worked to relieve the poor, support schools, send missionaries to Africa, or simply provide a place where friends might meet in good fellowship.[43]

[42] Browning, "Beginnings of Insurance Enterprise Among Negroes," pp. 417–32; *Constitution and By-Laws of the African Benevolent Society of Wilmington* (n.p., n.d.), in DelHR; *Constitution of the Union Burial Ground Society*, 23 January 1848, Broadside, VSL; WPA, Brown Fellowship Society Papers, SCHS; Petition from the Brotherly Association of Charleston, 1856, with "Report of Committee on Colored Population," 2 December 1856, SCLP; Phillips, *American Negro Slavery*, pp. 451–2.

[43] [Tyson], *Life of Elisha Tyson*, pp. 108–10; "Condition of the Coloured Population of the City of Baltimore," *Baltimore Literary and Religious Magazine*, IV (1838), 174–5; Handley Mobley to William McLain, 12 August 1851, ACS; Records of the Poor Saints Fund in Minutes of the First African Baptist Church, Richmond; Dorothy Porter, "The Organized Educational Activities of Negro Literary Societies," *Journal of Negro Education*, V (1936), 555–8, 573–6.

Most benevolent societies, like other insurance agencies, soon accumulated funds in excess of their immediate needs. Many associations agreed to lend money to members and became an important source of capital for black businessmen. Members of the African Benevolent Society of Wilmington could draw on the treasury whenever it held more than two hundred dollars. The Brown Fellowship Society regularly made loans, and adopted rules to provide for delayed repayment by those unable to retire their debts on time. Looking beyond their own membership, some associations sponsored Negro-owned businesses. A Baltimore free Negro reported that several of that city's fraternal organizations desired to invest in the Liberian trade.[44]

Like the African church, the benevolent and fraternal associations were centers of activity and interest in the black community. They too sponsored fairs, parades, concerts, suppers, picnics, and dances. In St. Louis, for example, the annual draymen's parade was a major event for freemen and slaves. Black carters bedecked their wagons with streamers and colorful posters, and the entire black community turned out to view the parade. Indeed, many of the activities of the church and the benevolent societies were so similar that the two organizations often were almost indistinguishable. Although some benevolent societies grew out of churches, others seemed to *function* as churches. The mayor of Richmond once warned the members of the Union Travellers Association against "singing, praying, reading the Bible [and] preaching" without the presence of a white minister. When Richmond police listened in on a meeting of another African benevolent society, they "could distinctly hear the preacher, with his Bible before him, giving a biographical sketch of Moses, from his birth to his death."[45]

Since only a handful of benevolent societies applied for state charters and most met clandestinely, the extent of black membership is difficult to gauge. But numerous fraternal or-

[44] *African Benevolent Society of Wilmington,* p. 3; Browning, "Beginnings of Insurance Enterprise Among Negroes," p. 426; C. C. Harper to R. R. Gurley, 9 April 1829, ACS.

[45] St. Louis *Daily Missouri Democrat,* 29 December 1853; Richmond *Daily Dispatch,* 22 June 1858, 11 April 1860.

ganizations existed in every black community, and many free Negroes belonged to more than one organization. In 1838, Baltimore boasted at least forty black benevolent societies ranging from workingmen's and literary associations to temperance and religious societies. Since many fraternal organizations grew up around the African church, the white ministers who were supposed to supervise them were probably more familiar with the fraternal orders than any other whites. Almost universally, white churchmen affirmed the enormous popularity of these associations. A Charleston clergyman reported that "they exist among those who are members of almost every Church in the City although without the cognizance or recognition of the constituted authorities of the Churches."[46]

Whites feared these secret societies perhaps more than the African churches and schools. The clandestine meetings, uniforms, secret signs, and passwords smacked of subversion. Yet attempts to disband these organizations came to nothing. Proscriptive laws were either modified or fell into disuse in the face of the freemen's persistent violations. Even where benevolent societies, like all meetings of more than half a dozen Negroes, were illegal, these associations flourished. Police continually broke up illicit meetings and uncovered caches of uniforms and the like, but to no avail. "Who has not heard of the 'burial society' among the negroes of Richmond?" exclaimed the *Enquirer* in 1858. "A *secret* and, for aught we know, oath bound mutual society for the interment of negroes with carriages, processions, and uniforms." Prodded by the *Enquirer*, police arrested several "Union Travellers" for meeting illegally. But the press denigrated the mayor's efforts. "There are some ten or twelve of these Societies in Richmond, and most of them meet to transact their business in the basement or private rooms of the African churches," complained another leading journal. The mayor's efforts, it added coldly, will "fall still-born on their ears, and are no more regarded

[46] "Condition of the Coloured Population of the City of Baltimore," pp. 174–5; William Wells Brown, *The Negro in the American Rebellion* (Boston, 1880), p. 189; *Proceedings Relating to Calvary Church*, p. 42; also see Porter, "Organized Activities of Negro Literary Societies," pp. 573–4; William H. Grimshaw, *Official History of Freemasonry Among the Colored People in North America* (Montreal, 1903).

than an idle wind of a March day." This display of skepticism was well merited. Two years later the paper noted "that negroes . . . despite the laws to the contrary, cannot resist the temptation of forming their own societies."[47]

Authorities trying to disband fraternal societies confronted not only the freemen's stiff-necked opposition but the hostility of many whites. Some whites simply could not bring themselves to smash organizations whose primary purpose was to bury the dead and sit up all night with sick friends. A Norfolk minister reported that African benevolent associations met openly in his city, distributed sick dues, and arranged elaborate funerals. "All this, though believed in violation of legislative authority, is sanctioned by the community generally, and encouraged by a portion of it."[48] Once again, black organizations thrived at the confluence of black demands and white acquiescence.

Like the black churches, benevolent and fraternal associations reflected the divisions within the black community, particularly within the free Negro caste. Although some associations mixed free Negroes and slave, many were composed exclusively of freemen. At the other end of the social scale, the wealthiest free Negroes generally stood apart from the benevolent organizations; just as they preferred to attend white churches and have their children educated by private tutors, they had no desire to be buried in the African graveyard or to mingle with the free Negro masses. Besides, these men of independent wealth had no need for the protective services that attracted less affluent freemen. When elite free Negroes did join fraternal associations, it invariably was with men of like standing. In seeking out friends with similar interests and styles of life, even the middle-class tradesmen and artisans organized their associations along class lines. Sometimes innocent groupings by occupation or interest masked inherent class biases. There were, after all, few poor men in the barber's fraternity and fewer uneducated men in the literary society. Thus the benevolent societies often tended to intensify the

[47] *Md. Laws,* 1842, c. 281, 1845, c. 284; *Louisville Daily Courier,* 12 August 1851; *Mobile Daily Advertiser,* 8 August 1860; *Richmond Enquirer,* 1 July 1858; Richmond *Daily Dispatch,* 19 June 1858, quotations in 22 June 1858, 11 April 1860.

[48] *Public Proceedings Relating to Calvary Church,* p. 77.

class, denominational, and sometimes even the color differences within the free Negro caste by giving them an institutional form. When successful Charleston free blacks found themselves barred from the exclusive Brown Fellowship Society, they organized the Humane Brotherhood and limited its membership to "Free Dark Men."[49]

But most benevolent society members were drawn from the same middle-ranking free Negroes who made up the bulk of the membership of the African church. These hard-working wage earners and shopkeepers had accumulated some property and needed protection against sudden disaster. While they were proud of their own status and achievements, they had many ties in the slave community. They mixed with slaves in their churches and in the marketplace. Many had friends and relatives in bondage, and some were former slaves. They saw benevolent societies not only as a source of protection and fraternity, but also as an opportunity to pull the black community together and improve the condition of their people. Richmond free Negroes organized the Union Burial Ground Society because of "a deep interest in the welfare of our race and the importance of advancing our morality." The Sons of Benevolence of New Castle, Delaware, joined together for "suppressing vice and immorality among their coloured brethren," and the Colored Benevolent Society of New Orleans hoped to inculcate "virtue among the class to which they belong."[50] In placing the church and the benevolent society at the center of black life and making them the primary institutions for black improvement, the middling tradesmen and artisans established their leadership within the black community. The names of some of the black fraternal organizations—the Friends of Order, the Perseverance Society, the Society of Economy and Mutual Assistance—suggest that the upward-mobile free Negroes who led these institutions hoped to imbue all blacks with the values of hard work, frugality, and strict morality, values they believed characterized their own success.

[49] Browning, "Beginnings of Insurance Enterprise Among Negroes," pp. 422–8.
[50] *Constitution of the Union Burial Ground Society*, 25 January 1848, Broadside, VSL; Petitions relating to Negroes and Slavery 1830, DelLP; W. H. Rainey, comp., *A. Mygatt & Co.'s New Orleans Business Directory* (New Orleans, 1858), app., p. 88.

The caste unity that these free Negro leaders fostered was reflected in the activities of many of the African churches and benevolent associations. The First African Baptist Church of Richmond donated a hundred dollars to help Fredericksburg freemen build a meetinghouse. Later it contributed smaller sums to free Negroes in Petersburg, Lynchburg, and Staunton for similar purposes. Occasionally African churches helped slaves purchase their freedom. Richmond's First African Church set aside one Sunday's collection to liberate Noah Davis, a Baltimore minister, and later it aided other slave members in purchasing themselves. Some African organizations were even bolder in helping slaves obtain their freedom. It was "known to the mayor and police," declared a Richmond newspaper, "that a negro man, owned by Mr. Grant, received money from one of these societies to take him North." Such charges are of course impossible to substantiate, but it was easy, as Denmark Vesey showed, for blacks planning an escape or plotting a rebellion to camouflage their activities within the bustle of the African church. Much to their chagrin, whites were constantly discovering free Negroes and slaves twisting to their own purposes the liberties that the African churches and benevolent associations provided. Robert Ryland belatedly found that some of the letters he casually distributed to his congregation from members who had migrated north contained detailed plans as to how slave friends might join them. The extent of this activity is impossible to measure, but the name of one Richmond benevolent society—the Union Travellers—suggests other objectives besides securing burial plots.[51]

African churches, schools, and benevolent societies were a reservoir of strength for the free Negro community. The holidays celebrated in these institutions reflected the freemen's powerful desire for racial unity and equality. In 1825, Baltimore free Negroes met at the house of a leading African Methodist minister to celebrate Haitian independence. William Watkins, the orator for the day, praised the rise of the black republic and declared it "an irrefutable argument to prove . . .

[51] Minutes of the First African Church, Richmond, 6 April 1849, 8 December 1850, 3 February 1852, 21 May 1854; Richmond *Daily Dispatch*, 22 June 1858; [Ryland], "Reminiscences of the First African Baptist Church," p. 323.

that the descendants of Africa never were designed by their Creator to sustain an inferiority, or even a mediocrity, in the chain of being; but they are as capable of intellectual improvement as Europeans, or any other nation upon the face of the earth." Later the celebration of Haitian independence spread to other Southern cities. In 1859, St. Louis masons rented a train to take them into the countryside to commemorate the abolition of slavery in Saint-Domingue. Free Negroes in several Southern cities joined their Northern brethren in celebrating the final abolition of slavery in New York. In Virginia, Fredericksburg freemen closed their dinner with an appropriate toast: "May the anchor now cast for freedom by the State of New York sink deeply in the breasts of our Southern States."[52]

[52] *Genius of Universal Emancipation,* IV (August 1825), 167–9; St. Louis *Daily Missouri Democrat,* 10 August 1859; New Orleans *Daily Picayune,* 15 January 1860, quoted in Benjamin Quarles, *Black Abolitionists* (New York, 1969), p. 121.

10

The Mechanics of White Dominance

> If Slavery were abolished . . . the negroes amongst us would be slaves to the social system, instead of slaves to individuals; the restrictions of the law would be more hard than the control of a master.
>
> John L. Carey, *Slavery in Maryland, Briefly Considered* (1845)

SOUTHERN race relations required that Negroes be powerless, submissive, and dependent. This allowed whites to extort slave labor and provided the basis for paternalistic rule. The free Negro's insistent drive for independence and respectability shook the ideological foundations of the slave society. It challenged white racial assumptions and created doubts about the beneficence of slavery. More dangerous still, it demonstrated to slaves that blacks could be free, control their own institutions, and improve their lives without whites. To meet these threats, whites continually pushed free Negroes closer to slavery and tried to keep them dependent on whites by harsh, proscriptive laws.

By the beginning of the nineteenth century, the legal foundation of white control was set. Southern law presumed all Negroes to be slaves, and whites systematically barred free Negroes from any of the rights and symbols they equated with freedom. Whites legally prohibited Negro freemen from moving freely, participating in politics, testifying against whites, keeping guns, or lifting a hand to strike a white person "except in defense against wanton assault." In addition, they burdened free Negroes with special imposts, barred them from certain trades, and often tried and punished them like slaves. To enforce their proscriptive codes and constantly remind free Negroes of their lowly status, almost every state forced free Negroes to register and carry freedom papers, which had to be renewed periodically and might be inspected by any suspicious white.

This system of proscription at first varied from state to state. But as the nineteenth century wore on, Southern legislators reviewed each other's statute books and gradually made their laws uniform. New states generally adopted the legal codes of the older states, thereby adding still greater uniformity to the system. By 1860, despite regional variations in racial ideology, the free Negro's legal status was strikingly similar in every Southern state.

Yet the details of these laws were constantly changing—almost always to the detriment of free Negroes. Although slave codes remained almost unchanged throughout the antebellum years, Southern legislatures constantly added to, modified, or simply reiterated free Negro laws. "Hardly a session of the legislature passes," observed a committee of the Maryland House of Representatives in 1843, "that some law is not enacted restricting them in their rights and privileges."[1]

New legislation gnawed at the freemen's already limited liberty. Various states prohibited free Negroes from assembling without white supervision, prevented them from holding certain jobs and owning slaves, tried them in courts of oyer and terminer, punished their criminal acts with greater severity than those of whites, and enslaved them for petty debts, misdemeanors, and failure to pay taxes or fines. In addition, Southern municipalities nudged free Negroes closer to slavery by subjecting them to slave curfews and by punishing free Negro criminals, like slaves, with the lash. Sometimes state and municipal codes left only trivial distinctions between free Negroes and slaves. In Norfolk, for example, slaves had to be in

[1] "Report of the Committee on Colored Population," *Maryland Legislative Documents,* 1843, doc. M, p. 47.

by nine o'clock in the summer, eight in the winter; free Negroes had a ten o'clock curfew.[2] As whites tried to equate freemen and bondsmen, even these minor distinctions disappeared.

Free Negroes might be pushed theoretically closer to bondage, but in practice they remained slaves without masters. Although Southern law precisely refined the status of a bondsman, slave discipline, for the most part, stayed in the hands of the slaveholder. During the nineteenth century, Southern legislators wrestled with the problem of controlling free Negroes without driving them from the South or into an insurrectionary alliance with slaves. Slowly new laws—the black codes of the tidewater Upper South and the guardianship laws of the Lower South—emerged to provide free Negroes with surrogate masters. The state would stand in the master's stead, and whites would be deputized to oversee these masterless blacks.

In rural areas, finding whites to assume control over free Negroes proved relatively easy. Most free Negroes lived and worked under conditions barely distinguishable from slavery. Their employers were familiar with slavery, and naturally treated them much like slaves. But the needs of urban employers and the problems of controlling urban freemen differed from those of the countryside. In the cities, businessmen demanded a more skilled and flexible work force than their rural counterparts, and, unlike farmers and planters, they generally eschewed the onerous task of disciplining and supervising forced labor. Even the requirement that free Negroes take white guardians did not fully satisfy the special problems of regulating free Negroes in the cities. The confusion of urban life placed Negro freemen outside the purview of the most vigilant guardian most of the time and allowed them a measure of liberty that exceeded the white man's standards of racial decorum.[3]

[2] *The Ordinances of the Borough of Norfolk . . . 1845* (Norfolk, Va., 1845), p. 244; *The Revised Ordinances of the City of Norfolk . . . 1852* (Norfolk, Va., 1852).

[3] Richard Arnold, the mayor of Savannah and legal guardian of many of the city's free Negroes, confessed he paid little attention to their affairs. When one of his wards was arrested for failing to register, he observed: "I knew

Municipal officials tried to meet this problem of reinforcing the basic mechanism of free Negro control. Almost uniformly, city governments enacted registration laws which supplemented and strengthened state regulations. Nashville authorities required all free Negroes who remained in the city more than forty-eight hours to register with the mayor. Free Negroes had to keep their papers on their person at all times and show them to city officials upon demand. In addition to having free Negroes register annually, Montgomery officials ordered them to report every time they "changed their place of sleeping," and in Baton Rouge, Negro freemen without proper papers but "styling themselves free" were deemed fugitives.[4]

Police supervision further strengthened the registration system. City officers periodically ordered police to check the papers of all newly arrived free Negroes. In a typical action, the Petersburg City Council required the master of police to obtain a list of newly registered free Negroes every three months and review their good character. If it was found wanting, free Negroes could be brought before the mayor, declared vagrants, and deported to their former residence. Other cities regularly instructed police to investigate Negro freemen who failed to register or lacked visible means of support. Raleigh required its constable to go over the whole city and suburbs at least two Sundays in every month and search every suspect house and alley to prevent strange free Negroes from moving into town.[5]

Despite the watchful eye of the police, basic problems of free Negro discipline persisted. Whites and blacks lived in close proximity, often with little to distinguish their styles of life. Urban conditions simultaneously eroded much of the phys-

---

nothing of it, as it is quite enough for me to act as general Guardian without attending to such details. Out of the great number for whom I act as Guardian, I have never done it for one but leave it to themselves." Shryock, ed., *Letters of Richard D. Arnold*, p. 72.

[4] *Laws of the Corporation of Nashville* (Nashville, Tenn., 1837), pp. 71, 74; John W. A. Sanford, comp., *The Code of the City of Montgomery* (Montgomery, Ala., 1861), pp. 89–90; *Digest of the Laws and Ordinances of the Police Jury of East Baton Rouge* (Baton Rouge, La., 1821), p. 50.

[5] *Acts of the General Assembly Relative to . . . the Town of Petersburg to which are Added, Bye-Laws and Regulations of the Corporation* (Petersburg, Va., 1824), c. 3; *Laws for the Government of the City of Raleigh . . . 1838* (Raleigh, N.C., 1838), pp. 48, 57.

ical distinction between the way whites and blacks lived and shrank the social distance between the races. Free Negroes constantly confronted whites who were stripped of the trappings of superiority. Whites never were able to dominate free Negroes in the cities as they did in the countryside. To compensate for their loss of mastery, urban whites tried to legislate the master's role by carefully codifying forms of racial deference often unspoken in the countryside. In Richmond, for instance, a free Negro could be whipped for being insolent to a white. The punishment, of course, was not unusual; impudence was a form of rebellion no white could tolerate. Although many slaveholders lashed "uppity" bondsmen as a matter of course, no Southern legislature ever thought it necessary to give that unspoken rule the force of law. Only in the cities, where free Negroes and slaves acting as free Negroes stood outside the direct control of whites, were such laws necessary.[6]

The detail in which city officials codified the forms of racial deference suggests the extent to which the state acted as a surrogate master. Several cities forbade free Negroes to walk on the city square, to smoke in the street, and even to carry a cane—a symbol of white authority that could not be allowed blacks.[7] In many cities, free Negroes who merely acted "in an indecent manner in the view of a white person" could be jailed or whipped. Municipal authorities carefully prescribed the details of the most commonplace instances of social intercourse. "A negro meeting, or overtaking, or being overtaken by a white person on the sidewalk," declared the Richmond code in exquisite detail, "shall pass on the outside; and if necessary to enable such a white person to pass, shall immediately get off the sidewalk."[8]

Even when it was codified and given legal sanction, whites

[6] *The Charter and Ordinances of the City of Richmond . . .* (Richmond, Va., 1859), p. 198; and see *Ordinances and By-Laws . . . of the City of Raleigh, 1803–1854,* p. 66; Kenneth M. Stampp, *The Peculiar Institution* (New York, 1956), pp. 145–6.

[7] *Charter of the City of Raleigh, Revised . . . 1856–1857* (Raleigh, N.C., 1857), c. 9; *Charter and Ordinances of Richmond,* pp. 194–8; Atlanta Ordinances, 25 April 1851, AHS; Sanford, comp., *Code of Montgomery,* pp. 85–6; Phillips, *American Negro Slavery,* p. 497.

[8] Sanford, comp., *Code of Montgomery,* p. 95; *A Collection of the Ordinances of the City Council of Charleston . . . 1818 to . . . 1823* (Charleston, S.C., 1823), pp. 9–10; *Charter and Ordinances of Richmond,* p. 196.

found Negro subordination difficult to maintain in the cities. To restore the ever-shrinking social distance between whites and blacks, whites physically separated themselves from Negroes whenever possible. The obvious inferiority of slaves made it unnecessary—indeed unprofitable—for whites to wall themselves off from slaves. Besides, the slave's lowly status seemed to assure whites of their racial superiority. In this context, the desire to live apart from blacks was never so strong as in the North. Northern visitors marveled at the comparative ease with which whites and blacks mingled in the South. Olmsted observed that "when the negro is definitely a slave it would seem the alleged natural antipathy of the white race to associate with him is lost."[9] But the ambiguity of the free Negroes' status, their growing numbers, wealth, and respectability, shook Southern confidence. No matter what law and custom said, Southern whites found it awkward to equate successful property-owning blacks with slaves. Nowhere was this contradiction more glaring than in the cities of the South. Frustrated by the presence of blacks who were not only free but obviously enjoying their liberty, whites lashed out at the free Negro: "I like a nigger . . . but I hate a damned free nigger."[10]

The free Negro's implicit challenge to white dominance made racial segregation imperative. If the South developed segregation more slowly than the North, it was nevertheless present from the emergence of the free Negro caste. During the Revolution, whites and blacks sometimes fought together, and in the years that followed they established a few mixed churches and schools, but these instances of racial mixing were short-lived. The separation and subordination implicit in slavery soon spread to churches, schools, militia drills, and burial grounds. By the beginning of the nineteenth century, whites had excluded free Negroes from the most important

[9] J. S. Buckingham, *The Eastern and Western States of America,* 3 vols. (London, 1842), III, 7–8; Olmsted, *Journey in the Seaboard Slave States,* p. 18, also pp. 315–16; also see Alexis De Tocqueville, *Democracy in America,* ed. Phillips Bradley, 2 vols. (New York, 1945), II, 360; Abdy, *Journal of a Residence,* II, 352–3; Ferguson, *America by River and Rail,* p. 111. Segregation in the North is discussed in Litwack, *North of Slavery,* pp. 97–9, 103–16, 120–3, 136–51, 168–70, 179–81, 191–211, 279. For the theoretical basis of segregation and a summary of the historiography of the controversy over its development, see Woodward, *American Counterpoint,* pp. 234–60.

[10] James Stirling, *Letters from the Slave States* (London, 1857), pp. 243–4.

Southern institutions, and blacks had begun to build their own separate organizations.

As the number and complexity of Southern institutions grew, segregation matured. Whereas there were few places whites and blacks might get together during the eighteenth century, there were many more possible common meeting grounds by 1860. The intervening years witnessed the establishment of schools, benevolent societies, and reform organizations. Southerners founded insane asylums, poorhouses, reformatories, and penitentiaries to care for the sick, destitute, and criminal, and museums, theaters, libraries, traveling shows, and menageries to educate and entertain the public. Regularly scheduled stage lines, steamboats, packets, and railroads necessitated depots and stations to serve an increasingly mobile society. As these institutions and facilities appeared and grew, whites applied their racial assumptions by systematically excluding Negroes from or segregating Negroes within them. The pattern of racial separation, confined to a few institutions during the early years of the Republic, expanded with the nation.

Many new institutions simply barred free Negroes. Schools and libraries served only whites, as did benevolent societies, reform groups, and workingmen's associations. Poverty doubtless kept the majority of free blacks from attending public entertainment even when available. But many public places formally excluded free Negroes except in a servile capacity. In 1831, the newly established Baltimore Zoological Institute warned that "coloured persons were not admitted unless accompanying families as servants." Similarly, the custodians of the Mississippi Lunatic Asylum refused to accept blacks because they "could not put them in the same apartments with white patients." No matter how lowly, the privileged position of whites had to be maintained. Since the benefits of the poorhouse were "specifically intended for destitute whites," the mayor of Charleston found it "repugnant to my feelings to suffer the introduction of blacks within it."[11]

[11] *Baltimore American,* 1 December 1831; "State Lunatic Asylum, Report of Trustees," *Journal of the Mississippi House of Representatives,* 1858, p. 188; Henry L. Pinckney, *A Report Containing a Review of the Proceedings of the City Authorities from . . . 1837, to . . . 1838* (Charleston, S.C., 1838), p. 40; also see *Report on the Free Colored Poor of the City of Charleston* (Charleston, 1842).

Some places barred blacks from regular participation, but set aside a special time or place for their attendance. A Louisville Mechanics Fair, which excluded Negroes, allowed them to attend one day just before it closed. "As this occasion will be somewhat extraordinary," noted the press, "the band and the Fountain will both play at the same time." The success of this special event induced white showmen to invite Negroes to a "panoramic exhibit of the Russian War . . . given exclusively for their benefit." The profits to be made serving blacks encouraged businessmen to build separate institutions for free Negroes. During the 1830s, a New Orleans railroad opened an exclusive resort for free people of color along the shores of Lake Pontchartrain. The spa attracted wealthy freemen from Natchez as well as New Orleans and proved an enormous success. Eventually, the railroad added segregated cars to carry the free Negroes to and from the resort.[12]

It was awkward and even impossible to bar free Negroes from some places. In 1800, when the Virginia penitentiary was opened, it apparently excluded all blacks. The obvious problem of dealing with Negro convicts forced state officials to ease the restriction, but pressure for exclusion continued. "Although the free white persons usually confined to the penitentiary, are for the most part from the lowest order of society," declared the superintendent in 1823, "yet the free Negroes and mulattoes are a grade or so below them, and should not be associated with them." An abortive attempt to sell free Negro prisoners left the penitentiary integrated and officials sputtering against racial mixing. "The will of God has declared the separation of the negro and the white man, and our laws and feelings approve it," blustered the governor in 1846. "Yet, most remarkably, this fundamental difference is disregarded in our punishment, and blacks and whites are thrown together in all respects upon terms of the most entire equality." Twelve years later, Virginia finally hit upon a profitable solution to this vexing problem and leased black convicts to canal and railroad

[12] *Louisville Daily Courier*, 18 October 1855; *Louisville Daily Democrat*, 12 January 1857; James P. Baughman, "A Southern Spa: Ante-Bellum Lake Pontchartrain," *Louisiana History*, III (1962), 15–16; Matilda C. F. Houstoun, *Texas and the Gulf of Mexico*, 2 vols. (London, 1844), II, 20; Hogan and Davis, eds., *William Johnson's Natchez*, p. 441.

companies by the year. Although Virginia, like other states, had long hired out freemen for fines and taxes, the convict-lease system was a striking innovation. Governor Henry Wise, quick to see a good thing, suggested that it might be applied to whites as well.[13]

Most institutions avoided the problems of the Virginia penitentiary by physically separating blacks within the institution. North Carolina legislators took this tack when they ruled that free Negroes might be admitted to a proposed state penitentiary, but "in no case shall be kept in the same apartment with white persons."[14] Cost and convenience made this kind of segregation—rather than outright exclusion—the most prominent form of racial separation, and it grew throughout the antebellum years.

Institutional growth spurred the physical separation of blacks and whites. Although legislators resisted the expense of duplicating existing facilities, new institutions generally incorporated the principles of racial segregation. In 1830, for example, a visiting physician found the almshouse in Anne Arundel County in southern Maryland bursting with inmates. Fifty whites and blacks lived packed into eight or nine rooms. "In order to remedy this inconvenience, as well as for the promotion of health," he declared, "it is indispensably necessary that a house should be erected for the accommodation of the Blacks—a log house with earthen floor will answer every purpose." The same sequence of growth, expansion, and segregation took place in every major Southern city. In 1859, the mayor of Nashville

[13] Palmer, ed., *Virginia State Papers,* IX, 135; "Report of the Committee to Examine the State Penitentiary," *Journal of the House of Delegates of Virginia,* 1822, app., p. 18, 1846–1847, pp. 3–4; *Va. Laws,* 1857–1858, c. 29; "Message III on Miscellaneous Subjects," *Journal of the House of Delegates of Virginia,* 1857–1858, app., p. cil. For the operation of the convict-lease system see, for example, "Annual Report of the Penitentiary Institute," *Virginia Legislative Documents,* 1859–1860, doc. XIII, pp. 5, 8; the expansion of the system to whites is discussed in the "Governor's Message," *ibid.,* doc. I, p. 44, and in *Va. Laws,* 1859–1860, c. 54. The development of the convict-lease system in Louisiana is traced in Mark T. Carleton, *Politics and Punishment: The History of the Louisiana State Penal System* (Baton Rouge, 1971), pp. 7–13.

[14] "Report of the Committee . . . to Improve County Prisons and Establish a House of Correction," *North Carolina Legislative Documents,* 1850–1851, doc. CIX, p. 720.

proudly reported that he had finally remedied the disgraceful condition of the city workhouse. "[The] prisoners of the city, amounting sometimes to forty or fifty, were crowded, without respect to sex or color, in two small rooms, [which were] badly ventilated." Now a new building that would separate sexes and races was nearing completion.[15]

Like the mayor of Nashville, reformers interested in ameliorating the condition of inmates commonly recommended racial segregation along with the separation of men from women, children from adults, and new from hardened offenders. In 1838, the reform-minded trustees of the Baltimore jail vowed to push ahead with their plan for racial separation despite the shortage of funds. The following year they boasted that "the three vacant cells in the north end of the jail will be made comfortable for keeping black prisoners, and separating them from whites, which is believed to have a beneficial influence upon their moral character."[16]

Segregation sometimes did improve the condition of white inmates, but generally at the expense of blacks. Whites were usually lodged in new houses while blacks languished in their old quarters. (Just as in the creation of African churches, blacks purchased secondhand white meetinghouses while white congregations moved on to new buildings.) Thus the process of physical separation usually left blacks worse off than before, for once they were isolated in separate prisons or asylums, white officials rarely bothered to improve their conditions.[17] Likewise, free Negro theatergoers were forced into the most distant corners and black travelers ordered to the lowest deck of steamboats and the baggage cars of railroads. Occasionally blacks boldly rejected these inferior conditions and took the places reserved for whites. More frequently, wealthy freemen bought their way out of such inferior quarters, but most free Negroes had neither the nerve nor the money to resist segre-

[15] Minute Book of the Anne Arundel County Alms House, 10 July 1830, MdHS; *Communication of His Honor the Mayor, Randall W. MacGavock, Transmitted to the City Council of Nashville, Tenn. . . . September 30th, 1859* (Nashville, 1859), p. 11.

[16] "Report of the Visitors of the Jail," *Ordinances of the Mayor and City Council of Baltimore,* 1838, app., p. 494, 1839, app., p. 24.

[17] *New Orleans Commercial Bulletin,* 17 March 1842.

gation. They stoically accepted it and, when they could, turned it to their advantage by creating all-black institutions.[18]

By the eve of the Civil War, segregation had extended to almost every corner of Southern life. Free Negroes, no matter how wealthy, were separated from whites in hospitals, theaters, parks, railroad cars, and omnibuses. One Southern municipality even legislated whites and blacks into separate brothels.[19] Most of these institutions were in the cities, where social mixing was extensive, but segregation was not solely an urban phenomenon. Whites thought it just as important in an isolated rural poorhouse as in a city jail—indeed, anywhere they felt the need to substitute physical space for social distance as a means of maintaining their racial hegemony. In some places where racial roles had become particularly confused, whites embellished physical separation with other distinctions to make sure that the differences between the races would not be lost. The New Orleans City Council not only separated black and white

[18] New Orleans *Louisiana Courier,* 30 July 1833; Hogan and Davis, eds., *William Johnson's Natchez,* p. 391; Benwell, *Englishman's Travels in America,* p. 173.

[19] Nearly all "correctional" institutions such as poorhouses, workhouses, penitentiaries, and mental hospitals either excluded blacks or segregated them. For hospitals and asylums: *Savannah Republican,* 18 April 1823, 6 May 1823; *Richmond Enquirer,* 30 December 1854; *Charleston Courier,* 11 September 1856; "Negro Hospital," *Charleston Journal and Review,* XII (1857), 134; Norman Dain, *Disordered Minds; The First Century of the Eastern State Hospital in Williamsburg* (Charlottesville, Va., 1971), pp. 19, 99, 105, 108–13. For theaters: New Orleans Resolutions and Ordinances, 8 June 1816, 30 December 1820, Minutes of the New Orleans City Council, 1820, *passim,* typescript, NOPL; New Orleans *Louisiana Courier,* 29 November 1820; New Orleans *Louisiana Advertiser,* 27 January 1826; New Orleans *Daily Picayune,* 4 November 1856; Schultz, *Travels on an Inland Voyage,* II, 196. For public parks and promenades: *Ordinances of the City of Charleston from . . . 1837, to . . . 1840* (Charleston, 1840), pp. 94–8; Savannah Ordinances, 2 August 1827, 11 October 1827, SCH. For railroads: New Orleans *Louisiana Courier,* 30 July 1833; Buckingham, *Slave States of America,* I, 479–80; Houstoun, *Texas and the Gulf of Mexico,* II, 20; *Charleston Courier,* 25 June 1848. For omnibuses: *Charleston Courier,* 12, 16 August 1853; *New Orleans Crescent,* 24 September 1861. For brothels: Henry J. Leovy, comp., *The Laws and General Ordinances of the City of New Orleans* (New Orleans, 1857), p. 358.

Nevertheless, the development of Southern segregation lagged behind that of the North. Even after the Civil War, Northern travelers continued to remark on the comparatively greater racial intermingling in the South. Still, by 1860 whites had set the basic patterns of racial separation; C. Vann Woodward, *The Strange Career of Jim Crow,* 2nd ed. (New York, 1966), especially chap. 2.

convicts, but also ordered blacks "to wear different clothes than do the whites." Likewise, Charleston churchmen pleading to establish an African church assured the city fathers they would provide a separate section for white visitors with "benches painted a different color from the others . . . and a wide space between them and the seats for the blacks." In the final analysis, that wide space was a physical embodiment of white racial attitudes. A Louisiana legislator admitted that "he might sit down and take refreshments at a free colored man's table, but never yet did he shake hands with one of them, because he thought there was social contagion in the touch."[20]

Racial segregation had its dangers. Depriving free Negroes of liberties and treating them like slaves united them with bondsmen and created explosive possibilities. Whites, who viewed free Negroes as incorrigible subversives, needed no lessons in the perils of such a combination. While segregating Negroes, Southern legislators issued a variety of prohibitions to keep Negro freemen and bondsmen from associating with each other. Some states barred free Negroes from gambling, trading, or meeting with slaves and from marrying them. The cities, where free Negroes and slaves lived in constant contact, naturally expanded these laws and made them more explicit. Various cities barred free Negroes from entertaining slaves in their homes and whipped both free and slave violators. "The whole purpose of the police laws," noted one Richmond newspaper, "is to prevent the association of free negroes and slaves."[21]

Laws alone could not control the free Negroes. They resisted the restrictive codes and violated them with impunity, so that whites frequently found it impossible to enforce their own regulations. Even the registration system, the key to controlling free Negroes, fell before the freemen's determined opposition. Many simply never bothered to register, and despite the obvious dangers probably few carried freedom papers. In

[20] Resolutions and Ordinances of the New Orleans City Council, 29 October 1827, typescript, NOPL; *Charleston Mercury*, 21 July 1849; *Journal of the Louisiana Senate*, 1857, pp. 7–8.

[21] Richmond *Daily Dispatch*, 9 May 1860.

1851, a colonization agent touring the Virginia countryside found that potential emigrants usually lacked proof of their freedom. "I have written evidence that Phillis Griggs is free," he wrote to the home office, "but I have difficulty to show that her children and grandchildren, 14 in number, belong to her. They never were registered." Surprised at this state of affairs, he investigated the local records. "A census of the county has been taken & of 300 hundred colored, only 51 are registered, the rest by the laws of the state have no rights"; over 80 percent of the county's free Negroes remained unregistered. Such flagrant violations were common. Extant registers of free Negroes show that only a fraction of the caste ever applied for certificates of freedom. In Amelia County, Virginia, for example, a consecutively numbered register of free Negroes kept between 1800 and 1865 listed about 150 freemen. In 1860, however, almost 200 resided in the county and many more had been born, had been manumitted, and had migrated into and out of the area during those years.[22]

In spite of more intensive surveillance, the registration system worked no better in the cities. Following the 1850 census and six years after Missouri adopted a comprehensive registration code, St. Louis officials discovered that less than half the city's free Negroes had applied for papers. Richmond authorities found themselves in the same bind: free Negroes migrated to the city and rarely bothered to establish their right of residence. When the mayor ordered a crackdown, the press hinted at the extent of the difficulty. "If this order is properly obeyed," declared a leading daily, "we have no doubts the police will have their hands full for months to come, for there are hundreds of such characters infesting our city."[23]

Free Negroes instinctively avoided white officials. Many had remained in the state illegally after manumission, worked at a prohibited trade, or failed to take a guardian, or perhaps were fugitives. But even those who had done nothing wrong might

[22] R. W. Bailey to William McLain, 21 June 1850, 28 November 1851, ACS; Amelia County Register of Free Negroes, VSL. In Savannah, less than 200 free Negroes registered in 1855, although there were about 700 living in the city; *Savannah Republican,* 13 August 1855.

[23] St. Louis *Missouri Republican,* 20 January 1851; Richmond *Daily Dispatch,* 25 November 1853.

well avoid a sheriff who could jail or enslave them for any one of a dozen piddling reasons. Free Negroes often found it best to do without papers or to use forged registries rather than chance a trip to the local courthouse. Forgeries were easy to come by. Many, of course, were crude copies and easily detected, but some were the work of a practiced hand. Wrinkled and smeared with grease and dirt, they were difficult to distinguish from the real thing. Richmond police picked up one free Negro and found his "torn register as obscure and undefinable, as the cabbage folios to which Sybil [*sic*] committed her prophecies." When they brought him to the courthouse to be reregistered, no record of his freedom could be found.[24]

When the police tried to enforce the law, some free Negroes reluctantly complied, but most disguised themselves or disappeared until the furor had passed. Elusive free Negroes proved so difficult to identify that Petersburg officials ordered the city guard to ascertain if municipal records listed free Negroes by the wrong name, by an alias, or "by any name." When pressure became too great, free Negroes simply slipped out of town. Police arrested one Richmond free Negro several times for remaining illegally in the city. Upon investigation, they discovered she was a long-time resident who had avoided discovery by periodically moving to Petersburg. Some free Negroes even passed themselves off as slaves to avoid detection.[25]

Whites complained bitterly about the ease with which free Negroes violated the law, and demanded that the police take stern action. "Our police regulations should either be rigorously executed or repealed," grumbled an angry Nashville citizen. Echoing these sentiments, a Virginia daily warned that "until the laws were uniformly enforced there was little hope of preventing negroes from all sections of the State from making their abodes in Richmond."[26] Actually, the police did what they could. In 1851, for example, Richmond city clerks issued over 750 registers and the police jailed or hired out fifty-nine

[24] *Richmond Whig*, 19 August 1853; Petition from Charleston, 1830, SCLP.

[25] *The Charter and Laws of the City of Petersburg* (Petersburg, 1852), c. 25; *Richmond Whig*, 11 November 1853; Richmond *Daily Dispatch*, 29 September 1854.

[26] *Nashville Republican Banner*, 21 December 1856; Richmond *Daily Dispatch*, 2 December 1858.

Negroes who lacked proper papers.[27] But the most sustained efforts never seemed to be enough. Even when local officers kept up the pressure, some free Negroes blithely continued to ignore the laws. In 1853, St. Louis authorities attempted to chase alien free Negroes out of the city and to force native free Negroes to register. Police raided well-known free Negro haunts, whipped unregistered freemen, and shipped them beyond the city limits. In this instance, police enthusiasm did not wane after the initial crackdown. The raids continued for almost a year, although they ended in failure. "There is hardly a day that passes in this court," noted one police reporter late in 1854, "but one or two negroes are called for examination and we cannot see why such persons continue in visiting our city and walking our streets, when the municipal law is imperative that they cannot be allowed within our midst. . . ."[28]

Inability, rather than a lack of desire, accounted for much of the failure to enforce the free Negro codes. Poor organization condemned rural slave patrols to a constant state of disrepair, and urban police forces, although regularly organized, were too small for their task. In 1859, five day officers and forty night watchmen protected Richmond, a city of over 38,000. Only two constables guarded Petersburg, although blacks composed better than half its population and police had other responsibilities besides watching free Negroes. Larger cities had many more police and they were better organized, but complaints about lack of protection were loud and frequent in some of the biggest Southern municipalities. "Think of the perfect absurdity of giving the peace of seventy-five thousand people into the charge of eight men," grumbled the leading Louisville daily, "or the more apparent folly of entrusting our lives to the watchful care of sixteen persons, who, no matter how faithful, cannot half discharge their duties."[29]

[27] Richard B. Morris, "The Measure of Bondage in the Slave States," *Mississippi Valley Historical Review*, XLI (1955), 238.

[28] St. Louis *Daily Missouri Democrat*, 24 December 1853, 19 October 1854; also see 18 February 1858.

[29] Howell M. Henry, *Police Control of the Slave in South Carolina* (Emory, Va., 1914); Richmond *Daily Dispatch*, 25 September 1852; *Petersburg Daily Democrat*, 9 July 1857; *Louisville Daily Courier*, 19 January 1855, also 9 April 1853; *Nashville Republican Banner*, 12 January 1855; *Memphis Daily Appeal*, 20 January 1858; *Report of James P. Screven*, p. 11; New Orleans *Daily*

Poorly paid, ill-trained officers had little incentive to keep free Negroes in line. Pay was so low for the Charleston city guard that one citizen doubted that even the most aroused officials could prevent them from "passing their watch in a comfortable sleep or before the cheering fire of a dram shop." Most of the Savannah night watch worked during the day and patrolled the city after dark to earn some extra cash. When they took their posts each evening, the mayor admitted they were "pretty well exhausted by their day's work." The lack of training or equipment further lowered police morale.[30] Naturally, saloon keepers, who often depended on the free Negro trade, found policemen easy prey for graft, and quick-witted freemen had little trouble outsmarting unqualified officers. In Petersburg, the city fathers belatedly discovered that most of their night watch was illiterate. Free Negroes confidently flashed passes which were "nothing more nor less than a small bill of sale belonging to one of our leading houses. The watchmen pretended to read it and allowed the negro to pass, being satisfied it was a *pass*."[31]

The inability of officials to enforce the registry codes paralleled difficulties in deporting newly manumitted blacks, proscribing free Negroes from certain trades, closing their churches, schools, and benevolent societies, and preventing their free movement around the South. Despite their numerous efforts, whites continually found the entire web of free Negro laws in disarray.

Yet the law, although largely unenforced, prescribed the boundaries of free Negro behavior. Free Negroes usurped considerably more liberty than the law allowed—perhaps just enough to prevent an explosive rebellion; whites nevertheless severely limited their freedom. Imperfect, almost random enforcement allowed free Negroes many liberties the law denied, but only at the expense of their security. A free Negro never knew when the law might be enforced. At any time, in any

---

Picayune, 26 December 1856; Messages of the Mayor of New Orleans, 1858, pp. 11–12, typescript, NOPL.

30 Charleston *City Gazette*, 10 November 1822; *Report of R. D. Arnold, Mayor of the City of Savannah, for the Year Ending September 30th, 1860* (Savannah, Ga., 1860), p. 8; *Louisville Daily Courier*, 1 September 1855.

31 *Petersburg Daily Democrat*, 9 July 1857.

place, any white might challenge his liberty. A routine check of freedom papers could reveal that a free Negro had been improperly manumitted, remained illegally in the state, or worked at an illicit trade. A gathering of friends to celebrate a wedding, to plan an outing, or simply to discuss old times might be broken up by the police, the participants arrested and dragged to the whipping post. Any minor infraction could lead to imprisonment or worse. The irregular enforcement of the law failed to stop offenders, but it constantly reminded free Negroes of the fragility of their liberty.

Whites played on the free Negro's insecurity by vigorously enforcing the free Negro codes upon occasion. Almost anything, no matter how trivial or distant, could trigger a sudden crackdown. In 1841, news that several Negroes had brutally murdered a white family in St. Louis incited what William Johnson called the "Inquisition" in Natchez. Incensed by the murders some six hundred miles up the Mississippi, Natchez whites slapped out at blacks. Public meetings fired off lengthy petitions to the legislature demanding that black rivermen not be allowed to land in the state. White workingmen, turning the hysteria to their own advantage, railed at the growing number of slaves permitted to hire their own time—"free slaves"—and urged new restraints on this practice. But eventually outraged whites settled on the free Negro, whom they equated with "the rogue, the incendiary, and the abolitionist." In the leading Natchez newspaper, "Civis" complained of the growing number of illegal manumissions and free Negro migrants who remained in the city without official permission. Soon after, a vigilance committee was formed "to rid the country of free Negro and 'free slave' population," and the board of police convened a special meeting for "recalling free negro licences." For over a month, free Negroes were ordered before the police board to prove they had the right to remain in the city. "All Sort of Tryals going on," Johnson glumly noted in mid-August. "The different Offices has been full all day and they Continue to arrest Still." At first, Natchez authorities limited themselves to deporting poorer free Negroes with few connections with whites, but soon some of Johnson's friends were called to account. By September, even the wealthy barber began to feel the heat. "Oh what a country we

Live in," he complained in the privacy of his diary. But just when Johnson expected the worst, white enthusiasm for the "Inquisition" suddenly waned. Johnson surmised that more vital political concerns, especially the resurgent debate over national banking policy, blunted interest in the free Negro. Whatever the reason, Natchez free Negroes gladly accepted the respite. However, the reverberations of the "Inquisition" continued to ring in Mississippi. The following year the legislature slapped new limits on manumission and free Negro liberty. The free Negro population of Natchez declined sharply thereafter and never recovered from the "Harrows of the Inquisition."[32]

Such terror gripped every free Negro community at one time or another. Crackdowns on free Negroes almost always followed in the wake of slave insurrections or insurrection scares, but often whites seemed to apply long-neglected laws merely as a way of redressing years of lax enforcement. Occasionally, a new mayor or constable used rigid enforcement to build his reputation. Yet whites found spasmodic crackdowns had their drawbacks. They disrupted business by driving off the most skilled and successful free Negroes while leaving those whom whites most feared. In 1850, when Mobile officials activated the twenty-year-old stricture against free Negro immigration, many of those free Negroes left the city. "Our churches are curiously affected, especially the Methodist and Baptist," noted one concerned citizen. "Their best, leading colored men have left—are leaving and must leave."[33] Fear of losing these "best men" sobered some whites and acted as a brake on white hysteria, but the periodic crackdowns continued and seemed to grow more frequent as the Civil War drew closer.

Free Negroes dreaded the chance confrontation with police and the periodic enforcement of some law that might sweep them from their homes into prison or servitude. Their anxie-

[32] *Trials and Confessions of Madison Henderson, Alias Blanchard, Alfred Amos Warrick and Others, Murderers of Jesse Baker and Jacob Weaver* (St. Louis, Mo., 1841); Natchez *Mississippi Free Trader,* 13, 20 May 1841, 7, 10, 12, 14 August 1841; *Natchez Courier,* 4, 28 August 1841; New Orleans *Daily Picayune,* 22 August 1841; Hogan and Davis, eds., *William Johnson's Natchez,* pp. 338–50; *Miss. Laws,* 1842, c. 4.

[33] Robert Nall to William McLain, 24 June 1850, ACS; also Orlando Brown to son, 23 September 1856, Orlando Brown Papers, FC.

ties were compounded by the harsh punishments they were bound to receive. In slavery, the lash stood as the ultimate symbol of white authority, and whites reserved it for free Negroes as well. In fact, as legislation and public pressure reduced punishments of white criminals during the nineteenth century, the whipping post became the Negro's exclusive preserve. By the 1850's, it was so rare for whites to be whipped that a Kentucky jury awarded six hundred dollars to a white thief who had been so punished. A Richmond newspaper agreed that "no man should use a cowhide on a white man. It is a cutting insult never forgiven by the cowhided party, because a white man's nature revolts at such degrading punishment."[34]

A punishment too degrading for whites was perfect for blacks. Southern officials routinely whipped free Negro offenders. "There was nothing of moment before 'His Honor' yesterday," casually noted a Richmond court reporter. "An average amount of niggerdom was ordered to be thrashed . . . for violations of the police regulations and city ordinances of so slight a character that it is hardly worthwhile publishing them in a newspaper." More than a punishment, the lash was a reminder to blacks and a reassurance to whites that freedom did not fundamentally alter the Negro's status. White officials used the lash to punish not only Negro criminals but "uppity" free Negroes as well. The mayor of Mobile awarded a free Negro boy ten lashes "for being impudent to a white man," and a New Orleans free Negro who struck a police officer was given "twenty-five lashes to teach him the difference between white and brown."[35]

Many condemned free Negroes considered themselves lucky to escape with only a whipping. Throughout the South, white officials sold free Negroes into terms of servitude for unpaid fines and jail fees, and in Maryland and Delaware free Negro criminals could be auctioned into long terms of virtual slavery. Typical of other courts in the two border states, the Baltimore Circuit Court sold free Negroes into servitude for up to five

[34] *Louisville Daily Courier*, 3 May 1855; *Richmond Enquirer*, 5 August 1858.

[35] *Richmond Enquirer*, 18 April 1860; *Mobile Daily Advertiser*, 18 July 1857; New Orleans *Daily Picayune*, 3 November 1860.

years for stealing shoes, a dress, a buggy harness, and a coffee pot. "The convicted negroes," observed one Maryland slaveholder, "commanded a more ready sale in Baltimore than any other commodity which could be placed on the market."[36]

Once arrested, free Negroes rarely escaped such terrifying punishments. Few could afford lawyers, and even when they could, their attorneys had little incentive to protect them. In 1837, a young Baltimore lawyer created a stir in the city courthouse by defending a free Negro with "exuberance of thought and feeling." "If, however, the accused had not been a poor, degraded negro," noted one observer, "but . . . some hitherto respectable and responsible white man, this defect would probably have not been noticed; but on the contrary, it would have been considered a decided merit." Even with the aid of the most enthusiastic attorney, free Negroes rarely received justice at the hands of all-white judicial systems. Blacks could expect stiffer punishments than whites for the most trivial crimes. Most free Negroes dared not protest this harsh justice for fear of further antagonizing whites, but after being sentenced to death one New Orleans free Negro blurted out what many felt, and boldly declared "he was going to be hung because he was a negro." A Baltimore attorney agreed and observed that local juries were "inclined to convict a man merely because he was black, as an English judge . . . condemned every Irishman, merely because he was of that nation."[37]

Brutal punishment, hard justice, and periodic crackdowns more than compensated for the inability of Southern officials to enforce the free Negro codes rigorously. The fear of imprisonment, the lash, or enslavement intimidated some free Negroes and probably limited the illegal activities of most. Even the boldest had to consider the grim consequences that might befall them if caught. Although this still failed to stop many free Negroes from violating the law, it limited the rebelliousness of most to that which increased their comfort but did not disturb white dominance. Thus much of the free

[36] For example, Baltimore *Sun*, 30 June 1837, 14 May 1839, 12, 18, 19 February 1842, 19, 28 May 1859, quotation in 18 January 1842.

[37] *New Orleans Crescent*, 22 January 1861; Baltimore *Sun*, 22 October 1839.

Negro code was unenforced because whites did not consider it vital to assure their rule. Free Negroes could work at proscribed trades, organize churches and schools, or travel without proper papers because some whites viewed these activities as harmless and some profited from them. Perhaps a few whites understood that many of the harsh free Negro laws—passed in the heat of the moment—did not need total enforcement to serve their purpose. Brutal (and expensive) repression, moreover, would be necessary to assure complete compliance with racial codes, and such measures would disrupt Southern society and might drive desperate free Negroes to violent revolt. Yet when free Negroes violated laws whites considered necessary to their security or seemed to threaten white dominance, Southern officials took prompt action and savagely punished offenders. Violent retribution emanated not only from the legal authorities but from white vigilantes who visited extralegal punishments on blacks who forgot "their place."

The master's concern for his valuable property generally protected slaves from white vigilantes, but they frequently terrorized free Negroes. In a typical action, a group of Virginia whites banded together in 1821 "for the purpose of chastising a set of free negroes in the county who were of bad fame and who had associated with them a white woman of foul character." Admittedly the freemen had not "publicly acted to make themselves punishable by law, yet their mischievous conduct and example in the neighbourhood" might produce serious evils. Although whites were most sensitive to violations of the sexual code, any threat to white control—real or imagined—might set vigilante terrorists in motion. The growth of the free Negro caste in one Tennessee community unleashed a wave of white terror. Although the free Negroes were as "well behaved as slaves," noted a local colonizationist, "their increase are [*sic*] producing uneasiness in the minds of some. This feeling is breaking out in whipping free negroes."[38]

Vicious intimidation demoralized many free Negroes. Freemen never knew when vigilante whites might strike or what might induce them to act. Partisans of the South Carolina Association of Charleston argued that their mere presence

[38] Petition from Amelia County, 11 December 1821, VLP; H. McMillan to William McLain, 3, 10 October 1856, ACS.

tended to have a beneficial effect on the habits and deportment of the people of color. Whites used vigilante tactics to keep free Negroes in a constant state of fear and destroy their will to challenge the oppressive racial codes. "Who does not know," casually declared one Virginian, "that when a free negro . . . has rendered himself obnoxious to a neighborhood, how easy it is for a party to visit him one night, take him from his bed and family, and apply to him the gentle admonition of a severe flagellation, to induce him to *consent* to go away? In a few nights the dose can be repeated, perhaps increased, until . . . the fellow becomes perfectly willing to go away."[39]

Most vigilante action was spontaneous and unorganized, but in some communities established bands of regulators stood ready to enforce free Negro subordination. Soon after the discovery of the Vesey conspiracy, some of the leading citizens of Charleston organized the South Carolina Association to end "the daily violation or evasion of the laws made to regulate the conduct of our colored population." The association arrested black seamen who dared leave their ships, hunted fugitives in the city, and enforced other rules of Negro deportment. Similar groups could be found throughout the South, although the pedigrees of their members were not as fine as those of the South Carolina Association.[40] When Lunsford Lane, a former slave, returned to Raleigh in 1845 to purchase his family, the police arrested him for entering the state illegally. Once Lane was in court, it quickly became clear that the charge was not immigration but his alleged abolitionist activities. Although a court acquitted Lane, a mob tarred and feathered him, and probably only his friendship with the governor saved his life. Following its success, the mob organized itself more tightly. "They call themselves the *Raleigh Regulators*," noted a visitor to the city, "and have issued handbills threatening those opposed to their lawless course with the fate of Lunsford Lane." About ten years later, white vigilantes established the "Rockette Regulators" on the outskirts of

[39] *Charleston Mercury*, 29 July 1823; *Richmond Enquirer*, 14 February 1832, also quoted in Jackson, *Free Negro Labor and Property Holding*, p. 23.

[40] *Charleston Courier*, 24 July 1823; also see *Charleston Mercury*, 29 July 1823, 25 August 1823, 9 September 1823, 8, 10 October 1823, 5 November 1823; *The Memorial of the Officers and Members of the South Carolina Association*, 1830, SCLP; *Charleston Courier*, 15 December 1859.

Richmond to get rid of "disgraceful characters by summary punishment." They began their reign of terror by visiting "a den in which a negro woman and a white man lived in the most intimate terms" and dragging the offending couple to the river to be "dunked and painted." The Regulators then proceeded to another "notorious shanty occupied by a white woman and a negro man, and after leading them to the river, [they] gave them the benefit of numberless plunges and let them loose, promising to repeat their visit if their association were continued."[41]

Extralegal terror was an integral part of the system of disciplining free Negroes. Southern leaders sometimes encouraged vigilante action against free Negroes when officials seemed unable or unwilling to enforce the code. With the failure of Richmond officials to close one notorious Negro cookshop, the editor of the *Daily Dispatch* implied that more direct action might be necessary. He suggested that "no one need be surprised, if the citizens themselves should take the matter into their own hands, and break up the vile nest in which had been hatched vice and villainy of almost every hue." Indeed, Southerners incorporated the right of whites to discipline any "uppity" Negro into their code of chivalry. After a Memphis mob lynched a fugitive slave who had killed a city official in attempting to escape, the city's largest newspaper admitted the act had been distasteful, but that those "who could have been here yesterday, and not felt as *all* here felt would have been *more* or *less* than a MAN." Extralegal punishments found sanction in the courts as well as the press. Southern judges generally upheld the right of any white to deliver summary punishment on an errant free Negro. If a free Negro was impudent, ruled the North Carolina Supreme Court, "a white man, to whom the insolence has been given, has a right to stop it in any extra judicial way."[42]

Free Negroes sought to protect themselves against legal and extralegal violence by building friendships with powerful

[41] Diary of Sidney Bumpas, 29 April 1845, Bumpas Family Papers, SHC; William G. Hawkins, *Lunsford Lane, or Another Helper from North Carolina* (Boston, 1863), pp. 147–55; Richmond *Daily Dispatch*, 28 June 1858.

[42] Richmond *Daily Dispatch*, 16 February 1858; *Memphis Eagle* quoted in *Louisville Daily Democrat*, 14 January 1851; Catterall, ed., *Judicial Cases Concerning Slavery*, II, 151, 350.

whites. White employers and customers might be depended upon to attest to their good character during a periodic crackdown or the rampaging of white regulators. Such friendships were crucial to most free Negroes, because few escaped without some challenge to their liberty. When the crisis came, the good offices of the leading whites provided the best protection. Free Negroes scurried around collecting certificates attesting to their good character from the most unimpeachable sources, hopeful that such "proof" would be enough to satisfy the local sheriff or vigilantes.[43]

Freemen sometimes formalized these arrangements and induced a white person to serve as their protector. Although the basis of this kind of agreement was usually unspoken, its general outline was well known. Free Negroes gave the correct degree of deference to leading white planters or businessmen whose sense of *noblesse oblige* or personal interests induced them to protect "their" Negroes. James Boon, a free Negro artisan who traveled throughout North Carolina seeking work, was always careful to secure a protector whenever he arrived in a new town. While working in Raleigh, Boon carried a pass from a leading white businessman declaring that "[James Boon is] under my protection and wishes to pass about where his business may call him at any time unmolested and rec'd fair treatment as a honable free man of culer." Without such a pass, a free Negro in a strange city was in a dangerous position. Boon's brother anxiously wrote from Wilmington that his protector refused to supervise the other free Negroes in his employ. "Please see Duke Harrison," he implored, "and get him to write to Mr. Jeffery and get him to be their protector as my Protecto[r] as he dont wanrts to be bothered with them. I offered to pay him money but he wonts act."[44]

[43] Hogan and Davis, eds., *William Johnson's Natchez,* p. 343; also see Madden Family Papers, UVa, and petitions from free Negroes asking relief from specific laws or the sudden enforcement of the law in VLP, NCLP, TLP, SCLP, and MLP.

[44] A pass from A. Kerning, 7 May 1848, Carter Evans to James Boon, 20 January 1848, James Boon Papers, NCA; John Hope Franklin, "James Boon, Free Negro Artisan," *JNH,* XXX (1945), 150–80; Franklin, *Free Negro in North Carolina,* pp. 153–4. One former free Negro, writing from the perspective of the twentieth century, remembered that "every white man in the South, in olden times, had his particular Negro, and every Negro had his particular white man. I remember Mayor Polk Brown [of Nashville], who

Many free Negroes, especially the elite, depended on white protectors to reduce the risks of living in a slave society and to improve their chances for material prosperity. They strengthened their relationships with whites by patronizing white merchants and tradesmen—and thereby retarding the development of Negro-owned businesses—by keeping whites informed of the activities of more rebellious blacks, and by deferring to whites on all occasions. In doing so, they satisfied the paternalist pretensions of upper-class whites. These whites gladly served as protectors and patrons because they understood it assured their dominance. Their ability to vouch for the good character of a free Negro, like their presence at a slave wedding or a gift to the hands at Christmas, symbolized the free Negro's continued dependence. By encouraging freemen to believe that the relations between whites and blacks were more important in assuring security and prosperity than the relations among blacks, whites stifled the development of the free Negroes' group consciousness.[45] Not all freemen could or did participate in the protector system, but by favoring their wards with privileges not generally accorded free Negroes, whites lured many of the most talented and ambitious into this relationship. In seeking security from whites, free Negroes implicitly renounced their objections to the Southern caste system.

Yet the legal and extralegal pressures that drove Negro freemen to take a protector merely reflected the workings of the Southern economy and social system, which forced free Negroes to depend on white employers for their jobs, on white customers to support their businesses, and on white ministers to supervise their churches. In this sense, the free Negro laws codified the demands that free Negroes be dependent on whites. The web of constraint which kept free Negroes in "their place" was woven into the fabric of Southern society.

---

was a great friend to my father in the ante-bellum days. Although we were free Negroes, it was hard to get permission for my mother to take me and my older brother to Ohio to school. Mayor Polk Brown interceded for us"; J. Merton England, "The Free Negro in Ante-Bellum Tennessee," *Journal of Southern History,* IX (1943), 58.

[45] Wolf, "Specific Aspects of Plantation Systems in the New World," pp. 168–9.

PART THREE

THE CRISIS OF THE 1850s

As we have before remarked, a *free* negro is an anomaly—a violation of the unerring laws of nature—a stigma upon the wise and benevolent system of Southern labor—a contradiction of the Bible. The status of slavery is the only one for which the African is adapted; and a great wrong is done him when he is removed to a higher and more responsible sphere.

Jackson *Semi-Weekly Mississippian*, 21 May 1858

11

The Best of Times, the Worst of Times

> Humanity, self-interest and consistency all require that we should enslave the free negro.
>
> George Fitzhugh, *What Shall Be Done with the Free Negro* (1851)

> If the [enslavement] policy . . . should be adopted and executed, it would be a disgrace to Kentucky—a disgrace to American civilization. It would call forth the cry of "shame!" "shame!" from the lips of the world.
>
> [Louisville?] *Journal*, quoted in the *Nashville Republican Banner*, 24 February 1860

THE onrushing sectional conflict pushed the free Negro caste to the edge of extinction. The threat of free Negro subversion, always present in the white mind, loomed ever larger as the South prepared for war. Southerners willing to defend to the death a society based on Negro slavery had no desire to live alongside blacks who were free. But the 1850s were also a time of unprecedented prosperity. With the exception of a brief financial panic in 1857, the South enjoyed a decade of continuous economic expansion, and many free Negroes shared in the good times. Like whites, free Negroes found that employment was easy to get and wages were generally high. Their prosperity contradicted the white man's most exalted racial beliefs. Rather than mitigating white hostility, the freemen's success only stoked it. Frustrated by their inability to force free Negroes to conform to their racial code, some whites demanded their forcible expulsion or enslavement.

During the 1850s, free Negroes prospered as never before. Their material success, despite all the obstacles whites threw in their path, was apparent in almost every community. In Charleston alone some seventy-five whites rented their homes from free Negro landlords, and one street took its name from the wealthy freeman who owned the houses that lined both sides of the block.[1] Much of this new wealth was an offshoot of the general prosperity which sent land values skyrocketing; free Negroes who had earlier invested in small parcels of land suddenly found themselves wealthy men. The flush times also allowed many free Negroes to climb into the property-holding elite for the first time. In 1860, Nashville boasted twenty-six free Negroes worth over a thousand dollars who had owned no property at all ten years earlier. Tax rolls and census enumerations in other Southern cities told similar success stories.[2]

Black wage earners also partook of the good times. In spite of numerous restrictions and growing competition from white immigrants, the general prosperity and the labor shortage drove wages up. Bemoaning the need for more workers, St. Louis businessmen observed that "every fresh pair of hands will here find quick employment." In the Upper South, where the drain of slaves southward aggravated the existing labor shortage, free Negroes used their strong bargaining position to abrogate year-long contracts and push for higher wages. When employers failed to meet their terms, free Negroes frequently refused to work. "Many farmers who have plantations to cultivate have not a single hand," lamented a rural Maryland paper in 1850; "this in great measure is owing to the free negroes who have been in the habit of hiring out, now refusing to do so." Five years later, another journal noted that wages had

1 Ford, comp., *Census of Charleston*, pp. 23–239.

2 England, "Free Negro in Ante-Bellum Tennessee," pp. 225–34; Jackson, *Free Negro Labor and Property Holding*, pp. 102–70; Wright, *Free Negro in Maryland*, pp. 184–6; Boucher, "Free Negro in Alabama," pp. 189–221, 368–507; Sweat, "Free Negro in Ante-Bellum Georgia," pp. 154–71; *List of the Tax Payers of the City of Charleston for 1859*, pp. 389–405; *List of the Tax Payers of the City of Charleston for 1860*, pp. 314–34; Provine, "Economic Position of Free Blacks in the District of Columbia," pp. 69–72.

almost doubled because free Negroes refused to sign yearly contracts. "Some farmers are paying as high as $120—the same hands a few years ago could have been hired for $75."[3]

Extravagant signs of free Negro affluence could be seen everywhere: free Negroes employing whites, owning their homes, donning the latest fashions, riding in fancy carriages, flaunting other trappings of success.[4] But nothing bespoke free Negro prosperity more than the bright new churches that dotted black communities throughout the South. During the 1850s, African churches multiplied rapidly. Newly organized congregations built churches, and older ones added galleries, remodeled decrepit buildings, and erected new meetinghouses. Typical of many black churches, the First African Baptist Church of Nashville enlarged its meetinghouse to a "size commensurate with the demands of their increasing congregation." In Louisville, the Fifth Street African Baptist Church completely overhauled its old hall so that even the white press admitted the church was "one of the most handsome edifices of the description in this place." Wealthier congregations did even more. In 1857, the pastor of the old Gillfield African Baptist Church of Petersburg cut the ribbon on a spanking new seven-thousand-dollar meetinghouse.[5]

The free Negroes' ability to thread their way through the maze of restrictive obstacles bolstered their confidence and nurtured a new militance. Although they remained a cautious and generally conservative caste, they seemed more willing to challenge white dominance than at any time since the Revolution. To whites, it appeared that the established racial order was under siege. In 1858, for instance, Richmond free Negroes petitioned the City Council for the repeal of the city's repressive municipal black code. The council rejected

[3] St. Louis *Daily Missouri Democrat,* 27 April 1857; *Kent News* quoted in Baltimore *Sun,* 15 January 1860; Chestertown *News* quoted in *ibid.,* 3 January 1855; also *ibid.,* 7 January 1856; Curtis W. Jacobs, *The Free Negro Question in Maryland* (Baltimore, 1859), pp. 15–16.

[4] Richmond *Daily Dispatch,* 24 January 1855; *New Orleans Crescent,* 10 July 1858; *Nashville Republican Banner,* 19 October 1858; *Charleston Courier,* 10 July 1858, 29 November 1859; Charleston Grand Jury Presentment, 7 January 1860, SCA.

[5] *Nashville Republican Banner,* 27 July 1859; *Louisville Daily Democrat,* 26 October 1854; Petersburg *Express,* 17 August 1859.

the petition almost out of hand, but the audacity of the challenge startled city officials. Before long other whites were shocked by similar challenges. A leading New Orleans journal summed up the common complaint when it noted that "impudence is beginning to be a feature of the grand order of the F.M.C.'s."[6]

Sensitized by the growing sectional dispute to the slightest deviation from racial etiquette, Southern whites saw Negro freemen striking out at their rule in the most common forms of daily intercourse. When a group of Richmond whites ordered a free Negro from their path, "he challenged them to a fight and said he had as good a right to be on the sidewalk as any of them." Whites detected the freemen's growing resistance at every turn. Whenever free Negroes see a white man coming, grumbled a citizen of Petersburg, "they plant themselves square in the middle of the walk, and nine cases out of ten they are slow to give way." The irate white man suggested a more liberal application of the lash, but neither white protests nor stiffer punishments seemed to have much effect. "The insolence with which many of our city's negroes locomote about the city is positively unbearable," lamented a Petersburg newspaper several years later. "We see many of them with cigars, puffing their disgusting smoke into the faces of ladies and gentlemen . . . with a degree of *sang froid*, which even the Boston community would not tolerate in a white person."[7]

Far more frightening to whites than these breaches of sidewalk etiquette was an awakening of the free Negro's political consciousness. Free Negroes were finally attuned to the growing sectional controversy. Listening in on their conversations, whites picked up frightening allusions to emancipation and equality. Previously innocent encounters between free blacks and whites suddenly took on new political meaning. In the autumn of 1856, several wagons filled with free Negroes returning from a picnic on the outskirts of Baltimore passed a

[6] Richmond *Daily Dispatch*, 12, 15 March 1858; Minutes of the Richmond City Council, 2, 9 March 1858, VSL; New Orleans *Weekly Picayune*, 17 September 1855.

[7] *Richmond Whig*, 19 July 1853; *Petersburg Daily Southside Democrat*, 25 September 1855; *Petersburg Daily Democrat*, 19 February 1856.

large party of Irishmen. The two groups exchanged racial slurs, and the inevitable fight broke out. The blacks quickly routed the Irishmen and, despite white reinforcements from nearby saloons, "armed themselves with stones and drove the white men entirely off." Flushed with victory, the blacks transformed the riot into a political rally. "For a time they took entire possession of the road," noted one observer, "and spying a political liberty pole, erected by the Democrats of that vicinity, they gave three cheers for Frémont and immediately attempted to pull the pole and the flag down."[8] Incidents such as these fed the gnawing fear of free Negro subversion.

The growing number of successful fugitives confirmed white fears. Slaveholders were sure these runaways were aided to freedom by free Negro or white sympathizers, and although many slaves needed no help, Negro freemen were caught helping fugitives often enough to reinforce white suspicions. A Kentucky sheriff discovered one free Negro with a satchel full "of the peculiar yellow paper used for free passes." Another black conductor on the Underground Railroad was found leading a slave to the Ohio River armed with a "bowie knife, a pistol, lucifer matches, and powder and ball in abundance." Throughout the South, but especially in the border states, militant free Negroes helped shrink the slave population.[9] "Every day but swells the number of absconding slaves from Maryland," complained a Baltimore journal in 1850. Attempts to stop the stream of fugitives leaving the South were often dramatic but generally ineffective.[10] As the number of successful fugitives grew, so did white fear of the free Negro caste.

Free Negroes sowed subversion, and whites feared they would reap a harvest of black discontent. The increase in runaways suggested how contagious free Negro militance could be. Some bondsmen demanded their liberty with astounding forcefulness. In 1853, John Scott, a Virginia slave, tried to sue for his freedom and that of over a hundred other bonds-

[8] *New Orleans Crescent*, 4 October 1860; *Baltimore American*, 9 September 1856.

[9] *Louisville Daily Courier*, 15, 16 December 1856; *Louisville Daily Democrat*, 12 January 1855, 19 June 1857. The activities of Northern free black members of the Underground Railroad in the South are discussed in Quarles, *Black Abolitionists*, pp. 159–67.

[10] Baltimore *Sun*, 7 January 1850; *Baltimore American*, 9 September 1858.

men by claiming they had been emancipated by the will of their late master. He hired several lawyers to get him a copy of the will, but complained that they deceived him and left him "fare from Africa the home of our forefathers." Frustrated by corrupt attorneys, Scott and twenty of his fellow bondsmen marched on Richmond City Hall, demanding to see the will. The mayor stalled them while a posse formed which drove the blacks off.[11] But such face-to-face confrontations left their mark. Whites searched for the source of this new militance. Reluctant to credit their slaves with the desire for freedom, they blamed the growing servile unrest on outsiders, particularly the free Negro. The more forcefully slaves demanded their liberty, the more dangerous free Negroes seemed. By the eve of the Civil War, after a decade of increasing unrest among slaves, free Negroes did not have to aid fugitives or pass abolitionist literature to be considered dangerous. "Their mere presence, the simple act of walking our streets, and travelling our highways by the farms of the countryside is sufficient to incite insurrection in the slaves . . . ," cautioned one Tennessee legislator in 1860.[12]

As the sectional crisis mounted, whites found the freemen's "mere presence" increasingly repugnant. Everything the free Negroes did offended and frightened whites. On one hand, they eroded the color line by accumulating property, building their own churches, demanding their rights, blending into the white caste by passing—in short, by acting just as whites suspected they themselves would act under similar circumstances. With no sense of irony, North Carolina slaveholders complained that free Negroes were "a perfect nuisance to civilized society," because they "hold themselves a grade above the slave population and attempt in divers ways to equalize themselves with the white population, not withstanding the legal restrictions . . . already thrown around them."[13] On the other hand, free Negroes disdained whites and joined with slaves, setting dread precedents for slaves to imitate. While some whites worried that the freemen's success would dissolve

[11] John Scott to William McLain, 19 September 1853, ACS; *Richmond Whig*, 19 July 1853.

[12] *Nashville Union and American*, 19 November 1860.

[13] Petition from Sampson County, 1852, NCLP.

the color line, others feared they would soon face slave armies led by free Negro rebels.

Fear of free Negro subversion was not new. Throughout the antebellum years, whites had answered these threats, real and imagined, by trimming free Negro liberty still further. The racially charged atmosphere of the 1850s again incited Southern lawmakers to devise new laws to limit free Negro mobility, punish their crimes more severely, tax them heavily, extract their labor, and generally equate them with slaves. "Every session of our Legislature," noted a New Orleans newspaper in 1859, "gives occasion for a new batch of statutes for the regulation of our free colored population, and the adoption of stringent measures for their control."[14] As had happened so often in the past, these legal assaults encouraged less scrupulous whites to attack Negro freemen more directly. Free Negroes increasingly found themselves the target of kidnappers and vigilantes.[15]

Among those who saw an opportunity to profit from the new attacks on free Negro liberty were white wage earners. Encouraged by the growing opposition to the free Negro, white workingmen openly assaulted their black competitors in occupations where free Negroes had long gone unchallenged. By the late 1850s, free Negroes had monopolized the caulking trade in Baltimore for more than a decade. Although whites had challenged the black caulkers several times, the freemen's skill and their ties with employers allowed them to hold their own. Exasperated by the free Negroes' success, whites determined to drive them off by force. Beginning in 1858, gangs of white "Tigers" roamed the Baltimore docks, beating black caulkers and harassing shipyards that employed them. Within the next two years, whites broke the free Negro monopoly and forced many free blacks to seek employment in other cities. Although free Negro caulkers were still too well

[14] New Orleans *Daily True Delta*, 16 March 1859.

[15] See, for example, St. Louis *Daily Missouri Democrat*, 27 November 1855, 28 January 1858; Richmond *Daily Dispatch*, 23 April 1858; H. McMillan to [William McLain], 6 October 1856, P. Slaughter to William McLain, 5 July 1858, ACS; *Opelousas* (La.) *Patriot*, 23 July 1859; Proceedings of the Savannah City Council, 5 December 1859, SCH; Earl W. Fornell, "The Abduction of Free Negroes and Slaves in Texas," *Southwestern Historical Quarterly*, LX (1957), 369–86.

entrenched to be driven off completely, their privileged position was lost. Before long, the example of the "Tigers'" success incited white workers in other trades to drive out blacks.[16]

Class conflict within the white caste further intensified hostility between white and free Negro workers. The general prosperity of the 1850s heightened labor militancy. Hard-pressed employers countered the demands for higher wages by relying increasingly on slave hirelings. The practice of renting slaves by the year or allowing bondsmen to peddle their labor by the week or month grew markedly in the cities of the South. Municipal officials frowned on the practice and frequently complained it undermined slavery, but slaveholders, who found hiring out extremely lucrative, and slaves, who liked the added freedom it afforded, conspired to evade the flaccid regulations.[17]

White laborers fumed at the growing competition from slave labor and the humiliation of having to work alongside blacks. They bitterly resented the fact that upper-class whites isolated themselves from Negro competition, while leaving white workers to fend for themselves. Since "free negroes are not allowed to be Doctors, Lawyers, Merchants, and Tradesmen," declared the Petersburg Mechanics' Association in 1857, "we consider they have no more right to compete with our employment, by undertaking mechanical arts, than they have to compete with any other branches of business or professions. . . ." A St. Louis workingman registered the same complaint. Lawyers would never permit blacks to practice their profession, but they refused to restrict Negro mechanics. "Now I want to know," he asked, "if it is any worse to put a negro pleading a case before the Judges of the Supreme Court than driving a dray upon the levee?" Legislators protected themselves and left workingmen defenseless. "I don't think there is any equality in that," he snapped, "and I, for one, don't think a lawyer or a doctor is better than a drayman." The demands of white workingmen for a general equality of whites ricocheted against free Negroes. When slaveholding legislators refused to

[16] *Baltimore American,* 5, 8 July 1858, 28 June 1859, 8 February 1860; Baltimore *Sun,* 3, 5 June 1858, 13 July 1858, 28 June 1859.

[17] Wade, *Slavery in the Cities,* pp. 38–54; Starobin, *Industrial Slavery in the Old South,* pp. 128–37.

restrict the use of skilled bondsmen or slave hirelings, white laborers turned their fury on the most visible and accessible target. Petitions that began with complaints against black competition generally almost always ended with an attack on the free Negro.[18] White wage earners were in the vanguard of the opposition to the free Negro caste throughout the 1850s.

New restrictions on free Negro liberty could not assuage white anxieties. In most places these proscriptions were already so comprehensive that new laws were simply redundant. Restating them more explicitly, adding penalties for second offenders, and providing incentives for enforcement spurred new crackdowns and created severe dislocations within free Negro communities. But free Negroes proved remarkably resilient. Before long they were again evading the law and often turning the new enactments to their own advantage. The inability to subjugate free Negroes frustrated whites and incited harsher repression, but still the free Negroes remained. And they multiplied.

In the Upper South, white anxieties were further inflamed by economic and social changes. The corrosive effects of manumission and sale to the Lower South continued to wear away at slavery in that region. Indeed, soaring cotton prices inflated demand for slaves during the 1850s and increased the flow of bondsmen from the Upper South. With prime hands selling upwards of $1,500 by the end of the decade, the temptation of selling off a few bondsmen was too much for many Upper South masters to resist. While thousands of slaves marched south in shackles, others fled north to freedom. The slaves' powerful desire for liberty and the efforts of Northern abolitionists and militant free Negroes were eliminating slavery on the northern fringe of the South. Between 1850 and 1860, the slave population of the counties bordering on the North declined by over 14,000 as they escaped to freedom or their masters removed them to safer ground. Henry Wise, the governor of Virginia, mused that only the solicitude with which

[18] *Richmond Enquirer,* 27 August 1857; St. Louis *Daily Missouri Democrat,* 29 July 1858. Also see Little Rock *Arkansas Gazette and Democrat,* 16 October 1858; *Baltimore American,* 10 June 1859; Petitions from Portsmouth, 25 February 1851, from Norfolk, 12 November 1851, VLP; "A Memorial to Encourage the Mechanics of North Carolina," *North Carolina Legislative Documents,* 1850–1, doc. CVI; Takaki, *Pro-Slavery Crusade,* pp. 44–50.

masters treated their slaves kept slavery alive in these areas.[19] With the decline of slavery, Yankee farmers began to trickle into the border region. Taking advantage of low land prices and using modern farming methods, they quickly found profit in previously forsaken land. But not all came for profit. Northern abolitionists, seeing slavery on the ropes, also began to move into the region. Eli Thayer, the founder of the Massachusetts Emigrant Aid Company and an ally of John Brown, sponsored the immigration of Northern farmers into Virginia, confident that free-labor competition would soon rout slavery. Northern free-soilers and later Radical Republicans eyed the possibility of developing an indigenous antislavery party in the border South.[20]

The "Friendly Invasion" of the Upper South cheered Southern emancipationists and unsettled slaveholders. Southern opponents of slavery took heart from these changing circumstances. Some spoke out boldly against slavery and boasted of its imminent demise. "Kentucky is now destined to be a free state," exclaimed one emancipationist following the Kentucky Constitutional Convention in 1849. "No earthly power can now prevent it."[21] Rabidly racist antislavery politicians made steady progress in the border states. Whereas earlier antislavery extirpationists had cloaked their opposition to slavery by aiming colonization at the free Negro, now some colonizationists openly proclaimed their hostility to slavery. By the end of the decade, free-soiler newspapers in Wheeling, Louisville, and St. Louis spoke of the virtues of ridding the South of all blacks, and antislavery politicians like the Blairs in Missouri and Maryland and Cassius Clay in Kentucky worked to establish the Republican Party in these border states. As free-soilers made inroads in Missouri and Maryland,

19 Wilbur Zelinsky, "The Population Geography of the Free Negro in *Ante-Bellum* America," *Population Studies,* III (1950), 397–9; "Governor's Message," *Virginia Legislative Documents,* 1859–1860, doc. I, p. 16. Also John Fee to Lewis Tappan, 30 October 1849, AMA Papers.

20 Richmond *South,* especially March through May 1857; George W. Smith, "Ante-Bellum Attempts of Northern Business Interests to 'Redeem' the Upper South," *JSH,* XI (1945), 177–213; Otis K. Rice, "Eli Thayer and the Friendly Invasion of Virginia," *ibid.,* XXXVII (1971), 575–96; Richard H. Abbott, "Yankee Farmers in Northern Virginia, 1840–1860," *VMH&B,* LXXVI (1968), 56–66; Foner, *Free Soil, Free Labor, Free Men,* pp. 269–70.

21 J. A. Jacobs to William McLain, 11 March 1849, ACS.

slaveowners found that slavery was "no longer being debated upon the high vantage ground occupied by the Southern States of the original rectitude and reciprocal blessings of African slavery; but it is reduced merely to the question of the practicability of emancipation." "It is simply a question of dollars and cents," echoed one Virginian. On that basis, many doubted that slavery could long survive in the Upper South. Given the present rate of decline, a leading Maryland jurist predicted, "the State would glide into a free condition within the next quarter of a century."[22]

Fears arising from the deterioration of slavery in the Upper South were not confined to that region. Although not directly threatened, Lower South whites worried that the Upper South would "lapse into free states" with the drain of slaves south. Once Maryland, Virginia, Kentucky, and Missouri went free, North Carolina and perhaps Tennessee would eventually follow. Increasingly the cotton states would be isolated, robbed of their political muscle within the Union, and so greatly outnumbered that they could not defend themselves outside the Union. Some Lower South politicians searched for ways to preserve slavery in the Upper South. They pressed for a reopening of the African slave trade, in part because the flood of newly imported Africans would decrease their dependency on Upper South imports and "force the border states to be pro-slavery." But few Southern whites would have welcomed the influx of thousands of strange "heathen" Africans into their midst, and the movement to reopen the transatlantic slave trade foundered.[23] Meanwhile, Lower South whites took cold comfort from the fact that some Northern antislavery politicians, reasoning as they did, worked to speed emancipation in the border region with the hope of driving slavery from the South entirely.

Many Upper South whites had long since accepted the eventual demise of slavery in their region. It was not a distant emancipation that worried them but the steady growth of the free Negro caste. Even without total emancipation, free Negroes might outnumber them. For years the decline of slavery

[22] Richmond *South,* 3, 10 July 1857; Baltimore *Sun,* 10 June 1859.

[23] Quote in Jackson *Daily Mississippian,* 17 December 1858; also *De Bow's Review,* XXVI (1859), 482; Takaki, *Pro-Slavery Crusade,* pp. 67–8, 117–21.

had been robbing white farmers of labor and forcing them to migrate west. Now white workers, unwilling to labor alongside blacks, were increasingly following suit. If the trend continued, the free Negro would soon dominate all. The fear of living surrounded by blacks who were free shook Upper South whites, yet the reality daily drew closer. The number of free Negroes fast approached equality with that of slaves in Maryland; in Virginia and Kentucky, slavery barely maintained itself against the pressures of sale, manumission, and flight; and Missouri politicians openly debated emancipation. Before the 1850 census documented what everyone sensed, whites had begun the almost ritual projection of the proportions of whites, slaves, and free Negroes who would someday inhabit the Upper South. The free Negro population of Virginia, calculated several anxious white petitioners in 1849, had increased over 400 percent in the past fifty years. "If nothing was done, they would form a population of 240,000 in the year 1900, a period that will arrive during the natural life of our children. In 1950 our grandchildren will encounter this population increased to a numerical force of about one million—thirty percent greater than our present white population—and our great grandchildren will see a free black population of 4,000,000 in Virginia."[24]

Once free Negroes outnumbered whites, the dreaded confrontation would become inevitable, and the outcome of the conflict was no longer sure. Viewing blacks as people like themselves, Upper South whites understood that white dominance grew increasingly precarious as their numerical superiority slipped away. "History furnishes no instance of one people residing in the midst of another people as a lower caste and excluded from an equality of civil rights," declared one Virginian, "that have stopped short of violence and rebellion so soon as their strength gave them reasonable hope of success." Surrounded by the signs of growing black militance, whites saw

[24] *African Repository,* XXV (March 1849), 73. Also *Richmond Enquirer,* 10 February 1858; "Reports of the Committee on Colored Population," *Maryland Legislative Documents,* 1852, 1860; Jacobs, *Free Negro Question in Maryland,* pp. 12–13, 16. Although over all the population of the Upper South was getting whiter with the drain of slaves and the influx of Irish and German immigrants, some backwater agricultural areas in the Maryland and Virginia tidewater continued to push closer to free black majorities; "Report of the Committee on Colored Population," *Maryland Legislative Documents,* 1852, doc. L, p. 4.

the bloody scenario being played out before them. Free blacks "will naturally be clamorous for privileges. They will be urgent in petition, then in argument, and then in demand. They will be first persuasive, then accusatory, and finally insolent. They are men, and even if we had no record of history, in which to read the future by the past, we may know what they will do!" As heirs to a revolutionary tradition and witnesses to the liberation struggles in Latin America and Europe, Southerners indeed had a record in which to read the future by the past. Predictions of "a war between the castes" ripped through the tidewater of the Upper South.[25]

Reacting almost instinctively, Upper South legislators reached for their perennial solution to the free Negro problem —deportation. After a burst of interest following the Nat Turner rebellion, public support for African colonization had waned. By 1840, state-sponsored colonization schemes had collapsed everywhere except in Maryland. The renewed fear of free Negro subversion revived interest in African removal. During the 1850s every Upper South state, except Delaware and North Carolina, instituted some colonization plan. Virginia, a reliable index of Upper South opinion, took the lead. In 1850, the state appropriated $30,000 annually for the next five years to send free Negroes and emancipated slaves to Liberia. Always suspicious of colonizationist intent, legislators earmarked the money for the deportation of Liberian emigrants at the rate of $30 a head. A tax on free Negroes added another $10,000 to the colonization fund. In 1852, colonizationists scored another victory in Maryland. The old deportation plan had been a dismal failure. After twenty years and an expenditure of over $200,000 in public funds, the number of Maryland free Negroes had continued to grow. Yet, state lawmakers renewed their support for another five years. Success in Virginia and Maryland warmed colonizationist prospects throughout the Upper South. In 1853, Tennessee approved a modified colonization scheme. Tightfisted legislators refused to appropriate removal funds, but they ordered all emancipated slaves shipped to Liberia. Those slaves whose masters failed to provide transportation would be hired out for two years and the proceeds

[25] *African Repository,* XXV (March 1849), 73–4; *Debates and Proceedings of the Maryland Reform Convention,* I, 194–8.

used for their removal. Two years later, Missouri and Kentucky enacted plans similar to that of Virginia with annual appropriations of $3,000 and $5,000 respectively.[26] Such miserly support assured the failure of these deportation plans, but the fact that Upper South lawmakers felt the need to make the gesture demonstrated again their rising fear of the growing free Negro caste.

Free Negroes had no illusions about the motives of the colonizationists. Whites wanted to get rid of them and cared little how they did it. "I am of the opinion," declared John Rapier, the brother of a future Alabama congressman, "they would not care if all the free negroes in the united states was at the Botom of the Sea so they was out of the united States." Yet repressive laws and vicious vigilantism drove some freemen into the arms of the deportationists. "Believe me sir I am serious in my idea of Emigrating," continued Rapier; "in this country I cannot live."[27]

While most free Negroes did not change their views about the colonizationists, emigration found an increasingly large following in the decade before the Civil War. "I believe that a man of color must seek and obtain a home [,] a peace [*sic*] of earth that he could call his own," declared a St. Louis free Negro in 1851, "and water it with the sweat of his brow, he must plant the tree of liberty and build a temple sacred to Religion and Justice." However noble that dream, whites had made it clear it could never be realized in the South. Blatant racism in the North made the free states a forbidding alternative. Reluctantly, some free Negroes looked for a new home where they might find a modicum of freedom, new opportunities, and a taste of manhood. "[I] cannot be a man heare and . . . I an ready to go if i live on bread and warter or die the never day i get there," declared a Liberia-bound black. "[I] think hit better to die a onebrel [honorable] death than

[26] *Va. Laws,* 1850, c. 6; *Md. Laws,* 1852, c. 10; *Tenn. Laws,* 1853, c. 50; *Ky. Laws,* 1855–1856, c. 274; *Mo. Laws,* Act of December 13, 1855. Some Lower South states tinkered with the idea of giving financial support to the American Colonization Society, but most remained unalterably opposed; *Journal of the Louisiana House of Representatives,* 1853, p. 231; *Savannah Republican,* 28 January 1858, 26 February 1856.

[27] John H. Rapier to William McLain, 18 January 1854, 5 March 1855, ACS.

to live a misreble life [,] that is the spearit that you may find me an in eney man that draws one breth of life."[28]

Emigration drew support from a broad spectrum of free Negro society. Many elite free Negroes who had previously shown little interest in Africa now had second thoughts. John Adams, one of the wealthiest free Negroes in Richmond, took a subscription to the *African Repository,* and a Nashville schoolteacher considered transferring his school to Liberia. J. B. Jordan, a long-time exponent of colonization, found black opinion in New Orleans totally transformed. Blacks who had once ridiculed his opinions now listened carefully, and some made plans to migrate to the African republic.[29] Other members of the free Negro elite prepared to move to Canada, Latin America, or the West Indies. In 1855, a wealthy New Orleans freeman sponsored free Negro settlements in Mexico and Haiti. Several years later, when Florida officials enforced the guardianship law, a large number of Pensacola creoles sailed for Haiti and other West Indian islands. Still, the bulk of the free Negro upper class showed no desire to leave the South.[30]

Against this background of rising interest in emigration, several prominent Baltimore free Negroes met in the spring of 1852 to consider their plight. After lengthy debate, the leaders of the group, James A. Handy, an African Methodist Episcopal minister, and John H. Walker, a local schoolmaster, issued a call for a convention of Maryland free Negroes to be held in Baltimore that summer. Quoting liberally from the Declaration of Independence, free Negroes bitterly condemned the disparity between the promise of American life and their dismal condition. The time had come, they concluded, "to take into serious consideration our present condition and our future

[28] N. D. Artist to William McLain, 5 October 1851, Lewis G. Whitten to William McLain, ? July 1855, Francis M. Sloggins to William McLain, [Ocober 1859], T. J. Bowers to R. R. Gurley, 27 November 1857, ACS.

[29] William H. Starr to William McLain, 16 February 1857, J. H. Martin to William McLain, 10 February 1861, J. B. Jordan to William McLain, 1 October 1850, ACS.

[30] Desdunes, *Nos Homme et Notre Histoire,* pp. 88–9; Barr and Hargis, "Voluntary Exile of Free Negroes of Pensacola," pp. 3–4; *Savannah Daily News,* 16 August 1852; J. W. Lugenbeel to [William McLain], 18 October 1852, ACS.

prospects in this country and contrast them with the inducement and prospects opened to us in Liberia, or any other country."[31]

In response to this call, about two months later representatives from six counties and several districts of Baltimore gathered in a stuffy Baltimore hall.[32] Angry delegates bitterly denounced white oppression. An Eastern Shore free Negro complained that white officials took the children of free Negroes they deemed improvident and bound them out to local farmers. Even swine were treated better than free Negroes, bellowed a militant Baltimore representative. "The hog law said at certain seasons they should run about, and at certain seasons be taken up; but the laws referring to the colored people allowed them to be taken up at any time." Another Eastern Shore delegate denounced the rigorous black codes which locked free Negroes into virtual peonage. Some freemen from his county had been hired and then sold for another year before the completion of their first term. "Who knows what the next legislature would do; if any arrangements could be made to better their condition, he was in favor of them."

Delegates universally agreed their position was deteriorating. Their fathers had been deemed citizens; the new state constitution stripped them of that status. The spirit of the age encouraged men to control their own affairs, develop their abilities, and unleash their aspirations, but for blacks "in this country, at all events, from present appearances, it is out of the question." Agitation to improve their condition only seemed to make it worse. "They were men," declared one anguished delegate, "but not recognized as men."

Leaders of the convention maintained that emigration was the solution to the freemen's oppression. The black colonizationists, led by Handy and Darius Stokes, another AME minister, introduced several resolutions calling for a return to Africa. Others rejected Africa in favor of Canada or Haiti, but the ministers insisted Liberia was the only place blacks could hope to find freedom. To Handy, Africa meant more than

[31] *Maryland Colonization Journal*, new ser., VI (June 1852), 193–5.

[32] The following account of the Baltimore Convention is drawn from the *Baltimore American*, 28, 29 July 1852; Baltimore *Sun*, 27–29, July 1852; *Maryland Colonization Journal*, new ser., VI (July 1852), 225–30.

greater liberty or expanded opportunities. It was their destiny. They must return to the fatherland and Christianize it so that Africa might be "resuscitated, renovated and redeemed."

Black colonizationists met with stiff opposition. Intimating they were in the pay of the white colonization society, anti-emigrationists packed the hall and tried to break up the meeting. When several confused representatives offered to withdraw if Baltimore free Negroes opposed the convention, their motion was greeted by wild applause and cries of "That's good!" Opposition grew so fierce inside the hall that many delegates resigned on the spot. Outside the building, an angry, anti-colonizationist black mob threatened to disperse the convention. Only the arrival of the police prevented a general melee.

Most free Negroes had not changed their minds about returning to Africa. It was the white man's idea of the proper place for them. Suspicious blacks preferred almost any locale to Liberia. Rising interest in Africa and a growing desire to escape the South could not overcome the taint of colonizationist racism. Although the number of emigrants to Liberia increased in the decade before the Civil War, colonizers found most free Negroes just as resistant to removal as before. A colonization agent accompanying sixty former slaves from western Virginia to Norfolk arrived with only half that number. He sadly reported that blacks were so opposed to Liberia that they took every opportunity to escape to the North.[33] Once in a port city, free Negroes remained remarkably inventive at finding excuses to delay their departure. "I shall, of course, try to keep up the steam among them," wrote a North Carolina agent to the home office, "but foolish creatures, they allow every little difficulty to thwart them. 'Can't sell my house.' 'Can't sell my lot.' 'Money owing to me, can't get it.' &c. &c." If potential emigrants needed help in escaping forceful colonizationists, local freemen quickly extended it. Colonization agents slowly relearned that no free Negro could be considered an emigrant until the ship had left port.[34]

[33] N. D. Artist to William McLain, 5 October 1851; ACS; Staudenraus *African Colonization Movement*, p. 251; *Petersburg Daily Intelligencier*, 12 May 1859.

[34] J. W. L[ugenbeel] to William McLain, 15 October 1852; also see William H. Starr to William McLain, 23 July 1853, W. D. Shumate to William McLain, 24 October 1857, ACS.

The free Negroes' refusal to emigrate and inadequate funds had once again foiled the colonizationists. The failure of these new voluntary removal efforts were all too apparent. In 1850, twenty-nine free Negroes left Virginia for Liberia under the Virginia plan. The following year, despite the frantic efforts of deportationists, only six freemen were transported out of the state under the act. Meanwhile, the 1850 census revealed a 7 percent increase in that state's free Negro population. The governor declared that the census proved colonization to be a dismal failure, and he demanded a more vigorous removal policy before the free Negro caste grew out of control.[35] If free Negroes would not leave the state voluntarily, they must be forced to go. Responding promptly to the governor's suggestion, some lawmakers proposed to hire out all free Negroes for five years. The funds raised from their labor would be used to deport to Liberia all but a few freemen by 1858. Any free Negro who refused to leave would be sold into slavery, and the state would be cleared of the despised caste.[36]

John Rutherfoord, a powerful Democratic assemblyman from a county just west of Richmond, championed the forcible expulsion of free Negroes from the state. Rehearsing long-standing charges, he condemned free Negroes as hopeless idlers who filled the courts with culprits and the jails with convicts, who consumed more than they produced and diminished rather than added to the state's wealth. White disdain for blacks and the presence of racial servitude forever barred freemen from improving their lowly status. Allowing free Negroes to elevate themselves would only make them more obnoxious and dangerous. "They have proved most troublesome where their privileges have been the greatest." However, throughout Rutherfoord's condemnation of the free Negro and his insistent demand for expulsion, he nowhere dipped into the increasingly popular positive-good ideology. It was not the free Negroes' innate character but their social circumstances that made exclusion necessary: "Morally and economically, they are unfit

[35] "Report of the Auditor of Public Accounts," *Virginia Legislative Documents*, 1850–1851, doc. II, p. 16, 1852, doc. II, p. 9; *Journal of the House of Delegates of Virginia*, 1852 (January session), p. 16.

[36] The bill is outlined in *Maryland Colonization Journal*, new ser., VI (June 1852), 198.

for freedom among whites." But they were fit for freedom. Like the colonizationists, Rutherfoord lauded the freemen's African prospects. As citizens of the Liberian Republic, free Negroes would shake off the shabby vices that characterized black life in Virginia. Those who recoiled at the idea of ordering free Negroes from their homes might take consolation from Rutherfoord's assurances that free Negroes would "be made the agents, under Providence, of a vast and noble work of human good—the suppression of the slave trade, which has so long desolated Africa, and the final civilization and enlightenment of her unhappy and benighted millions."[37]

Rutherfoord's proposal stood midway between the familiar ideas of voluntary emigration and the militant demands for the enslavement of free blacks which would soon ring throughout the South. Indeed, the Virginia lawmaker went out of his way to condemn an enslavement measure that had been introduced into the legislature about the same time. He carefully noted that his own plan threatened enslavement as a last resort, to be used only when free Negroes had shown they would not leave voluntarily. Since he believed free Negroes, like all men, loved liberty, he was sure the threat would never have to be carried into effect.[38] Steeped in the necessary-evil argument, Rutherfoord had simply lifted colonizationist ideas intact and added compulsion.

Not even the familiar colonizationist rhetoric could hide the radical character of expulsion. Paying the free Negroes' way to Africa and encouraging migration by taxing them more heavily or proscribing their activities more severely was drastically different from ordering them from their homes or clapping them into bondage. Rutherfoord, sensing opposition to driving the free Negroes from the state, offered to moderate his demands by postponing the threatened enslavement until 1869. But still he insisted that the law of "self-protection and self-preservation" made expulsion necessary.[39]

The opposition Rutherfoord had expected was quick to form.

[37] *Speech of John C. Rutherfoord of Goochland in the House of Delegates of Virginia, on the Removal from the Commonwealth of the Free Colored Population* (Richmond, 1853).

[38] *Ibid.*, pp. 8–10, 16.

[39] *Ibid.*, p. 10.

Contending that deportation would wreck the state's labor-short economy, one Virginian blasted expulsion as not only unwise but counterproductive. Far from assuring their safety or securing slave property, expulsion would disrupt society and further undermine slavery. The laborers who replaced free Negroes would be more degraded than the freemen or be opposed to slavery. As one opponent pointed out, "it would be vain to expect industrious and respectable laborers to come among our slaves and labor with them. They would not do it." Those who did migrate into the state could hardly be expected to defend slavery. "[It is] a perfect certainty," declared another opponent of the bill, "that this labor must be *white* and anti-slavery in its feelings," and consequently most likely to champion abolition.[40]

Free Negroes, so long condemned as vicious malcontents, had suddenly found a host of ardent defenders. Freemen were not criminals, argued one Richmond newspaper. "On the contrary, they number among them men of the highest character and respectability—men of piety—men of substance—men of considerable intelligence." The majority of free Negroes were ignorant and degraded, but they were not offensive and rebellious. "The idea that the free negro disaffects the slave, renders him rebellious," declared another opponent of the bill, "is a mere dream without foundation in fact, whose laments Mr. Rutherfoord cannot have analyzed." Free Negroes composed a disproportionate number of the state's criminals, and many were indeed incorrigible idlers, but what else could be expected of a people barred from education and proscribed from all areas of gentility? Crimes were always higher among the lower classes, and "the laws against free negroes are even more severe, and are executed with much more severity than the laws against white men."[41]

The debate over the expediency of free Negro expulsion was a standoff. Some Virginians believed the economy would be shattered by the deportation of so many workers, while others thought it would flourish and slavery would be secured by the free Negro's departure. Again, many Virginians thought free

[40] Richmond *Daily Dispatch*, 15 February 1853; *Richmond Whig*, 25 January 1853.

[41] Richmond *Daily Dispatch*, 15 February 1853, 9 March 1853.

Negroes were incurable criminals and fiendish revolutionaries, while others believed them innocuous and ineffectual. On balance, most whites doubtless would just as soon have eliminated the free Negro caste, but Southerners did not decide political questions on mere expediency; they weighed their acts on other scales besides convenience. Virginians did not doubt that expulsion would work a hardship on freemen. Even Rutherfoord had apologized for the harshness of his plan and had modified it by delaying deportation. Still, the proposed legislation provided no sure destination for free Negroes. The North would not have them, and freemen would not have Africa. "Every man must have a country," observed one opponent, "and if this is not the free Negro's country, where is it?"[42]

Expulsion offended the Virginians' delicate sense of right. Free Negroes were not embraced by the state's bill of rights and the new constitution permitted forcible deportation, but "there are some things all mankind will take for granted," declared an anguished opponent. "They *are* embraced by a more comprehensive code of Human Rights and 'imperfect obligations.'" Another opponent of the bill ran the gamut of arguments against expulsion and concluded that "the great plea . . . is humanity." Free Negroes were a responsibility as well as a burden. "We believe the Almighty sent negroes here to be civilized, and we cannot, at will, doff that responsibility He has imposed."[43]

Pangs of conscience mixed with the need for free Negro labor to defeat expulsion. Rutherfoord's proposal rattled around in the General Assembly for almost a year. Amendments ameliorated its harshest features and pushed the date of final deportation still farther into the future. But when the bill finally came to a vote in the spring of 1853, a substitute extending the old colonization law replaced Rutherfoord's scheme and passed easily.[44]

The failure of the Virginia expulsion proposal was rooted in the premises of its leading proponent. Rutherfoord never dis-

[42] *Ibid.*, 15 March 1853.

[43] *Ibid.*, 9 March 1853; also *Richmond Whig*, 25 January 1853, 4 February 1853.

[44] *Journal of the House of Delegates of Virginia*, 1852, p. 458, 1852–1853 (adjourned session), pp. 104–76, 235–6, 338, 536; *Va. Laws*, 1852–1853, c. 56.

puted that expulsion would impose hardships on free Negroes and on the white farmers who depended on their labor. But he maintained that the threat of free Negro subversion overwhelmed any short-term dislocations expulsion might cause. By making expulsion contingent on the extent of the freemen's threat or the depth of the dislocations that removal might cause, Rutherfoord made it a matter of open debate, and when the smoke cleared, expulsion had been badly defeated. Yet, even as Virginia lawmakers were rejecting forcible deportation, other Southerners were insisting that the liquidation of the free Negro caste was not a matter for dispute but a natural and necessary extension of Southern principles.

The belief that slavery was beneficial to white and black alike grew in power during the 1850s. Isolated in an antislavery world, their nerves rubbed raw by constant criticism, Southerners looked for some way to justify their social order and prove that slavery, not "free labor," made for the best of all possible societies. The positive-good argument not only provided such a rationale but eased the nagging doubts Southerners felt about the benefits of their peculiar institution. Ransacking the Bible, dredging up the lessons of history, searching the sciences, Southern ideologues molded an amalgam of often contradictory race and class theories into a powerful defense of the status quo. Previously confined to the Lower South, positive-good thought spread into the Upper South, where George Fitzhugh gave it its most coherent statement. By the end of the decade, Upper South politicians were vying with each other in ridiculing Jeffersonian ideas of the universality of liberty. Ideological attachments did not vanish overnight, and sectional differences continued to exist within the South. A Virginia woman traveling to Charleston on the eve of the Civil War could still display shock at hearing slavery defended as a good.[45] Although there were many dissenters, positive-good thought had become the leading edge of Southern opinion in the decade before the war.

In earlier years, the positive-good theory had mitigated white fear and hatred of the free Negro. Whites sure of their superiority did not have to fear the congenitally inferior blacks or degrade free blacks to demonstrate white mastery. But the

[45] *Richmond Enquirer,* 15 August 1857; Anne Rice to R. R. Gurley, 19 April 1860, ACS.

crisis atmosphere of the 1850s transformed this once-powerful buffer into a heady stimulant of racial antagonism. The South was under attack, and Southerners demanded that their social order be made consistent with their ideology.

The growing power of the positive-good argument heightened racial tensions. The new hostility was reflected in the increased difficulties light-skinned free Negroes encountered when trying to slip under the color line. Many whites were no longer willing to tolerate the silent passage of mixed-bloods into the white caste. In Virginia, the old mixed-blood law, which had permitted hundreds of fair-skinned persons of African ancestry to prove they were less than one-quarter black in court and thereby escape their legal disabilities, met increased opposition. Richmond whites were especially aroused because mixed-bloods used the law to evade the stiff punishments meted out to violators of the municipal black code. Persons who would have been routinely ordered to the whipping post for minor infractions escaped by brandishing their special status. The mayor grumbled that the mixed-blood law befogged caste lines and undermined white supremacy. It not only relieved mixed-bloods from the threat of the lash, but it also allowed persons of African ancestry to travel freely without a pass, to preach, to hold office, and even legally to marry whites. There were only two castes, white and black, stormed one Richmond journal. If the legislature wanted to make a third, it should prescribe their status; otherwise, mixed-bloods would soon "become governors, judges, jurors, soldiers, or lawyers."[46]

Whites feared mixed-bloods would destroy caste distinctions. "What is a negro?" asked a Charlottesville editor. He did not believe, as some had recently maintained, that an inferior race could "be entirely obliterated by breeding towards a superior one." A white and a black produced a mulatto, a mulatto and a white a quadroon, a quadroon and a white a mustee, a mustee and a white a *white,* but what kind of white man could be "manufactured" from a Negro? He might have fair skin, but close examination would reveal "black and curly hair, nails

[46] For the use of the mixed-blood law see Richmond *Daily Dispatch,* 15 September 1853, 24 October 1853, 1 December 1853, 28 January 1854; *Richmond Enquirer,* 1 September 1853, 24 February 1854; *Richmond Whig,* 16 February 1855; *Richmond Examiner* quoted in Richmond *Daily Dispatch,* 25 August 1858.

dark and ill-shaped, feet badly formed, and much of the negroes propensities." A Richmond newspaper played a variation on the same theme. Some persons might have less than one-quarter Negro blood "and yet betray the essential character of a Negro," it stated. Still the law denied they were black, and if it continued the state would soon have a new caste, like Northern Negroes, recognized and elevated by law, despised and degraded by society. Virginians wanted "no such nondescript class here, and no such conflict between law and society." The journal warned the legislature to repeal the law or be guilty of encouraging amalgamation. "The blood of the Caucasian cannot continue pure and undefiled while the law compels a fellowship with negroes."[47]

Yet the General Assembly remained unmoved by the growing controversy. Light-skinned freemen continued to escape their caste proscription legally and many doubtless passed for white, but the legislature turned aside attempts to repeal the act. Finally, the harried mayor of Richmond took summary action and announced that mixed-bloods might be relieved of their disabilities, but since the legislature had never intended "to make white persons out of this class, or to create a third class in this State," he intended to treat them as free Negroes until an appellate court ruled otherwise.[48]

These skirmishes over the mixed-blood law in Virginia reflected the anxieties of many whites. Throughout the South, the fear grew that free Negroes would wander over the color line and usurp white privileges. Even in Louisiana, where wealthy creole freemen had long been passing into the white caste, lawmakers denounced the practice and demanded new safeguards to keep the social order consistent with Southern ideology.[49]

Anxious to affirm their most cherished beliefs, whites searched everywhere for confirmation of the positive-good argument. Southern newspapers filled their columns with stories

[47] *Richmond Enquirer,* 3 January 1854, 31 December 1853.

[48] Richmond *Daily Dispatch,* 1 September 1858. Later some light-skinned freemen used the law to escape impressment into Confederate service; James H. Brewer, *The Confederate Negro: Virginia's Craftsmen and Military Laborers, 1861–1865* (Durham, N.C., 1969), p. 169, n. 7.

[49] *Journal of the Louisiana Senate,* 1856, p. 6; New Orleans *Daily Picayune,* 20 February 1857; *Ga. Laws,* 1851, c. 161.

about the dismal condition of free Negroes in the North, the decline of sugar production in Jamaica after emancipation, and the failure of black self-government in Haiti. But nothing more surely verified the sanctity of their ideals than a free Negro voluntarily requesting enslavement. During the 1850s, many Southern states facilitated enslavement by providing legal mechanisms for free Negroes to renounce their liberty. Unfortunately for white hopes, only a few Negroes took advantage of these elaborate preparations. Most who did were paupers decrepit with age.[50] Yet whites celebrated each case as a victory for slavedom. Newspapers throughout the South avidly spread enslavement stories. The disproportion of interest to reality suggests that they searched these stories out as jewels to be collected, polished, and displayed as evidence of the beneficence of their society. Such gems were doubly valuable if the free Negro had returned from the North to accept bondage. Nothing, observed one Richmond newspaper with obvious relish, "furnished strong[er] evidence in favor of the comfortable and contented condition of the Southern slave." "These negroes know what their own best interest is," chimed in J. D. B. De Bow.[51]

Just as Southerners continually affirmed the rightness of slavery, they constantly stamped out contradictions of the positive-good litany. Manumission was no longer a wrong-headed act by a softhearted master. In the 1850s, it was outright sedition. If free Negroes "be qualified for liberty," declared George Fitzhugh with his usual logic, "so are our slaves, and we are acting morally wrong in retaining in bondage, beings who would be better off as freemen." Manumission not only undermined the foundation of Southern society, it did a

[50] *Va. Laws,* 1856, c. 46; *Tenn. Laws,* 1856, c. 45; *Texas Laws,* 1857, c. 63; *Fla. Laws,* 1858, c. 860; *La. Laws,* 1859, c. 275; *Ala. Laws,* 1859–1860, c. 71; *Md. Laws,* 1860, c. 332. Between 1856 and 1859, $2,853 was paid into the Virginia treasury as a result of slaves voluntarily sold into slavery. Even if they were sold for $200 apiece, only fourteen Negroes accepted enslavement during those four years. "Report of the Treasury of Virginia," *Virginia Legislative Documents,* 1857–1858, doc. VI, pp. 10, 12, 1859–1860, doc. VI, pp. 10, 12; also John Hope Franklin, "The Enslavement of Free Negroes in North Carolina," *JNH,* XXIX (1944), 401–28.

[51] *Farmville Journal,* quoted in *Richmond Enquirer,* 2 April 1858, and *Richmond Whig,* 16 April 1858; *De Bow's Review,* XXVIII (1860), 481.

great disservice to the slave. Once released from bondage, the Negro would slide backward on the great chain of being. He would revert to type; the sambo would become a savage. Incapable of caring for themselves in freedom, emancipated Negroes were doomed to a premature death. "The responsibilities of freedom are too great for them," exclaimed a Tennessee legislator; ". . . hence, the man that emancipates his slave entails upon him a curse."[52]

Likewise, colonization was not only hopelessly impractical but morally wrong. Liberia survived only because of the presence of a handful of mulattoes whose white ancestry allowed them to persevere and the continued infusion of American money. Instead of providing black emigrants with opportunities unobtainable in the United States, colonizationists only assured them of lifelong poverty and degradation. Such anticolonizationist sentiment had long been present in the Lower South, but now it spread to the Upper South along with other positive-good ideas. Free Negroes who migrated to Africa, observed one writer in the Richmond *South*, "will be doomed either to early death . . . or, if escaping that, will be rendered more worthless in every respect, and far less happy, than they and their descendants would have been had they continued as slaves in Virginia, with the possible evils and afflictions incident to that condition."[53] Only under the watchful eye of a good master could the Negro live a comfortable, useful life.

Yet, it was the free Negro who most offended the logic of the positive-good ideology. If slavery was the Negro's natural state and freedom somehow was unnatural, then the free Negro was a veritable contradiction in terms, whose very existence challenged every premise in the positive-good argument. According to the logic of this argument, free Negroes should have happily renounced their liberty for the life of a slave, but instead they clung tenaciously to freedom. They should have slowly been driven into poverty by white competition, yet many free Negroes thrived. Indeed, since Negroes could not

[52] George Fitzhugh, *What Shall Be Done with the Free Negroes* (Fredericksburg, Va., 1851), p. 6; *Nashville Union and American*, 9 December 1859.

[53] *De Bow's Review*, X (1851), 331–2; quotation in Richmond *South*, 27 January 1858.

cope with liberty, the caste should have slowly become extinct. Yet, each census revealed an increase in their numbers.

The free Negro threatened to unravel the moral basis of the slave society. The justification of the institution of slavery rested on the innate inferiority of black people, their unfitness for freedom, and their incapacity to govern themselves. However much whites condemned free Negroes as hopelessly depraved, indolent, and criminal, their success in mastering white society demonstrated that blacks could take care of themselves. The danger was not only that slaves would learn this from the freemen's example, but that whites would. "The very same arguments that show it a measure of inhumanity [to enslave a free Negro]," reasoned one Tennessee legislator, "will prove that it is inhumane to hold slaves."[54] The positive-good argument, thrust forward to counter fears of slave rebellion and soothe the Southern conscience, created new conflicts in the white mind.

Free Negroes threatened the stability of Southern society in other ways as well. Black slavery provided a floor beneath which no white could fall and laid the foundation for racial solidarity in a society rife with class divisions. As long as any white, no matter how lowly, could look down on the Negro, those class divisions did not seem quite so formidable. Racial unity allowed nonslaveholding whites to treasure their liberty and support slavery. While planters monopolized the best land and dominated Southern society, they boasted that slavery provided the foundation for white democracy. Under the best of conditions, whites did not like sharing their proudest possession with blacks. But when slavery became the basis for Southern democracy, the liberty of some blacks became particularly odious. If some blacks were free—could live by themselves, care for their families, accumulate wealth, and even own slaves—precisely what was the value of a white skin? The free black called into question the racial foundations of Southern democracy and threatened to undermine racial unity at a time of growing class conflict among whites. Such reasoning exacerbated white racism and heightened opposition to the free Negro. A Maryland lawmaker, arguing that abolition would doom democracy in the South, demanded that "*all*

[54] *Nashville Union and American,* 6 April 1860.

negroes . . . be slaves in order that all whites may be free."[55]

Whites were free, blacks were slaves; as the positive-good ideology became the badge of Southern orthodoxy, whites were less willing to bear the ambiguity of the freemen's middle position. But whereas the logic of the necessary-evil argument only seemed to frustrate Southern whites and magnify their fears, positive-good thought suggested a solution to the heightened demands for ideological purity. "The truth is," exclaimed one Southern ideologue, "if the status of slavery is right, and best for the African, then of course, the status of the free negro is the worst; and it is the duty of those under whose care and control this class is, to do [that] which is best to promote their welfare—which is, to enslave them."[56]

Enslavement struck a sympathetic chord in the Southern mind. Many Southerners saw enslavement, like the reopening of the African slave trade, as the logical outgrowth of slavery and a final solution to their frustrating inability to make free Negroes conform to the logic of white racial thought. Besides, if slavery was benevolent and freedom a tyranny for the Negro, the truly moral man would want to help the free Negro find happiness. The failure to enslave free Negroes would be more than a mere careless blunder; it would be morally wrong.

Driving free Negroes from the South or into bondage would have practical benefits as well. Positive-good theorists believed that eliminating them from the border areas would help secure slavery in that region and ultimately protect it throughout the South. Slaves would be less likely to escape to the North if there were no free Negroes to aid their flight.[57] While free Negro removal would stabilize slavery in the South, the wholesale migration of Negro freemen to the North would cool the sectional conflict. Secure in their knowledge that most Northerners shared their racial attitudes, many Southerners believed that "colonizing abolitiondom" with free Negroes would cure fa-

[55] Fredrickson, *Black Image in the White Mind*, pp. 61–4; William B. Hesseltine, "New Aspects of the Pro-Slavery Argument," *JNH*, XXI (1936), 1–14; quotation in Curtis W. Jacobs, *Speech of Curtis W. Jacobs, on the Free Colored Population of Maryland, Delivered in the House of Delegates . . . 1860* (Annapolis, 1860), p. 10.

[56] *Petersburg Daily Democrat*, 9 February 1858.

[57] *Richmond Enquirer*, 11 August 1857.

natical Yankees of their antislavery ideas. "The strongest argument we can send the North in favor of Southern institutions would be our free Negro population," declared one proponent of expulsion. If the North barred the entry of Southern free Negroes, as some "free" states already had, "we will convict them before the world of their hypocrisy, and explode the humbug of their philanthropy, showing them to be inconsistent knaves and unprincipled scoundrels."[58] Finally, additions to the slave population would help satiate the need for labor in the South. Some enslaved free Negroes could be put to work in the cotton fields of the Lower South, and others might be sold to those whites not so fortunate as to share in slavery. Indeed, some enslavement proposals purposefully limited sale of free Negroes to nonslaveholders or provided that the receipts from their sale be given to the local school fund. One Tennessee legislator boasted that enslavement "would take money out of the coffers of the wealthy and give the poor man's children the benefit of it." By spreading slavery among nonslaveowners and funding white schools with black liberty, planters hoped to defuse the submerged conflict between slaveholding and nonslaveholding whites.[59]

Demands for enslavement spread through the South. In 1858, when the Virginia colonization law expired, the state legislature again debated forcibly removing free Negroes from the state under threat of enslavement. The movement for expulsion failed again, but the tone of the debate revealed a much more favorable attitude toward enslavement than before. Many legislators now demanded enslavement of free blacks, not as a last resort, but as the first, and even after forcible removal had been defeated, the old colonization law was not renewed.[60] Virginia colonizers felt the chill of changing opinion in the Commonwealth. Those who had once hoped to see all blacks swept from the state by a combination of manumission, sale

[58] New Orleans *Bee*, 16 April 1858; *Richmond Enquirer*, 20 August 1857.

[59] *Baltimore American*, 10 June 1859; Jacobs, *Free Negro Question in Maryland*, p. 22; quotation in *Nashville Union and American*, 18 January 1860.

[60] For the 1857–8 Virginia debate, see the Richmond *South* and the *Richmond Enquirer*, August–September 1857; "Message III on Miscellaneous Subjects," *Journal of the House of Delegates of Virginia*, 1857–1858, app., doc. I, pp. 101–3, 1857–1858, pp. 165, 230, 239–40, 246, 249–51, 256, 260–3, 275–83, 292.

southward, and voluntary removal to Liberia lowered their expectations. "If we can keep the free negroes from being enslaved," noted one long-time colonizationist, "& preserve the slaveholders right to emancipate their slaves & send them to Liberia we shall not labor in vain."[61] Pleas to push free Negroes into slavery rang out in other states. In 1858, North Carolina and Missouri lawmakers debated expulsion for the first time and Arkansas freemen felt the full fury of aroused Southern opinion.[62]

Arkansas, with one of the smallest free Negro populations of all Southern states, had long been a center of hostility to freemen. William Woodruff, editor of the state's largest newspaper and an ardent racist, had called for enslavement as early as 1835. By the 1850s, legislators were regularly tendering bills to force free Negroes out of the state or into bondage.[63] These proposals were easily turned aside, partly because hysterical complaints about free Negro subversion made no sense to lawmakers who rarely saw a freeman. But events of the 1850s reinforced the demands to expel free Negroes. In 1856, a measure threatening to enslave all free Negroes who did not leave the state within a year was barely defeated when its constitutionality was called into question.[64] Within a year, however, the United States Supreme Court in the *Dred Scott* decision had eliminated the slender protection of constitutional guarantees by stripping free Negroes of their citizenship.

Dred Scott breathed new life into the expulsion movement. In July 1858, a large public meeting in Little Rock called for the immediate removal of free Negroes from the state. Rehashing the positive-good argument, whites declared it "insane to

[61] Philip Slaughter to William McLain, 17 April 1858, ACS.

[62] Franklin, *Free Negro in North Carolina,* pp. 213–17; *Journal of the House of Representatives of the State of Missouri,* 1858 (adjourned session), pp. 50–1, 468–70, 473–6; *Journal of the Senate of the State of Missouri* (adjourned session), 1858, pp. 450, 491, 494.

[63] Little Rock *Arkansas Gazette,* 7 July 1835, 17 November 1835. By 1858, Woodruff had retired but the new owners generally followed his policies. *Journal of the Arkansas House of Representatives,* 1850, pp. 51, 68, 73, 90–100, 127, 138; Margaret Ross, *Arkansas Gazette: The Early Years, 1819–1866* (Little Rock, Ark., 1969), pp. 126, 184, 278, 325–6.

[64] *Journal of the Arkansas House of Representatives,* 1856, pp. 67, 121, 176, 315–22; Little Rock *True Democrat,* 2, 9, 23, 30 December 1856.

teach the slave . . . by allowing the free man of his own color and race to *be* free, to deal and trade as a free man, to hold property and sue in court, that he *is* fit to be free, and *can* take care of and govern himself; while in words we preach a different doctrine."[65] Little Rock workingmen soon joined the movement to expel the free Negro. Seeing an opportunity to rid themselves of unwanted black competitors, they lashed out at free Negro mechanics and claimed that their ability to work at skilled trades promoted racial equality. "If the negro is fit for the mechanic arts, he may aspire to belle letters. If he is made to associate the equal of mechanics, let him be taught the languages, mathematics—let him aspire to the graces and accomplishments, music, drawing, dancing, and become a patron at once in society."[66] Elias Conway, the newly elected governor, was also quick to perceive the political capital that might accrue from opposition to the free Negro. In November, in his annual message, he added his weight to the growing demands for expulsion and warmly offered slavery to any Negro freemen who desired to remain in the state.[67]

Under pressure from the governor, the state's leading newspaper, white workingmen, and petitions from various public meetings, the legislature hastily ordered Negro freemen to leave the state by 1 January 1860. All free Negroes found in Arkansas after that date would be allowed to choose a master or would be sold into slavery, with the benefits of their sale going to the state school fund.[68] As word of the legislature's decision spread, free Negroes quickly packed their belongings and fled. Some went north to the free states and Canada, others traveled down the Mississippi to Memphis and New Orleans, and a few tried to escape whites altogether by migrating into the Indian territory. Despite the painful separation from enslaved relatives and countless memories, apparently

[65] Washington (Ark.) *Telegraph,* 4 August 1858; Little Rock *True Democrat,* 22 September 1858.

[66] Little Rock *Arkansas State Gazette and Democrat,* 9, 16 (quotation) October 1858; Little Rock *True Democrat,* 23, 29 September 1858.

[67] *Journal of the Arkansas House of Representatives,* 1858, pp. 32–3.

[68] Debates can best be followed in the Little Rock *True Democrat,* December 1858–February 1859; Orville Taylor, *Negro Slavery in Arkansas* (Durham, N.C., 1958), pp. 255–8; *Ark. Laws,* 1858, c. 151.

none chose slavery. In 1860, only 144 mostly elderly free Negroes remained in the state.[69]

News from Arkansas shot through the South and sparked still another wave of assaults on the freemen's liberty. During the next two years nearly every slaveholding state wrestled with the question how to force free Negroes from its borders. As usual, opposition to free Negroes was most intense along the tidewater of the Upper South. In 1859, Maryland slaveholders held another convention to deal with their frighteningly large free Negro population. But the fears previously confined to the border states spread throughout the South. If something is not done, complained the mayor of Nashville, "we will very soon . . . encounter the same troubles experienced by the people of Maryland and other states." Legislators in states with but a fraction of Maryland's free Negro population debated expulsion and enslavement with all the fury of tidewater slaveholders. As more states took up the issue, rumors that free Negroes had been expelled or enslaved in still other states began to fly. "Texas has adopted some very strong regulations to free herself from this population. Virginia is perfecting a plan to cure this evil, so is Mississippi, South Carolina, Georgia, and Alabama," noted one rural Louisiana journal. "Shall Louisiana remain an idle spectator to this great work of safety and reformation, and make no move in self defense, though experiencing the effect of this curse upon her population?"[70] By the fall of 1859, the movement to rid the South of free Negroes had picked up momentum of its own.

John Brown's raid added an unprecedented sense of urgency to the demands for free Negro expulsion. The blacks who had accompanied Brown demonstrated the danger of free Negro subversion as perhaps no one else could. Even more frightening was the enthusiasm with which many free blacks celebrated Brown's assault upon slavery. When Baltimore police broke into the annual caulker's ball, they discovered the hall bedecked with pictures of Brown and a bust inscribed "The

[69] Little Rock *True Democrat,* 7 March 1860; Jackson *Daily Mississippian,* 21 January 1860.

[70] The debates of the Maryland Slaveholder's Convention are reported in the *Baltimore American* and the Baltimore *Sun,* 9, 10 June 1859; *Communication from His Honor the Mayor, Randall W. MacGavock,* p. 17; *Opelousas* (La.) *Patriot,* 15 January 1859.

martyr—God bless him." Chalked on the floor was an outline of Governor Henry Wise straddled by "a huge Ethiopian," surrounded by "inscriptions unfit for publication."[71] It was a chilling sight.

The supercharged atmosphere created by John Brown's raid pushed the free Negro question to the fore. In what would be their final sessions before the war, Missouri and Florida lawmakers ordered free Negroes from their states under threat of enslavement. The Mississippi General Assembly read and passed a similar bill twice, and in January 1860 it awaited the usually perfunctory approval of a third reading. The Tennessee House of Representatives endorsed a similar measure, and in the early months of 1860 it too only awaited ratification by the state Senate. Following the Slaveholder's Convention, Maryland legislators again wrestled indecisively with the free Negro question and passed the issue directly on to the people. In the best democratic tradition, Maryland lawmakers provided for a referendum in which whites might vote blacks into slavery. Ongoing debates in Kentucky, South Carolina, Georgia, Alabama, and Louisiana hinted that these states might soon follow suit.[72] Virginia and North Carolina, where expulsion had only recently failed, now stood aloof from the rush to new expulsion measures; but if other states acted, it would be difficult for them to resist.

Just as Southern radicals stood on the verge of expelling the free Negro, they were challenged by a surge of popular

[71] Baltimore *Sun*, 14 December 1859.

[72] MISSOURI: W. P. Johnson to J. F. Snyder, 21 December 1859, MoIHS; *Columbia* (Mo.) *Statesman* and the St. Louis *Daily Missouri Democrat*, March 1860. FLORIDA: Tallahassee *Floridian and Journal*, December 1859–January 1860. MISSISSIPPI: Jackson *Daily Mississippian*, Natchez *Mississippi Free Trader*, and *Natchez Daily Courier*, November 1859–February 1860. TENNESSEE: *Nashville Republican Banner*, *Nashville Union and American*, and *Nashville Daily News*, December 1859–April 1860. MARYLAND: *Baltimore American* and Baltimore *Sun*, January and February 1860. KENTUCKY: *Journal of the Kentucky House of Representatives*, 1859–1860, pp. 312, 668–74, 696–9, 720, 761, 809. SOUTH CAROLINA: Grand Jury Presentments, 1858–1860, SCA; *Charleston Courier* and *Charleston Mercury*, December 1859. GEORGIA: *Savannah Republican*, December 1859 and again in November–December 1860. ALABAMA: *Mobile Daily Advertiser* and *Montgomery Daily Confederation*, January 1860. LOUISIANA: *Opelousas* (La.) *Patriot*, December 1858–July 1859; Alexandria *Louisiana Democrat*, December 1859; Baton Rouge *Weekly Gazette and Comet*, February–May 1859; *New Orleans Crescent*, September–December 1859.

opposition. Southern ideologues discovered that many of their fellow citizens not only failed to follow their reasoning but disagreed with their premises. Making liberty a felony, punishing innocent free Negroes along with the guilty, destroying African churches, and breaking up free Negro families—as a matter of conscious policy—offended the sense of right of many Southerners. "Argument is unnecessary to show," observed one Mississippi representative, "the injustice and inhumanity of requiring such as these to be driven suddenly from their homes, and without means of support, or sometimes even of transportation into another State. . . ." Throughout the South, expulsion met the same cries of inhumanity, injustice, and barbarism which had earlier defeated it in Virginia. While some whites gloried in the prospect of returning free Negroes to their natural state, most shrank back in horror. "For the South, for Maryland, we say no," exclaimed one outraged Baltimore minister. "It is revolting to justice, shocking to humanity, and will be an eternal disgrace to any people." Legislators who had expected to be greeted as heroes for finally cleansing the South of this unwanted caste found themselves castigated for pandering to the basest elements in the community.[73]

Such reasoning mystified the defenders of slavery. "Every day we hear our slaves pronounced the happiest people in the world," noted a Savannah newspaper. "Why then this lamentation over putting the free negro in his only proper . . . condition?" The suggestion that white lawmakers had no power to deprive blacks of their liberty or that it was unjust to enslave Negroes had no place in Southern society. The dangers of these arguments were all too apparent to Southern radicals. "If it is too harsh and inhuman to reduce a Free Negro to slavery," reasoned a Florida journal, "upon what ground can the African Slave Trade, the keeping of a single negro in slavery be justified?"[74] Angered by the dangers of such slipshod reasoning, positive-good theorists ripped into those con-

[73] *Natchez Daily Courier,* 6 December 1859; Andrew H. Cross, *To Mr. Jacobs, Chairman of the Committee on Colored Population in House of Delegates of Maryland, a Few Thoughts* (n.p., 1860), p. 4; New Orleans *Daily True Delta,* quoted in Baton Rouge *Weekly Gazette and Comet,* 1 May 1859.

[74] *Savannah Republican,* 15 December 1859; Tallahassee *Floridian and Journal,* 21 January 1860.

fused liberals who thought a free Negro better off than a slave. "If any Southern conscience is so tender . . . that it cannot bear the idea of conferring the blessing of slavery upon a wretched free negro," sneered one fire-eating newspaper, "then in the name of consistency, why does its owner not turn amateur crusader and preach regeneration and disenthralment throughout a land afflicted with such a curse?"[75] Even an abolitionist would be better than a Southern hypocrite.

Most Southerners were neither hypocrites nor abolitionists. It was not merely their horror of enslaving free blacks but also the free Negro's entrenched position in Southern society which prevented whites from acting. While free Negroes were given no voice in the debates over their future, their sentiments were clear. Throughout the South, free Negroes voted with their feet. Maryland newspapers reported hundreds of blacks emptying their bank accounts, selling their property, and heading north. Others left for Africa, Canada, and Latin America. "Scarcely a week passed but a large number of free persons [of color] leave this port for Mexico or Hayti," noted a New Orleans newspaper in 1860.[76] Once again Southerners were threatened with the loss of an important part of their labor force. The familiar exaltation of free Negro workers replaced complaints about black indolence, criminality, and subversion wherever free Negroes were numerous.[77]

Fear of massive economic dislocation was reinforced in the border states by the inroads of the free-labor system. Reliance on free labor, even free Negro labor, spawned different values than did slavery. Many of the farmers and businessmen who

[75] *Petersburg Daily Democrat*, 9 February 1858.

[76] Wright, *Free Negro in Maryland*, p. 315; *Nashville Union and American*, 17 February 1860; T. C. Stuart to R. R. Gurley, 7 February 1860, James Purviance to R. R. Gurley, 2 April 1860, ACS. For the large migration of New Orleans freemen to Haiti, see New Orleans *Daily Picayune*, 22, 23 June 1859, 15 July 1859, 14 August 1859, 24 December 1859, 15 January 1860, 21 October 1860, 11 November 1860, 28 February 1861; quotation in *New Orleans Daily Delta*, 16 January 1860. Other free Negroes, thinking expulsion laws had been enacted, pleaded for legislative exemptions or petitioned to be permitted to take masters who would allow them *de facto* freedom; MLP, Box 107.

[77] *Baltimore American*, 7 February 1860, 8 March 1860; *Daily Baltimore Republican*, 16 February 1860; clipping from *Richmond Whig*, n.d., with W. H. S [tarr] to ?, February 1859, ACS; *Nashville Republican Banner*, 15 January 1860; New Orleans *Daily Picayune*, 16 July 1859; Jackson *Daily Mississippian*, 7 December 1859.

had come to depend on free Negro workers no longer looked upon slavery as the linchpin of a distinctive way of life, but viewed it simply as an inefficient (and even an unjust) economic system that burdened them with unwanted responsibility. "I *prefer* to employ them as present," insisted one Baltimore businessman. "Employment and reward for industry and a discharge if otherwise. I don't want to be *forced* into other relations, at least with no more emergency than at present." The use of free labor, moreover, portended an entirely different pattern of development from slavery. Some border-state politicians feared expulsion of so many laborers would jeopardize the orderly development of the state.[78]

The freemen's strategic position in the Southern economy allowed them the leverage needed to defend their own liberty. The wealth and social standing free Negroes had accumulated over the years had earned them the respect of many whites. During the enslavement crisis, Southerners suddenly found reasons to describe free Negroes as "industrious," "honest," "wealthy," "pious," and "respectable," words previously reserved for whites only. Those pressing for enslavement found the stereotype of the indolent, degraded free Negro challenged in the most embarrassing ways. When a Maryland enslavement leader declared that free Negroes were lazy and a burden on the community, an Eastern Shore legislator quietly asked why Baltimore workingmen petitioned the General Assembly for relief from free Negro competition. "If he doesn't work, how does he compete with white men?"[79]

The intimate relations between light-skinned free Negroes and whites, particularly in the Lower South, added to the solicitude many whites felt toward the freemen's liberty. "There is hardly one in ten that is of unmixed blood," observed John Catron, the United States Supreme Court Justice from Tennessee. "Some are half white; many have half white mothers, and white fathers, making a caste that is 87½–100th of white blood; many have a third crop in which negro blood

[78] *Baltimore American,* 21 February 1860; *Journal of Missouri House of Representatives,* 1860 (special session), p. 126.

[79] New Orleans *Daily Picayune,* 16 July 1859; *Charleston Courier,* 18 December 1859; *Natchez Daily Courier,* 10, 16, 20 December 1859; quotation in *Daily Baltimore Republican,* 16 February 1859.

is almost extinct."[80] Clearly, many whites bridled at the enslavement of their children and grandchildren, brothers and sisters—indeed, of any people who looked so much like themselves.

Finally, Southern whites feared that any attempt to enslave or expel free Negroes would destroy the very institutions they were trying to save. They understood it would be most dangerous to mix a people who had tasted freedom with slaves. Bitter about the loss of their liberty, free Negroes would be a constant source of slave unrest. And even if swept from the South, free Negroes would plot to liberate their friends and relatives entrapped in bondage and retake their native land. Moreover, the physical removal of free blacks would encourage the immigration of other workers "far more dangerous to the institution of slavery and the security of slave property than the free negroes themselves." Whites would come south not only as laborers but as voters with a "known antipathy to slavery," observed one Maryland newspaper. They would use their political power to "abolish the 'peculiar institution' in our midst, and thus while depriving us of our slaves, would restore the evil of free-negroism of which we now complain."[81] Free Negro removal, however accomplished, threatened to leave the South worse off than before.

In the shadow of secession and the creation of a slaveholding republic, one Southern state after another drew back from expelling or enslaving the free Negro. The governors of Florida and Missouri vetoed the expulsion enactments which had so easily sailed through the legislatures of those states. Soon after, Mississippi lawmakers quietly refused to approve the third reading of a similar measure. The Tennessee Senate procrastinated until the waning days of the session and then rejected the House bill in favor of stricter free Negro regulations. When

80 *Nashville Union and American,* 8 December 1859. Catron's outspoken letter apparently had the intended effect in the Lower South, where it was widely reprinted; but in the Upper South, where most free Negroes were of unmixed racial origins, many whites were outraged. P. F. Howard to James Hall, 17 January 1860, Letters Received, MdSCS Papers.

81 *Maryland Colonization Journal,* new ser., X (February 1860), 137–45; *Baltimore American,* 10 June 1859, 14 February 1860; *Nashville Union and American,* 8 December 1859, 21 February 1860; Frederick (Md.) *Examiner,* 1 June 1859; Cumberland (Md.) *Democratic Alleganian,* 18 February 1860.

the two houses failed to compromise their differences, the legislature went home without enacting new laws on the subject. Finally, Maryland voters overwhelmingly rejected their enslavement option.[82] With the movements for expulsion and enslavement collapsing throughout the South, states that had only begun to debate the issues quickly backed off. In the end, only Arkansas, where free Negroes had been too few to be of any economic importance and too recently arrived to have developed binding ties with whites, was able to chase the free blacks out of the state. But with the general failure of expulsion throughout the South, even Arkansas lawmakers relented. Just as the law was scheduled to go into effect, the legislature postponed its operation until 1863. Although most free Negroes had already fled the state, the expulsion law never became operative.[83]

As the Civil War drew closer, the necessity of cleansing Southern thought and institutions of contradictions had never seemed clearer to the theorists of the slave society. They rightly understood that their failure to press the free Negro into slavery or at least expel him from the South weakened the whole logic of secession. "The Legislature talks one way and acts another," grumbled one South Carolina planter in January of 1861. "They secede on account of free negro influence in the North and advocate and defend free negroism here in So. Ca."[84] But when faced with the task of transforming theory into practice, Southern radicals failed. The cries of inhumanity which greeted their calls for enslavement and expulsion revealed the hidden power of the free Negro caste and the weakness of positive-good ideology. The free Negroes' entrenched position in Southern society protected them in their moment of greatest danger.

[82] Tallahassee *Floridian and Journal,* 31 December 1859; *Journal of Missouri House of Representatives,* 1860 (special session), pp. 123–9; Jackson *Daily Mississippian,* 7 February 1860; T. C. Stuart to R. R. Gurley, 2 March 1860, ACS; *House Journal . . . State of Tennessee,* 1859–1860, pp. 480–4, 1096, 1134, 1174; *Baltimore American,* 17 November 1860. One Maryland county approved the enslavement referendum, but apparently never put it into effect.

[83] *Ark. Laws,* 1860, c. 99.

[84] David Gavin Diary, 26 January 1861, copy, SHC.

Epilogue

Freemen and Freedmen

The ex-slave was not a free man; he was only a free Negro.

George Washington Cable, *The Negro Question* (1888)

BORN in the equalitarian enthusiasm of the American Revolution, the free Negro caste perished in the libertarian spirit of the Civil War. Ironically, freedom did what all the harsh proscriptions and threats of enslavement could not. With the Emancipation Proclamation and the Thirteenth Amendment, free Negroes lost their special status. Freedom was no longer an anomalous condition for Southern blacks.

The war eliminated the free Negro caste, but it could not erase the experience of freedom which generations of blacks had enjoyed. Their years of liberty were crucial to the development of black life in the postwar South. In like fashion, whites did not forget the struggle to force free Negroes to conform to their racial standards and the methods they had evolved to make free Negroes toe the line.

The long experience in dealing with blacks who were free provided crucial lessons for Southern whites confronting the new postwar realities. During the antebellum years, they had created the institutions, standards of personal relations, and patterns of thought which helped them control free Negroes, extort their labor, and maintain social distance between the races. Faced with a greatly enlarged free black population after the Civil War, whites almost instinctively applied the lessons of the past. Perhaps through trial and error they might have developed the same pattern of race relations even had there been no antebellum free Negro caste. Various forms of debt peonage, for example, entrapped blacks in nearly every post-emancipation slave society in the Americas.[1] But with almost a century of experience to draw on, whites had little need to grope.

As Southern whites transformed the slave system into a caste system, some of the antebellum institutions first developed to control free Negroes reappeared with scarcely a hint of disguise. Fearful of losing the benefits of black labor, many of the recently defeated Confederate states enacted black codes that replicated those passed by Maryland and Delaware twenty-five years earlier. Like the antebellum laws, these new enactments allowed whites to force blacks into long terms of service on the flimsiest of pretenses. In addition, newly emancipated blacks found their liberty burdened with restrictions against traveling freely, testifying against whites, and enjoying the suffrage—all proscriptions familiar to the antebellum free Negro caste. Although many of these laws had long been in the statute books of Southern—and indeed, some Northern—states, they incensed Northerners who were determined to protect the fruits of their victory and were angry at the arrogance of Southern lawmakers. The new black codes fell as Radical Republicans rose to power in the North. But even as these laws were being swept from the statute books, other more subtle forms of social control were replacing them, tieing blacks to their employers, to landlords, or to the planter-merchants who rented them land and provided credit while their crops still had to be harvested. Like the black codes and the convict-lease system, which also became increasingly popular in the Southern states, sharecropping and debt peonage were no strangers to the antebellum free Negro caste.[2]

[1] David Lowenthal, "Post-Emancipation Race Relations: Some Caribbean and American Perspectives," *Journal of Inter-American Studies,* XIII (1971), 367–75.

[2] Theodore B. Wilson, *The Black Codes of the South* (University, Ala., 1965); James B. Browning, "The North Carolina Black Code," *JNH,* XV (1930), 461–73; Morris, "Course of Peonage in a Slave State," pp. 261–3;

Segregation, or at least the formal separation of the races, developed more slowly. Not until the end of the nineteenth century was the system of "cradle-to-grave" separation given full legal sanction. However, the informal pattern of separation, well entrenched long before Emancipation, persisted. Long-segregated institutions like churches, schools, and graveyards continued as such. Indeed, segregation in churches increased as newly liberated blacks, re-enacting the free Negroes' antebellum experience, withdrew from white-dominated congregations and established their own. In other institutions—penitentiaries, asylums, railroad terminals, theaters, and the like—segregation developed at a more leisurely pace, but generally according to the established antebellum mode: that is, whites applied the principles of racial segregation as they established new institutions and enlarged or remodeled older ones. As always, whites widened the physical distance between the races whenever blacks threatened to shrink the social distance between themselves and their former masters.[3]

The antebellum pattern of social relations between free Negroes and whites also persisted into the postwar era. Common living and working conditions continued to breed close friendships between the races at both ends of the social spectrum. The general Emancipation increased the opportunities for blacks and whites to meet as equals, strike up friendships, and enjoy each other's company. Many clandestine relationships begun in the antebellum years flourished in the postwar South. But Emancipation also brought blacks and whites into more direct competition for housing, jobs, and political office. This competition, carried on in an atmosphere of endemic

---

Williamson, *After Slavery*, pp. 72–9, 169–75; George B. Tindall, *South Carolina Negroes, 1877–1900* (Columbia, S.C., 1952), pp. 105–14; Peter Kolchin, *First Freedom: The Responses of Alabama's Blacks to Emancipation and Reconstruction* (Westport, Conn., 1972), pp. 30–55; C. Vann Woodward, *Origins of the New South, 1877–1913* (Baton Rouge, La., 1951), pp. 180–4, 205–8, 212–15, 232–4.

[3] Woodward, *Strange Career of Jim Crow*, especially chs. 1–3, maintains that the rigid system of racial separation, supported by statute, was not established until the 1890s. His chronology has been challenged by a number of historians, and this and other related questions are debated in Joel Williamson, ed., *The Origins of Segregation* (Lexington, Mass., 1968). See Woodward's sensible rejoinder and shift in the emphasis of the debate from when to why in his *American Counterpoint*, pp. 234–60.

racism, aroused distrust and contempt more often than it created understanding and respect. As during the antebellum years, the closer blacks came to equality with whites, the more whites felt a need to assert their superiority. When it seemed that freedmen, aided by their Northern allies, might topple white supremacy, Southern whites resorted to naked force to beat them back. For years, white regulator organizations had taken it upon themselves to discipline free Negroes who dared violate the Southern racial code. During the Reconstruction era, white vigilantes rampaged across the land.[4] To escape white terror, many freedmen sought the protection of powerful whites. As in the past, elite whites gladly satisfied their paternalist pretensions by trading the promise of protection for the Negro's deference. And after Emancipation, blacks had more to offer than mere submission. They could also bargain their labor and their votes in return for the right to purchase land, enjoy steady employment, or safely raise their families. Such unspoken bargains between upper-class whites and blacks provided the social basis for an alliance which, for a time, dominated Southern politics.

Yet the most important antebellum legacy was the white man's idea of the black as a free man. For years whites had been building an image of the free Negro, and now that all blacks were free that vision proved all the more important. The belief that blacks were naturally lazy, criminal, lustful, and seditious and that those without masters refused to work, stole uncontrollably, and rebelled frequently provided an easy justification for the harsh laws and brutal vigilantism. It enabled whites to preserve their good image of themselves while imposing the stringent racial code. The idea of the free Negro formed during the years of slavery served whites well in freedom.

Free Negroes also drew on their antebellum experience. Blacks who had enjoyed freedom before the war generally remained at the top of the new black society. Throughout the postbellum South, they controlled a disproportionate share of black wealth, skill, political power, and social leadership. In

[4] Allen W. Trelease, *White Terror: The Ku Klux Klan Conspiracy and Southern Reconstruction* (New York, 1971).

1868, a survey by a leading Nashville newspaper found that more than half the leading "colored men of property" in that city had been free before the general Emancipation.[5] Their heritage of liberty, accumulated wealth, skill, and knowledge gave free Negroes the self-confidence to grab political power when a shift in national policy threw open the doors of public office to blacks. Only 1 black person in 9 was free in 1860, but at least 10 of the 22 blacks who served in Congress between 1869 and 1900 were drawn from the old free Negro caste. The freemen's disproportionate influence was also felt on the local level. Of the 102 blacks to hold state office in Virginia between 1867 and 1890, 43 had been free before the war. In the states of the Lower South, where free people of color were not as numerous but enjoyed a comparatively higher social status, their postwar predominance was often overwhelming. All but 20 of the 111 black delegates to the Louisiana Republican Convention in 1865 were freeborn. Likewise, of the 59 black delegates to the 1868 South Carolina Constitutional Convention who were natives of the state, at least 18 and perhaps as many as 21 were former free Negroes. Another 14 had been born in freedom in other parts of the nation, thereby giving the old free Negro caste a clear majority of the black delegation.[6]

[5] Nashville *Daily Press and Times,* 4 April 1868. Free Negroes did not everywhere so dominate the new black upper class, but even where they composed a small part of the new elite, it generally was proportionately larger than their share of the black population in 1860; Kolchin, *First Freedom,* p. 141, n. 51. On the other hand, not all free Negroes survived the Civil War with their fortunes intact and some of them, notably slaveholders, saw their status slip badly as a result of Emancipation; "Romance of Little Wassaw," UGa; Kolchin, *First Freedom,* pp. 140–2.

[6] Samuel D. Smith, *The Negro in Congress, 1870–1901* (Chapel Hill, N.C., 1940), p. 8. In addition to the 9 free Negroes cited by Smith, Joseph H. Rainey of South Carolina had also been free before the war; Williamson, *After Slavery,* p. 369. Also see Luther P. Jackson, *Negro Office-Holders in Virginia, 1865–1895* (Norfolk, Va., 1945), pp. 1–43, 50; Donald E. Everett, "Demands of the New Orleans Free Colored Population for Political Equality, 1862–1865," *Louisiana Historical Quarterly,* XXXVII (1955), 62; Williamson, *After Slavery,* pp. 376–7. Even where there were few free Negroes before the war, freemen still emerged as disproportionately influential. In Alabama, where fewer than 1 black in 200 was free in 1860, at least 4 of the 17 blacks to attend the 1867 state constitutional convention were former free Negroes; Kolchin, *First Freedom,* pp. 163–7. Also Margaret L. Callcott, *The Negro in Maryland Politics, 1870–1912* (Baltimore, 1969), pp. 157–8.

Some of these free Negroes flaunted their former status. Styling themselves "bona-fide free" or "old issue free," they stood scornfully aloof from the mass of former bondsmen. Early in the war, many members of the old elite had rushed to the defense of the Confederacy to take up arms for the new slaveholders' regime. As they later complained, these freemen were frequently forced into Confederate service by threats to themselves and their families. Others no doubt hoped to extract new privileges from whites, as they always had whenever whites were threatened and needed their help. But the enthusiasm and alacrity with which wealthy, light-skinned free Negroes volunteered for Confederate service suggest that many came forward to protect their property and their privileged positions. Free Negroes who filled the ranks of the colored militia units were overwhelmingly slaveholding planters and successful tradesmen. One rural Louisiana newspaper described them as "the flower of that description in the State," and Benjamin Butler, who later mustered the Louisiana Native Guard into Union service, was astonished to find that the darkest of them was "about the complexion of the late Mr. Webster."[7] Some of these elite freemen feared for their lives if the slaves were freed. In the ports of the Lower South, where many free people of color were just one generation removed from the rebellion that had sent their fathers flying from Saint-Domingue, these anxieties were especially real. A

Free Negroes also made up a disproportionate share of the emerging black intelligentsia at the end of the nineteenth century. Of the 18 members of the American Negro Academy known to have attended the 1897 organization meeting, 13 were born before 1865. Of these, 6 had been born free in the United States, 2 had been born free in Canada, and another 2 had free fathers. Horace Mann Bond, "A Study of Factors Involved in the Identification and Encouragement of Unusual Academic Talent Among Underprivileged Populations," U.S. Department of Health, Education, and Welfare, Project no. 5-0859 (1967), p. 26; also Robert A. Bone, *The Negro Novel in America* (New Haven, Conn., 1958), p. 15, n. 4.

[7] *Nation,* I (14 September 1865), 332; Carter G. Woodson, *Free Negro Heads of Families in the United States in 1830* (Washington, D.C., 1925), pp. lvi–lvii; Williamson, *After Slavery,* pp. 316–17; Mary F. Berry, "Negro Troops in Blue and Gray: The Louisiana Native Guard, 1861–1863," *Louisiana History,* VIII (1967), 165–90; Charles H. Wesley, "The Employment of Negroes as Soldiers in the Confederate Army," *JNH,* IV (1919), 242–5; Sellers, *Slavery in Alabama,* pp. 387–9, 397–8; Luther P. Jackson, "Free Negroes of Petersburg, Virginia," *JNH,* XII (1927), 387–8; quotations in Pointe Coupee (La.) *Democrat,* 16 May 1861, and Berry, "Negro Troops in Blue and Gray," p. 173.

few light-skinned free Negroes were so scornful of black slaves that they openly doubted whether blacks could survive without a master. John Rapier, an Alabama free Negro who had sat out the first years of the war in the West Indies, despaired of the effects of Emancipation on those islands. "I am now ultra pro slavery," he wrote from Haiti in 1861, "and am satisfied that a greater curse could not be imposed upon the United States or any other country than the emancipation of negro slaves. For once free, he literally lays down the shovel and the hoe, takes his fiddle, banjo and tambour, and devotes him[self] to dancing, drinking and playing, only interrupting these occupations to steal something to eat to support him in his idleness." Rapier swore he would never live with blacks, except where they were slaves.[8] Later he reversed himself, joined the Union army, and served with distinction, but the actions of other upper-class free Negroes in rushing to the Confederate standard gave force to Rapier's harsh words.

When the tide of battle turned, the free Negro elite scurried to exchange their Confederate gray for Union blue. But they could not shed their old attitudes with the same ease. In 1864, a Union officer wrote William Lloyd Garrison from New Orleans that the free people of color, "with all their admirable qualities, have not yet forgotten that they were, themselves, slaveholders." Many remained bitterly "hostile to the black, except as slaves." An upcountry visitor to Charleston observed that the old free Negro elite disassociated themselves from the "parvenu free." Rather than attend church with the new freedmen, they formed their own congregation, hired a white minister, and let it be known that "no black nigger [was] welcome." While newly liberated blacks slighted whites at every turn to flaunt their freedom, many of the old elite continued to defer to whites and tried to repair the damage done by Emancipation. "They are exceeding respectful to the Charleston gentlemen," noted the same visitor, "taking their hats off and expressing their pleasure in seeing them again, but regret that it is under such circumstances."[9]

[8] John H. Rapier to James P. Thomas, 25 February 1861, Rapier Papers, HUL. For Rapier's army career see Schweninger, "James Rapier and Reconstruction," chap. 1.

[9] Everett, "Demands of New Orleans Free Colored for Political Equality," pp. 43–64, quotation on pp. 54–5; Williamson, *After Slavery,* pp. 316–17;

The free people of color of the Lower South had long stood further apart from slaves and closer to whites than Upper South free Negroes, but Upper South observers noted the same division between freemen and freedmen. "The feeling existing between these two classes of the colored population of this city is not of the most harmonious character," wrote a Petersburg editor in 1867. "The latter, though the most numerous, seems to be looked upon by the former as a degree inferior to themselves, and as naturally subject to their control. . . ."[10] Doubtless whites, trying to divide blacks as they had during the prewar years, exaggerated the differences between those who had formerly been slaves and those who had been free. But not even the grossest overstatement could hide the fact that antebellum prejudices had no more disappeared among blacks than they had among whites.

The animosities inherited from the antebellum era festered and grew after the war. Fearful of being thrown together with the ragtag, destitute former slaves who were fleeing the plantations with little more than the clothes on their backs, some members of the elite retreated still further to themselves, cursed the general Emancipation, and yearned for the old days. Elite free Negro organizations like the Brown Fellowship Society of Charleston and the Creole fire companies of Mobile continued to meet on the old exclusive basis. The light-skinned scions of the free Negro caste continued to marry among themselves, imitate the style of life of the white upper class they so admired, and boast of their white ancestry. Honing their taste for the high life through education and travel, they seemed to be preparing themselves for the moment they might be accepted into the dominant part of the dominant caste. Although subject to much of the same racial oppression that entrapped poorer blacks, this "*crème de la crème* of the Southern light colored aristocracy" rarely joined the movement for racial uplift. Instead, sustained by the hope that class would

---

Tindall, *South Carolina Negroes*, pp. 195–7, 200, 207–8; Kolchin, *First Freedom*, pp. 142–3; Howard A. White, *The Freedmen's Bureau in Louisiana* (Baton Rouge, 1970), p. 7., n. 3; George P. Rawick, comp., *The American Slave: A Composite Autobiography*, 19 vols. (Westport, Conn., 1972–   ), II, pt. 1, 36.

[10] Alrutheus A. Taylor, *The Negro in the Reconstruction of Virginia* (Washington, D.C., 1926), p. 7.

prevail over race, they sought to convince whites they were a caste apart from blacks or, at least, to renew the alliance with upper-class whites which had given them their privileged position during the antebellum years. Charles Chesnutt, a free Negro, captured their spirit in his sardonic story entitled "A Matter of Principle." "If we are not accepted as white," declared "Brotherhood" Clayton, Chesnutt's protagonist, "we can at any rate make it clear that we object to being called black. Our protest cannot fail in time to press itself on the better class of white people; for the Anglo-Saxon race loves justice. . . ."[11]

Lower-class blacks envied the elite's wealth, its high style of life, and its ability to escape many of the racial restrictions that pelted them full force. An upcountry freedman of extremely light complexion decided to test out the rumors he had heard about the Charleston church "dat all de society folks of my color went to." He was impressed: "Ah, how they did carry on, bow and scrape and ape de white folks. I see some pretty feathers, pretty fans, and pretty women dere!" Yet, he was ill at ease amongst all the finery. "I was uncomfortable all de time . . . 'cause they was too 'hifalootin' in de ways, in de

[11] E. Horace Fitchett, "The Status of the Free Negro in Charleston, South Carolina, and His Descendants in Modern Society," *JNH*, XXXII (1947), 439–46; Kolchin, *First Freedom*, pp. 141–3; Tindall, *South Carolina Negroes*, p. 200; E. Franklin Frazier, *Negro Family in the United States*, pp. 393–419, and *Black Bourgeoisie: The Rise of a New Middle Class in the United States* (Glencoe, Ill., 1957), pp. 31–41, 98–103. Frazier writes: "In some small communities in the South, a single family with this social and cultural background would live in complete isolation rather than associate with the masses of Negroes"; *Black Bourgeoisie*, p. 99. Also see Charles W. Chesnutt, *Wife of His Youth* (Boston, 1899), p. 95, and *The House Behind the Cedars* (Boston, 1900).

Throughout the antebellum years, the elevated position of the generally light-skinned free Negro upper class had been based on their color as well as their wealth. This too carried into the postwar years, and "mulatto consciousness" among blacks may have increased as the overwhelmingly black former slaves challenged the brown elite's leadership. Although the question of color—brown and black—has not been nearly as crucial in determining the pattern of race relations in the United States as it has in parts of Latin America, its importance has generally been underestimated. While most whites perceived the United States pattern as a two-caste system, many Negroes, both black and brown, viewed it as a three-caste system. For an excellent survey of the literature on this little-studied question, see Robert Brent Toplin, "Reinterpreting Comparative Race Relations: The United States and Brazil," *Journal of Black Studies*, II (1971–2), 145–9.

singin', and all sorts of carryin' ons." Many freedmen sensed the rejection of blacks implicit and often explicit in the elite's exclusivist ways, and they returned it at every opportunity. One Alabama Radical Republican expressed the feelings of many newly liberated slaves when he blasted the old light-skinned creole caste who, "inflated with pride at their supposed superiority to 'common niggers,' have assumed such airs that sensible people are heartily disgusted at them."[12] The haughty attitudes of this remnant of the free Negro elite were a continuing source of disunity within black ranks.

Black life from Reconstruction to the present cannot be fully understood without taking into account the long-standing differences between these free Negroes and the masses of former slaves. Well into the twentieth century, the descendants of the free Negro elite maintained their lofty status within black society. During the 1940s, sociologist E. Horace Fitchett queried Howard University students as to the status of their ancestors during slavery. Of the 180 students who returned his questionnaires, fully half claimed descent from free Negroes. Twenty years later, Horace Mann Bond, conducting a similar survey, was "astonished to discover how largely the 10 percent of Negroes who were free in 1860 have dominated the production of Negro professionals (and intellectuals) up to the present day." His study, entitled "Factors Involved in the Identification and Encouragement of Unusual Academic Talent Among Underprivileged Populations," ironically and somewhat hyperbolically had demonstrated that "Negro academic doctorates were not in fact from an 'underprivileged' population. Indeed, they are from one of the most 'privileged' populations in America."[13] Frequently, these privileged descendants of the free Negro upper class expressed the same scorn for poorer blacks that their grandfathers and great-grandfathers had felt toward the slaves. The children of newly enfranchised slaves who rose to positions of power within the black community did not soon forget the slights

[12] Rawick, comp., *American Slave*, II, pt. 1, 34–6; Kolchin, *First Freedom*, pp. 142–3.

[13] Fitchett, "Status of the Free Negro in Charleston," pp. 447–8; Bond quoted in Andrew Billingsley, *Black Families in White America* (Englewood Cliffs, N.J., 1968), pp. 117–18.

they had received at the hands of this light-skinned elite. Robert Abbott, editor of the *Chicago Defender,* went out of his way to hire blacks as opposed to mulattoes because of his ostracism by the "blue veined elite" of his native Savannah. In the 1920s, Marcus Garvey, a West Indian black finely attuned to black-mulatto differences, seized on these racial animosities and used them to promote the growth of his Pan-African movement. While members of the "Talented Tenth" were scandalized by his crude appeal, Garvey electrified the black masses with his denunciation of mulattoes as whites trying to pass for black.[14] Some years later, E. Franklin Frazier, a leading black sociologist, delivered a slashing attack on the lack of race consciousness of the black bourgeoisie, who had adopted many of the exclusivist tendencies of the antebellum free Negro caste. While the Negro press vilified Frazier, he reported that black workingmen accosted him on the street to thank him for saying what too long had gone unsaid.[15]

The legacy of the free Negro caste was not confined to these lingering enmities. Most free Negroes did not belong to the elite and felt little sympathy for its pretensions. Tied closely to former slaves by blood, marriage, religious affiliation, and work habits and alienated from whites, the vast majority of free Negroes greeted Emancipation with the same wild enthusiasm as did the mass of enthralled blacks. If freedom within the slave society had made free Negroes leaders without a following, Emancipation restored their constituency. Newly liberated blacks could patronize Negro-owned businesses, support black ministers, and before long, vote for black politicians. Rather than feeling threatened by the general Emancipation, most free Negroes saw only new opportunities to assert their leadership, strengthen African churches, and achieve the

[14] Roi Ottley, *The Lonely Warrior: The Life and Times of Robert S. Abbott* (Chicago, 1955), pp. 35–7, 68–9, 75–6, 85; Edmund David Cronon, *Black Moses: The Story of Marcus Garvey and the Universal Negro Improvement Association* (Madison, Wis., 1955).

[15] Frazier, *Black Bourgeoisie,* especially his account of the black reaction to his book, pp. 7–14. Although Frazier was caustic in his condemnation of the new black middle class, his attitude toward the old elite was ambivalent. He clearly found something attractive in their genteel tradition. In this light, it is interesting to compare *Black Bourgeoisie* to his earlier evaluation of the new middle class in *Negro Family in the U.S.,* pp. 420–46.

equality they had long desired. Even though initially reluctant, many members of the free Negro caste were soon won over to this position. Much to their dismay, Southern whites found that some of the most loyal Confederate freemen were not to be depended upon. Those free Negroes who continued to stand apart from the newly liberated slaves, perhaps hoping to win concessions from whites, were often driven into the arms of the black masses by the actions of whites who lumped all blacks together regardless of their wealth, color, or former status. "Our future is indissolubly bound up with that of the negro . . . and we have resolved [to] rise or fall with them," declared one New Orleans freeman in the summer of 1864. "We have no rights which we can reckon safe while the same are denied to the fieldhands on the sugar plantations."[16]

Economic changes unleashed by Emancipation also pushed freemen and freedmen together. Emancipation eroded the paternalism which had encouraged whites to patronize free Negro tradesmen by depriving these whites of the gratification they received from being served by those of lower status than themselves. At the same time, the stigma of "nigger work," which had protected free Negro jobs during the antebellum years, was no longer as potent a deterrent to white competition. Whites began to muscle into many of the trades free Negroes had monopolized before the war. Even black barbers found many of their old customers switching their allegiance to whites, as a growing number of whites took up that trade. Thus Emancipation forced black businessmen to look for new customers for the services they had long supplied whites, and newly freed blacks provided the surest market. The mutual dependence of the marketplace reinforced the growing political ties between former free Negroes and former slaves. A visitor to South Carolina soon after the war noted that the "wealthy slaveholding mulatto families of Charleston are fully identified in interest with the mass of the colored people, and are becoming the leaders among them, while the old jealousy between

[16] Vernon L. Wharton, *The Negro in Mississippi, 1865–1890* (Chapel Hill, N.C., 1947), pp. 141–2, 144, 147, 150; Everett, "Demands of New Orleans Free Colored for Political Equality," pp. 55–64; Williamson, *After Slavery*, p. 317; quotation in Clara L. Campbell, "The Political Life of Louisiana Negroes, 1865–1890," unpublished doctoral dissertation, Tulane University, 1971, p. 19.

blacks and mulattoes is disappearing."[17] If important differences between free and slave, brown and black, survived Emancipation, blacks were united as never before.

Free Negroes worked to strengthen black life. Not only did they become black political leaders, but they also helped expand African churches, schools, and benevolent societies so that former slaves might benefit from the institutions that had served freemen so well during the antebellum years. New black churches sprang up by the dozens; these churches joined together to form black associations and conferences and elected state and national officers. Schools, which had carried much of the burden of free Negro hope and ambition during the slave period, flourished as never before. Fraternal organizations and benevolent societies likewise increased in number, and some of the larger ones mushroomed into insurance companies offering protection for thousands and jobs for hundreds. After the fraternal orders had lost much of their social-welfare function to the insurance organizations, they still served as centers for the black community and a source of support for aspiring black politicians. The institutions that were the core of free Negro life now spread throughout the black community.[18]

Even as blacks pulled together to improve themselves and achieve equality, differences in means and ends appeared. These divisions transcended the withdrawal of one part of the free Negro elite from black affairs, or the well-meaning but nonetheless painful condescension with which free Negroes occasionally treated newly liberated blacks, and instead were rooted in the unique experience of the free Negro caste. Throughout the antebellum years, free Negroes had been an extremely cautious group. Their fragile liberty had made them chary of offending whites because they had something real to lose and understood that whites were always looking for an excuse to grab it. All too often their social advancement hinged on their ability to distinguish themselves from slaves and ingratiate themselves with whites. Their insecurity bred

[17] Tindall, *South Carolina Negroes*, pp. 129, 140–1; *Nation*, I (14 September 1865), 332.

[18] Williamson, *After Slavery*, pp. 180–208; Tindall, *South Carolina Negroes*, pp. 186–208; Kolchin, *First Freedom*, pp. 107–27.

ambivalence and was reflected in their role as race leaders. Although they protested white racism at every turn, free Negroes had been careful to protect their one claim to privilege. They might aid a fugitive or help a relative purchase his or her freedom, but few chanced all for universal black liberty. Rather than challenge whites directly, they developed other strategies for improving themselves. They accumulated property, worked at trades on which whites depended, and made alliances with these same whites to protect their liberty. When free Negroes assumed positions of leadership after the war, they often continued this same cautious strategy of race improvement. "Let us be patient," advised one former free Negro when the Supreme Court struck down the Civil Rights Act of 1875. "The objection of our commingling unreservedly with whites, can be overcome, by education, and by such personal methods as will make us more presentable. . . . This cannot be done in a day, or in a year. It will take time. . . ."[19]

Freedom changed many things, and former free Negroes were frequently in the ranks of the most militant blacks. But even then they aimed their militance at goals that grew out of their special experience in freedom. Free Negroes had long yearned for full acceptance into American society. After the war, the complete integration that civil, political, and social equality presaged appealed more to them than to the mass of former slaves. For one thing, they were far better prepared to compete as equals in the white world than those just released from plantation bondage. Educated, skilled, and confident of their abilities, they wanted only the opportunity to rise to the top. Free Negro leaders naturally pressed hardest for measures that would break down the walls of caste and assure equality to all. On the other hand, they showed little interest in fundamentally reordering the society they hoped to join. Massive expropriation and redistribution of land aroused little enthusiasm among black leaders who had been free before the war. They had already imbibed too much of the ethos of hard work, underconsumption, and property accumulation to subscribe wholeheartedly to the doctrine of forty acres and a mule. They did not wish to revamp the

[19] Tindall, *South Carolina Negroes*, p. 292.

structure of society just when their knowledge of the social order would benefit them. If the mass of newly liberated slaves wanted economic, political, and social equality, in that order, the priorities of the black elite—composed disproportionately of free Negroes—were precisely the opposite.[20]

Thus whites and blacks carried their antebellum expectations and ideals into the post-Emancipation world. Confronted with the new opportunities and problems created by freedom, both races drew on their antebellum experience. Often the legacy of freedom was as important as the heritage of slavery.

[20] Kolchin, *First Freedom*, pp. 144–6, 151–83; August Meier, "Negro in the First and Second Reconstruction of the South," *Civil War History*, XIII (1967), 114–30.

Appendix 1

SLAVE AND WHITE POPULATIONS

Table A

Slave Population, 1755–1860

	Pre-1790	*1790*	*1800*	*1810*
United States		697,897	893,041	1,191,354
North		40,370	35,946	27,500
South		657,527	857,095	1,163,854
Upper South		521,169	648,051	810,523
Lower South		136,358	209,044	353,331
Delaware		8,887	6,153	4,177
D.C.		—	3,244	5,395
Kentucky		11,830	40,343	80,561
Maryland	43,495[a]	103,036	105,635	111,502
Missouri		—	—	3,011
North Carolina		100,572	133,296	168,824
Tennessee		3,417	13,584	44,535
Virginia		293,427	345,796	392,518
Alabama		—	—	—
Arkansas		—	—	—
Florida		—	—	—
Georgia		29,264	59,404	105,218
Louisiana	4,519[b]	[16,544][c]	[12,920][d]	34,660
Mississippi		—	3,489	17,088
South Carolina		107,094	146,151	196,365
Texas		—	—	—

[a] 1755
[b] 1769
[c] 1785
[d] ca. 1803

Sources: *Gentlemen's Magazine and Historical Chronicle,* XXXIV (1764), 261; Lawrence Kinnaird, ed., *Spain in the Mississippi Valley, 1765–1794* in *Annual Report of the American Historical Association for the Year 1945,* 4 vols. (Wash-

1820	*1830*	*1840*	*1850*	*1860*
1,538,125	2,009,043	2,487,455	3,204,313	3,953,760
19,108	3,568	1,129	262	64
1,519,017	2,005,475	2,486,326	3,204,051	3,953,696
965,514	1,159,670	1,215,497	1,395,283	1,530,229
553,503	845,805	1,270,829	1,808,768	2,423,467
4,509	3,292	2,605	2,290	1,798
6,377	6,119	4,694	3,687	3,185
126,732	165,213	182,258	210,981	225,483
107,397	102,994	89,737	90,368	87,189
10,222	25,091	58,240	87,422	114,931
205,017	245,601	245,817	288,548	331,059
80,107	141,603	183,059	239,459	275,719
425,153	469,757	449,087	472,528	490,865
41,879	117,549	253,532	342,844	435,080
1,617	4,576	19,935	47,100	111,115
—	15,501	25,717	39,310	61,745
149,654	217,531	280,944	381,682	462,198
69,064	109,588	168,452	244,809	331,726
32,814	65,659	195,211	309,878	436,631
258,475	315,401	327,038	384,984	402,406
—	—	—	58,161	182,566

ington, D.C., 1946), II, pt. 1, 196; *Appendix to an Account of Louisiana Being an Abstract of Documents in the Offices of the Departments of State and the Treasury* (Philadelphia, 1803), pp. 84–7; *Annals of Congress,* 8th Cong., 2nd Sess., pp. 1574–6; *Population of the United States in 1860* (Washington, D.C., 1864), pp. 598–605.

TABLE B

WHITE POPULATION, 1755–1860

	Pre-1790	*1790*	*1800*	*1810*
United States		3,172,464	4,304,501	5,862,004
North		1,900,976	2,601,521	3,653,219
South		1,271,488	1,702,980	2,208,785
Upper South		1,078,424	1,399,868	1,791,840
Lower South		193,064	303,112	416,945
Delaware		46,310	49,852	55,361
D.C.		—	10,066	16,079
Kentucky		61,133	179,871	324,237
Maryland	108,193[a]	208,649	216,326	235,117
Missouri		—	—	17,227
North Carolina		288,204	337,764	376,410
Tennessee		32,013	91,709	215,875
Virginia		442,115	514,280	551,534
Alabama		—	—	—
Arkansas		—	—	—
Florida		—	—	—
Georgia		52,886	101,678	145,414
Louisiana	6,540[b]	[14,215][c]	[21,244][d]	34,311
Mississippi		—	5,179	23,024
South Carolina		140,178	196,255	214,196
Texas		—	—	—

[a] 1755
[b] 1769
[c] 1785
[d] ca. 1803

SOURCES: *Gentlemen's Magazine and Historical Chronicle*, XXXIV (1764), 261; Lawrence Kinnaird, ed., *Spain in the Mississippi Valley, 1765–1794* in *Annual*

1820	*1830*	*1840*	*1850*	*1860*
7,861,931	10,537,378	14,195,695	19,553,114	26,957,471
4,970,371	6,886,620	9,563,165	13,330,696	18,860,008
2,891,560	3,650,758	4,632,530	6,222,418	8,097,463
2,250,965	2,711,743	3,187,918	4,085,134	5,154,206
640,595	939,015	1,444,612	2,137,284	2,943,257
55,282	57,601	58,561	71,169	90,589
22,614	27,563	30,657	37,941	60,763
434,644	517,787	590,253	761,413	919,484
260,223	291,108	318,204	417,943	515,918
55,988	114,795	323,888	592,004	1,063,489
419,200	472,843	484,870	553,028	629,942
399,927	535,746	640,627	756,836	826,722
603,087	694,300	740,858	894,800	1,047,299
85,451	190,406	335,185	426,514	526,271
12,579	25,671	77,174	162,189	324,143
—	18,385	27,943	47,203	77,747
189,566	286,806	407,695	521,572	591,550
73,383	89,441	158,457	255,491	357,456
42,176	70,443	179,074	295,718	353,899
237,440	257,863	259,084	274,563	291,300
—	—	—	154,034	420,891

Report of the American Historical Association for the Year 1945, 4 vols. (Washington, D.C., 1946), II, pt. 1, 196; *Appendix to an Account of Louisiana Being an Abstract of Documents in the Offices of the Departments of State and the Treasury* (Philadelphia, 1803), pp. 84–7; *Annals of Congress,* 8th Cong., 2nd Sess., pp. 1574–6; *Population of the United States in 1860* (Washington, D.C., 1864), pp. 598–605.

TABLE C

PERCENT INCREASE OF SLAVES, 1755–1860

		1790–1800	*1800–1810*
United States		28.0%	33.4%
North		−11.0	−23.5
South		30.4	35.8
Upper South		24.3	25.1
Lower South		53.3	69.0
Delaware		−30.8	−32.1
D.C.		—	66.3
Kentucky		241.0	100.0
Maryland	136.9%[a]	2.5	5.6
Missouri		—	—
North Carolina		32.5	26.7
Tennessee		297.5	227.8
Virginia		17.8	13.5
Alabama		—	—
Arkansas		—	—
Florida		—	—
Georgia		103.0	77.1
Louisiana	266.1[b]	[−21.9][c]	[168.3][d]
Mississippi		—	389.8
South Carolina		36.5	34.4
Texas		—	—

[a] 1755–1790
[b] 1769–1785
[c] 1785–ca. 1803
[d] ca. 1803–1810

SOURCES: *Gentlemen's Magazine and Historical Chronicle*, XXXIV (1764), 261; Lawrence Kinnaird, ed., *Spain in the Mississippi Valley, 1765–1794* in *Annual*

1810–1820	*1820–1830*	*1830–1840*	*1840–1850*	*1850–1860*
29.1%	30.6%	23.8%	28.8%	23.4%
−30.5	−81.3	−68.4	−76.8	−75.6
30.5	32.0	24.0	28.9	23.4
19.1	20.1	4.8	14.8	9.7
56.7	52.8	50.3	42.3	34.0
7.9	−27.0	−20.9	−12.1	−21.5
18.0	− 4.0	−23.3	−21.5	−13.6
57.3	30.4	10.3	15.8	6.9
− 3.7	− 4.1	−12.9	.7	− 3.5
239.5	145.5	132.1	50.1	31.5
21.4	19.8	.1	17.4	14.7
79.9	76.8	29.3	30.8	15.1
8.3	10.5	− 4.1	5.2	3.9
—	180.7	115.7	35.2	27.2
—	183.0	335.6	136.3	135.9
—	—	65.1	52.9	57.1
42.2	45.4	29.2	35.9	21.1
99.3	58.7	53.7	45.3	35.5
92.0	100.1	197.3	58.7	40.9
31.6	22.0	3.7	17.7	4.5
—	—	—	—	213.9

Report of the American Historical Association for the Year 1945, 4 vols. (Washington, D.C., 1946), II, pt. 1, 196; *Appendix to an Account of Louisiana Being an Abstract of Documents in the Offices of the Departments of State and the Treasury* (Philadelphia, 1803), pp. 84–7; *Annals of Congress,* 8th Cong., 2nd Sess., pp. 1574–6; *Population of the United States in 1860* (Washington, D.C., 1864), pp. 598–605.

Table D

Percent Increase of Whites, 1755–1860

		1790–1800	*1800–1810*
United States		35.7%	36.2%
North		36.9	40.4
South		33.9	29.7
Upper South		29.8	28.0
Lower South		57.0	37.6
Delaware		7.6	11.1
D.C.		—	59.7
Kentucky		194.2	80.3
Maryland	92.8%[a]	3.7	8.7
Missouri		—	—
North Carolina		17.2	11.4
Tennessee		186.5	135.4
Virginia		16.3	7.2
Alabama		—	—
Arkansas		—	—
Florida		—	—
Georgia		92.3	43.0
Louisiana	117.4[b]	[49.4][c]	[61.5][d]
Mississippi		—	344.6
South Carolina		40.0	9.1
Texas		—	—

[a] 1755–1790
[b] 1769–1785
[c] 1785–ca. 1803
[d] ca. 1803–1810

Sources: *Gentlemen's Magazine and Historical Chronicle,* XXXIV (1764), 261; Lawrence Kinnaird, ed., *Spain in the Mississippi Valley, 1765–1794* in *Annual*

1810–1820	*1820–1830*	*1830–1840*	*1840–1850*	*1850–1860*
34.1%	34.0%	34.7%	37.7%	37.9%
36.7	38.6	38.9	39.4	41.5
30.9	26.3	26.9	34.3	30.2
25.6	20.5	17.6	28.1	26.2
53.6	46.6	53.8	47.9	37.8
– .1	4.2	1.7	21.5	27.3
40.6	21.3	11.2	23.6	60.2
34.1	19.1	14.0	29.0	20.8
10.7	11.7	9.0	31.3	23.1
225.0	105.0	182.1	82.8	79.6
11.4	12.8	2.5	14.1	13.9
57.5	57.1	19.6	18.1	9.2
9.3	15.1	6.1	20.8	17.0
—	122.8	76.0	27.2	23.4
—	104.1	200.6	110.2	99.9
—	—	52.0	68.9	64.7
30.4	56.6	37.4	27.9	13.4
113.9	21.9	77.2	61.2	39.9
83.2	67.0	154.2	65.1	19.7
10.9	8.1	.5	6.0	6.1
—	—	—	—	173.2

Report of the American Historical Association for the Year 1945, 4 vols. (Washington, D.C., 1946), II, pt. 1, 196; *Appendix to an Account of Louisiana Being an Abstract of Documents in the Offices of the Departments of State and the Treasury* (Philadelphia, 1803), pp. 84–7; *Annals of Congress,* 8th Cong., 2nd Sess., pp. 1574–6; *Population of the United States in 1860* (Washington, D.C., 1864), pp. 598–605.

Appendix 2

MANUSCRIPT SOURCES CONSULTED

Alabama State Department of Archives and History, Montgomery
Executive Papers
Atlanta Historical Society, Atlanta, Georgia
City Council Minutes, 1851–1860
Ordinances, 1854–1862
Amistad Research Center, Dillard University, New Orleans
American Missionary Association Papers
Baltimore City Hall
Municipal Records
Delaware Hall of Records, Dover
Legislative Papers, Petitions on Negroes and Slavery
Ridgely Family Papers
Duke University Library, Durham, North Carolina
Anonymous Diary of Natchez to Texas Journey, 1838
Robert Carter Papers, typescript
Michael Collins Papers
Dismal Swamp Land Company Papers
Alfred Huger Letterbooks
William R. Johnson Papers
Lee Family Papers
Robert Leslie Account Books and Papers
Julia L. N. Loveland Journal
Alexander Randall Papers
Davis Richardson Ledgers and Papers
John Rutherfoord Papers
Edward Telfair Papers
Peter Vial Papers
Benjamin L. C. Wailes Diaries and Papers
George Walton Papers
Filson Club, Louisville, Kentucky
Orlando Brown Papers

First African Baptist Church, Richmond, Virginia
Church Minute Books and Papers
Garrett Theological Seminary Library, Evanston, Illinois
Ezekiel Cooper Papers
Georgia Department of Archives and History, Atlanta
Baldwin County Inferior Court Minutes, Trials of Slaves, 1812–1826
County Registers of Free Negroes
Milledgeville Police Court Minutes, 1854–1870, 1856–1893
Georgia Historical Society, Savannah
R. D. Arnold Papers
Chatham County Registers of Free Negroes
Chatham County Inferior Court Minutes, Trials of Persons of Color, 1813–1827
Savannah Tax Rolls, 1860
Gillfield Baptist Church, Petersburg, Virginia
Church Minute Book
Guilford College Library, Guilford, North Carolina
Quaker Collection
Historical Foundation of the Presbyterian and Reformed Churches, Montreat, North Carolina
Papers Relating to John Chavis
Historical Society of Delaware, Wilmington
Abolition Society of Delaware Minute Books and Papers, 1801–1807
African School Society Papers, 1809–1861
Africana School Society Papers, 1819–1823
Brown Collection
Female African School Society Papers, 1833–1861
Lea Mills Account Book and Letterbooks, 1773–1879
William D. Lewis Diary
Milligan-McClaure Papers
C. A. Rodney Papers
Thomas Rodney Papers
Slavery Collection
Society for the Encouragement of Free Labor Papers, 1826–1828
Historical Society of Pennsylvania, Philadelphia
Abolition Society of Delaware Minute Books, 1801–1819
Miscellaneous Papers of the Three Lower Counties
Pennsylvania Society for Promoting the Abolition of Slavery Papers
Howard University Library, Washington, D.C.
Rapier Family Papers
Altetha Tanner–Jane Eleanor Datcher Papers
Library of Congress, Washington, D.C.
American Colonization Society Papers
Robert Carter Papers
Myrtilla Minor Collection
Jonathan Roberts Family Papers
Michael Shiner Diary

Carter G. Woodson Collection

Louisiana State University Library, Baton Rouge

Norbert Badin Papers
Louis A. Bringier Papers
James Brown Papers
Atala Chelette Papers
Dupre and Metoyer Account Book
E. John Ellis Papers
François Escoffer Papers
Nathaniel Evans Papers
Elizabeth Jefferson Reminiscences
William Johnson Papers
Robert M. Livingston Papers
Adeleda Metoyer Papers
Auguste Metoyer Papers
Meullion Family Papers
New Orleans Municipal Papers
John H. Randolph Papers and Account Books
Slavery Collection
A. P. Walsh Papers
Joseph Watson Papers
WPA transcripts, Parish Police Jury Minutes

Maryland Diocesan Library, Baltimore

Miscellaneous Sermons and Papers

Maryland Hall of Records, Annapolis

Anne Arundel County Manumission Records, 1790–1864
County Register of Free Negroes

Maryland Historical Society, Baltimore

Anne Arundel County Almshouse Minute Book
Bloomsbury Mills Ledger
Robert Carter Papers
Cushing Account Book
Robert Franklin Account Book
Gittings Account Book
Charles Howard Papers
Cornelius Howard Account Books and Papers
Thomas Jones Papers
Thomas Law Papers
Maryland State Colonization Society Papers
Richard Vansant Ledger

Mississippi Department of Archives and History, Jackson

Executive Papers, 1856–1860
Legislative Papers, 1817–1860
Wade-Ross Family Papers

Missouri Historical Society, St. Louis

California-Oregon Papers
St. Louis Free Negro Bonds and Registers, Tiffany Collection

Mobile City Hall, Mobile, Alabama

Common Council Minutes, 1851–1859, typescript

Interesting transcriptions from City Documents, 1815–1859, typescript

Interesting transcriptions from the Mayor's Court Records, 1820–1835, typescript

Interesting transcriptions from the Miscellaneous Books of the Probate Court, 1819–1884, typescript

Tax Books, 1860

National Archives, Washington, D.C.

Charleston Manuscript Census, 1850, 1860, RG 29

Mobile Manuscript Census, 1850, 1860, RG 29

Orleans Territorial Papers, Records of the Department of State, RG 59

Payroll Ledgers, Bureau of Yards and Docks and Records of the Naval Shore Establishment, RG 71

Payroll Ledgers, Naval Records Collection, RG 45

Richmond Manuscript Census, 1850, 1860, RG 29

New Orleans Public Library

First Municipality, Petitions for Emancipation, 1835–1846

First Municipality, Resolutions and Ordinances, 1840–1841, 1844–1845, typescript

First Municipality, Messages of the Mayor, 1835–1852, typescript

Mayor's Complaint Book, 1856–1859

Messages of the Mayor, 1805–1845, typescript

Proceedings of the City Council, 1803–1829, typescript

Records of Cases Before the Mayor's Court, 1823–1827

Resolutions and Ordinances, 1805–1835, typescript

Registers of Free Coloured Persons Enabled to Remain in the State, 1840–1864

Third Municipality, Messages of the Mayor, 1836–1842, typescript

Third Municipality, State v. Free Persons of Color, 1840–1851

Third Municipality, Proceedings of the City Council, 1845–1852

North Carolina State Department of Archives and History, Raleigh

Bonds for Emancipated Slaves, Craven County Papers

James Boon Papers

Capitol Building Manuscripts, Comptrollers' Papers

Executive Papers and Letterbooks

James Henry Harris Papers

Internal Improvement Manuscript, Comptroller's Papers

Legislative Papers

Minutes of the New Bern Town Council, 1797–1828

Perquimans County Slave Papers

Ebenezer Pettigrew Papers

Raleigh First Baptist Church Minute Book

D. S. Reid Papers

Stokes County Slave Papers

Calvin H. Wiley Papers
Jonathan Worth Papers

Savannah City Hall, Savannah, Georgia
Ordinances
Proceedings of the City Council

South Carolina Archives Department, Columbia
Documents Relating to Free Moors
Executive Papers
Grand Jury Presentments
Journal of the South Carolina House of Representatives
Journal of the South Carolina Senate
Legislative Papers Relating to Slavery and Free Negroes
Miscellaneous Records of the Secretary of State
Trial Records of the Denmark Vesey Insurrection

South Carolina Historical Society, Charleston
Charleston Alms House Records
Philippe Noisette Papers
Notes on the Brown Fellowship Society
Pineville Association Patrol Book
Rusticus Papers

South Caroliniana Library, Columbia
Charleston Free Negro Registers
Noisette Family Papers

Southern History Collection, University of North Carolina,Chapel Hill
John M. Berrien Papers
Bertie County Papers
Bumpas Family Papers
Cape Fear and Deep River Navigation Company Papers
Cupola House Papers
Philip R. Fendall Papers
David Gavin Diary, typescript
Paul Green, "Autobiography of Sam Morphis," typescript
Greenfield Fisheries Papers, Hayes Collection
Earnest Hayward Collection
John Hubbard Papers
William Lord London Collection
Louisa Furnance Day Book
North Carolina Manumission Society Papers
Henri Masson Journal
Pettigrew Family Papers
University of North Carolina Papers
William D. Valentine Diary
John Walker Diary
Calvin H. Wiley Papers

Syracuse University Library, Syracuse, New York
Gerrit Smith Papers

Tennessee Historical Society, Nashville
Henry Hollingsworth Journal
Montgomery Bell Papers, Nannie Seawell Boyd Collection
Tennessee State Library and Archives, Nashville
George H. Clark Papers
Legislative Papers
Mill Creek Baptist Church Minute Book
John Sumner Russworm Papers
Tulane University Library, New Orleans, Louisiana
B. H. Latrobe Papers
John McDonogh Collection
Pontchartain Railroad Company Minute Book
St. Rosalie Plantation Journal
University of Georgia Library, Athens
"Romance of Little Wassaw," typescript
University of Virginia Library, Charlottesville
Alexandria Common Council Minutes
Charles L. Bankhead Papers
Muscoe R. H. Garnett Papers
Graham Family Papers
Madden Family Papers
Richmond Police Day Book
David Shaver Papers
Virginia Baptist Historical Society, Richmond
Carmel Baptist Church Minute Book
Cedar Run Baptist Church Minute Books
Colosse Baptist Church Minute Book
Emmaus Baptist Church Minute Book
First Baptist Church of Richmond Minute Books, typescript
Fork Baptist Church Minute Book
Gillfield Baptist Church Minute Book, copy
Liberty Baptist Church Minute Book
Long Branch Baptist Church Minute Book
Mount Hermon Baptist Church Minute Books
Round Oak Baptist Church Minute Book
Robert Ryland Papers
Upper Essex Baptist Church Minute Book
Walnut Grove Baptist Church Minute Book
Zion Hall Baptist Church Minute Book
Virginia Historical Society, Richmond
Robert Carter Papers and Account Books
Robert Leslie Account Books
Lower Lunenburg County Register of Free Negroes
John Page Commonplace Book
David Ross Papers and Letterbooks
Edmund Ruffin Papers

Tayloe Family Papers
Jourdon Woolfolk Account Books

Virginia State Library, Richmond

Charles J. F. Bohannan Account Book
County Registers of Free Negroes
County Order Books
County Overseer of the Poor Papers and Account Books
William C. Bruce Papers, John Randolph Collection
Executive Papers, Letterbooks and Other Communications
First Baptist Church of Richmond Minute Book, typescript
John Floyd Diary
Legislative Papers
William McKean Letterbook, Roslin Plantation Papers, copy
Petersburg Hustings Court Minute Books
Richmond Common Council Minute Books
Richmond Hustings Court Minute Books
Staunton Common Council Minute Books
Tredegar Iron Works Papers

Western Historical Collection, University of Missouri, Columbia

County Free Negro Registers
Maramec Iron Works Papers, Lucy Worthington James Collection

INDEX